Psychology Survey
No. 4

Psychology Survey
No. 4

Edited by John Nicholson and Brian Foss

The British Psychological Society

Published by The British Psychological Society
St Andrews House, 48 Princess Road East, Leicester, LE1 7DR

ISBN 0 901715 21 2

Printed in Great Britain by Lavenham Press Ltd

FOREWORD

For those readers who are not familiar with the aims of the Psychology Survey series we cannot do better than quote from the relevant sections of the Foreword to the first volume:

> The series is aimed at keeping psychologists and psychology students abreast of the way the subject is developing. Each volume will be made up of a sample of topics from the total cross-section of psychology. The topics will be dealt with in different ways, varying in breadth and depth according to the following plan. Most undergraduate courses include subjects which are thought of as part of the core of academic psychology - perception, learning, memory, thinking and so on. Some aspects of these core subjects will be dealt with in almost all volumes of the Survey, so the authors have been asked to write at some depth about a particular area in which they are expert and which is of special current interest. Then there are chapters on typical 'options', where authors have been asked to cover a relatively wide area, drawing attention to some of the better general references, and, where appropriate, dealing with a few special topics in a little more detail, especially when they seem to be developing in a way which may shape future research. Finally, a few chapters deal with subjects which are not central to most psychology syllabuses but which may interest students who are choosing subjects for research. Some will also be relevant to psychological careers.

In this volume, chapters 1-4 deal with specific aspects of core subjects; chapters 5, 6, 7, 9 and 10 deal with what might be thought of as optional subjects; and chapters 8, 11, 12 and 13 are more peripheral. Two of them, chapter 11 (Psychology and Music) and chapter 12 (Psychology and Mathematics) bridge disciplines, and will be easier reading for students with a knowledge of music and mathematics respectively.

We are delighted that The British Psychological Society has taken over the publication of the series. Readers will now be getting very up-to-date information, since the BPS production process is so streamlined that publication is possible within four months of us receiving the last of the contributors' typescripts. We are very grateful to Anna Karbik of the BPS for her efficient and imaginative editorial assistance, and to Kathryn Metzenthin of the Bedford College Psychology Department, who undertook all the correspondence.

John Nicholson
Brian Foss

CONTENTS

Chapter 1

HUMAN VISUAL DEVELOPMENT

Janette Atkinson and Oliver Braddick

Although human infants appear very immature and helpless in many respects, even to a casual observer they show a variety of active visual behaviour. In the last decade this has provoked a flood of research, which has led to a picture of a remarkable development of visual competence in the first months of life. In this chapter we shall concentrate on this early development, although there is no doubt that perceptual processes continue to develop later in childhood.

In the first part of our chapter we look at how the infant develops the basic sensory mechanisms of contrast, colour, movement and binocular vision. New knowledge about the physiology of the eye and visual pathway has helped our understanding of these processes, and has led to hypotheses about the links between neural developments and the development of visual behaviour. We have also learnt from clinical and animal data on how the course of development can be changed by visual experience.

In the later part of the chapter we shall look at some evidence on how infants can put together this basic visual information. Vision serves several vital functions for the adult: it allows the environment to be perceived as an arrangement of objects and surfaces in three-dimensional space; it provides information on the observer's own position and movement; it enables objects to be recognized; and it helps to establish and regulate interactions with other people. The beginnings of all these uses of vision can be seen in infants' perceptual abilities.

Any one of the sub-headings in this chapter could be (and has been) the subject of a chapter in itself, so where possible we refer the reader to reviews which can do more justice to these flourishing areas of research than we have space for here.

1

METHODS OF STUDYING INFANT VISION

Recent advances in our knowledge of infant vision have largely depended on variants of a few basic techniques. One of the most widely used is <u>preferential looking</u> (PL), originated by Fantz (1961), in which two patterns are presented side by side. The infant's ability to discriminate them is inferred from the tendency to fixate one pattern in preference to the other (figure 1). Of course, the method depends on the existence of a marked preference: the commonest example is the preference for a patterned over a uniform screen, which can be used to show that particular patterns, e.g. fine striped gratings, are detectable. Originally, preference was measured by comparing the time or number of fixations. More recently, the method of 'forced-choice preferential looking' (Teller, 1979) has been used. The 'forced choice' here is on the part of a trained observer, who, without knowing on which side a pattern has been presented, has to make a judgement (left or right) based on observation of the infant's eye movements and general behaviour. The percentage of correct judgements can be used to estimate the infant's 'threshold' in a similar way to estimation of adult psychophysical thresholds.

If infants show no intrinsic preference between two stimuli, it may be possible to create one temporarily by the method of habituation/recovery. In this, the infant's looking time, or some response by which the infant controls exposure of the stimulus (Siqueland and DeLucia, 1969), declines as the same pattern is shown repeatedly to the infant, i.e. habituation occurs. Following such a sequence a new pattern is presented. If responsiveness reappears, then the infant must be able to detect the difference between the old and new patterns; if the old and new patterns are treated as equivalent, habituation will continue. The method depends on an increased responsiveness to novelty (which may, of course, not always be a correct assumption: under some circumstances the familiarity of a stimulus might produce a preference for it or some novel stimuli might be positively aversive). Nevertheless, a particular version of the method ('infant control procedure': Horowitz, 1975) has proved useful in finding out about discriminations by newborns, an age group for whom behavioural methods generally are difficult (Maurer and Barrera, 1981; Slater, Morison and Rose, in press).

Habituation, PL, and other techniques share the problem that they can yield positive evidence for a discriminative capability, but failure to show a differential response might be due to an absence of preference rather than a failure to discriminate. Consequently, the conclusions drawn from them must be conservative. Negative results are of most significance in close association with positive ones. For example, if a bright green stripe and a dimmer green stripe presented against a white background both elicit a preference, but an intermediate brightness of green did not, then it is conceivable that infants disliked that particular intensity of green, but more likely that it became less detectable to them because it merged with the background of equivalent luminance.

PL and habituation/recovery techniques work best for ages up to six months, when infants are usually alert but relatively passive, although some studies have tested an extended age range (Gwiazda, Brill, Mohindra and Held, 1980; Atkinson, Braddick and Pimm-Smith, 1982). It is more difficult to work with older infants who become rapidly bored with repetitive exposures to visual stimuli and who want to play a more active role. Operant procedures have been applied (e.g. Mayer and Dobson, 1982), but have not yet yielded as extensive results as those obtained at younger ages.

Some of our knowledge about infant vision comes not from behaviour, but from measures of electrical activity in the nervous system (Sokol, 1979). Visual evoked potentials (VEPs) are recorded from electrodes on the scalp, and are identified as caused by a visual stimulus because they are time-locked to it. The occurrence of VEP indicates that sensory information is transmitted to the brain. However, our understanding of how VEPs are generated is very limited, and since they are gross potentials combining the activity of vast numbers of nerve cells, they are very crude indicators of what kind of sensory processing is going on. Furthermore, although they do not depend on a behavioural measure directly, satisfactory VEP recordings do depend on behavioural attention to the stimulus.

These behavioural and electrophysiological methods can tell us what sensory information is available to the infant. They do not tell us how the infant is capable of using it, or assigning meaning to it. These questions require more complicated and specific experimental designs, which require a lot of care in interpretation. An infant detects and encodes sensory events; perceptual and cognitive processes connect this incoming information to meanings; and appropriate motor actions must be initiated and controlled. Our particular research interest may be focussed on one of these levels, but processes at any one or more levels may be important in determining the visual behaviour we observe in an infant.

The leaps of inference needed to test a specific hypothesis may not always be justified. To take a single

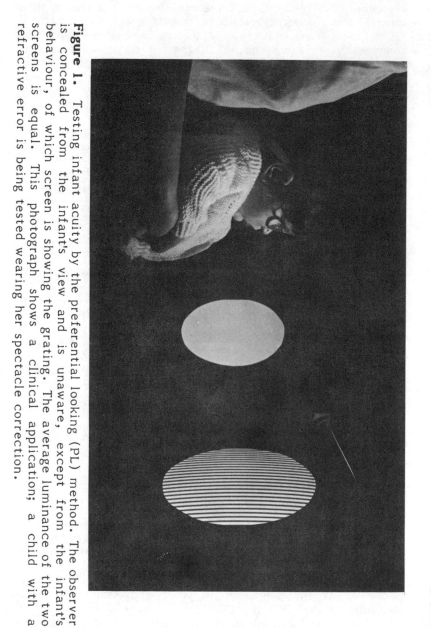

Figure 1. Testing infant acuity by the preferential looking (PL) method. The observer is concealed from the infant's view and is unaware, except from the infant's behaviour, of which screen is showing the grating. The average luminance of the two screens is equal. This photograph shows a clinical application; a child with a refractive error is being tested wearing her spectacle correction.

4

example, if an adult subject was asked to track an oscillating target, and the motion suddenly stopped after a number of cycles, we might observe that he briefly continued his eye movement along the expected path. We would probably suggest that he was showing a learnt 'predictive' pattern of eye movements, rather than that he lacked the concept of an object with an identity independent of any movement in space, or that he was unable to perceive the change in stimulus direction (although, strictly, we would need further experiments to establish this). Yet investigators have attempted to draw inferences about the infant's object concept from analogous observations. This is not to assert that the infant's behaviour must be a result of oculomotor control systems rather than knowledge of object properties, simply that such experiments do not have an unambiguous interpretation.

MEASURES OF VISUAL FUNCTION

The simple question 'how much can a baby see' requires some quantitative measure of visual performance if it is to be answered. The most familiar measure is visual acuity, that is, the finest detail that can be resolved. For infants, the usual test is to distinguish a black-and-white pattern from a uniform grey of equal luminance, where acuity is stated in terms of the minimum stripe width in minutes of arc visual angle. One minute is conventionally taken as normal adult acuity (corresponding to 6/6 in clinical notation), 10 minutes or 6/60 would represent acuity one tenth as good, and so on. It is important to realize that the smallest resolvable is not the same as the smallest visible object: a single spot or line can be visible as a blur against the background even when it is smaller than the acuity limit. For this reason, these discrete targets are not suitable for testing acuity, in infants or adults (Atkinson, Braddick, Pimm-Smith, Ayling and Sawyer, 1981).

Acuity specifies only how well the visual system handles very fine detail. The quality of vision depends also on how well coarser, but possibly fainter, patterns of light and dark can be detected. The contrast sensitivity function (see Atkinson and Braddick, 1981a; Banks and Salapatek, 1981) provides this more general measure. It is tested using grating patterns which have a sine-wave distribution of light intensity rather than sharp-edged stripes, the fineness of the grating being measured in the number of cycles (paired dark and light stripes) per degree visual angle (spatial frequency). High spatial frequency means narrow stripe width; low spatial frequency means broad stripes. The amount of contrast between light and dark stripes needed to make the grating just visible varies with spatial frequency. As the grating is made finer, more contrast is required for it to be visible. Acuity corresponds to the spatial frequency where even 100 per cent contrast only just reaches visibility: the conventional adult value of one minute of arc is 30 cycles/ degree in spatial frequency terms. In adults, increasing contrast is also required for detection as the stripes become very broad, i.e. very gradual changes in luminance across a pattern are hard to detect. This is referred to as the low spatial frequency cut in sensitivity. There is a maximum contrast sensitivity at intermediate spatial frequencies (around three cycles/degree), where the adult can detect contrasts as low as 0.5 per cent.

DEVELOPMENT OF ACUITY AND CONTRAST SENSITIVITY

There is a rapid improvement in pattern vision, as measured by acuity and contrast sensitivity, during the first year of life. However, even at birth the infant has useful pattern vision. Estimates of the newborn's acuity are around 30 min arc, with 50 per cent contrast as the lowest which can be shown to be detected (see Atkinson and Braddick, 1982). These levels, very low by adult standards, must be seen in relation to the infant's visual needs. For example, they are adequate to detect the major features and outline of a face at a distance of half a metre (see figure 2). At one month, acuity estimates are in the range 15-30 min arc, and at 2-3 months 6-15 min arc (the ranges reflect not just differences between studies but also considerable variations between individual infants (Atkinson and Braddick, 1981a)). Contrast sensitivity improves over these months to a similar degree. By six months, contrast sensitivity to the lower spatial frequencies is close to that of adults, though acuity is generally somewhat lower at 2-3 min arc. (Detailed documentation of this course of development can be found in recent reviews by Dobson and Teller, 1978; Held, 1979; Salapatek, 1979; and Atkinson and Braddick, 1981a.)

Because of the difficulties of working with older infants, we do not know at what age adult acuity is attained, and in any case it is probably approached asymptotically over quite a long period. By age three to four, grating acuity is essentially adult (Atkinson, French and Braddick, 1981). This is found also for acuity measured by identification of single letters, but even older children show reduced acuity for letters spaced closely together (Atkinson and Braddick, in press). This 'crowding effect' implies that the visual system's ability to handle spatial detail accurately continues to mature beyond the age at which basic transmission of fine detail information has reached adult levels.

ACCOMMODATION AND REFRACTION

The first requirement for good acuity is that the eye itself form a sharp optical image. When the focussing (ciliary) muscles of the eyes are completely relaxed (which can be achieved with cycloplegic drugs) most young infants are hyperopic or longsighted, which means that they are focussed beyond infinity. This does not mean that they can only see things clearly that are very far away, because infants are normally actively accommodating, that is contracting the ciliary muscles to focus the eye at a nearer distance. How accurately they focus depends on their age, state of alertness and the properties of the object they are looking at (for example, how contrasting the object is with its background). Very young infants tend to set their focus close in around 20-30 cm (Haynes, White and Held, 1965), although even at birth they do change their focussing appropriately but rather inaccurately for targets at different distances (Braddick, Atkinson, French and Howland, 1979; Banks, 1980). By six months this adjustment is as accurate as the adult's. At no stage in infancy are the errors of focussing likely to limit acuity, as infants are always tested at fairly close distances from the stimuli.

Rather than optical focus limiting acuity, the relationship may well be the other way around. To be able to adjust accommodation accurately, the infant must be able to distinguish the blurred image produced by defocus from the sharp image of a well-focussed eye. If acuity is limited by immaturity of the neural pathway, information about image sharpness will be degraded in transmission to the brain. This will impair the accuracy with which accommodation can be adjusted to the stimulus distance. However, there also seem to be limitations of visual attention which contribute to infants' difficulties in focussing on distant objects (see below).

One feature of infant's optics is that their eyes are commonly astigmatic (Mohindra, Held, Gwiazda and Brill, 1978; Howland, Atkinson, Braddick and French, 1978). This means that the focussing power of the eye is different for horizontal and vertical lines in the image. A large fraction of three- to

7

Figure 2. The effect of infant's limited acuity. These photographs simulate viewing of a life-size face at a distance of about 50 cm with a degree of optical blur that removes detail (high spatial frequencies) beyond the infant's acuity limit. (a) sharp image (b) blur removes all spatial frequencies beyond one-month-old's acuity limit (c) blur removes all spatial frequencies beyond three-month-old's acuity limit. The remarkably small loss of useful visual information in (c) and even in (b) depends on the short viewing distance; high acuity is principally important for distance vision, or for very fine manipulative skills and reading.

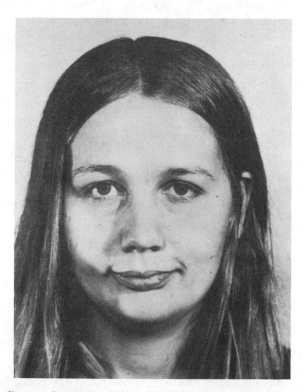

Above: figure 2a; top right: figure 2b; bottom right: figure 2c

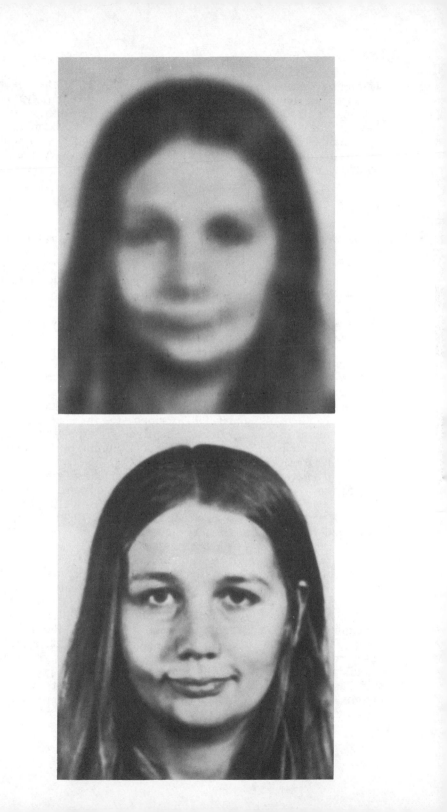

six-month infants have enough astigmatism to affect their measured acuity significantly (Atkinson and French, 1979), although it is unlikely to impair the visual information that they actually need from their surroundings, for example in recognizing faces. This astigmatism normally reduces to adult levels in the course of the first two years (Atkinson, Braddick and French, 1980).

PHYSIOLOGICAL BASIS FOR VISUAL SENSITIVITY

If the development of acuity is determined by neural rather than optical development, what is it that develops? Probably several kinds of neural maturation are taking place together. The highest acuity of the human eye is provided by the densely packed receptors and numerous ganglion cells of the central fovea. Anatomical evidence suggests that these special features of the fovea develop over the first few months of life (Mann, 1964; Abramov, Gordon, Hendrickson, Hainline, Dobson and LaBossiere, 1982). High acuity also depends on the organization of neural connections, as reflected in the receptive fields of nerve cells at the various levels of the visual pathway. One pointer to this development is the shape of the contrast sensitivity function. The low spatial frequency cut described above is generally ascribed to the presence of lateral inhibition in retinal receptive fields: nerve cells effectively measure the difference of illumination between nearby regions and so are relatively insensitive to very gradual transitions from light to dark over large areas. This low spatial frequency cut is present in the contrast sensitivity of two-month-olds but not of one-month-olds (Atkinson, Braddick and Moar, 1977a; Banks and Salapatek, 1978), implying that inhibitory neural connections are developing in the retina over the first few months.

Neural development is not limited to the retina. The visual cortex of the brain shows a striking increase in the richness of its connections over the first few months (Conel, 1939, 1947). This development may not be the primary factor in development of acuity, since acuity changes (parallel to those in human infants) are seen at precortical levels of the monkey visual pathway (Blakemore and Vital-Durand, 1979). The cortical connections must be important, though, in determining the organization of cortical cells responses to pattern properties such as orientation. This has been studied most fully in kittens, where such organization is present at birth but is very incomplete (Blakemore, 1978).

SENSITIVITY TO MOTION AND FLICKER

Movement and change are effective in eliciting visual attention in young infants (Haith, 1966, 1978; Tronick, 1972; Volkman and Dobson, 1976; Bushnell, 1979). Does the infant have a special sensitivity to these stimuli? Various aspects of sensitivity to temporal change have to be distinguished. Atkinson, Braddick and Moar (1977b) compared contrast sensitivity for static and moving gratings. They found that one- to three-month infants showed higher sensitivity to low- and medium-spatial-frequency gratings when they were moving at moderate rates, which may help to explain infants' attention to moving stimuli. However, a comparable difference is found in adults at these spatial frequencies. That is, there was no indication of any different balance between the systems detecting moving and static stimuli ('transient' and 'sustained': Kulikowski and Tolhurst, 1973) in infant and adult. On the other hand, the infant's sensitivity to temporal change (presumably mediated by the transient system) extends to remarkably high flicker frequencies. Regal (1981) found in a PL experiment that the maximum flicker rate detected by one-month-olds was 75 per cent of the adult's, suggesting a system which in this respect may be almost fully mature at birth. (Compare this with detection of <u>spatial</u> modulation, i.e. acuity, which is less than 10 per cent of adult performance at the same age.)

Motion in the visual field plays an important part in our awareness of objects' form and layout in space. Infants' ability to use this information will be discussed in the section on perceptual constancies.

COLOUR VISION

As colour vision is a conspicuous feature of our mature visual experience, it is natural to ask whether young infants see differentiated colours in the same way as ourselves. Normal colour vision depends on the existence of three types of cone receptors in the retina, differing in their sensitivity to different wavelengths. From recordings of electrical activity in the retina (ERG) some cone activity is present in newborns (Maurer, 1975; Werner and Wooten, 1979). Adult-like spectral sensitivity functions have been obtained for two-month-olds using behavioural techniques and VEP measurements (Peeples and Teller, 1978; Dobson, 1976; Moskowitz-Cook, 1979), although these do not prove whether all three cone types are operating, and whether the infant's visual system can separate and compare their signals for colour discriminations.

In any demonstration of colour discrimination, it is important to show that the discrimination performance could not be based on differences in brightness. Since an individual infant's brightness matches between different colours are difficult to establish, it is best to show that a discrimination between two colours holds over a range of relative intensities that are closely spaced enough to include the unknown point where the colours match in brightness. This was done, for instance by Teller, Peeples and Sekel (1978) who used the PL method to test whether two-month-olds could detect a coloured stripe against a white surround. Most colours, they found, were discriminated from white over the full range of relative intensities, but there were 'neutral points' in the spectrum where the babies' behaviour showed no discrimination. In adults, neutral points indicate dichromacy, the form of colour blindness where only two rather than three cone types contribute to colour vision. However, the infants' neutral points were not those characteristic of the adult system missing any one of the normal three mechanisms. Further evidence that two- to three-month infants are not like adults with the common forms of red-green colour deficiency (either dichromatism or a milder anomaly) comes from Hamer, Alexander and Teller (1982) who showed that the red-green mixture needed to match a yellow background (again assessed by PL) was similar to that expected from normal adult long- and medium-wavelength cone mechanisms.

In adults, individual cone mechanisms can be isolated by testing threshold on various coloured adapting background (see Mollon, 1982). Pulos, Teller and Buck (1980) used this method to look for evidence in infants of thresholds controlled by the third 'short-wavelength' cone mechanism. They found such evidence in three-month-olds but not in two-month-old infants. Are the younger infants tritanopic, i.e. restricted to colour information from long- and medium-wavelength cones? (Their neutral points are somewhat different from those of the rare adult tritanopes.) The possibility has implications beyond colour vision, since primate physiology (see Mollon, 1982) suggests that tritanopia might be expected in a visual system using the information that goes to the superior colliculus but not that going to the visual cortex.

Strictly, to detect a coloured patch against a white of differently coloured background, as in the experiments mentioned, the infant visual system would not have to compare signals from different types of cone: it would be enough to process information from each cone type separately and find that the signals from adjoining areas were different within any one cone mechanism. A test of colour vision in a truer sense is provided by the habituation-recovery method, since this tests whether the infant recognizes as different two colours presented at separate times. Such experiments (Bornstein, Kessen and Weiskopf, 1976; Bornstein, 1976) show that three- to four-month infants can perform a variety of colour discriminations, including some that would not be expected for a red-green dichromat. Of course, this method requires the infant to encode colour properties in memory as well as to discriminate them.

Habituation experiments have also been used (Bornstein, Kessen and Weiskopf, 1976) to argue that the infant divides colours into the categories red, green, blue and yellow. The implications of this kind of 'categorical perception', however, are controversial (Werner and Wooten, 1979; Bornstein, 1981): in adults at least, the divisions between these colour categories are not always consistent across individuals, and do not bear much relation to which colour discriminations are easiest.

In summary, no major differences have yet been found between the colour discriminations of a three-month infant and those of a normal adult. There are developmental changes before that age, which probably reflect neural processing of colour information rather than any peripheral lack analogous to the common forms of 'colour blindness'.

At low light levels, vision depends on the rod receptors which are of a single type and so cannot differentiate colours. One-month infants have been shown to have this system also (Powers, Schneck and Teller, 1981). The absolute dark-adapted sensitivity shown by this PL experiment is about 50 times lower for one-month-olds, and 10 times lower for three-month-olds, than for adults. While these may sound like large differences, they still represent remarkably high sensitivity for the infants: in comparison, it must be remembered that adult sensitivity can be reduced a millionfold by light adaptation.

DEVELOPMENT OF EYE MOVEMENTS

Eye movements are an integral part of the process of spatial vision. Saccadic movements are abrupt jumps to bring an object of interest on to the fovea. The slower smooth pursuit movements allow the eyes to maintain a steady image of a moving object. In both these kinds of movement, the two eyes move in the same way. Movements which change the convergence of the two eyes will be discussed under 'binocular vision'.

Saccadic eye movements are present from birth, and the success of the PL method shows that they are directed towards visual targets (even though the fovea, onto which a fixated target is imaged, is immature). However, the control of directed saccades is not adult-like in the infant of two months or less. The infant's initial saccade is normally in the correct direction, but may cover only a fraction of the distance to the target. Fixation is then attained by a series of saccades which are of a standard amplitude rather than being matched to the target distance (Aslin and Salapatek, 1975).

In contrast to saccades, the smooth pursuit system does not begin to function until about two months (Aslin, 1981a). Younger infants will track a slowly moving stimulus, but this 'tracking' is achieved by a series of saccades. However, when a large part of the field of view is filled with uniformly moving patterns, optokinetic nystagmus (OKN) occurs even in newborns (in whom it has been used, e.g. by Dayton, Jones, Aiu, Rawson, Steele and Rose (1964), to test acuity for the moving pattern). OKN is a repetitive cycle of slow following motions interleaved with saccade-like returning flicks. If young infants have a response mechanism that can generate the OKN slow phase, why are they incapable of the dynamically very similar smooth pursuit? One possibility is that they are incapable of using a single pursuit target to initiate this mechanism, when the rest of the field is filled with competing stationary contours.

One respect in which OKN of young infants is not adult-like is its asymmetry. This appears when the infant is viewing with one eye only: OKN can be elicited by pattern moving temporal-to-nasal (i.e. moving towards the nose) and not in the reverse direction. (There is no asymmetry in binocular OKN because the left eye will drive left-to-right OKN and the right eye right-to-left.) By about three months, monocular OKN can be driven in both directions (Atkinson and Braddick, 1981b). Animal studies (see Hoffman, 1979) suggest that the temporal-to-nasal direction of OKN is controlled by an entirely subcortical pathway: the attainment of symmetry must reflect development of some aspect of cortical function.

VISUAL FIELDS AND ATTENTION

Under what conditions can a visual target elicit a fixation movement from an infant? The pattern variables that determine fixation will be discussed below. Once a target has 'captured' visual attention, infants under two months show great difficulty in releasing their gaze from it. This is shown by an apparently very narrow visual field: a second target has to appear within 15 to attract a fixation. If the initial fixation target disappears as the peripheral target appears, then newborns will shift further out, to 25 and seven-week-olds to 35 (Harris and MacFarlane, 1974). This is still a very restricted field compared to an older infant or adult. However, it is probable that the restriction is a matter of the mechanisms controlling the infant's visual attention rather than any basic limitation on the area of visual sensitivity. The use of a moving or flashing target increases the effective visual field (McKenzie and Day, 1976), while competing activities such as sucking a dummy decrease it.

The effectiveness of a stimulus in capturing a young infant's attention also depends on its distance. Even for an object subtending a constant angle, fixation probability decreases with increasing distance (McKenzie and Day, 1972, 1976; De Schonen, McKenzie and Bresson, 1978). This is probably a major factor in the difficulty of infants under three months accurately accommodating at distances over 75 cm. It also implies that these infants can discriminate near from far distances even for a constant angular target.

BINOCULAR VISION

Three-dimensional perception is traditionally discussed in terms of 'cues', that is specific properties of the visual input that give information about depth. For the cue of bino-cular disparity or stereopsis we know most about the sensory mechanisms, and study of their development helps us to understand about more general problems of plasticity in the visual system. However, binocular disparity is only one amongst a number of sources of depth information (motion parallax, texture gradient, linear perspective, etc.), and there is no reason to suppose that it is primary either in development or in the developed system. We shall return to the infant's use of depth information more generally after discussing binocular function.

In adults, the two eyes move together ('conjugate movement') and can be adjusted to converge on an object of interest. This enables the visual system to bring together corresponding information from the two eyes. The small differences between their two views (binocular disparity) can then be used as a sensitive indicator of the relative depth of surfaces and objects (stereopsis). Aslin and Dumais (1980) provide a thorough review of the foundations of binocular function in infancy.

Even in newborns, almost all eye movements are conjugate. The young infant's eyes generally appear divergent, but this is probably the result of a systematic error in the corneal reflex method of measuring eye position (Slater and Findlay, 1975a). It is difficult with any available method to assess the exact alignment of the eyes, but changes in alignment (vergence movements) can be recognized. Newborns can show convergence changes in the correct direction in response to changes in target distance (Slater and Findlay, 1975b), but these improve a good deal in consistency and quantitative accuracy over the first three months (Aslin, 1977).

Can the infant's visual system combine information from the two eyes? Binocular function can be distinguished from purely monocular visual processing by the use of random dot patterns. In a random-dot correlogram an ever-changing pattern of dots is displayed to each eye, which may either be identical (correlated), or the left eye's image may be the negative of the right (anticorrelated). When the pattern switches from the correlated to the anticorrelated phase, the appearance (to a binocular adult observer) changes from a clearly fused surface to an incoherent array of dots that are poorly localized in depth. This perceptual change is accompanied by a measurable evoked potential, which must originate in nerve cells that combine inputs from the two eyes, since neither eye alone can detect the change. Such evoked potentials can be recorded from most infants over three months, some two-month-olds, but not from younger infants (Braddick, Atkinson, Julesz, Kropfl, Bodis-Wollner and Raab, 1980; Petrig, Julesz, Kropfl, Baumgartner and Anliker, 1981; Braddick and Atkinson, in press). Positive results with correlograms show that the infant's visual system can match the images coming to the two eyes, but do not directly prove that it is sensitive to the disparities between these images that are the basis of stereoscopic depth perception. This can be tested with random-dot stereograms, in which the dots in one region are displaced in the left eye's view compared to their positions as seen by the right eye, so that to an observer with stereopsis the region appears to stand out in depth from its surround. Fox (1981) reviews work from his laboratory showing that, from four months of age on average, infants track a region of binocularly disparate dots when it moves across a random dot pattern. This evidence of disparity detection is reinforced by the findings of Held, Birch and Gwiazda (1980) that infants in a PL experiment fixate a three-line target, where the centre line is disparate, in preference to one where all three lines lie in the same stereoscopic plane.

All these studies concur that evidence of binocular function is first found, on average, around three to four months of age (although there are individual differences). It is difficult to exclude the possibility that the neural apparatus of binocular vision is present earlier, but that the eyes are not well enough aligned to make use of it. However, the observations of convergence control mentioned above make this unlikely, and Birch, Gwiazda and Held (in press) have confirmed their PL results on the development of disparity sensitivity with stimuli which are designed to be unaffected by errors of eye alignment.

BINOCULAR PLASTICITY AND CRITICAL PERIODS

Binocular vision is the aspect of vision which most often goes wrong in early development. A proportion which has been estimated between 2-8 per cent of children develop strabismus (squint) in which the two eyes become permanently misaligned, and/or amblyopia (where one eye suffers a functional loss of vision in competition with the other, which cannot be improved by spectacle correction).

Neurophysiological studies of the cat and monkey (reviewed by Blakemore, 1978; Mitchell, 1981; and Movshon and Van Sluyters, 1981; see also Wiesel, 1982) have shown phenomena that may be related to these disorders. If one eye of an animal is covered, or its image grossly blurred, during early life, that eye loses almost all its connections to cells of the visual cortex. If the two eyes are covered alternately, or if an artificial deviation of one eye is produced, so that the two eyes do not see correlated images, then although each eye maintains its separate input to the cortex, no cortical cells are found which combine signals from the two eyes. These studies have emphasized the idea of a critical period in which the binocular system is modifiable or plastic, since the changes described only occur if the eye is covered during a particular period of development (e.g. approximately three weeks to three months postnatal in kittens). If modifications are made in that period, they cannot be reversed by visual experience after the critical period. These findings immediately provoke the question: when does the critical period of human visual development begin and end? One approach to this question has been to look psychophysically for evidence of cells with binocular input, in individuals who suffered squint at various ages (Banks, Aslin and Letson, 1975). This study suggests that the plasticity of the human binocular system is greatest at ages up to two years, and declines rapidly after that, although the system may not be completely fixed at age five. This is broadly in line with clinical experience, although systematic quantitative clinical data is rare and it is doubtful just how far the physiological evidence from animal experiments provides a model for clinical disorders and treatment. For example, physiological evidence on how many cells receive input from each eye cannot be straightforwardly related to the usual clinical measure of the acuity of each eye. Direct evidence of plasticity in the first year, based on infant acuity measurements, is starting to become available (Mohindra, Jacobsen, Thomas and Held, 1979).

An indirect and more speculative argument is that the period in which the visual system is developing most rapidly is likely to be the period when it is most susceptible to modification and disruption by anomalous input (Hickey, 1981). On these grounds, anatomical and performance data would suggest that the human visual system is most modifiable during the first year.

Several cautions need to be borne in mind when thinking about visual critical periods. First, it is almost certain that plasticity declines gradually, rather than there being an age which marks the 'end of the critical period'. Given that, the practical questions 'when is it too late to reverse any effects of deprivation?' on the one hand, and 'what is the age at which the visual system is most acutely susceptible?' on the other, are likely to focus attention on very different ages. Second, this discussion has concentrated on the plasticity of binocular function. However, other aspects of visual function have been shown to be modifiable, such as sensitivity to orientation and direction of movement. The critical periods for modification of different functions probably do not coincide (Daw, Berman and Ariel, 1978).

PERCEPTION OF DEPTH

We can ask two distinct questions about infants' processing of visual depth information. First, can infants distinguish differences in depth cues? Second, do these differences signify differences in depth to the infant? For instance, the results of the stereoscopic experiments described above show that four-month infants can discriminate between different binocular disparities (question one above), but do not indicate whether infants perceived this difference as one of depth. Similarly, the finding by Fantz (1961) that one-month-olds fixate a solid textured sphere in preference to a flat disk shows that one or more of the differences between these targets (shadowing, texture gradient, motion parallax or binocular disparity) can be discriminated, but does not indicate whether these cues provide any sense of depth.

To answer the second question, it is necessary to show either that the infant recognizes an equivalence between similar depth arrangements even when signalled by different cues ('stimulus convergence') or that depth cues determine a response which is appropriate to the location in three-dimensional space ('response convergence') (Yonas and Pick, 1975). In practice, most experiments have investigated infants' spatially appropriate responses. A well-known example is the 'visual cliff' (Walk, 1966), where infants who are old enough to crawl avoid an apparently deep drop off a platform and in preference crawl to the apparently shallow side. Other experiments have used responses which can be observed earlier in infancy, and have investigated individual depth cues.

Experiments on infants' responses to stereoscopic stimuli have generally used the 'virtual objects' produced by a binocularly disparate pair of shadows (figure 3). Five-month-olds show reaching responses which vary with the distance of a virtual object, implying perceived depth from disparity information, but there is controversy over the significance of the less well directed arm movements produced by younger infants in this situation (Yonas, 1979; McDonnell, 1979).

If the object producing shadows in the apparatus of figure 3 moves, it can simulate the image changes due to an object approaching the infant (with or without disparity information). Yonas (1979, 1981) reviews evidence that infants respond to this depth information signalling collision. Bower and his colleagues have reported that infants as young as one week show head withdrawal, but it has proved difficult to distinguish between a true withdrawal response and an upwards head movement tracking the top edge of the moving object. However, by 15-20 weeks, infants reliably make blinking and withdrawal responses specifically to the optical changes specifying collision.

Yonas, Cleaves and Pettersen (1978) studied differential reaching responses to determine infants' sensitivity to 'pictorial' depth cues, i.e. cues not depending on motion or binocular vision. Specifically, they looked at the perspective cues of size difference between the two ends of a rotated

19

rectangular shape. They found that at 26-30 weeks, infants reached for the apparently nearer side, either for a rectangle that was really tilted in space or for a trapezoidal shape presented head on. At 20-22 weeks they responded to real depth but not the 'pictorial' depth of the trapezoid.

By six months, then, infants can use a range of cues to obtain information about depth. The limited evidence available so far suggests that motion information is used first, followed by stereoscopic disparity and then perspective information. Experiments on the perceptual constancies (see below) also imply the ability to use depth information between three and six months.

Classically, the development of spatial perception has been a prime area for the dispute between nativist and empiricist views. In the traditional empiricist view, the perception of depth is a result of learnt associations between visual stimuli and other sensations, e.g. tactile or kinaesthetic. The infant's motor experience is very limited up to six months, but it is difficult to exclude the possibility of this kind of learning, since the use of response convergence to test the infant's sense of space means that some visuo-motor experience must have occurred. There is a great deal more possibility, of course, of learnt associations between visual stimuli or between different properties of the same stimuli.

A modern opponent of the associationist view is J. J. Gibson, who sees space perception as the direct pickup of high level properties of the optical array. In the Gibsonian view, these properties do not have to acquire meaning through association; their meaning is intrinsic, although they have to become more finely differentiated in development. On this view the distinction between detection of a depth cue and its use in space perception is not a valid one. It is difficult to see how these questions on the role of learning in space perception can be experimentally resolved unless cases can be found where infants (human or otherwise) have been exposed to different structures of stimulus associations.

The physiological work on visual plasticity in the critical period cannot answer questions about the meaning of visual cues, but it does alert us to the possible subtleties of the interaction between innate structure and visual experience. The newborn visual cortex appears to contain, at least in outline, the basis of its mature organization, but this organization requires certain visual experience to develop normally and even the organization present at birth can be disrupted by anomalous experience. There is a wide range of possible relationships between genetic and experiential determinants of

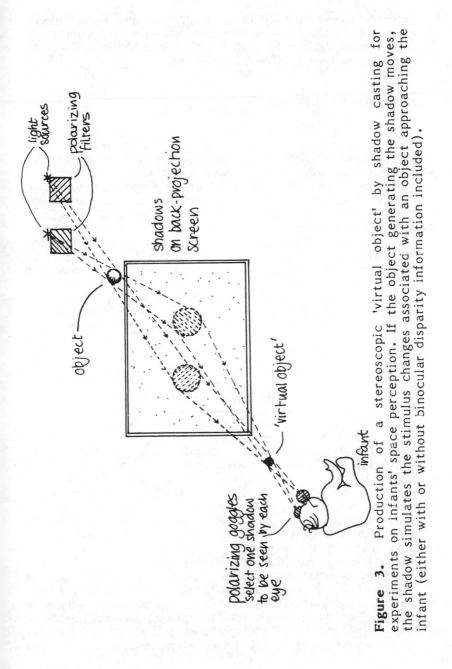

Figure 3. Production of a stereoscopic 'virtual object' by shadow casting for experiments on infants' space perception. If the object generating the shadow moves, the shadow simulates the stimulus changes associated with an object approaching the infant (either with or without binocular disparity information included).

perception (see Aslin, 1981b), which must now be considered instead of a simple dichotomy between nature and nurture. Furthermore, it is likely that different interactions will be found for different perceptual functions.

PATTERN PERCEPTION

The fact that infants from birth show a marked preference for fixating a patterned rather than an unpatterned field, has encouraged investigators to study what properties of patterns produce this preference. Pattern 'complexity' has been proposed as a variable, but it is almost impossible to define independently of contour density and pattern area (Karmel and Maisel, 1975; Haith, 1978). Banks and Salapatek (1981) apply a more sophisticated and realistic analysis in which they use the infant's contrast sensitivity function to determine the effectiveness of different spatial frequency components in simple patterns for the infant's visual system and hence to predict preferences.

All these approaches are essentially looking for a variable which reflects 'amount of pattern'. This implies that the form or configuration of the pattern is not relevant for infants' visual preferences. Are newborns really unable to discriminate differences in configuration, and if so, when does this ability develop?

The physiology of the visual cortex (Hubel and Wiesel, 1977) suggests that contour orientation is one of the most basic pattern variables. Evidence for differential responses to orientation has been found at birth (Slater and Sykes, 1977) and at one to three months (McKenzie and Day, 1971; Leehey, Moskowitz-Cook, Brill and Held, 1975). It is possible that horizontal-vertical differences in eye scanning or in the optics of the eye (astigmatism) could produce these effects without true sensitivity to orientation. However, an experiment by Maurer and Martello (1980), showed discrimination of opposite obliques by five- to six-week-olds, that could only be accounted for by orientation detection. All these experiments have used straight lines, presenting only one orientation within each stimulus. Curved lines contain a range of orientations, and it is therefore interesting that infants show a preference for fixating patterns of curves over straight line patterns matched for contour length and area (Fantz, Fagan and Miranda, 1975; Hopkins, Kagan, Brachfeld, Hans and Linn, 1976). This preference is shown by newborns (Fantz and Miranda, 1975). It may be explained as a preference

22

for the pattern giving more stimulation, if multiple orientations within the pattern are processed separately, i.e. it implies the existence at birth of orientation-selective systems, presumably in the visual cortex.

Some experiments have looked at infants' discriminations of more complex forms such as discrimination between a triangle and a cross (Slater, Morison and Rose, in press). It has generally been difficult to prove satisfactorily that infants are sensitive to complex properties of a configuration, since there have frequently been variations in lower level pattern properties such as orientation, contour length or contrast, which could have served as the basis of discrimination or preference.

FACE PERCEPTION

One visual configuration which has been felt to be of special significance to the infant is the human face. The early work of Fantz (1963) suggested that a schematic face was a highly preferred stimulus for neonates. Most of the more recent work suggests that if simple variables like contour density, contrast and symmetry are kept constant, infants under four months do not show any preference for a natural arrangement of facial features over a scrambled arrangement. Maurer and Barrera (1981) used a habituation/recovery measure which might be expected to show discriminative ability not revealed as a preference, and showed a face/scrambled face discrimination by two-month-olds but not by one-month-olds. However, one report (Goren, Sarty and Wu, 1975) does seem to provide unequivocal evidence for this discrimination in newborns. Of course, even if this performance represents an intrinsic sensitivity to a face-like form, we do not know what significance, if any, the newborn attaches to this stimulus. The possible innate sensitivity to faces may be linked to 'face detecting cells' found in monkey cortex (Perrett, Rolls and Caan, 1979), although nothing is yet known about the developmental history of these cells.

The ability to distinguish one individual's face from another might be expected to be much more subtle than the ability to recognize a configuration as face-like. None the less, a number of studies have shown discrimination between photographs of different faces around 20 weeks (e.g. Fagan, 1972; Cornell, 1974; Cohen, De Loache and Pearl, 1977), and even in infants as young as 13 weeks (Barrera and Maurer, 1981a) and five to seven weeks (Bushnell, 1982). The ability to distinguish between individuals is also found very early in other sensory modalities (Mills and Melhuish, 1974; Macfarlane, 1975). A discrimination of comparable subtlety, which infants are also able to make by three months of age, is between facial expressions of the same individual (Young-Browne, Rosenfeld and Horowitz, 1977; Barrera and Maurer, 1981b).

From what part of the face do infants obtain the information they use in recognition? Measurements of eye scanning patterns show that infants under two months spend most time fixating near the outer contour of the face. Beyond this age infants, like adults, concentrate their fixations in the region of internal features, particularly the eyes (Maurer and Salapatek, 1976; Haith, Bergman and Moore, 1977). When information from the outer contour of the face (the hairline) is deleted, five- to seven-week-olds can no longer discriminate between faces, whilst older infants can use internal features (Bushnell, 1982).

THE 'EXTERNALITY' EFFECT

Young infants' concentration on the outer boundary of a form is not restricted to faces. There is evidence that one month olds' fixations tend to cluster on the outer boundary of a geometrical figure while two-month-olds fixate internal features (Salapatek, 1975) (although some of the age differences in scanning patterns have not appeared in a more systematic study by Hainline and Lemerise (1982)). Discrimination evidence is more direct than that from eye movements: Milewski (1976) showed that five-week-olds, after habituation to a figure consisting, for example, of a triangle within a square, showed a response to novelty if the external form was changed but not to a change in the internal form. Three-month-olds would respond to either change. The inability to use internal features does not seem to be a consequence of limited acuity. Nor is it due simply to an inability to process more than one feature at a time: if the internal features are made more conspicuous by motion, five-week-olds will respond to shape changes in either internal or external figures (Bushnell, 1979). The insensitivity to features within an outer boundary has a suggestive similarity to the behaviour of monkeys lacking a striate cortex (Humphrey, 1974).

PERCEPTUAL CONSTANCIES AND CATEGORIES

The ability to recognize the invariant form of an object, despite changes in the retinal image due to viewing angle (shape constancy) and distance (size constancy), requires both an ability to recognize shapes and the appreciation of three-dimensional spatial relations. Bower (1966a) reported that two-month infants could respond equivalently in an operant task to a rectangle at various slants, and differentiate it from a frontally presented trapezoid giving the same retinal shape; he also reported a similar ability to generalize a response to the same object at different distances (Bower, 1966b). These experiments implied a surprisingly sophisticated perceptual integration by the infant. More recent studies have used habituation techniques. Day and MacKenzie (1973) found that eight-week and 14-week infants habituated over a series of presentations of a cube in different orientations as rapidly as to a single view, suggesting shape constancy. This experimental design is open to the criticism that it does not demonstrate any ability to discriminate shape differences in the three-dimensional forms (Cook, Field and Griffiths, 1978). However, fuller habituation-recovery studies by Caron, Caron and Carlson (1978, 1979) show the ability of 12-week-olds both to discriminate changes in slant and shape, and to recognize the novelty of a new shape after exposure to a habituation stimulus in a variety of tilted positions. Unlike these confirmations of shape constancy quite early in infancy, Bower's finding of size constancy has not been replicated: McKenzie, Tootell and Day (1980), using a habituation-recovery method, showed discriminations based on object size and distance in infants over six months of age but not in four-month-olds.

The studies described above presented infants with static views of objects. When an object is in motion, its image undergoes a continuous transformation between such views. Gibson, Owsley and Johnston (1978) showed that five-month infants, after habituation to a variety of rigid motions, recognized the novelty of a non-rigid 'squashing' transformation. They went on to show (Gibson, Owsley, Walker and Megaw-Nyce, 1979; Walker, Owsley, Megaw-Nyce, Gibson and Bahrick, 1980) that three-month-olds recognized the nature of rigid motion across a variety of objects, recognized object identity across various rigid motions, and recognized that various non-rigid deformations were distinct from rigid motion. These results imply that three- to five-month infants are sensitive to the properties of objects that are invariant under rigid motion, and to the quality of motion that preserves these invariants. Gibson and her colleagues argue that these invariants of a dynamic optical array should be considered as basic in perception, rather than the 'snapshot' geometry of static retinal images. However, infants' object recognition can be hindered, rather than helped, by rigid transformations of more complex objects (Ruff, 1982); the infant may have grasped the basic property of invariance under motion, but that does not mean it will be recognized in every case.

In the spatial constancies, different stimuli are treated as in some respect equivalent. This does not mean that they are indiscriminable: several of the experiments reviewed above demonstrated discriminations between the same object presented with different slants, distances, or motions. To demonstrate constancies, therefore, many of these experiments had to use designs where the habituation stimulus varied on successive exposures, so that all the infant could habituate to was the common invariant property. This experimental design clearly has possibilities beyond the spatial constancies: it can be used to test the infant's formation of a general 'concept' which includes a selected set of stimuli (Cohen, 1979). For example, an experiment by Cohen and Strauss (1979) included tests at several levels of generality. Thirty-week-old infants, habituated to a single face picture, responded to the novelty of a different photograph of the same face, or to a different face. These discriminations could be based on a number of visual properties. Infants habituated to a series of different pictures of the same face responded to the novelty of a different face, but not to a new picture of the familiar face. This can be regarded as a demonstration of shape constancy of a fairly complex kind. Finally, infants habituated a series of different female faces showed no recovery to a new female face, implying the habituation of a category 'female faces in general' or perhaps 'faces in general'. Younger (18- and 24-week) infants showed novelty responses in every case, suggesting that they did not generalize across different views or different members of the face category. Clearly, this technique has possibilities for explaining the development of infants' perceptual categorizations of many kinds and at various levels.

No clear dividing line can be drawn between the recognition of invariant visual properties and the assignment of an object to an abstract cognitive category, although there are examples of categories which we would not regard as having any common visual properties. We are also working on the borderlines of perception and cognition in another sense: it is not clear how far findings in habituation experiments should be regarded as telling us about infants' visual perception and how far as about visual memory (many are reviewed, for example in Werner and Perlmutter's (1979) chapter on infant memory). It is plausible that, in development, perceptual processes of generalization may serve as prototypes for concept formation of a more abstract kind. As a central example, the perception of an object as having an invariant shape may provide a foundation for the more general 'object concept', i.e. the idea that an object has a continued unitary existence even when it disappears from the child's view.

OVERVIEW

The first months of life are a period of radical development in human vision. In particular, we have seen a set of striking changes that occur between the first and third months of life: the low-spatial-frequency cut appears in the contrast sensitivity function; smooth pursuit eye movements begin; switches of visual attention occur more readily; OKN becomes symmetrical; binocular function emerges; the externality effect is overcome; various pattern preferences become manifest (Fantz, Fagan and Miranda, 1975). We do not know what underlying development causes these changes, or how far they have a common cause. A number of them would be accounted for by the emergence of function in the visual cortex, and Bronson (1974) has proposed that visual behaviour before two months is controlled by the superior colliculus, a midbrain structure that is believed to be involved primarily in orientating behaviour and eye movement control, with relatively little capacity for pattern recognition. However, the pattern discriminations that the newborn and one-month infants can perform are beyond those that are believed possible for primates lacking striate cortex. Specific physiological theories of partial cortical function are possible (e.g. Maurer and Lewis, 1979), but we do not yet understand the function of different physiological systems well enough to test them in any detail (Atkinson and Braddick, 1982).

We have expressed these changes in terms of sensory processes. However, they coincide with equally radical changes in the infant's social behaviour (Trevarthen, 1980). It is not difficult to imagine how the development of fixation patterns that lead to eye contact can have an impact on interaction in a social dyad, and how the ability to shift visual attention may be a necessary component of the development of social turn taking. The basic sensory mechanisms of acuity, colour, motion, and binocular vision appear to be established by three months, although they may show great quantitative improvements after that age. In some respects it is remarkable how soon the use of these mechanisms in spatial and social perception follows on their basic establishment. It is difficult to avoid the conclusion that the human visual system is, from the start, well prepared for its essential perceptual tasks. We have yet to understand how the maturation of sensory systems, experience of the regularities of the visual world, and innate organizing principles interlock, and we do not know whether the nature of this interlocking relationship will be at all similar for each of the diverse perceptual functions we have considered. These remain major intellectual and experimental challenges for the future.

REFERENCES

Abramov, I., Gordon, J., Hendrickson, A., Hainline, L., Dobson, V. and LaBossiere, E. (1982). The retina of the newborn human infant. Science, 217, 265-267.

Aslin, R. N. (1977). Development of binocular fixation in human infants. Journal of Experimental Child Psychology, 23, 133-150.

Aslin, R. N. (1981a). Development of smooth pursuit in human infants. In D. F. Fisher, R. A. Monty and J. W. Senders (eds), Eye Movements: Cognition and visual perception. Hillsdale, NJ: Erlbaum Press.

Aslin, R. N. (1981b). Experiential influences and sensitive periods in perceptual development: a unified model. In R. N. Aslin, J. R. Alberts and M. R. Petersen (eds), The Development of Perception: Psychobiological perspectives. Volume II: The Visual System. New York: Academic Press.

Aslin, R. N. and Dumais, S. T. (1980). Binocular vision in infants: a review and a theoretical framework. In L. P. Lipsitt and H. W. Reese (eds), Advances in Child Development and Behaviour, 15. New York: Academic Press.

Aslin, R. N. and Salapatek, P. (1975). Saccadic localization of peripheral targets by the very young human infant. Perception and Psychophysics, 17, 293-302.

Atkinson, J., Braddick, O. and Moar, K. (1977a). Development of contrast sensitivity over the first 3 months of life in the human infant. Vision Research. 17, 1037-1044.

Atkinson, J., Braddick, O. and Moar, K. (1977b). Contrast sensitivity of the human infant for moving and static patterns. Vision Research, 17, 1045-1047.

Atkinson, J. and Braddick, O. (1981a). Acuity, contrast sensitivity, and accommodation in infancy. In R. N. Aslin, J. R. Alberts and M. R. Petersen (eds), The Development of Perception, Volume 2: The Visual System. New York: Academic Press.

Atkinson, J. and Braddick, O. (1981b). Development of optokinetic nystagmus in infants: an indicator of cortical binocularity? In D. F. Fisher, R. A. Monty and J. W. Senders (eds), Eye Movements: Cognition and visual perception. Hillsdale, NJ: Erlbaum Press.

Atkinson, J., Braddick, O. and French, J. (1980). Infant astigmatism: its disappearance with age. Vision Research, 20, 891-893.

Atkinson, J. and Braddick, O. (1982). Sensory and perceptual capacities of the neonate. In P. Stratton (ed.), Psycho-biology of the Human Newborn. Chichester: Wiley.

Atkinson, J. and Braddick, O. Assessment of visual acuity in infancy and early childhood. Acta Ophthalmologica. In press.

Atkinson, J. and French, J. (1979). Astigmatism and orientation preference in human infants. Vision Research 19, 1315-1317.

Atkinson, J., French, J. and Braddick, O. (1981). Contrast sensitivity function of preschool children. British Journal of Ophthalmology, 65, 525-529.

Atkinson, J., Braddick, O. and Pimm-Smith, E. (1982). 'Preferential looking' for monocular and binocular acuity testing in infants. British Journal of Ophthalmology, 66, 264-268.

Atkinson, J., Braddick, O., Pimm-Smith, E., Ayling, L. and Sawyer, R. (1981). Does the Catford Drum give an accurate assessment of acuity? British Journal of Ophthalmology, 65, 652-656.

Banks, M. S. (1980). The development of visual accommodation during early infancy. Child Development, 51, 646-666.

Banks, M. S., Aslin, R. N. and Letson, R. D. (1975). Sensitive period for the development of human binocular vision. Science, 190, 675-677.

Banks, M. S. and Salapatek, P. (1978). Acuity and contrast sensitivity in 1-, 2- and 3-month-old human infants. Investigative Ophthalmology and Visual Science, 17, 361-365.

Banks, M. and Salapatek, P. (1981). Infant pattern vision; a new approach based on the contrast sensitivity function. Journal of Experimental Child Psychology, 31, 1-45.

Barrera, M. E. and Maurer, D. (1981a). Discrimination of strangers by the three-month-old. Child Development, 52, 558-563.

Barrera, M. E. and Maurer, D. (1981b). The perception of facial expressions by the three-month-old. Child Development, 52, 203-206.

Birch, E. E., Gwiazda, J. and Held, R. The development of vergence does not account for the onset of stereopsis. Perception. In press.

Blakemore, C. (1978). Maturation and modification in the developing visual system. In R. Held, H. W. Leibowitz and H. L. Teuber (eds), Handbook of Sensory Physiology VIII: Perception. New York: Springer Verlag.

Blakemore, C. and Vital-Durand, F. (1979). Development of the neural basis of visual acuity in monkeys. Transactions of the Ophthalmological Society of the UK, 99, 363-368.

Bornstein, M. H. (1976). Infants are trichromats. Journal of Experimental Child Psychology, 21, 425-445.

Bornstein, M. H. (1981). 'Human infant color vision and color perception' reviewed and reassessed: a critique of Werner and Wooten (1979). Infant Behaviour and Development, 4, 119-150.

Bornstein, M. H., Kessen, W. and Weiskopf, S. (1976). The categories of hue in infancy. Science, 191, 201-202.

Bower, T. G. R. (1966a). Slant perception and shape constancy in infants. Science, 151, 832-834.

Bower, T. G. R. (1966b). The visual world of infants. Scientific American, 215, 80-92.

Braddick, O. and Atkinson, J. The development of binocular function in infancy. Acta Ophthalmologica. In press.

Braddick, O. J., Atkinson, J., French, J. and Howland, H. C. (1979). A photorefractive study of infant accommodation. Vision Research, 19, 1319-1330.

Braddick, O., Atkinson, J., Julesz, B., Kropfl, W., Bodis-Wollner, I. and Raab, E. (1980). Cortical binocularity in infants. Nature, 288, 363-365.

Bronson, G. (1974). The postnatal growth of visual capacity. Child Development, 45, 873-890.

Bushnell, I. W. R. (1979). Modification of the externality effect in young infants. Journal of Experimental Child Psychology, 28, 211-229.

Bushnell, I. W. R. (1982). Discrimination of faces by young infants. Journal of Experimental Child Psychology, 33, 298-308.

Caron, A. J., Caron, R. F. and Carlson, V. R. (1978). Do infants see objects or retinal images? Shape constancy revisited. Infant Behaviour and Development, 1, 229-243.

Caron, A. J., Caron, R. F. and Carlson, V. R. (1979). Infant perception of the invariant shape of objects varying in slant. Child Development, 50, 716-721.

Cohen, L. B. (1979). Our developing knowledge of infant perception and cognition. American Psychologist, 34, 894-899.

Cohen, L. B., De Loache, J. S. and Pearl, R. A. (1977). An examination of interference effects in infants' memory for faces. Child Development, 48, 88-96.

Cohen, L. B. and Strauss, M. S. (1979). Concept acquisition in the human infant. Child Development, 50, 419-424.

Conel, J. L. (1939, 1947). The Postnatal Development of the Human Cerebral Cortex. (Volumes 1 and 3). Cambridge, Mass.: Harvard University Press.

Cook, M., Field, J. and Griffiths, K. (1978). The perception of solid form in early infancy. Child Development, 49, 866-869.

Cornell, E. H. (1974). Infants' discrimination of photographs of faces following redundant presentations. Journal of Experimental Child Psychology, 18, 98-106.

Daw, N. W., Berman, N. E. J. and Ariel, M. (1978). Interaction of critical periods in the visual cortex of kittens. Science, 199, 566-567.

Day, R. H. and McKenzie, B. E. (1973). Perceptual shape constancy in early infancy. Perception, 2, 315-320.

Dayton, G. O., Jones, M. H., Aiu, P., Rawson, R. A., Steele, B. and Rose, M. (1964). Developmental study of coordinated eye movements in the human infant. I: Visual acuity in the human newborn: a study based on induced optokinetic nystagumus recorded by electro-oculography. Archives of Ophthalmology, 71, 865-870.

De Schonen, S. McKenzie, B. and Bresson, F. (1978). Central and peripheral object distances as determinants of the effective visual field in early infancy. Perception, 7, 499-506.

Dobson, V. (1976). Spectral sensitivity of the 2-month infant as measured by the visual evoked cortical potential. Vision Research, 16, 367-374.

Dobson, V. and Teller, D. Y. (1978). Visual acuity in human infants: a review and comparison of behavioral and electrophysiological studies. Vision Research, 18, 1469-1485.

Fagan, J. F. (1972). Infants' recognition memory for faces. Journal of Experimental Child Psychology, 14, 453-476.

Fantz, R. L. (1961). The origin of form perception. Scientific American, 204, 66-72.

Fantz, R. L. (1963). Pattern vision in newborn infants. Science, 140, 296-297.

Fantz, R. L. and Miranda, S. B. (1975). Newborn infant attention to form of contour. Child Development, 46, 224-228.

Fantz, R. L., Fagan, J. F. and Miranda, S. B. (1975). Early visual selectivity. In L. B. Cohen and P. Salapatek (eds), Infant Perception: From sensation to cognition, Volume I. New York: Academic Press.

Fox, R. (1981). Stereopsis in animals and human infants. In R. N. Aslin, J. R. Alberts and M. R. Petersen (eds), Development of Perception: Psychobiological Perspectives. Volume 2: The Visual System. New York: Academic Press.

Gibson, E. J., Owsley, C. J. and Johnston, J. (1978). Perception of invariants by five-month-old infants: differentiation of two types of motion. Developmental Psychology, 14, 407-415.

Gibson, E. J., Owsley, C. J., Walker, A. and Megaw-Nyce, J. (1979). Development of the perception of invariants: substance and shape. Perception, 8, 609-619.

Goren, C. C., Sarty, M. and Wu, P. Y. K. (1975). Visual following and pattern discrimination of face-like stimuli by newborn infants. Pediatrics, 56, 544-549.

Gwiazda, J., Brill, S., Mohindra, I. and Held, R. (1980). Preferential looking acuity in infants from two to fifty-eight weeks of age. American Journal of Optometry and Physiological Optics, 57, 428-432.

Hainline, L. and Lemerise, E. (1982). Infants' scanning of geometric forms varying in size. Journal of Experimental Child Psychology, 33, 235-256.

Haith, M. M. (1966). The response of the human newborn to visual movement. Journal of Experimental Child Psychology, 3, 235-243.

Haith, M. M. (1978). Visual competence in early infancy. In R. Held, H. Leibowitz and H. L. Teuber (eds), Handbook of Sensory Physiology, Volume VIII: Perception. Berlin: Springer Verlag.

Haith, M. M., Bergman, T. and Moore, M. J. (1977). Eye contact and face scanning in early infancy. Science, 198, 853-855.

Hamer, R. D., Alexander, K. R. and Teller, D. Y. (1982). Rayleigh discriminations in young infants. Vision Research, 22, 575-587.
Harris, P. L. and Macfarlane, A. (1974). The growth of the effective visual field from birth to seven weeks. Journal of Experimental Child Psychology, 18, 340-348.
Haynes, H., White, B. L. and Held, R. (1965). Visual accommodation in human infants. Science, 148, 528-530.
Held, R. (1979). Development of visual resolution. Canadian Journal of Psychology, 33, 213-221.
Held, R., Birch, E. and Gwiazda, J. (1980). Stereoacuity of human infants. Proceedings of the National Academy of Sciences of the USA, 77, 5572-5574.
Hickey, T. L. (1981). The developing visual system. Trends in Neurosciences, 4, 41-44.
Hoffman, K. P. (1979). Optokinetic nystagmus and single-cell responses in the nucleus tractus opticus after early monocular deprivation in the cat. In R. D. Freeman (ed.), Developmental Neurobiology of Vision. New York: Plenum Press.
Hopkins, J. R., Kagan, J., Brachfeld, S., Hans, S. and Linn, S. (1976). Infant responsivity to curvature. Child Development, 47, 1166-1171.
Horowitz, F. D. (1975). Infant attention and discrimination: methodological and substantive issues. Monographs of the Society for Research in Child Development, 39 (5-6, serial no. 158), 1-15.
Howland, H. C., Atkinson, J., Braddick, O. and French, J. (1978). Infant astigmatism measured by photorefraction. Science, 202, 331-333.
Hubel, D. H. and Wiesel, T. N. (1977). Functional architecture of macaque monkey visual cortex. Proceedings of the Royal Society of London Section B, 198, 1-59.
Humphrey, N. K. (1974). Vision in a monkey without striate cortex: a case study. Perception, 3, 241-256.
Karmel, B. Z. and Maisel, E. B. (1975). A neuronal activity model for infant visual attention. In L. B. Cohen and P. Salapatek (eds), Infant Perception: From sensation to cognition. Volume 1. New York: Academic Press.
Kulikowski, J. J. and Tolhurst, D. J. (1973). Psychophysical evidence for sustained and transient detectors in human vision. Journal of Physiology, 232, 149-162.
Leehey, S. C., Moskowitz-Cook, A., Brill, S. and Held, R. (1975). Orientational anisotropy in infant vision. Science, 190, 900-902.
Macfarlane, A. (1975). Olfaction in the development of social preferences in the human neonate. Parent-infant

interaction. CIBA Symposium 33, 103-113. Amsterdam: Ciba Foundation.

Mann, I. C. (1964). The Development of the Human Eye. London: British Medical Association.

Maurer, D. (1975). Infant visual perception: methods of study. In L. B. Cohen and P. Salapatek (eds), Infant Perception: From sensation to cognition. Volume 1. New York: Academic Press.

Maurer, D. and Barrera, M. (1981). Infants' perception of natural and distorted arrangements of a schematic face. Child Development, 52, 196-202.

Maurer, D. and Lewis, T. L. (1979). A physiological explanation of infants' early visual development. Canadian Journal of Psychology, 33, 232-252.

Maurer, D. and Martello, M. (1980). The discrimination of orientation by young infants. Vision Research, 20, 201-204.

Maurer, D. and Salapatek, P. (1976). Developmental changes in the scanning of faces by young infants. Child Development, 47, 523-527.

Mayer, D. L. and Dobson, V. (1982). Visual acuity measurements in young children, as assessed by operant preferential looking. Vision Research, 22, 1141-1151.

McDonnell, P. M. (1979). Patterns of eye-hand coordination in the first year of life. Canadian Journal of Psychology, 33, 253-267.

McKenzie, B. and Day, R. H. (1971). Orientation discrimination in infants: a comparison of visual fixation and operant training methods. Journal of Experimental Child Psychology, 11, 366-375.

McKenzie, B. and Day, R. H. (1972). Object distance as a determinant of visual fixation in early infancy. Science, 178, 1108-1110.

McKenzie, B. and Day, R. H. (1976). Infants' attention to stationary and moving objects at different distances. Australian Journal of Psychology, 28, 45-51.

McKenzie, B. E., Tootell, H. E. and Day, R. H. (1980). Development of visual size constancy during the first year of human infancy. Developmental Psychology, 16, 163-174.

Milewski, A. E. (1976). Infants' discrimination of internal and external pattern elements. Journal of Experimental Child Psychology, 22, 229-246.

Mills, M. and Melhuish, E. (1974). Recognition of mother's voice in early infancy. Nature, 252, 123-124.

Mitchell, D. E. (1981). Sensitive periods in visual development. In R. N. Aslin, J. R. Alberts and M. R.

34

Petersen (eds), Development of Perception. Volume 2: The Visual System. New York: Academic Press.

Mohindra, I., Held, R., Gwiazda, J. and Brill, S. (1978). Astigmatism in infants. Science, 202, 329-331.

Mohindra, I., Jacobsen, S. G., Thomas, J. and Held, R. (1979). Development of amblyopia in infants. Transactions of the Ophthalmological Society of the UK, 99, 344-346.

Mollon, J. D. (1982). Color vision. Annual Review of Psychology, 33, 41-85.

Moskowitz-Cook, A. (1979). The development of photopic spectral sensitivity in human infants. Vision Research, 19, 1133-1142.

Movshon, J. A. and Van Sluyters, R. C. (1981). Visual neural development. Annual Review of Psychology, 32, 477-522.

Peeples, D. and Teller, D. Y. (1978). White-adapted photopic spectral sensitivity in human infants. Vision Research, 18, 49-53.

Perrett, D. I., Rolls, E. T. and Caan, W. (1979). Temporal lobe cells of the monkey with visual responses selective for faces. Neuroscience Letters Supplement, 3, S358.

Petrig, B., Julesz, B., Kropfl, W., Baumgartner, G. and Anliker, M. (1981). Development of stereopsis and cortical binocularity in human infants: electrophysiological evidence. Science, 213, 1402-1405.

Powers, M. K., Schneck, M. and Teller, D. Y. (1981). Spectral sensitivity of human infants at absolute visual threshold. Vision Research, 21, 1005-1016.

Pulos, E., Teller, D. Y. and Buck, S. L. (1980). Infant color vision: a search for short-wave-sensitive mechanisms by means of chromatic adaptation. Vision Research, 18, 1137-1147.

Regal, D. (1981). Development of critical flicker frequency in human infants. Vision Research, 21, 549-555.

Ruff, H. A. (1982). Effect of object movement on infants' detection of object structure. Developmental Psychology, 18, 462-472.

Salapatek, P. (1975). Pattern perception in early infancy. In L. B. Cohen and P. Salapatek (eds), Infant Perception: From sensation to cognition, Volume 1. New York: Academic Press.

Salapatek, P. (1979). Behavioral and electrophysiological evaluation of the infant contrast sensitivity function. In E. Jampolsky and L. Proenza (eds), Proceedings of the Symposium on Applications of Psychophysics to Clinical Problems. Washington, DC: National Academy of Sciences.

Siqueland, E. R. and DeLucia, C. A. (1969). Visual reinforcement of nonnutritive sucking in human infants. Science, 165, 1144-1146.
Slater, A. M. and Findlay, J. M. (1975a). The corneal reflection technique and the visual preference method: sources of error. Journal of Experimental Child Psychology, 20, 240-247.
Slater, A. M. and Findlay, J. M. (1975b). Binocular fixation in the newborn baby. Journal of Experimental Child Psychology, 20, 248-273.
Slater, A., Morison, V. and Rose, D. (submitted). Perception of shape by the newborn baby.
Slater, A. and Sykes, M. (1977). Newborn infants' visual responses to square wave gratings. Child Development, 48, 545-554.
Sokol, S. (1979). Pattern visual evoked potentials: their use in pediatric ophthalmology. International Ophthalmology Clinics, 20, 251-268.
Teller, D. Y. (1979). The forced-choice preferential looking procedure: a psychophysical technique for use with human infants. Infant Behavior and Development, 2, 135-153.
Teller, D. Y., Peeples, D. R. and Sekel, M. (1978). Discrimination of chromatic from white light by 2-month-old human infants. Vision Research, 18, 41-48.
Trevarthen, C. (1980). The foundations of intersubjectivity: development of interpersonal and co-operative understanding in infants. In D. R. Olson (ed.), The Social Foundations of Language and Thought: Essays in honor of Jerome S. Bruner. New York: Norton.
Tronick, E. (1972). Stimulus control and the growth of the infant's effective visual field. Perception and Psychophysics, 11, 373-375.
Volkmann, F. C. and Dobson, M. V. (1976). Infant responses of ocular fixation to moving visual stimuli. Journal of Experimental Child Psychology, 22, 86-99.
Walk, R. D. (1966). The development of depth perception in animals and human infants. Monographs of the Society for Research in Child Development, 31, 82-108.
Walker, A. S., Owsley, C. J., Megaw-Nyce, J., Gibson, E. J. and Bahrick, L. E. (1980). Detection of elasticity as an invariant property of objects by young infants. Perception, 9, 713-718.
Werner, J. S. and Perlmutter, M. (1979). Development of visual memory in infants. In H. W. Reese and L. P. Lipsitt (eds), Advances in Child Development and Behavior, 14. New York: Academic Press.

Werner, J. S. and Wooten, B. R. (1979). Human infant color vision and color perception. Infant Behaviour and Development, 2, 241-274.

Wiesel, T. N. (1982). Postnatal development of the visual cortex and the influence of environment. Nature, 299, 583-591.

Yonas, A. (1979). Studies of spatial perception in infancy. In A. D. Pick (ed.), Perception and its Development: A tribute to Eleanor Gibson. Hillsdale, NJ: Lawrence Erlbaum.

Yonas, A. (1981). Infants' responses to optical information for collision. In R. N. Aslin, J. R. Alberts and M. R. Petersen (eds), Development of Perception: Psychobiological perspectives. Volume 2: The Visual System. New York: Academic Press.

Yonas, A., Cleaves, W. T. and Pettersen, L. (1978). Development of sensitivity to pictorial depth. Science, 200, 77-79.

Yonas, A. and Pick, H. (1975). An approach to the study of infant space perception. In L. B. Cohen and P. Salapatek (eds), Infant Perception: From sensation to cognition, Volume II. New York: Academic Press.

Young-Browne, G., Rosenfeld, H. M. and Horowitz, F. D. (1977). Infant discrimination of facial expressions. Child Development, 48, 555-562.

Chapter 2

OPERANT CONDITIONING

D. E. Blackman

To many outsiders an operant conditioner is a hard-nosed experimentalist who spends endless hours in the enthusiastic analysis of cumulative records from one or two subjects, attacks anything that seems even mildly theoretical or physiological, ridicules anyone who has ever used statistics of the R. A. Fisher variety and ignores the work of any psychologist who does not publish in JEAB (Journal of the experimental Analysis of Behavior). Not since J. B. Watson's time has any band of behaviorists seemed so assertive in its likes and dislikes and so convinced that its techniques and experimental approach will not only change psychology but in the process reshape the world (Hearst, 1967).

This evaluation of operant conditioners was offered some 16 years ago. This chapter addresses the question of whether Hearst's comments would capture the flavour of operant conditioners' contributions to contemporary psychology. It begins by reviewing the essential features of operant conditioning. It then reviews the impact of two recent developments, first the increased experimental interest in phylogenetic, as opposed to ontogenetic, influences on behaviour, and second the increasing willingness of some learning theorists to bring cognitive explanations to bear on the conditioned behaviour of animals. The strident isolation of earlier operant conditioners seems to have been muted. The chapter therefore ends by considering briefly what operant conditioning has to offer psychology today.

THE EXPERIMENTAL ANALYSIS OF BEHAVIOUR

Operant conditioning has, of course, developed from Skinner's early experimental studies (Skinner, 1938). Skinner made his first significant contribution to the study of learning by inventing a new technology, typified in what is now ubiquitously termed 'the Skinner box'. Animals, usually pigeons or rats, are placed in an enclosed and controlled environment. They are free to behave in any way, though in truth the limitations of their environment do not prompt a wide range of activities. If the animal happens to behave in a specified way, certain consequences may occur, perhaps every time the behaviour is emitted or perhaps only occasionally. Thus access to food may be allowed to a pigeon every time it pecks a disc, or access to water may occasionally be given to a rat when it presses a lever. If these consequences affect the frequency with which the behaviour occurs, then operant conditioning is said to have taken place, and the specified act can be described as operant behaviour. If operant behaviour increases in frequency, the consequence related to it is termed a reinforcer. If the operant behaviour decreases in frequency, the consequence is termed a punisher. In either case, the frequency of operant behaviour can be seen to be a function of the environmental conditions to which the animal is exposed.

It should be emphasized here that operant behaviour and reinforcers or punishers are defined in relation to each other. Properly, behaviour is not described as operant unless its frequency of occurrence is affected by environmental consequences, and events are not described as reinforcers or punishers unless they affect the frequency of the behaviour to which they are specifically related. This point may perhaps seem esoteric, but it is fundamental to the theoretical or interpretative scheme advocated by Skinner. In their analysis of behaviour in general, Skinner and other contemporary behaviourists put their explanatory emphasis on the relationships between operant behaviour and reinforcers or punishers defined in this functional way.

Nevertheless, it should also be pointed out here that different interpretative schemes can be used with respect to the experimental procedures developed by Skinner. Some psychologists emphasize, for example, the hedonic or rewarding qualities of the programmed consequences of behaviour in a Skinner box, or their physiological effects on the internal mechanisms of the animal. It is possible to investigate the frequency of occurrence of classes of behaviour defined topographically rather than in functional terms. It might seem pedantic to resist the use of the term 'operant conditioning' to describe experiments using the methods developed from Skinner's work but formulated in different theoretical terms from his. It is for this reason that the Skinner box was described earlier as a technological development in the experimental study of behaviour. It allows extended and detailed analysis of environmental influences on behaviour without the intrusive inter-trial intervals typical of studies with mazes, runways or jumping-stands.

The Skinner box also allows the study of the effects of different rules by which events are related to behaviour, schedules of reinforcement. The apparently endless fascination of operant conditioners for the behavioural effects of small differences in reinforcement schedules has contributed to the image of them with which this chapter opened. The use of automated experimental procedures has made it possible to indulge this interest. The string and ceiling wax of the early innovators in this field of experimental psychology quickly gave way to control and recording by means of electrical switches, timers and counters, then to on-line control and analysis by digital computers, and now to the use of microprocessor technology. Operant conditioning has thus become technically demanding, with some of the trappings of the laboratories of more established sciences. This fact does not, of course, in itself make operant conditioning more scientific than other areas of experimental psychology.

A crucial component in the early automation of operant conditioning experiments was provided by cumulative recorders. These devices automatically plot the occurrence of operants against time, thereby producing continuous time-graphs of the behaviour of individual animals during extended experimental sessions. Cumulative recorders, therefore, provide a detailed visual display of the primary datum of operant conditioning experiments, the rate at which operant behaviour is emitted as a function of the reinforcement schedules to which an animal is exposed. Operant conditioners put great store on the uncontaminated and direct nature of cumulative records, and the reporting of pioneering studies of the effects of schedules of reinforcement relied on them almost exclusively (e.g. Ferster and Skinner, 1957). Although cumulative records can seem a little intimidating to the uninitiated, the excitement should not be underestimated of watching orderly patterns emerge over time through the continuous recording of the operant behaviour of individual animals. It seems that this feedback acts as a potent reinforcer, to judge from the marked enthusiasm of operant conditioners for their studies.

In a brief review such as this, it is not possible even to summarize the findings of 45 years of operant conditioning research except by recourse to an undocumented list of wide empirical generalizations. The widest of these is simply that in a well-conducted experiment the operant behaviour of animals does occur at predictable frequencies as a function of the environmental contingencies to which the animals are exposed. Some events (reinforcers) increase or maintain the frequency of operant behaviour to which they are related, whilst others (punishers) decrease it. The reinforcing or punishing effects of events are not intrinsic characteristics of these events, but depend critically on the experimental circumstances or conditions in which they are delivered. So food is not necessarily a reinforcer, even to a food-deprived rat, and painful events do not necessarily act as punishers in the functional sense. Similarly, originally neutral events such as noises or lights may in some conditions acquire reinforcing or punishing effects, and are then termed 'conditioned' reinforcers or punishers. It is an empirical matter to identify the conditions in which any event influences the rate of operant behaviour to which it is related. The nature of the control exerted by reinforcers or punishers depends critically on the schedules by which they are related to behaviour. This schedule-control is shown in strikingly different patterns of conditioned behaviour.

Gradual and systematic changes in the contingencies of reinforcement (known as shaping) can lead to the development of remarkably complex, accurate or extended sequences of operant behaviour. The similarities between the patterns of operant behaviour engendered by sensitive operant conditioning experiments with individual animals or even with different species of animal are often more striking than are the differences between them. If schedules of reinforcement are differentially accompanied by other environmental events, like noises or lights, these events come to set the occasion or cue for the appropriate schedule-controlled behaviour (discriminative control). Such control can be introduced gradually (fading), can be exploited to develop complex sequences of behaviour, or can lead to a repertoire of different patterns of operant behaviour in different discriminative conditions, even within individual animals.

All the above statements arise from a vast amount of detailed research in which the phenomena have been studied extensively (see Blackman, 1974). Operant conditioning has provided a technology by which behaviour can be modulated experimentally by means of schedules of reinforcement and differential discriminative control. This technology has been valuable not merely in identifying the basic elements of environmental influences on behaviour listed above. It has also provided controlled behavioural baselines, against which further independent variables of interest to psychologists can be studied, such as drugs or physiological interventions. The technology has also made it possible to study the perceptual capacities of animals. The literature of operant conditioning is, therefore, extensive. It has been authoritatively reviewed by the contributors to two edited volumes (Honig, 1966; Honig and Staddon, 1977), which provide some indication of the diversity and achievements of operant conditioning experiments.

Operant conditioning provides, then, a technology for an experimental analysis of behaviour. It should be noted, however, that its pervasive influence in experimental psychology rests essentially on a limited laboratory model of behaviour. It focusses on arbitrary behavioural acts which are readily emitted by the experimental subjects at high or low frequencies, and whose occurrence can easily be sensed automatically by the apparatus which controls the experiment. These acts are usually pressing a lever or pecking a key. The animals whose behaviour is investigated are those who adapt readily to laboratory conditions and experimental procedures, and which are easily obtained and handled, usually rodents or pigeons, occasionally primates. The events whose reinforcing or punishing effects are studied are normally drawn from a very limited range of stimuli and can be easily controlled and manipulated by the experimenter, usually food, water, lights and noises, perhaps low-intensity electric shocks, occasionally drugs. The technology provided by operant conditioning is then to a large extent based on the scientific investigation of rats pressing levers or pigeons pecking keys for food or water. The generalizations drawn from such studies are couched in terms, however, of the effects of environmental conditions on behaviour, and such generalizations even assume, at least for contemporary behaviourists, the force of an explanatory system within psychology as a whole. It is clear that operant conditioning experiments provide a clear example of how the search for general psychological principles is based by some psychologists on the intensive study of a limited laboratory model. Operant conditioning experiments, in a more limited context, form part of the search for general laws of learning.

It was not simply operant conditioners' enthusiasm for studying rats or pigeons repeatedly behaving in an unchanging environment for occasional reinforcers that attracted Hearst's (1967) sardonic comments about them. The technology of operant conditioning has long been closely associated with a distinctive research strategy based on the intensive study of individual subjects rather than on statistical comparisons between experimental and control groups. For example, the

identification of the patterns of operant behaviour characteristically maintained by the various schedules of reinforcement
results from exposing individual animals to those schedules
repeatedly until their behaviour becomes predictable, when the
behaviour has, as it were, reached a stage of equilibrium with
its environmental circumstances.

The research strategy employed in experiments using Skinner boxes is not necessarily of this nature, and statistical
designs and modes of inference are as readily available for
such experiments as for any other kinds of experimental psychology. One might, for instance, design an experiment on the
effects of reinforcement frequency in which rats from one
group are exposed to a schedule which delivers reinforcers
after a lever-press on average every 30 s, while those from
another group receive reinforcers only once every 60 s on
average (variable-interval 30 s or 60 s schedules). A statistical comparison of the rates of lever-pressing might reveal
that these were significantly higher with the group of rats
exposed to the higher reinforcement frequency. However, the
unusual degree of environmental control exerted in operant
conditioning experiments over repeated sessions leads to the
possibility of the alternative research strategy. Here individual animals would be repeatedly exposed to alternating
periods of the two reinforcement schedules, each schedule
being associated with a separate discriminative cue. Eventually, each rat may come consistently to press the lever more
frequently in the presence of the cue associated with the
higher rate of reinforcement. The generality of such a finding
can be extended beyond the individual rat by means of an
inductive argument if the relationship between rates of lever-
pressing and frequency of reinforcement is exhibited by each
of a small number of individual rats exposed to the multiple
schedule. With such a strategy, recourse to conventional
Fisherian statistical analyses can be obviated, for each
individual subject acts as its own control by being exposed to
each experimental condition. Operant conditioning lends itself
to such a strategy by means of the behavioural predictability
which arises with individual subjects as a result of extended
exposure to experimental conditions.

Sidman (1960) has considered in some detail some of the
research strategies which can be developed to exploit the
behavioural control of operant conditioning experiments in
order to develop generalizations based on the study of individual subjects. We shall return later to the implications of
such generalizations in experimental psychology. For the
moment, however, it is sufficient to note that this is a

fundamentally different research strategy from the dominant mode of statistical design and analysis. Operant conditioners who adopted single-subject research strategies found themselves unappreciated, and it is interesting to note that the Journal of the experimental Analysis of Behavior was founded in 1958 explicitly to cater for research reports emanating from single-subject research designs. This journal in fact quickly became the authoritative medium for reports of operant conditioning experiments using this research strategy, to such an extent that the case can be made that it contributed to a growing isolation of some operant conditioners within experimental psychology (Krantz, 1971).

As noted earlier, operant conditioning experiments are often associated with the theoretical stance in psychology advocated by Skinner and sometimes known as radical behaviourism. The term behaviourism has become a constant source of confusion in theoretical psychology. Some commentators seem to assume that Watson's writings of 60 years ago have defined behaviourism for ever and that behaviourists therefore of necessity eschew any reference to experience or inner life. Others use the term to denote those psychologists (still the great majority) who consider behaviour to be the primary focus of their studies, if only for methodological reasons. Within contemporary psychology there is a smaller group who, with Skinner, emphasize the relationships between environmental events and behaviour in their attempts to explain behaviour and experience (Blackman, 1980; Skinner, 1974). In bald terms, their accounts interpret behaviour as the result of environmental influences, emphasizing that behaviour can be explained as being causally determined by environmental circumstances. It is obvious that operant conditioning experiments tend to provide empirical support for such a stance. As the operant behaviour of animals comes to be identified experimentally as the outcome of reinforcement schedules and discriminative control, support is provided for the general proposition that behaviour can be understood and explained in terms of environmental influences. The more sensitive or subtle the relationships established experimentally between behaviour and environmental conditions, the greater is the support for the general theoretical stance in psychology of radical behaviourism or functional analysis.

In fact, operant conditioning experiments have investigated the effects of increasingly complex environmental conditions, extending their empirical analyses to the necessary and sufficient conditions for behaviour to occur which could be thought to reflect 'preference' between alternatives, 'choice', 'awareness', 'attention' or 'self-control' (see Rachlin, 1976). Paradoxically, it is this increasing complexity of operant conditioning experiments which gives rise to an issue which will be discussed later, namely the adequacy of functional analyses of behaviour to resist the encroachment of more cognitive interpretations.

Whilst operant conditioning experiments can sit happily in the general theoretical framework of radical behaviourism, the above comment emphasizes that such a theoretical stance is by no means necessary. In fact, as noted, operant conditioning procedures can provide excellent techniques for investigating physiological or pharmacological determinants of behaviour, as well as for investigating what some describe as the cognitive mechanisms of animals.

This brief review identifies three separable aspects of what has been termed, divisively, 'the experimental analysis of behaviour'. First, operant conditioning can be described as the experimental study of the effects of reinforcers or punishers and discriminative stimuli on the rate of occurrence of a specified act, usually the lever-pressing of rats or the key-pecking of pigeons. Second is the research strategy, which seeks to make general statements through the intensive study of the behaviour of individuals rather than the statistical comparison of groups. Third is the philosophical stance in psychology, radical behaviourism, which seeks to explain behaviour in terms of environmental influences rather than in terms of internal processes. These three aspects are separable: operant conditioning experiments can be conducted with statistical designs or in different theoretical contexts. However, taken together they form a powerful approach to psychology in general, and the caricature of operant conditioners by Hearst (1967) clearly invokes all three aspects of the experimental analysis of behaviour. We may now evaluate the impact of some recent developments in operant conditioning.

PHYLOGENETIC INTRUSIONS

In the previous section, operant conditioning was presented as part of the search for general laws of learning by means of controlled experiments with arbitrary patterns of behaviour, reinforcers and species of animal. This long-dominant theme in learning theory has been very severely challenged in the last 15 years, by the discovery that species differences can exert a profound influence on the effects of environmental events on behaviour. The litany is too long to rehearse here, but Selig-man and Hager's (1972) seminal collection of papers suggested that the laws of learning uncovered by studies of rats press-ing levers for food may not be general laws at all. Animals bring to experiments specialized attributes which have been developed by evolutionary pressures on their species, includ-ing differential susceptibilities to environmental influences. Thus, Breland and Breland (1961) long ago showed that some patterns of behaviour are not readily influenced by reinforce-ment contingencies with some species, and suggested that there is a tendency for any initially conditioned behaviour to 'drift' towards a form of behaviour characteristic of the species. Garcia and Koelling (1966) were the first to suggest that animals show a biological preparedness to form specific associations faster than others, as for example between a novel taste and illness. Since these pioneering studies of instrumental and of classical conditioning, interactions between biological dispositions and learning have been in-creasingly researched. For example, Shettleworth (1973) inves-tigated the effects of contingencies of reinforcement on different patterns of behaviour exhibited by golden hamsters, namely face-washing, digging, rearing, 'scrabbling' and lever-pressing. She found clear evidence for differential suscepti-bilities of different patterns of behaviour to environmental contingencies. While such work has contributed to a very desirable rapprochement between ethologists and experimental psychologists, it has inevitably left traditional operant conditioners somewhat exposed. This section briefly considers some phylogenetic intrusions into conventional operant condi-tioning experiments in Skinner boxes.

When animals are exposed to a schedule of intermittent reinforcement, patterns of behaviour other than the specified operant are sometimes induced, occasionally to such an extent that they disrupt operant conditioning. A good example of such schedule-induced behaviour is the excessive drinking reliably shown after food reinforcement by rats which have not been deprived of water (Falk, 1971). Such 'schedule-induced poly-dipsia' is both robust and puzzling. In one experimental session animals may drink as much as three times their normal daily intake, even though they have not previously been de-prived of water, and it is difficult to see either what pur-pose the phenomenon serves or indeed what gives rise to it. The drinking is not required by the experiment, yet it deve-lops reliably and excessively, even with adulterated water or solutions of drugs, and it has appeared to be hard to elimi-nate. Schedule-induced polydipsia is the clearest and most studied example of a number of patterns of behaviour which can develop 'spontaneously' in the periods after reinforcement in operant conditioning experiments, including patterns of attack towards other animals and running in a wheel (see Staddon, 1977). As noted, such intrusions can interfere with the orderly patterns of 'arbitrary' operant behaviour which would be expected to emerge from exposure to schedules of intermittent reinforcement.

The nature of schedule-induced behaviour remains a matter for theoretical debate. Falk (1971) has suggested that it is the result neither of operant nor of classical conditioning processes. He termed the behaviour 'adjunctive' and drew an analogy with the displacement activities which have long been studied by ethologists. These patterns of behaviour illustrate that the animals used in operant conditioning experiments bring dispositions to the experimental situation which interact with the contingencies of reinforcement set up by the experimenter.

Perhaps more embarrassing for conventional operant conditioners has been the increasing recognition that the 'arbitrary' patterns of behaviour which they select for intensive study may also be heavily influenced by phylogenetic factors. This seems particularly to be the case with key-pecking by pigeons. Using a discrete trials procedure analogous to classical conditioning but in Skinner boxes, Brown and Jenkins (1968) first showed that pigeons had a marked propensity to peck at a key which was lit just before food was presented, even though such pecking was not specified as a requirement for food to be delivered. Initial enthusiasm shown by operant conditioners for exploiting this discovery as a means of 'automatically shaping' an operant response was tempered when it was shown by Williams and Williams (1969) that pigeons persisted in pecking at a lit key even if such pecks prevented food from being delivered. Far from being an arbitrary operant, the pecking of keys by pigeons appeared to be generated in the absence of contingencies of reinforcement and to persist despite a schedule which might be expected to punish it.

Such 'sign-tracking' behaviour (Hearst and Jenkins, 1974) may perhaps be better considered as an example of classical conditioning, an interpretation emphasized by the discrete-tetrials procedure of early work. However, the removal of contingencies of reinforcement (response-dependencies) from conventional free operant conditioning experiments served to extend the impact of this further biological intrusion in the supposedly arbitrary world of the Skinner box. For example,

Gamzu and Schwartz (1973) carried out an experiment with pigeons which is more reminiscent of conventional operant conditioning procedures but in which no specified response was required. They found, in general terms, that pigeons would peck a key at sustained and high rates when it was lit by a stimulus which accompanied periods in which food was occasionally presented when that stimulus alternated with one which accompanied periods in which food was presented less frequently or not at all. In short, despite the absence of a response requirement in this experiment, differential rates of key-pecking developed to the two stimuli which are reminiscent of the rates of key-pecking engendered by a similar but conventional multiple schedule of reinforcement, in which there is a formal requirement for operant responses to be emitted if food reinforcement is to be delivered.

Findings such as these suggest that key-pecking by pigeons, the operant conditioners' paradigm case of an arbitrarily defined operant response is, in fact, an example of what Seligman (1970) described as biologically 'prepared' patterns of behaviour. One implication to be drawn from this observation is that the 'laws of learning' which emerge from the study of pigeons' key-pecking are not general laws, but relate specifically to 'prepared' patterns of behaviour.

Schedule-induced behaviour and sign-tracking by pigeons illustrate nicely the puzzlement or even embarrassment that can be caused to traditional operant conditioners by our new awareness of biological factors in conditioning experiments. One way of trying to limit the impact of these findings is by appeal to the concepts of adventitious reinforcement or superstitious behaviour. It must, of course, be admitted that the patterns of behaviour develop in the absence of a programmed relationship between them and reinforcers. Nevertheless, the inevitable close proximity between the occurrence of such behaviour and the delivery of food is such that a reinforcement contingency may be established by chance and then gain control over behaviour.

This argument has been considered by Staddon (1977), but he finds it unconvincing, even to the extent of suggesting that the response contingency is an unnecessary complication in the experimental analysis of behaviour. The rates of both schedule-induced behaviour and sign-tracking appear resistant to the imposition of delays between their occurrence and the delivery of a reinforcer, the traditional test of the effects of adventitious reinforcement. In any case, operant conditioners would still have to face the fact that particular kinds of behaviour (i.e. drinking or pecking) are most likely to occur in such a way that adventitious reinforcement can exert its effects. In other words, it would remain true that some patterns of behaviour are more susceptible to reinforcement than others, although this could perhaps result simply from their greater probability of spontaneous occurrence. This point is in fact supported empirically by Staddon and Simmelhag's (1971) demonstration that patterns of behaviour are not selected from an animal's behavioural repertoire at random by adventitious reinforcement, as well as by Shettleworth's (1973) investigations mentioned earlier.

Staddon (1977) has put forward a classification of the patterns of the behaviour seen in a typical Skinner-box experiment which is very different from the traditional analysis. He argues that the traditional emphasis on a single instrumental response is misplaced. He discusses instead the momentary effects of biologically important events on interacting parts of an animal's total behavioural repertoire. Different kinds of behaviour which the animal brings to an experimental situation are differentially sensitive to the effects of these events, regardless of whether the experimenter formally programmes a relationship or contingency between them. Staddon terms the patterns of behaviour which change in frequency immediately _after_ the delivery of an important event 'interim activities', and these of course include what was earlier termed schedule-induced behaviour. Other parts of the behavioural repertoire are differentially affected if they occur just before the biologically important event is likely to occur, whether or not a formal contingency between them is programmed by the experimenter. Such behaviour is called by Staddon 'terminal activity', and includes the sign-tracking by pigeons discussed above. Finally, a third class ('facultative activities') occurs at other times, and includes such behaviour as grooming. With an analysis such as Staddon's, the task of experimenters becomes that of unravelling the effects of environmental events on the dynamic interactions occurring between the components of the behavioural repertoire which characterizes animals of a given species.

Although studies such as those reviewed here have a considerable _empirical_ impact on operant conditioning, their _conceptual_ impact is also worth noting. At a simple level, for example, the language of operant conditioning, which defines reinforcers only in terms of their effects on the behaviour to which they are immediately related, and which defines operant reponses only in terms of the effects of reinforcers, is confronted with difficulties here. In the light of the influential studies reported here, there has been much recent interest in the effects of 'response-independent reinforcers', and it is not always recognized that such terminology in itself can produce confusion. The point becomes more forceful perhaps when the effects are considered of arranging an over-all correlation between the frequency of lever presses and the frequency of biologically important events such as food or shock. In such situations, the frequency with which the be-haviour occurs is affected by these correlations (Baum, 1973; Herrnstein and Hineline, 1966). Such findings have prompted Baum to develop what he called a 'correlation based law of effect' which emphasizes the functional importance of cor-relations between responses and reinforcers rather than the usual relationship of temporal contiguity between them. It will be necessary to return to the data which prompted such a theory in the next section of this chapter. For the moment, the point to be emphasized is that the thrust of what have been termed phylogenetic intrusions in operant conditioning experiments has been to limit the impact of contingencies of reinforcement in the analysis of behaviour. While this is undoubtedly true at an empirical level, it is perhaps even more important that it is true at a conceptual level too.

COGNITIVE INTERPRETATIONS

The second current source of pressure on 'the experimental analysis of behaviour' is to be found in the new willingness of some contemporary learning theorists to interpret the data of operant conditioning experiments in essentially cognitive terms. As described above, operant conditioners working within the framework of the experimental analysis of behaviour have traditionally attempted to understand behaviour in terms of its relationship with environmental events without recourse to physiological or cognitive concepts. According to Dickinson (1980), 'it turns out that most interesting behavioural capa-cities are just not susceptible to this kind of explanation'. Mackintosh (1978), in a clear and succinct summary of the perceived need for a cognitive learning theory, has argued that 'it is time that psychologists abandoned their outmoded view of conditioning and recognized it as a complex and useful process whereby organisms build an accurate representation of their world'.

The nub of contemporary cognitive learning theory is simply that the complexities of the relationships between behaviour and environment now studied in conditioning experi-ments demand that explanations be couched in terms of the central information-processing capacities of animals. Some of the force of this argument arises from recent studies of classical conditioning which are not strictly relevant to the present chapter (though one may note a little ruefully that the sign-tracking behaviour discussed above is now widely used as a classical conditioning procedure in this context: see Locurto, Terrace and Gibbon, 1981). This brief discussion is confined to the impact of cognitive learning theory on inter-pretations of operant conditioning experiments, and a fuller critique may be found elsewhere (Blackman, 1983).

Operant conditioning experiments have long progressed well beyond the exploration of the behavioural effects of simple schedules of reinforcement. One area of the research which has attracted much attention over many years, for example, is described as the study of choice behaviour. A rat or pigeon may be confronted with two manipulanda concurrently, each giving access to a different schedule of reinforcement. It is usually found that animals in such situations come to match the proportion of responses on each manipulandum with the relative frequency of reinforcers available on each (see Rachlin, 1976). That is to say, if reinforcers may occur twice as frequently for responses on key A than for responses on key B, then the rate of responding on key A will be twice that on key B. This simple matching law is the basis of much of con-temporary quantitative analyses of operant behaviour, and the generality and limitations of this simple law have been exten-sively explored in many different situations and with dif-ferent measures (see Bradshaw, Szabadi and Lowe, 1981). It is surely convenient to describe such studies as investigations of 'choice behaviour', thereby emphasizing that the animal has two alternative patterns of behaviour available. In this sense, responding on simple schedules of reinforcement might also be said to reflect a choice between responding and not-responding at any given moment. To speak in this way, however, has not by tradition been taken to imply that recourse to some cognitive 'choosing' mechanism within the animal is either necessary or desirable in order to explain the observed be-haviour. On the contrary, conventional operant conditioners were pleased to be able to specify the necessary and suffi-cient conditions for the relative rates of responding on the two keys, thereby in their view extending their environmental explanations of behaviour to a more complex situation. How-ever, the use of the cognitively loaded term 'choice' to des-cribe the behaviour on the two keys can lead to an increased readiness to explain the behaviour in terms of the cognitive or internal mechanisms of choice which could be said to lead to this allocation of responding.

This process has been exacerbated as operant conditioners have investigated increasingly complex environmental circumstances and their effects on behaviour. As an example, consider in general terms experiments on delayed matching to sample (e.g. Kendrick, Rilling and Stonebreaker, 1981). Pigeons may be presented with a colour on one key; this is then removed and replaced after an interval with two colours presented on two different keys; if the pigeon pecks the key with the colours previously presented, reinforcement is given. With careful training, pigeons are capable of performing this task appropriately. The opportunity therefore arises to investigate the critical parameters of the task. First, it may be easier to establish the behaviour if the bird is required to peck the initial stimulus before it is removed. Second, the interval between the removal of the sample and the presentation of the two subsequent test stimuli may be important, as may be the environmental conditions in the interval between the sample and test stimuli. These and other empirical questions emerge within the tradition of the experimental analysis of behaviour and can be addressed by means of experimental manipulations. Perhaps it is easier to describe the experiment in different terms, however: the pigeons need to attend to the sample stimulus, remember it when it is removed, compare their memory of it with the two test stimuli despite any interference, discriminate between the test stimuli, and choose the correct stimulus. If this language is used, the experimental manipulations can be said to investigate attention, short-term memory, consolidation, choice and so on. It is sufficient for our present purposes merely to note here that these concepts are, in fact, increasingly being used to handle the complexities of the procedures used in operant conditioning experiments. As a result, and with a similar process at work in the field of classical conditioning, learning theorists have felt it necessary to use cognitive terms in an effort to explain complex relationships between behaviour and environment, and have then dared to extend such explanations back to simpler behavioural situations.

A recent, edited volume on cognitive processes in animal conditioning illustrates this process clearly (Hulse, Fowler and Honig, 1978). Of particular interest is a paper by Church (1978) which presents the results of an extensive series of experiments investigating how the behaviour of rats becomes functionally related to the passage of time. Church himself asserts that his experiments provide ample evidence that there is an empirical relationship between time and behaviour. However, he chooses to explain this relationship by recourse to a hypothetical internal clock. Thus it is said that 'the rat reads the value of the clock and makes a decision to respond' (Church, 1978). It seems that the clock runs, stops or runs at different speeds, but cannot run backwards. The following more extensive quotation illustrates the process of concern in the present chapter:

> When we began research on timing ... the concept of internal clock was, for us, simply a metaphor. As our research progressed, however, we found ourselves searching for the properties of the internal clock. After we discovered some characteristics of the internal clock, our attitude toward it gradually began to change. The concept was no longer a metaphor; we began to believe that the clock actually exists (Church, 1978).

As suggested above, this willingness to explain admittedly complex relationships between environmental events and behaviour by recourse to hypothetical constructs has been extended to more simple relationships. It is here that Baum's (1973) correlation-based law of effect discussed in another context earlier becomes relevant once more. Baum found that behaviour was maintained at high rates by a schedule in which there was no more than an overall correlation between the occurrence of such behaviour and an increased frequency of food. In an earlier experiment, Herrnstein and Hineline (1966) found that rats' lever-pressing was maintained by a schedule in which this behaviour led to a decrease in the frequency (but not elimination) of shocks. This negative correlation between responding and the frequency of shock can be said to identify quite satisfactorily the necessary and sufficient conditions for operant behaviour to be sustained by negative reinforcement, though subsequent research has shown that other variables can be important too. To this extent, the correlation explains the behaviour. Within the tradition of 'the experimental analysis of behaviour', such findings can be said to make it necessary to widen the range of relationships between behaviour and environment which must be incorporated into a functional analysis or explanation of behaviour beyond the usual response contingencies. For cognitive learning theorists, on the other hand, data such as these make it necessary to assume 'that animals are calculating variations in the overall rate of shock per session, and correlating these with variations in their own patterns of responding' (Mackintosh, 1974).

This assertion illustrates clearly the difference between traditional behaviour analysts and contemporary cognitive learning theorists. Their different interpretations of behaviour can readily be extended to all the phenomena of operant conditioning. For example, the frequently demonstrated functional relationships between the frequency of operant behaviour and the frequency of positive reinforcement in interval schedules can be accepted as a satisfactory explanatory relationship in itself, or can be taken as an indication that animals compute the available frequencies of reinforcement and make decisions about appropriate rates of responding. Ultimately, even the traditional unit of analysis can be considered in these different ways. In a conventional, continuous reinforcement schedule the lever press can be said to increase in frequency because of its 1:1 relationship with food, thereby fitting into a functional analysis based on the concepts of operant and reinforcement. Alternatively, the lever press can be taken as a reflection of the rats' internal representation of and need for food reward.

Operant conditioning experiments are, therefore, one current focus of theoretical conflict between two different approaches to the explanation of behaviour. As was seen at the start of this chapter, operant conditioners have traditionally been closely associated with functional analyses of behaviour, which find in empirically demonstrated relationships between behaviour and environment a satisfactory level of explanation in psychology. Others, here represented by contemporary learning theorists, find a need to explain psychological data in terms of processes occurring within the organism. The conflict is almost as old as is psychology as a distinct discipline, and it is not likely to be resolved by any specific experimentation or empirical work. As a result, it could be said in one sense that operant conditioning, as defined in an earlier section of this chapter, is hardly affected by the current theoretical controversy. In another sense, however, the impact of theoretical debate has been profound, for reports of experiments using operant conditioning techniques, including those published in the Journal of the experimental Analysis of Behavior, are now often replete with references to cognitive processes even in animals, despite some spirited objections (e.g. Branch and Malagodi, 1980; Pierce and Epling, 1980). Indeed, Ferster (1978) has commented on the creeping cognitivism in many of the contributions even to the most recent authoritative review of operant conditioning (Honig and Staddon, 1977).

CONCLUSION

An attempt has been made in the previous section of this chapter to indicate two contemporary sources of pressure on any operant conditioners who would adequately have been described in the peroration by Hearst with which this discussion opened. We are now in a position to consider briefly the status of operant conditioning in contemporary psychology.

First, it is fair to suggest that the techniques of operant conditioning have established for themselves an important role in contemporary experimental psychology. In many research programmes the use of Skinner boxes is adopted without debate, so superior are their procedures to alternative methods of studying the effects of environmental influences on the behaviour of animals. The rigorous and uninterrupted control of the experimental environment, together with the ability to set up and sustain complex contingencies between stimuli or between stimuli and responses has, in fact, made operant conditioning a standard technique in experimental psychology. Thus operant conditioning procedures have proved invaluable in the comparative study of perceptual processes in animals (Blough and Blough, 1977) and of physiological processes (Mogenson and Cioe, 1977). Indeed, as noted above, even classical conditioning experiments are now often based on the key-pecking of pigeons in Skinner boxes. It could be argued that the technology of operant conditioning has been indispensable in allowing empirical studies to develop in some fields. An example is to be found in psychopharmacology. Thus drug infusions have been scheduled in various ways dependent on operant behaviour, and the schedule-controlled behavioural baselines have considerably extended the analysis of the environmental circumstances in which drugs exert reinforcing effects (Johanson, 1978). The behavioural baselines established by schedules of reinforcement have contributed much greater psychological sophistication to the interdisciplinary study of the effects of drugs on behaviour (McKearney and Barrett, 1978). As an experimental technique, operant conditioning is alive and well, and has added considerably to the empirical basis of many fields of contemporary psychology.

Operant conditioning continues to be unusual in contemporary psychology in using such rigorous procedures in the study of behaviour that it is possible to substitute experimental control for the ubiquitous statistical forms of control, thereby making scientifically respectable statements which are based on the behaviour of individuals rather than on comparisons between the behaviour of groups. Bakan (1967) has distinguished between what he calls 'aggregate propositions' and 'general propositions' in psychology. The former are statements about groups of subjects considered as a whole, as in statistical designs. The latter are statements which are intended to relate to each and every member of a designable class. It is interesting to note the dominance of aggregate propositions in psychology, and even the assumption sometimes made that scientific method in psychology demands statistical methods. Bakan suggests that the distinctions between the two kinds of proposition are potentially important but often blurred, and it may be noted that in an applied context psychologists in particular are often interested in the behaviour of individuals rather than of statistical groups. The various experimental designs which have been adopted in operant conditioning owe much to Sidman's writing (1960), which has not received the general recognition it deserves in discussions of methodology in psychology. Sidman discusses various ways in which the challenge may be faced of obtaining meaningful data from individual subjects. His work has been supplemented by Hersen and Barlow's (1976) discussion of single-subject research designs, in this case in applied settings though still interpreted within a broadly behaviouristic stance. It is interesting to note also that the use of operant conditioning techniques with single-subject designs often seems to distinguish 'behaviour analysts' from 'learning theorists' of a cognitive persuasion, who normally favour statistical designs for their studies of operant conditioning. This difference may reflect another fundamental difference between the two groups not discussed before: cognitive learning theorists tend to be more interested in transitional or dynamic states of behaviour ('learning'), whereas behaviour analysts are primarily interested in the patterns of behaviour which ultimately reflect the state of equilibrium between environmental conditions and operant behaviour (i.e. conditioned behaviour).

It is when the third strand is added of 'the experimental analysis of behaviour', namely the theoretical stance of radical behaviourism, that the impact of recent empirical work in operant conditioning should be most carefully considered. As part of the experimental analysis of behaviour, operant conditioning has for long acted as the empirical base on which radical behaviourism is built, and radical behaviourism has in turn given rise to applied behaviour analysis in clinical, educational and other settings (see Blackman, 1981). As noted earlier, experimental demonstrations of functional relationships between behaviour and environment may serve as general support for the philosophical approach to psychology which radical behaviourism represents and which underpins applied behavioural analysis. It was argued in the previous section, however, that empirical investigations in themselves will probably not resolve the argument between radical behaviourists and cognitive learning theorists, for psychologists from both schools will work assiduously to interpret the data within their own theoretical scheme. In this sense, the battle between the two armies is inconclusive. On the other hand, there can be no doubt that contemporary cognitive learning theory has produced many important findings which extend our knowledge of the relationships between behaviour and environment. These studies may prompt ever more cognitive interpretations of behaviour, but they also provide further challenges for radical behaviourist accounts (see Blackman, 1983).

Some may feel that it is the phylogenetic intrusions discussed in this chapter which have the greater impact on the experimental analysis of behaviour. Certainly, some of the empirical data obtained in operant conditioning experiments suggest that environmental contingencies are not the only influences on behaviour and that one must bear in mind the 'nature' of the creature whose behaviour is studied. This nature must, of course, be the result of evolutionary pressures on the species. Once more, we see that behaviour can only be considered as the result of interactions between phylogeny and ontogeny, between inheritance and environment. How could it be otherwise? It is perhaps most constructive to see the 'intrusions' reviewed above not so much as embarrassing slaps in the face for behavioural analysis but rather as long overdue contributions of data from a synthesis of psychology and biology. It should be added that such a synthesis is by no means anathema to contemporary versions of behaviourism (see for example Skinner, 1966, 1977). Perhaps the conceptual impact of 'phylogenetic intrusions' leads to a different kind of reassessment. At present, the functional analyses of behaviour favoured by contemporary behaviourists attempt to explain behaviour in terms of its relationship with the environment, and in this connection the terms operant, reinforcer/punisher, and discriminative stimulus play a crucial role. The data reviewed briefly above are sufficient to prompt some searching conceptual questions. For example, should the terms operant and reinforcer be extended to include the behaviour and food presentation in experiments in which there is a correlation but no immediate contiguity between them? Even more difficult to resolve is the question of whether the terms 'operant' and 'reinforcer' should be used when behaviour increases as a function of food delivered independently of behaviour. The relationships between behaviour and environment which these examples represent might appropriately be incorporated in a general functional analysis of behaviour, but we do not currently have an adequate vocabulary on which to base the theoretical implications of such a development.

It seems then that an old philosophical chestnut provides an appropriate end to a review of operant conditioning: 'It all depends on what is meant by operant conditioning'. There are certainly empirical riches still to be found in Skinner boxes. The phylogenetic intrusions in operant conditioning experiments and the cognitive interpretations of conditioned behaviour which have been prominent in recent years do not invalidate functional analyses of behaviour, but they raise conceptual issues which deserve detailed attention.

REFERENCES

Bakan, D. (1967). On Method. San Francisco: Jossey-Bass.

Baum, W. H. (1973). The correlation based law of effect. Journal of the experimental Analysis of Behavior, 20, 137–153.

Blackman, D. E. (1974). Operant Conditioning: an Experimental Analysis of Behaviour. London: Methuen & Co.

Blackman, D. E. (1980). Images of man in contemporary behaviourism. In A. J. Chapman and D. M. Jones (eds), Models of Man. Leicester: The British Psychological Society.

Blackman, D. E. (1981). The experimental analysis of behaviour and its relevance to applied psychology. In G. C. L. Davey (ed.), Applications of Conditioning Theory. London: Methuen & Co.

Blackman, D. E. (1983). On cognitive theories of animal learning: extrapolation from humans to animals? In G. C. L. Davey (ed.), Animal Models of Human Behavior. Chichester: Wiley.

Blough, D. S. and Blough, P. (1977). Animal psychophysics. In W. K. Honig and J. E. R. Staddon (eds), Handbook of Operant Behavior. Englewood Cliffs, NJ: Prentice-Hall.

Bradshaw, C. M., Szabadi, E. and Lowe, C. F. (eds) (1981). Quantification of Steady-State Operant Behaviour. Amsterdam: Elsevier/North-Holland Biomedical Press.

Branch, M. N. and Malagodi, E. F. (1980). Where have all the behaviorists gone? The Behavior Analyst, 3, 31-38.

Breland, K. and Breland, M. (1961). The misbehavior of organisms. American Psychologist, 61, 681-684.

Brown, P. L. and Jenkins, H. M. (1968). Auto-shaping of the pigeon's key-peck. Journal of the experimental Analysis of Behavior, 11, 1-8.

Church, R. M. (1978). The internal clock. In S. H. Hulse, H. Fowler and W. K. Honig (eds), Cognitive Processes in Animal Behavior. Hillsdale, NJ: Erlbaum Associates.

Dickinson, A. (1980). Contemporary Animal Learning Theory. Cambridge: Cambridge University Press.

Falk, J. L. (1971). The nature and determinants of adjunctive behavior. Physiology and Behavior, 6, 577-588.

Ferster, C. B. (1978). Is operant conditioning getting bored with behavior? A review of Honig and Staddon's Handbook of Operant Behavior. Journal of the experimental Analysis of Behavior, 29, 347-349.

Ferster, C. B. and Skinner, B. F. (1957). Schedules of Reinforcement. New York: Appleton-Century-Crofts.

Gamzu, E. and Schwartz, B. (1973). The maintenance of key pecking by stimulus-contingent and response-independent food presentation. Journal of the experimental Analysis of Behavior, 19, 65-72.

Garcia, J. and Koelling, R. A. (1966). The relation of cue to consequence in avoidance learning. Psychonomic Science, 4, 123-124.

Hearst, E. (1967). The behavior of Skinnerians. Contemporary Psychology, 12, 402-404.

Hearst, E. and Jenkins, H. M. (1974). Sign-tracking: The stimulus reinforcer relation and directed actions. Austin, Texas: Monograph of the Psychonomic Society.

Herrnstein, R. J. and Hineline, P. N. (1966). Negative reinforcement as shock-frequency reduction. Journal of the experimental Analysis of Behaviour, 9, 421-430.

Hersen, M. and Barlow, D. H. (1976). Single Case Experimental Designs. New York: Pergamon Press.

Honig, W. K. (ed.) (1966). Operant Behavior: Areas of research and application. New York: Appleton-Century-Crofts.

Honig, W. K. and Staddon, J. E. R. (eds) (1977). Handbook of Operant Behavior. Englewood Cliffs, NJ: Prentice-Hall.

Hulse, S. H., Fowler, H. and Honig, W. K. (eds) (1978). Cognitive Processes in Animal Behavior. Hillsdale, NJ: Erlbaum Associates.

Johanson, C. E. (1978). Drugs as reinforcers. In D. E. Blackman and D. J. Sanger (eds), Contemporary Research in Behavioral Pharmacology. New York: Plenum.

Kendrick, D. F., Rilling, M. and Stonebraker, T. B. (1981). Stimulus control of delayed matching in pigeons: directed forgetting. Journal of the experimental Analysis of Behavior, 36, 241-251.

Krantz, D. C. (1971). Schools and systems: the mutual isolation of operant and non-operant psychology as a case study. Journal of the History of the Behavioral Sciences, 7, 86-102.

Locurto, C. M., Terrace, H. S. and Gibbon, J. (eds) (1981). Autoshaping and Conditioning Theory. New York: Academic Press.

McKearney, J. W. and Barrett, J. E. (1978). Schedule-controlled behavior and the effects of drugs. In D. E. Blackman and D. J. Sanger (eds), Contemporary Research in Behavioral Pharmacology. New York: Plenum.

Mackintosh, N. J. (1974). The Psychology of Animal Learning. London: Academic Press.

Mackintosh, N. J. (1978). Conditioning. In B. M. Foss (ed.), Psychology Survey No.1. London: George Allen & Unwin.

Mogenson, G. and Cioe, J. (1977). Central reinforcement: a bridge between brain function and behavior. In W. K. Honig and J. E. R. Staddon (eds), Handbook of Operant Behavior. Englewood Cliffs, NJ: Prentice-Hall.

Pierce, W. D. and Epling, W. F. (1980). What happened to analysis in applied behavior analysis? The Behavior Analyst, 3, 1-9.

Rachlin, H. (1976). Behavior and Learning. San Francisco: W. H. Freeman.

Seligman, M. E. P. (1970). On the generality of the laws of learning. Psychological Review, 77, 406-418.

Seligman, M. E. P. and Hager, J. L. (eds) (1972). Biological Boundaries of Learning. New York: Appleton-Century-Crofts.

Shettleworth, S. J. (1973). Food reinforcement and the organization of behavior in golden hamsters. In R. Hinde and J. Stevenson-Hinde (eds), Constraints on Learning. London: Academic Press.

Sidman, M. (1960). Tactics of Scientific Research. New York: Basic Books.

Skinner, B. F. (1938). The Behavior of Organisms. New York: Appleton-Century-Crofts.

Skinner, B. F. (1966). The phylogeny and ontogeny of behavior. Science, 153, 1205-1213.

Skinner, B. F. (1974). About Behaviorism. New York: Knopf.

Skinner, B. F. (1977). Herrnstein and the evolution of behaviorism. American Psychologist, 32, 1006-1012.

Staddon, J. E. R. (1977). Schedule-induced behavior. In W. K. Honig and J. E. K. Staddon (eds), Handbook of Operant Behavior. Englewood Cliffs, NJ: Prentice Hall.

Staddon, J. E. R. and Simmelhag, B. (1971). The superstition experiment: a reexamination of its implications for the principles of adaptive behavior. Psychological Review, 78, 3-43.

Williams, D. R. and Williams, H. (1969). Auto-maintenance in the pigeon: sustained pecking despite contingent non-reinforcement. Journal of the experimental Analysis of Behavior, 12, 511-520.

Chapter 3

AGE DIFFERENCES AND AGE CHANGES

S. M. Chown

INTRODUCTION

It is not easy to identify the effects of aging on performance: many other causes of change get in the way. With age,
senses may become less acute, neurological and physiological
processes may become less reactive, and an increase in chronic
ailments may occur. Some of these changes have implications
for apparent cognitive or social functioning, and elderly
people taking part in an experiment are usually not chosen to
represent the superbly well-preserved. Some of their physical
problems will have been noticed and ameliorated by deaf aids,
spectacles, or tablets to control high blood pressure, but
other problems will be less obvious and untreated. Most gerontologists have at some point in their careers asked themselves
whether there are any inevitable age changes beyond those due
to basic bodily alterations. While this question cannot yet be
answered with certainty, it is worth noting that Birren and
Spieth (1962) gave tests of intelligence and speed to 161
healthy air pilots and traffic controllers and found that
their psychomotor performance still showed age effects in
spite of excellent physical condition. Moreover, Botwinick and
Birren (1963) found that an extremely healthy sample of men
over 65, while they showed no age effect on simple reaction
time, did show differences on more complex information processing tasks.

A further difficulty in research on aging has long been
recognized. Differences between age groups may include effects
of differences in upbringing and education as well as those
due to the aging process. On the other hand, longitudinal
studies are limited to people willing to be retested (biassed
to the initially more able), and results will include the
effects of any changes in the cultural ethos as well as those
due to aging.

Schaie and Baltes (1975) have discussed research strategies. Whereas cross-sectional studies look at many age groups

at one time of testing, and longitudinal investigations examine one birth cohort over many years of testing, they advocate cross-sequential studies. These follow up many birth cohorts over many years: either retesting the same people, or drawing new samples to represent the cohorts at each testing. Analysis of test scores according to any two of birth cohort, age at time of testing, and year of testing allows results to be attributed to the aging process, to differences between generations, or to cultural change. The impact of this technique has been very great. On those topics where test programmes have been carried out for long enough, it has become possible to identify aging-process effects, and to see just how much influence generation differences and cultural changes have had.

The complex organization of the individual also causes difficulties for research on age changes. Each person and his or her world together form a unique system: change in any part of the system is bound to result in adjustments elsewhere until a new stability is achieved. Changes in one respect or another are likely to be fairly frequent: indeed, some people desire change and initiate it in their own system by such means as taking a new job or learning to meditate. Gerontologists hope to study personal changes or changes in life contexts likely to affect many elderly people; they trust that the resulting adjustments in each person's system will be similar or at least classifiable into types. As recent research has been concentrated upon the individual's cognition and personality and, from the social context, upon life events, these three areas will be reviewed further in this chapter. (There has been a growth of interest in analysing the effects of physical surroundings, too; good reviews are to be found in Lawton, 1977; Parr, 1980.)

A human being is not just part of an objective system, but possesses a subjective evaluation of each component of that objective system. The subjective evaluations may influence each other, and may also interact with the objective elements. Attempts to assess the individual's behavioural responses to changes in self or circumstances have resulted in measures of 'adjustment'. However, people's opinions about themselves or their situations have given rise to scales of 'well-being', 'morale', and 'life satisfaction'. One or other of these is often regarded as the dependent measure in studies on aging where quality of life is an issue. Research examining satisfaction with life will be a further focus in this chapter.

COGNITION

Memory

Recent work on memory has been reviewed by Craik (1977), Hartley, Harker and Walsh (1980) and in the series of chapters edited by Poon, Fozard, Cermak, Arenberg and Thompson (1980). Their conclusions are that, while some age deficit occurs in sensory (immediate) memory, little loss, if any, can be shown in primary memory (i.e. that amount of material within the memory span). Fall-off in long-term memory with age seems most certainly attributable to acquisition difficulties, notably to poor encoding of material, but may also be due to retrieval problems. The latter are difficult to study because acquisition cannot readily be equated across age groups.

Recent work has again shown age differences in sensory memory, both in absorption time (Cerella, Poon and Fozard, 1982) and in visual persistence (Kline and Schieber, 1981). Some doubts have recently been expressed about the intactness of primary memory in older groups by Parkinson, Lindholm and Inman (1982) and Wright (1982) but rather little work has been done on the topic, which is difficult to keep free from contamination by secondary memory.

With respect to secondary long-term memory, attention has been focussed yet again on encoding. Charness (1981) neatly showed that chess players in their 50s appeared to have more difficulty in encoding chess diagrams than did players aged around 20. Zacks (1982) noted the less common use of encoding strategies by 70-year-olds compared with 20-year-olds in a complex 'running memory' task. Howard, McCandrews and Lasaga (1981) reported less category clustering of words in a free recall task by subjects of 70 than by subjects in their late 20s.

Encoding differences do not account for all age differences: Riege and Inman (1981) found that older people were worse than young or middle-aged ones when the stimuli were visual, auditory or tactile materials which could not easily be labelled. However, the age difference on attempts to reproduce and recognize such items did not become significant until 60. Nor are the old helped or hindered relative to the young by the use of visual rather than verbal material (Shelton, Parsons and Leber, 1982; Winograd, Smith and Simon 1982).

The effects of lack of encoding on later retrieval were shown by Bowles and Poon (1982), who gave a verbal recognition task to subjects in their 20s and 70s. The average performance of the two age groups did not differ significantly, but the distribution of scores for the older subjects was bimodal. The lower mode was much worse than the single mode for younger subjects, the higher mode was about equal to that for the younger subjects. Further analysis took verbal ability into account. Young and old subjects with high vocabulary scores did equally well on recognition; young and old subjects with low vocabulary scores differed on recognition, the old being poorer. Bowles and Poon say that encoding had gone awry for the elderly poor performers but not for the good ones.

Another factor influencing memory is undoubtedly familiarity with the material. Barrett and Wright (1981) found that word lists of old-fashioned words which were more familiar to 70-year-olds than to 20-year-olds were better remembered by the older group. New, modern words were more successfully remembered by the young. (In this task, the age groups had actually chosen to spend longer doing a preliminary task on the unfamiliar words than on the lists familiar to them, but they nevertheless remembered fewer of the former.)

As may have been apparent from this brief outline, nearly all these experiments have compared the performance of only two age groups, usually young adults and people in their 60s or 70s. Little can be gleaned about the possible age of onset of memory difficulties from such experiments. (NB: Riege and Inman's work (1981) using non-codable material was an exception to this, and onset of deficit was quite late.) Two recent studies are particularly welcome. One is an analysis of longitudinal results on some aspects of memory (though with an entirely aged sample) and the other checks age differences within generations against differences between generations across the adult age range.

McCarty, Siegler and Logue (1982) followed up members of the Duke longitudinal sample (aged 60 to 94 at the start of the study) on the Wechsler memory scale sub-tests. A period of up to 16 years was covered in some cases. Selective attrition of subjects occurred in this study, and results of those with one retest, five retests and 10 retests are quoted. Logical memory (immediate and delayed recall) and easy associative memory did not show declines even for people who were over 70 when first tested. (Indeed, logical memory showed some improvement on first retest.) However, memory for hard associations and visual reproductions did decline both for people over 70 and those under 70 at first test.

Arenberg (1982) has analysed the data collected between 1960 and 1976 from 894 men aged 17 to 96, members of the

Baltimore longitudinal study, on the Benton Visual Retention Test. He looked at within age groups slopes as well as slopes within age cohorts. Older men (those over 53 when first tested) made more errors than younger ones, and increasingly so at later ages, even allowing for a general cohort effect whereby later-born people did slightly better, age for age, than earlier-born people.

Elderly persons are prone to complain of poor memory; two recent studies suggest that they underestimate their own difficulties in learning new material. Murphy, Sanders, Gabriesheski and Schmitt (1981) asked 69-year-old and 20-year-old subjects to say how ready they were to recall line drawings. The younger group did better at this; the old overestimated their readiness. Interestingly, when allowed to spend as much time as they wanted on the material, the young subjects took longer than the old (and performed better). Those older subjects who were trained to 'chunk' and to rehearse material did better than the rest of their age group. Making the older subjects spend a longer time learning (though less than one minute per item) proved to be the most help to their performance. Bruce, Coyne and Botwinick (1982) asked three age groups, in their 20s, 60s and 70s, to estimate their performance in learning word lists of 20 words. Estimates did not differ with age, but actual performance was worse with increase of age group. With overlearnt material the situation was different. Lackman and Lackman (1980) found that female school teachers' general knowledge remained firm well beyond the 40s and so did efficiency of recall of that knowledge; and the teachers were accurate in their self-assessment for this task. People can, it seems, rely upon their overlearnt stock of information to carry them through.

Recent work on memory, then, has continued to explore the type of task causing memory difficulties, but has thrown little new light on the loci of deterioration in memory, and even now comparatively little is known about the age of onset of memory difficulties for different kinds of tasks.

Information Processing

So far, no large-scale longitudinal studies have been carried out on information processing and so little can be said about age changes in the individual. Cross-sectional studies have indicated a reduced capacity with increased age to cope with complicated material at speed. Welford (1965) used information theoretic measures to quantify the complexity of the stimuli.

Some assumptions had to be made, but the resulting equations gave a useful comparison of relative performance between age groups. An unsolved problem has remained: how to quantify the amount of information in those tasks where a measure of 'bits' cannot readily be assigned to the stimuli. Cerella, Poon and Williams (1980) have suggested the use of the processing time (latency of response) needed by various age groups compared with the processing time taken by subjects in their 20s. This suggestion uses processing time as a double measure, first to reflect task complexity, then to reflect age handicap. It demands very careful choice of the 20-year-olds who are to form the standard. Cerella and his colleagues believe they have shown, in data culled from a number of studies using the technique, that sensori-motor and mental processing times are greater by a factor of 20 per cent for people in their 40s and 50s; that sensori-motor performance differs little more in older groups; but that mental processing is worse in the 60s and 70s by a factor of 60 per cent when compared with the baseline. This may well turn out to be a useful way of describing results, though it lacks the theoretical under-pinning of Welford's analysis of complexity.

In the last two years, a number of papers have continued to report that elderly people are differentially worse than young adults at tasks which involve the mental processing of complex information. The use of simultaneous competing tasks (Wright, 1981), paced tasks (Perone and Baron, 1982), visual search tasks (Plude and Hoyer, 1981), and identification of tilted patterns (Cerella, Poon and Fozard, 1981) are but a few examples. A variation (Salthouse and Somberg, 1982) used accuracy as the basic measure. People around 20 and people over 60 were compared for accuracy in a simple classification task when required to react within strict time limits. Progressive overload was introduced by bringing in ever shorter time limits. Accuracy decreased at very similar rates in the two age groups as speed demands went up, but there was a difference of about 50 ms in the mean time necessary for them to achieve 50 per cent (or 100 per cent) accuracy. The authors suggest that this constant age differential arose because the old group needed longer to integrate information and prepare a response, not because of an age difference in rate of receiving information.

It remains to be seen whether the consistent age effects found in cross-sectional work on information processing will prove to owe anything substantial to cohort differences, and whether greater initial ability will give a longitudinal advantage. This is a topic where longitudinal and cross-sequential results are much needed.

Intelligence

Cross-sectional studies of problem solving and reasoning have long shown that age of peak performance varies, depending upon the type of task and the extent to which previous experience can be invoked. Recent work has continued to highlight these points.

Hartley (1981) found that deductive reasoning among college students and graduates did not differ until after 40; but it is more common to find, as did Denney and Palmer (1981), that abstract problem solving was linearly poorer with increase in age group although people in their 40s and 50s did best at making practical suggestions to deal with everyday human and mechanical predicaments (scored for number of suggestions and amount of self-reliance shown). It has once again been reported that divergent thinking abilities are highest in middle age (Jaquish and Ripple, 1981), although they found age had rather little absolute effect, and that scores were somewhat more related to subjects' self-esteem in the middle-aged and older groups.

Thought processes often differ in emphasis between age groups. Denney and Denney (1982), whose subjects ranged from 30 to 90, found that older people were increasingly more likely to pair pictures by complementarity rather than similarity, and also that, on a 20-questions task, their older subjects were less likely to ask exploratory, constraint-fixing questions and more likely to go for direct hypothesis-testing questions. Procedures open to different age groups may well vary, encouraging different methods of attacking problems. Camp (1981) reported that, when faced with questions about public events and dates, subjects aged about 70 made more use of inference to try to reach answers than did subjects in their 20s; but then, the older group were able to use reference to events they personally remembered rather than to academic 'history'. From such results, it seems that people generally prefer, as they get older, to rely upon wisdom and experience rather than upon reasoning ability.

In the last decade, longitudinal and cross-sequential studies have begun to yield results. The largest study, with most comparisons and controls, has been that by Schaie and his colleagues (1973, 1974, 1977, 1979). They used the Primary

Mental Abilities battery which assesses reasoning, spatial ability, number, verbal meaning and word fluency. Their subjects were all members of a group health organization. So far, longitudinal results have been reported from two samples each tested twice (1956-1963, 60 per cent retested; 1963-1970, 42 per cent retested) and a further follow-up of the earlier sample (1956-63-70, when 32 per cent of the initial sample completed the third test). Age effects appear much later than in cross-sectional work. Except for one of the samples on the highly-speeded word fluency test, the Primary Mental Abilities held up for individuals until the 60s.

As part of the same study, Schaie, Labouvie and Buech (1973) also tested independent samples from the same generations at seven-year intervals. Age effects showed up at 60 or a little before: but this is still a good deal later than has been found in traditional, cross-sectional work.

All Schaie's results have shown, to a greater or lesser extent, a generation difference (cohort effect) such that earlier-born people tend to do worse than later-born ones when those later-borns reach the same chronological age. The effect shows most clearly on the space sub-test of the PMA, rather less clearly on reasoning and verbal meaning, and hardly at all on number and word fluency. (The effect for word fluency appears to be reversed for one sample.) Naturally, in cross-sectional studies, each older group is from an older generation so any cohort decrements add on to aging-process effects and give greater apparent fall-off with age.

Two aspects of Schaie's results therefore need comments; the lateness of changes with age in longitudinal PMA scores, and cohort effects. Botwinick (1977) reviewed Schaie's findings very carefully with respect to lateness of onset of age changes. He pointed out that the samples have suffered, just as all other longitudinal samples have, from the effects of loss of subjects from retest groups. Loss is biassed, always being greater among those people who initially made lower scores. Thus, longitudinal results only describe what happens to initially able people. This trend, Botwinick showed, became more marked with each retest. Botwinick's own longitudinal data on people over 60 (Siegler and Botwinick, 1979) also show that the more able stay with research longer and show declines later. It would certainly seem reasonably safe now to predict that an able person is likely to maintain his or her own level of intellectual ability, including ability to reason, through middle age at least: and this is indeed a change from the prediction one would have felt obliged to make 10 years ago. A decline may begin in reasoning in the later 50s or 60s, and this decline may take place well before death. The older subjects tested three times in Schaie's work showed a decline by the second time of testing and thereafter survived for seven years: so a sudden drop in ability level, one to five years before death (Kleemeier, 1962), cannot account for these declines, though of course some physical and health changes may well underlie them (Spieth, 1964; Schaie, 1979).

However, what happens to initially less able people is not yet known; it cannot yet be assumed that their ability also holds up as they age. A question still to be answered is whether use of reasoning ability helps to maintain it. This is a difficult question in that people who do maintain a high level of ability to reason will be highly likely to continue to use it, but it is one on which longitudinal data may yet prove helpful. That cognitive test results may be linked to types of life style has been shown by Gribben, Schaie and Parham (1980) in a further ramification of Schaie's work. They clustered answers to a questionnaire about background and way of life and showed that cognitive abilities tended to reflect life style, or vice versa, depending upon one's outlook. They also showed that downward changes in ability were more likely in some life styles than others (Schaie, 1981). Analyses are still needed where initial ability is matched, and later 'use' has been varied. People may well be able to manage in their daily lives with very little recourse to reasoning. As Schuster and Barkowski (1980) showed, there are many occasions in the everyday affairs of adult life when having local information and relevant experience is more immediately helpful to competent performance than is intelligence. If extent of 'use' were found to have no effect on people initially of high ability, then it would become more reasonable to expect that individuals initially of low ability would also maintain their scores as they aged.

Cohort effects are a new feature of results on aging and deserve attention in their own right. How are they to be accounted for? It is possible that each succeeding seven-year cohort through this century has been more used to thinking for itself, more accustomed to intelligence being assessed, more used to working against the clock, and more research-orientated, than the one before it. This is indeed Schaie's view (1979). If this is the case, will the trend continue or will there come a limit to the improvement?

However, it is just worth asking whether cohort effects could be artifactual, perhaps due to self-selection of subjects and their attrition rates over time. Botwinick (1977) noted that, as attrition rates rose, so the remainder of the sample tended to do better. Are attrition rates evenly distributed across age groups? From experience it seems to be easier to persuade middle-aged persons to continue to co-operate in research on aging than young people. Inspection of the figures given by Schaie (1979, table III) shows that this seems to have happened in his samples, for attrition rates are higher in the young groups than in the middle-aged. Such self-selection would suggest that a comparatively more able younger group remains, but the point cannot be laboured too far: figures given in Schaie, Labouvie and Barrett (1973) show that the difference on initial tests between those later retested and those who dropped out was nearly always least in the youngest groups and became progressively greater through the age groups. Also, some cohort effects appear in Schaie's independent samples, each tested in one of 1956, 1963 or 1970 and then grouped by cohort, though the effects are not as marked as in the longitudinal samples. One could argue that these might be due to initial self-selection, but on balance the probability is that cohort effects are actual generation differences. They vary in extent from test to test and cannot be presumed always to be favourable to later-born cohorts, but they usually augment aging effects. They seem to be more pronounced on problem-solving tasks which require reasoning on the spot: in fact, on the 'fluid' abilities. These are the ones which show, not individual declines as used to be thought, but long-established differences between generations. To improve performance would require the overcoming of some effects of socialization. These might turn out to be early and serious influences such as type of upbringing, narrow education, or severe curtailment of encouragement to think; or perhaps less serious factors, such as test sophistication and practice with type of puzzles set in the tests. Recent efforts to train older subjects on figural relations and reasoning have shown some transfer of training which held for one to six months, but no younger groups were included for comparison (Blieszner, Willis and Baltes, 1981; Willis, Blieszner and Baltes, 1981). Other workers who gave practice and training on a coding task to young as well as old subjects found that both age groups improved and age differences were not diminished (Beres and Baron, 1981; Erber, Botwinick and Storandt, 1981). Cohort differences are probably going to be difficult to eliminate, but they do present a possible target for attack.

PERSONALITY

A comprehensive review of personality and age (Neugarten, 1977) noted the many recent studies of age-group differences on a wide range of personality variables. The effect most consistently recorded is of greater introversion with increase in age group. There have been a few recent longitudinal reports.

A longitudinal study of performance on a single questionnaire, the Guilford Zimmerman Temperament Survey, was reported by Douglas and Arenberg (1978). Their subjects were 915 men aged 17 to 98 from the Baltimore longitudinal sample, and test results were collected during a 16-year period. After a seven-year interval, 336 of the men were retested. In a cross-sectional analysis, general activity, masculinity and ascendance decreased with age, while restraint and co-operative tolerance increased. Cross-sequential analyses suggested that true age changes occurred only in masculinity and activity (from 50) which both decreased with age; and that earlier cohorts (older generations) scored lower on ascendance and higher on restraint. Thoughtfulness, personal relations, and co-operative tolerance showed cultural changes.

Another longitudinal study was that by Schaie and Parham (1976) who factored a 75-item questionnaire, primarily intended to measure rigidity and social responsibility, which was given to all their subjects in 1963 and 1970. They obtained a structure which shadowed many of the factors of the 16 PF. They first carried out two analyses of variance on the factor scores using cohort and time of measurement as the main variables. In the seven years (which represented age changes) excitability and untroubled adequacy decreased; dominance, practicality and self-sentiment increased. As cultural pressures might have caused change in the seven years, an analysis by age and time of testing was carried out. (Time of testing here represented cultural alterations.) Significant effects for time of testing were found on untroubled adequacy, dominance, practicality and self-sentiment, leaving only lower excitability as a certain age effect with no cultural or generational influences. Cohort effects consistently emerged for eight variables. Older cohorts were more excitable, less outgoing, less internally restrained, less suspicious, lower on super-ego strength, more practical, less group-dependent and had lower self-sentiment.

Thus both studies indicate rather few true age effects and suggest the importance of cultural pressures, either long-term on cohorts, or short-term on whole populations. One interesting result common to both studies is that they throw doubt on the status of introversion with respect to age. In the one study, no age decline in sociability occurred, assertiveness was cohort-related, and only part of the increase in thinking introversion was attributable to age. In the other, outgoingness and group-dependence were cohort-related, not age-related. Will it turn out to be the general case that 'increase in introversion with age' is a cohort difference rather than due to the process of aging?

A group of longitudinal studies referred to by Neugarten (1977) were carried out by the Institute of Human Development at Berkeley, following up cohorts born in Oakland in 1920-21 and Berkeley in 1928-29. Results from the years of early adolescence to the late 40s, have recently been collected into a book (Eichorn, Clausen, Haan, Honzik and Mussen, 1981). Here the basic data are details of life history, ratings and performance measures. Since the studies were originally separate, comparability was obtained by getting independent assessors for each age group to read the original protocols for each person and to carry out Q sorts for 90 carefully defined psychological characteristics. A technique of longitudinal principal components analysis has been used to delineate a common factor structure on which age trends can be examined.

Of the six factors which emerged, only 'degree of emotional control' showed no change with age. Age appeared to increase 'cognitive investment', 'openness to self', 'nurturance' and 'self-confidence'. (It also increased individual differences in openness to self.) Age appeared to decrease 'sexual expressiveness' until the late 40s, when scores for the factor rose somewhat. (Age appeared to diminish individual differences in this factor.) No clear-cut differences were found between the two cohorts, though there were some sex differences as females were more nurturant, less self-confident and less sexually controlled than males. Factors correlated more closely within adolescence (14 and 17) and within adulthood (37 and 47) than across the broad gap of 20 years between them. However, the factor scores correlated significantly even over the 20-year span on all the factors (for women) and on cognitive investment (for men). Considerable consistency of personality clearly existed. A study of 53 mothers of these subjects (Mussen, Honzik and Eichorn, 1980) gave results of Q sort assessments based on interviews with them when they were 30 and 70. Most characteristics were relatively stable over the 40 years and kept their Q sort positions. Few assessments could be regarded as unstable; these were self-assurance, satisfaction with life, and

73

(perhaps reassuringly in view of the time interval) attitude to their child.

In the middle-aged, different aspects of personality became determiners of psychological health as situations altered. This was most marked for women. At 37 (when young families were the norm) psychological health went with nurturance. At 47 (when work was becoming more important) psychological health favoured dominance. For men, psychological health at all ages was predicted by intellectual competence and responsibility.

Career achievement in men was predicted by adolescents' dependability, productiveness, effectiveness, ambitiousness and high cognitive investment. For women, nearly all of whom were married with children, it was necessary to look at subgroups of life patterns: homemakers, those committed to careers, those with dual roles of home and work (but not career) and those who had only had paid employment in the past. Among those who had not been to college, adolescents who became homemakers proved to have been higher in cognitive and social skills. Among college-educated women, adolescent personality also differentiated out the eventual homemakers: they were more conservative, conventional, feminine in style, dependent, submissive, placid and power-orientated. The small number of women committed to a career (10 out of 65) were, as adolescents, higher than the rest on anxiety, self-pity, feeling victimized and being basically hostile. This depressing list is illuminated by the fact that they were not then considered physically attractive or feminine. Even at 30 they were self-critical and self-defeating. However, at 40, these same females were distinguished for their cognitive involvement, incisiveness, independence, ambition and lack of irritability; and they equalled the homemakers on warmth and sympathy. This sequence of development demonstrates the interplay between personality and situation. The unattractive teenagers no doubt reacted to lack of social success with hostility and self-doubt, which melted only when they eventually achieved a successful situation in life.

These two cohorts, eight years apart in age, have responded to the particular times in which they have lived; the outstanding thing is that in most cases a good match seems to have been found between teenage personality and later life pattern. For a few people such a match was not readily forthcoming in adolescence, and there were signs of disruption in personality. In the years to come will there be other difficulties for some of the subjects, and if so, will these lead to disruptions of personality?

LIFE STAGES AND LIFE EVENTS

All societies have customs relating to birth, child rearing, adult living, ill-health and death. Any categorization of stages of life owes much to the cultural context. Events or experiences seen as a hurdle in one society may be taken for granted in another, and a time of life glorified in one society may be regarded as quite inglorious in another. Societies alter - sometimes rapidly - and so do expectations about behaviour. Against the background of way of life there will be the impact of life events, triumphs and disasters and changes, some sought by individuals and others imposed on them. (For a more detailed discussion see Bengtson, Kasschau and Ragan, 1977; and Lowenthal, 1977.)

Erikson (1959) talked of stages of life, each with a conflict to be resolved; those of the mature adult and old person being respectively generativity vs. stagnation and ego-integration vs. despair. Jacques (1965) stressed the mid-life crisis, reached when a person realized the limitations of time left (see Cytrynbaum, Blum, Patrick, Stein, Wadner and Wilk, 1980). Some health problem or family or social event may trigger this crisis (e.g. Vaillant, 1977) which is said to lead to a reappraisal of self and of aims in life. Levinson and his colleagues (Levinson, Darrow, Klein, Levinson and McKee, 1978) argued that destructuring and restructuring occur approximately once a decade as goals are achieved (or not) and new ones set. This seemed the pattern for their subjects: 40 American men aged 35 to 45.

But how generally are such patterns of crisis undergone? In a study of a representative sample of 461 people aged 29 to 58 in a small English provincial town, Nicholson (1980) found that most of his middle-aged subjects seemed to adapt to such changes as loss of further prospects of promotion gradually and smoothly. Their worries were material or about other people - offspring or parents - rather than for themselves. Most anticipated the future with pleasure rather than dismay. This finding may well partly reflect differences between American and British culture, but it may also owe something to the form of the study. People were asked about their present attitudes, including worries, and about general changes in their lives over the years, but probing was limited. However, an additional in-depth study bore out the main findings.

The possibility of both smooth adaptation and disturbance has been found by Lowenthal, Thurner and Chiriboga (1975), who studied American people who were at four points of life likely to demand adaptation. They found that young men, ambitious yet still uncertain of themselves, were the most unhappy group, the next most unhappy being middle-aged women who were uncertain of their aims as children departed and marriages were re-examined. What was particularly interesting was that styles of reacting could be identified. Some people had had, objectively, a great deal of disturbance in their lives; of these, some had quailed under it, others met it with resilience. (The latter tended to have deeper relationships with other people.) Other people had had comparatively few stresses to face. While many of these considered themselves lucky, there were others who were nevertheless overcome by their troubles. (The latter tended to be more neurotic.) Individual differences in reaction are important in this field, and interest has recently turned to the study of reactions to specific life events as distinct from stages.

Developments from the pioneer work of Holmes and Rahe (1967) have been used to assess the effects of stressful life events on the elderly. In general, men and women agree closely about the relative stressfulness of events, but women rate all events as more stressful than do men. Older and younger people also agree closely, but younger ones give higher weighting to many stresses relating to death and separation (Chiriboga and Dean, 1978; Masuda and Holmes, 1978; Sands and Parker, 1979-80; Horowitz and Wilner, 1980). Even here there may have been a change over time. In 1961, Friedsam found that elderly people expressed more hopelessness and loss of purpose after a flood had destroyed all their possessions than did younger people. Recently, however, Bell (1978) found that younger victims of a tornado seemed to have been more upset than older ones, in terms of anxiety, physical stress levels and changes in personal relationships; Huerta and Horton (1978) also found that older victims in a dam disaster reported fewer adverse emotional effects and fewer feelings of relative deprivation. It may be that the length of time since the disaster is an important variable, since the two latter investigations began respectively 18 weeks and 6 months after the event, but it would also be worth examining the expectations of the age groups and how these may have altered in the last two decades.

People expect that past events will cause less current stress than more recent events (Horowitz and Wilner, 1980), but events cast long shadows forward; Brown and Harris (1978) have shown that vulnerability to depression in middle-aged women was associated with pre-adolescent loss of mother, although a stressful current event actually sparked off the depression. Brown believes that a careful interview is necessary to find out the degree of stress which each person is experiencing, and to explore the background factors sufficiently to discover the complex interactions between them.

Are there characteristic ways of meeting stresses? Chiriboga and Dean (1978) reported five- and seven-year follow-ups of the people described by Lowenthal, Thurner and Chiriboga (1975). Positive stress (i.e. stress of an inherently pleasant event) increased in the middle-aged group but went down in retirement. Four groups of people were identified: there were those for whom both positive and negative stress decreased ('avoiders'); those with increased positive stress but decreased negative stress ('lucky'); those with decreased positive stress but increased negative stress ('overwhelmed'); and those for whom both kinds of stress went up ('stress prone'). Personal interests and activities had been noted five years before and they did differ slightly for each stress-change group for younger and older men and younger women (though not for older women). The investigators went on to relate recent changes in life satisfaction, depression, health (doctor's visits), and emotional problems, to the type of worries currently suffered by the different age and sex groups. There were discriminators, but these were not self-evident predictors (except in the case of health worries and doctor's visits). The work raises hopes that links exist between past experience and stress, and between stress and reaction, but the pattern is still far from clear in detail.

The impact of stress on personality characteristics may, it seems, not normally be very great. Leon, Kamp, Gillum and Gillum (1981) worked with 96 men whom they re-evaluated after an interval of 30 years. They found that personality scores on the MMPI remained fairly stable, and that the interactions of past personality and present life-stress did not predict present personality functioning.

One would expect that personality plus stress would normally lead to some typical mode of coping rather than to personality change. Mode of coping can take a variety of forms, but, once more, age does not seem a relevant influence (Vaillant, 1977; Folkman and Lazarus, 1980; McCrae, 1982), apart from a tendency for middle-aged and elderly people to avoid hostile reactions and escapist fantasies. What has not yet been demonstrated is whether there is any continuity over time in preferred methods of coping with stress, and whether personality and stress do interact to give a prediction of coping style.

SATISFACTION WITH LIFE

A person's evaluation of his or her life is likely to be influenced by past and present objective situations and by his or her own assessments of them (see Bengtson, Kasschau and Ragan, 1977; Chown, 1977).

Not surprisingly, recent work continues to find that good health, high activity, high social status and good income tend to be associated with high life satisfaction, morale or adjustment (Palmore and Kivett, 1977; Thomae and Kranzhoff, 1979; Felton, Hinrichsen and Tsemberis, 1981; Herzog and Rodgers, 1981). These predictors seem to be stronger in urban areas than in suburban or rural places (Felton, Hinrichsen and Tsemberis, 1981; Fengler and Jensen, 1981). Liang (1982) postulated a complex system of interrelationships between background factors and morale, with the most immediate influences being health, finance and subjective social integration. Objective social integration and social status were expected to have an effect by influencing the other three variables. The main linkages were indeed present. The less direct linkages were not as potent as expected.

Social interaction has continued to attract attention. Mutran and Reitzes (1981) reported findings for 1,055 men aged 55 and over, and found that involvement in community activities was most strongly related to feelings of well-being (measured on the Bradburn Affect Balance Scale), other important influences being visiting friends and state of health. Role-loss (Elwell and Maltbi-Crannell, 1981) and childlessness among widows (Beckman and Houser, 1982) affected social interaction and lowered well-being as assessed by the Philadelphia Morale Scale. Loneliness, reported by a quarter of 70-year-olds in a Swedish study (Berg, Mellstrom, Persson and Svanborg, 1981), went with lack of friends, depression and negative self-assessment of health (though not lower objective health). However, in a study of people living in two high-rise buildings where old people were not isolated, life satisfaction was not always greater among those with most social interaction (Mancini, Quinn, Gavigan and Franklin, 1980). The possibility is that availability of social interaction is a necessary but not sufficient factor in keeping up morale.

If this is so, then environments that give plenty of opportunity for social interaction might be expected to have inhabitants with, on average, higher morale than socially isolating environments; but in comparisons between 'sociable' environments the more 'sociable' might not be the more satisfying because other factors might then become important.

Windley, Arch and Scheidt (1982) carried out an investigation among people over 65 in 18 towns in Kansas. They asked each person about perceived environmental constriction (how much they liked the community, how much residents were involved with each other and the town) and also about the degree of satisfaction with their own homes. Both measures turned out to be useful in predicting a composite of morale, affect balance, and freedom from symptoms of mental disturbance. They were not so useful in predicting contact with friends and relatives. While this is not a direct test of the hypothesis previously mentioned, the results are certainly in line with it.

On the other hand, individual abilities and characteristics also prove to be influential in raising or lowering morale. Milligan, Powell and Furchtgott (1981) noted that, in a group of veterans aged 55 to 70, a positive attitude to aging and greater life satisfaction were correlated with better serial learning ability and faster reaction time (though which is cause and which effect here is difficult to say). Three studies provide longitudinal data showing relationships between personality and subsequent measures of well-being. Costa, McRae and Norris (1981) obtained Guilford Zimmerman Temperament Survey scores from men aged 17 to 97, and showed that introversion and neuroticism not only correlated with low concurrent personal adjustment, but that the personality scores predicted adjustment scores obtained 2 to 10 years later or between 10 and 17 years later. Costa and McCrae (1980) used introversion and neuroticism assessed by the 16 PF and EPI and these, too, predicted low subjective well-being 10 years later to a significant extent. Mussen, Honzik and Eichorn (1982) looked at ratings of current life satisfaction made from interview records obtained from elderly parents of the Berkeley longitudinal sample. This assessment of life satisfaction was correlated with assessments of personality characteristics obtained from records of 40 years before. Women who, 40 years before, had been mentally alert, cheerful, satisfied with their lot, self-assured, and not fatigued, tended to be high on life satisfaction at 70. For men, emotional and physical health at 30 were significant predictors, whereas their personality characteristics at that time were not. It was the emotional stability of their wives at age 30 which was a good predictor of the men's own life satisfaction at 70.

In examining variables which affect life satisfaction, the administrator is likely to pay most attention to objective factors which are external to the individual and which might be altered; indeed, he or she may prefer to concentrate upon detailed studies of the environment (see Parr, 1980). Many psychologists are likely to be more intrigued by the findings on ability and personality, and to suspect that these may be linked to differences in subjective interpretations of similar objective situations, so that morale differences will remain even when objective conditions have been made as good as possible.

CONCLUSION

Research in gerontology made a slow beginning in the early 1900s, expanded in the 1950s, and has undergone a further dramatic increase in the late 1970s and early 1980s. (Useful references are Birren, 1959; Birren and Schaie, 1977; Poon, 1980.) Until recently, concentration has been upon age-group differences. It is indeed useful to start with such work when exploring a new topic in gerontology: but it seems poor strategy to remain at that stage once age differences between groups have been found. The study of age changes in individuals used to seem the next essential step, once preliminary explorations had been made. Now cross-sequential analysis has provided a powerful tool which can yield even more information and, on some topics at least, with the need for only comparatively small longitudinal samples to check on the results from independent samples. It is certainly still costly because collection of data must be from a large number of people and spread over years; it requires long-term planning and long-term finance. Not all age-group differences will turn out to be cohort-related, but prior assumptions cannot be made. For instance, how far will 'cautiousness' in decision-making turn out to be cohort-related, and how far culture-influenced, and how far dependent upon the aging process? Results of applying cross-sequential analyses to the topics of intelligence and personality have shown that surprises will occur. The method is useful because it clarifies the traditional view of the effects of aging, and thus prepares the way for further investigations of 'causes' of both age-process and cohort-related differences between age groups.

REFERENCES

Arenberg, D. (1982). Estimates of age changes in the Benton Visual Retention Test. Journal of Gerontology, 37, 87-90.
Barrett, T. R., and Wright, M. (1981). Age related facilitation in recall following semantic processing. Journal of Gerontology, 36, 194-199.

Beckman, L. J., and Houser, B. B. (1982). The consequences of childlessness on the sociopsychological well-being of older women. Journal of Gerontology, 37, 243-250.

Bell, B. (1978). Disaster impact and response. Gerontologist, 18, 531-540.

Bengtson, V. L., Kasschau, P. L., and Ragan, P. K. (1977). The impact of social structure on aging individuals. In J. E. Birren and K. W. Schaie (eds), Handbook of the Psychology of Aging. New York: Van Nostrand Reinhold.

Beres, C. and Baron, A. (1981). Improved digit symbol substitution by older women as a result of extended practice. Journal of Gerontology, 36, 591-597.

Berg, S., Mellstrom, D., Persson, G. and Svanborg, A. (1981). Loneliness in the Swedish aged. Journal of Gerontology, 36, 342-349.

Birren, J. E. (ed.), (1959). Handbook of Aging and the Individual. Chicago: University of Chicago Press.

Birren, J. E. and Schaie, K. W. (eds), (1977). Handbook of the Psychology of Aging. New York: Van Nostrand Reinhold.

Birren, J. E. and Spieth, W. (1962). Age, response speed and cardiovascular functions. Journal of Gerontology, 17, 390-391.

Blieszner, R., Willis, S. and Baltes, P. B. (1981). Training research in aging on the fluid ability of inductive reasoning. Journal of Applied Developmental Psychology, 2, 247-265.

Botwinick, J. (1977). Intellectual abilities. In J. E. Birren and K. W. Schaie (eds), Handbook of the Psychology of Aging. New York: Van Nostrand Reinhold.

Botwinick, J. and Birren, J. E. (1963). Cognitive processes: mental abilities and psychomotor responses in healthy aged men. In J. E. Birren, R. N. Butler, S. W. Greenhouse, L. Sokoloff and M. R. Yarrow (eds), Human Aging. Washington, DC: Public Health Service Publication, no. 986.

Bowles, N. and Poon, L. W. (1982). An analysis of the effects of aging on recognition memory. Journal of Gerontology, 37, 212-219.

Brown, G. and Harris, T. (1978). Social Origins of Depression: A study of psychiatric disorder in women. London: Tavistock.

Bruce, P. R., Coyne, A. C. and Botwinick, J. (1982). Adult age differences in metamemory. Journal of Gerontology, 37, 354-357.

Camp, C. J. (1981). The use of fact retrieval vs. inference in young and elderly adults. Journal of Gerontology, 36, 715-721.

Cerella, J., Poon, L. W. and Fozard, J. L. (1981). Mental rotation and age reconsidered. Journal of Gerontology, 36, 620-624.

Cerella, J., Poon, L. W. and Fozard, J. L. (1982). Age and iconic read out. Journal of Gerontology, 37, 197-202.

Cerella, J., Poon, L. W. and Williams, D. (1980). Age and the complexity hypothesis. In L. W. Poon (ed.) Aging in the 1980s. Washington, DC: American Psychological Association.

Charness, N. (1981). Visual short term memory and aging in chess players. Journal of Gerontology, 36, 615-619.

Chiriboga, D. A. and Dean, H. (1978). Dimensions of stress. Journal of Psychomatic Research, 22, 47-55.

Chown, S. M. (1977). Morale, careers and personal potentials. In J. E. Birren and K. W. Schaie (eds), Handbook of the Psychology of Aging. New York: Van Nostrand Reinhold.

Costa, P. T. and McCrae, R. R. (1980). The influence of extraversion and neuroticism on subjective well-being. Journal of Personality and Social Psychology, 38, 668-678.

Costa, P. T., McCrae, R. R. and Norris, A. (1981). Personal adjustment to aging: longitudinal prediction from neuroticism and extraversion. Journal of Gerontology, 36, 78-85.

Craik, F. M. (1977). Age differences in human memory. In J. E. Birren and K. W. Schaie (eds), Handbook of the Psychology of Aging. New York: Van Nostrand Reinhold.

Cytrynbaum, S., Blum, L., Patrick, R., Stein, J., Wadner, D. and Wilk, C. (1980). Midlife development: a personality and social systems perspective. In L. W. Poon (ed.), Aging in the 1980s. Washington, DC: American Psychological Association.

Denney, N. W. and Denney, D. R. (1982). The relationship between classification and questioning strategies among adults. Journal of Gerontology, 37, 190-196.

Denney, N. W. and Palmer, A. M. (1981). Adult age differences on traditional and practical problem solving measures. Journal of Gerontology, 36, 323-328.

Douglas, K. and Arenberg, D. (1978). Age changes, cohort differences and cultural changes in the GZTS. Journal of Gerontology, 33, 737-747.

Eichorn, D. H., Clausen, J. A., Haan, N., Honzik, M. P. and Mussen, P. H. (1981). Present and Past in Middle Life. London: Academic Press.

Elwell, F. and Maltbi-Crannell, A. (1981). The impact of role loss upon coping resources and life satisfaction in the elderly. Journal of Gerontology, 36, 223-232.

Erber, J. T., Botwinick, J. and Storandt, M. (1981). The impact of memory on age differences in digit symbol performance. Journal of Gerontology, 36, 586-590.

Erikson, E. H. (1959). Identify and the life cycle. Psychological Issues, Monograph 1.

Felton, B. J., Hinrichsen, G. A. and Tsemberis, S. (1981). Urban-suburban differences in the prediction of morale among the aged. Journal of Gerontology, 36, 214-222.

Fengler, A. and Jensen, L. (1981). Perceived and objective conditions as predictors of the life satisfaction of urban and nonurban elderly. Journal of Gerontology, 36, 750-752.

Folkman, S. and Lazarus, R. S. (1980). An analysis of coping in a middle-aged community sample. Journal of Health and Social Behaviour, 21, 219-239.

Friedsam, H. (1961). Reaction of older persons to disaster caused losses: a hypothesis of relative deprivation. Gerontologist, 1, 34-37.

Gribben, K., Schaie, K. W. and Parham, I. A. (1980). Complexity of life style and maintenance of intellectual abilities. Journal of Social Issues, 36, 47-61.

Hartley, A. A. (1981). Adult age differences in deductive reasoning processes. Journal of Gerontology, 36, 700-706.

Hartley, J. T., Harker, J. O. and Walsh, D. A. (1980). Contemporary issues and new directions in adult development of learning and memory. In L. W. Poon (ed.), Aging in the 1980s. Washington, DC: American Psychological Association.

Herzog, A. R. and Rodgers, W. L. (1981). The structure of subjective well-being in different age groups. Journal of Gerontology, 36, 472-479.

Holmes, T. H. and Rahe, R. H. (1967). The social readjustment rating scale. Journal of Psychomatic Research, 11, 213-218.

Horowitz, M. J. and Wilner, N. (1980). Life events, stress and aging. In L. W. Poon (ed.) Aging in the 1980s. Washington, DC: American Psychological Association.

Howard, D. V., McCandrews, M. P. and Lasaga, M. (1981). Semantic priming of lexical decision in young and old adults. Journal of Gerontology, 36, 707-714.

Huerta, F. and Horton, R. (1978). Coping behaviour of elderly flood victims. Gerontologist, 18, 541-546.

Jacques, E. (1965). Death and the mid-life crisis. International Journal of Psycho-Analysis, 46 502-514.

Jaquish, G. A. and Ripple, R. E. (1981). Cognitive creative abilities and self esteem across the adult life span. Human Development, 24, 110-119.

Kleemeier, R. W. (1962). Intellectual changes in the senium. In Proceedings of the Social Statistics Section of the American Statistical Association.

Kline, D. W. and Schieber, F. (1981). What are the age differences in visual sensory memory? Journal of Gerontology, 36, 86-92.

Lackman, J. L. and Lackman, R. (1980). Age and actualization of world knowledge. In L. W. Poon, J. L. Fozard, L. S. Cermak, D. A. Arenberg and L. W. Thompson (eds), New Directions in Memory and Aging. Hillside, NJ: Lawrence Erlbaum.

Lawton, M. P. (1977). The impact of the environment on aging and behaviour. In J. E. Birren and K. W. Schaie (eds), Handbook of the Psychology of Aging. New York: Van Nostrand Reinhold.

Leon, G. R., Kamp, J., Gillum, R. and Gillum, B. (1981). Life stress and dimensions of functioning in old age. Journal of Gerontology, 36, 66-69.

Levinson, D., Darrow, C. N., Klein, E. B., Levinson, M. H. and McKee, B. (1978). Seasons of a Man's Life. New York: Knopf.

Liang, J. (1982). Sex diffences in life satisfaction among the elderly. Journal of Gerontology, 37, 100-108.

Lowenthal, M. F. (1977). Toward a sociological theory of change in adulthood and old age. In J. E. Birren and K. W. Schaie (eds), Handbook of the Psychology of Aging. New York: Van Nostrand.

Lowenthal, M. F., Thurner, M. and Chiriboga, D. (1975). Four Stages of Life: A comparative study of women and men facing transition. San Fransisco: Jossey Bass.

Mancini, J., Quinn, W., Gavigan, M. and Franklin, H. (1980). Social network interaction among older adults: implications for life satisfaction. Human Relations, 33, 543-554.

Masuda, M. and Holmes, T. H. (1978). Life events, perceptions and frequencies. Psychomatic Medicine, 40, 236-261.

McCarty, S. M., Siegler, I. C. and Logue, P. E. (1982). Cross sectional and longitudinal patterns of three Wechsler Memory Scale subtests. Journal of Gerontology, 37, 169-181.

McCrae, R. R. (1982). Age differences in the use of coping mechanisms. Journal of Gerontology, 37, 454-460.

Milligan, W. L., Powell, D. A. and Furchtgott, E. (1981). Learning and reaction time performance in older veterans: relationship to attitudes and life satisfaction. International Journal of Aging and Human Development, 13, 151-168.

Murphy, M. D., Sanders, R. E., Gabriesheski, A. S. and Schmitt, F. A. (1981). Metamemory in the aged. Journal of Gerontology, 36, 185-193.

Mussen, P., Honzik, M. and Eichorn, D. (1980). Continuity and change in women's characteristics over four decades. International Journal of Behavior Development, 3, 333-347.

Mussen, P., Honzik, M. and Eichorn, D. (1982). Early adult antecedents of life satisfaction at age seventy. Journal of Gerontology, 37, 316-322.

Mutran, E. and Reitzes, D. C. (1981). Retirement, identity and well-being: re-alignment of role relationships. Journal of Gerontology, 36, 733-740.

Neugarten, B. (1977). Personality and aging. In J. E. Birren and K. W. Schaie (eds), Handbook of the Psychology of Aging. New York: Van Nostrand Reinhold.

Nicholson, J. (1980). Seven Ages. Isle of Man, UK: Fontana.

Palmore, E. and Kivett, V. (1977). Change in life satisfaction: a longitudinal study of persons aged 46-70. Journal of Gerontology, 32, 311-316.

Parkinson, S. R., Lindholm, J. M. and Inman, V. (1982). An analysis of age differences in immediate recall. Journal of Gerontology, 37, 425-431.

Parr, J. (1980). The interaction of persons and living environments. In L. W. Poon (ed.), Aging in the 1980s. Washington, DC: American Psychological Association.

Perone, M. and Baron, A. (1982). Age related effects of pacing on acquisition and performance of response sequences - an operant analysis. Journal of Gerontology, 37, 443-449.

Plude, D. J. and Hoyer, W. J. (1981). Adult age differences in visual search as a function of stimulus mapping and processing load. Journal of Gerontology, 36, 598-604.

Poon, L. W. (ed.) (1980). Aging in the 1980s: Psychological issues. Washington, DC: American Psychological Association.

Poon, L. W., Fozard, J. L., Cermak, L. S., Arenberg, D. A. and Thompson, L. W. (1980). New Directions in Memory and Aging. Hillside, NJ: Lawrence Erlbaum.

Riege, W. and Inman, V. (1981). Age differences in nonverbal memory tasks. Journal of Gerontology, 36, 51-58.

Salthouse, T. A. and Somberg, B. L. (1982). Time accuracy relationships in young and old adults. Journal of Gerontology, 37, 349-353.

Sands, J. D. and Parker, J. (1979-80). A cross sectional study of the perceived stressfulness of several life events.

International Journal of Aging and Human Development, 10, 335-341.

Schaie, K. W. (1979). The primary mental abilities in adulthood, an exploration in the development of psychometric intelligence. In P. B. Baltes and O. G. Brim (eds), Life-Span Development and Behaviour, Volume 2. New York: Academic Press.

Schaie, K. W. (1981). Psychological changes from midlife to early old age: implications for the maintenance of mental health. American Journal of Orthopsychiatry, 51, 199-218.

Schaie, K. W. and Baltes, P. B. (1975). On sequential strategies in developmental research. Human Development, 18, 384-390.

Schaie, K. W. and Labouvie, G. V. (1974). Generation versus ontogenetic components of change in adult cognitive behavior: a fourteen-year cross-sequential study. Developmental Psychology, 10, 305-320.

Schaie, K. W., Labouvie, G. V. and Barrett, T. J. (1973). Selective attrition effects in a fourteen-year study of adult intelligence. Journal of Gerontology, 28, 328-334.

Schaie, K. W., Labouvie, G. V. and Buech, B. U. (1973). Generational and cohort specific differences in adult cognitive functioning: a fourteen-year study of independent samples. Developmental Psychology, 9, 151-166.

Schaie, K. W. and Parham, I. A. (1976). Stability of adult personality: fact or fable? Journal of Personality and Social Psychology, 34, 146-158.

Schaie, K. W. and Parham, I. A. (1977). A cohort sequential analysis of adult intellectual development. Developmental Psychology, 13, 649-653.

Schuster, M. and Barkowski, D. (1980). Intelligence or relevant knowledge: prerequisites for coping strategies in old age. Zeitschrift für Gerontologie, 13, 385-400.

Shelton, M. D., Parsons, O. A. and Leber, W. R. (1982). Verbal and visuospatial performance and aging: a neuropsychological approach. Journal of Gerontology, 37, 336-341.

Siegler, I. C. and Botwinick, J. (1979). A long-term longitudinal study of intellectual ability of older adults: the matter of selective subject attrition. Journal of Gerontology, 34, 242-245.

Spieth, W. (1964). Cardiovascular health status, age and psychological performance. Journal of Gerontology, 19, 277-284.

Thomae, H. and Kranzhoff, H. E. (1979). Perceived certainty of health and economic stress, a contribution to a cognitive theory of adjustment to aging. Zeitschrift für Gerontologie, 12, 439-459.

Vaillant, G. E. (1977). Adaptation to Life. Boston: Little, Brown.

Welford, A. T. (1965). Performance, biological mechanisms and age: a theoretical sketch. In A. T. Welford and J. E. Birren (eds), Behavior Aging and the Nervous System. Springfield, Ill: Charles Thomas.

Willis, S. L., Blieszner, R. and Baltes, P. B. (1981). Intellectual training research in aging: modification of performance on the fluid ability of figural relations. Journal of Educational Psychology, 73, 41-50.

Windley, P. G., Arch, D. and Scheidt, R. J. (1982). An ecological model of mental health among small town rural elderly. Journal of Gerontology, 37, 235-242.

Winograd, E., Smith, A. D. and Simon, E. W. (1982). Aging and the picture superiority effect in recall. Journal of Gerontology, 37, 70-75.

Wright, R. E. (1981). Aging, divided attention and processing capacity. Journal of Gerontology, 36, 605-614.

Wright, R. E. (1982). Adult age similarities in free recall: output order and strategies. Journal of Gerontology, 37, 76-79.

Zacks, R. T. (1982). Encoding strategies used by young and elderly adults in a keeping track task. Journal of Gerontology, 37, 203-211.

Chapter 4

SOCIAL INFLUENCE PROCESSES IN GROUPS

Peter B. Smith

The process whereby members of groups influence one another's behaviour has been close to the heart of social psychology since its inception. In the early days of the subject, interest was focussed on the process of social facilitation, in other words, the enhancement or inhibition of task performance caused by the presence of other people. Interest in this topic continues to the present (e.g. Zajonc, 1980), but for the most part social psychologists have found it more interesting to look at various different types of social influence one at a time, rather than all at once. For many years, a rather firm distinction has been drawn, for instance, between the process of leadership and the process of conformity. Studies of each of these processes have generated a vast literature, but in each case the findings have proved to be somewhat less useful than researchers had earlier anticipated. Perhaps for this reason, still other methods of studying social influence have been devised and evaluated. Prominent among these have been the series of studies of the phenomenon initially termed the 'risky shift' and later renamed group polarization. These studies attempt to show why decisions taken in groups are frequently not simply the average of the views of group members on the issue to be decided. Work on this topic reached a peak of popularity in the late sixties and has tailed off since. Another series of studies has focussed on 'groupthink' (Janis, 1972), which means the process occurring in some policy-making groups whereby social influence processes within the group serve to exclude crucial information which is available to the group from outside.

It will be argued in this chapter that an adequate understanding of social influence processes in groups must rest on research undertaken within all of these diverging series of research studies. The factors which have served to separate each tradition have mostly derived from failure to question arbitrary distinctions which are implicit in everyday common-sense. For example, some of the research to be reviewed later suggests that the distinction between conformity and leadership may be a hindrance to our thinking. Furthermore, the politics of academic publication have favoured the pursuit of studies which are quick and simple, such as risky shift studies, rather than those which shed more light on longer-term social influence processes. This chapter will both separate out these fields and also attempt to show their interrelation.

GROUP POLARIZATION

In 1961, Stoner reported a study comparing individual and group decision making by management students. The students were asked to complete a questionnaire concerning a series of hypothetical problems involving risk. For each problem, they selected the level of risk which they felt acceptable, first individually and then as a group. He found that the decisions taken by groups were very frequently more risky than the average of individuals' choices. This effect quickly became known as the risky shift and numerous successful replications of it were reported. Writers at this time often stressed that the inherent interest of the risky shift effect was that it contradicted the commonsense view that the effect of groups such as committees on individuals was to render them more cautious. Another reason for the very rapid growth of interest in the topic was the lucid exposition of the various possible explanations for the effect offered by Brown (1965).

Subsequent research, such as that by Moscovici and Zaval-loni (1969), has made clear that the effects of the group are by no means always towards greater risk-taking. The shift to risk is obtained only on decision items on which the individual choices already favour some degree of risk-taking. Items which evoke initially cautious individual choices yield still more cautious group decisions. Thus the effect of the group is to polarize or make extreme members' views rather than to move them towards risk. This was true even for the original items in Stoner's Choice Dilemmas Questionnaire, 10 of which showed movements to risk and two to caution.

The group polarization literature has thus established that groups have certain rather predictable influences on their members within a precisely specifiable experimental setting. Whether or not this effect is of lasting interest depends on whether the effect is a product of the rather artificial research setting in which it was initially found, or whether it can be shown to have a much wider applicability. On the face of it, the prospects are not good. Group polarization studies are typically done with groups of newly-assembled strangers, often students, who discuss and make decisions on the problems for only a few minutes, without the benefit of any established leadership structure in their groups. Groups in everyday life are longer-lasting, have more firmly established leadership structures and take decisions on matters which have tangible consequences. Lamm and Myers (1978) none the less show that group polarization effects can be clearly discerned in reports of many types of non-experimental study. In particular, they cite studies of student change while going through college, community conflicts, simulated juries and religious sects.

Since there is evidence that group polarization occurs in natural as well as experimental groups, it is worthwhile to consider the various possible explanations which have been advanced. The early researchers into the risky shift argued that the effect was not explicable as a conformity effect, since conformity pressures should produce a convergence towards the mean, rather than a polarization. Equally, they argued that leadership theories could not account for the effect, since appointing one of the members as group leader did not change the effect found. Some of the alternative explanations advanced here have not stood up to the test of time. For instance, Wallach, Kogan and Bem (1962) saw the effect as caused by a 'diffusion of responsibility', which occurred between members of groups. Obviously, this explanation cannot cope with the later discovery that group polarization can occur towards either extreme, not just towards risk.

According to Lamm and Myers (1978), two explanations of the effect remain viable. First, discussion may cause group polarization because it provides members with additional information relevant to the risks they are assessing. Tape recordings of groups discussing their preferences have shown that where the majority of individuals initially favour risk, then it is predominantly risk-orientated information and arguments which are brought forward during the discussion period. Conversely, when the majority of individuals initially favour caution, it is caution-orientated information and arguments which predominate (Burnstein and Vinokur, 1975). Thus the effect of group discussion is to accentuate or polarize whatever initial emphasis there is in the group. The initial spread of opinions serves as a filter of whatever additional views or information are brought into the group.

The second explanation for which Lamm and Myers find continuing support is that based on social comparison theory. Originally proposed by Festinger (1954), the theory proposes that people have a drive to evaluate their abilities. They prefer to do this by objective, non-social means, but where such non-social means are not available, then the next best possibility is to compare one's performance with others who are as similar as possible to oneself. In order to apply such a theory to the group polarization field one needs to assume that the drive to evaluate oneself extends not only to abilities but also to opinions. From the viewpoint of this theory then, what happens during the discussion period is that individuals are seeking to present themselves to others in a manner which shows them in the best possible light. On certain issues, the advocacy of risk is socially desirable, as reflected in the distribution of individual choices. On other issues, caution is more desirable. Group decisions reflect members' awareness of these desirabilities and their response to it. The strongest evidence in favour of this theory is the repeated demonstration that group polarization effects can be equally obtained without any actual group discussion (Myers and Kaplan, 1976). All that is required for group polarization to occur is that the individuals in the group become aware of the preferences which the others in the group have expressed. Even awareness of the average of others' views is enough to obtain an effect. Since these types of study do not provide the individuals with any additional information or arguments about the risks they are assessing, it is clear that an adequate explanation of group polarization effects must include some reference to social comparison processes as well as to information exchange.

The conclusions of Lamm and Myers would not be accepted by all students of group polarization (Brandstatter, Davis and Stocker-Kreichgauer, 1982), but they none the less represent the predominant recent view. Two things are striking about this view: first, that the two most favoured explanations of group polarization are extremely similar to the two most favoured explanations of the process of conformity, as studied 20-30 years ago (Deutsch and Gerard, 1957); and second, that most recent writers on group polarization tend to regard a conformity explanation as out of the question.

There are various ways of exploring more fully this rather odd situation. The one which will be adopted here is to argue that failures to conceptualize the process of conformity adequately have led to its premature abandonment as an explanatory concept. In order to sustain this viewpoint, we now turn to the literature on conformity.

CONFORMITY

The experimental study of conformity was popularized by Sherif (1935) and Asch (1951). Sherif made use of the so-called autokinetic effect, whereby a stationary point source of light appears to move when viewed in a totally dark room. When groups of subjects viewed the light together, he found that they tended over time to agree more and more as to the direction and degree of movement of the light. Sherif's study was thus concerned with a highly ambiguous situation, and he attributed the effects obtained to the development of a shared frame of reference between different judges. The study by Asch, on the other hand, asked subjects to identify which of a series of lines matched each other in length. When done individually there is no ambiguity as to the correct answers. What Asch did was to ask subjects to make their judgements in the presence of a number of others who were supposedly doing likewise. In fact, these other subjects were Asch's accomplices, and they had been instructed on certain of the trials to give responses which were unanimous, but incorrect. The Asch paradigm proved highly attractive to researchers for many years, particularly after Crutchfield (1955) devised a version of it which dispensed with the need for actual stooges. In his version, each of the subjects in the experiment records his or her judgements on a machine and each is misled by the machine into believing that the judgements he or she is making are the last in a sequence of judgements by others. The machine feeds spurious data to the subject which purports to be the judgements of subjects deciding earlier. Thus although there is no difference in principle between the design of the Asch and Crutchfield experiments, the Crutchfield one is much easier to stage once it has been set up.

For many years, Asch-type experiments have been seen as the way to study conformity pressures in groups (Allen, 1965, 1975). While the original design was certainly an ingenious one, it has become increasingly clear that the peculiar circumstances of experiments of this type call into question the generality of the findings obtained from them. The first problem is one that was readily apparent to Asch himself: yielding to the majority judgements by the naive subjects only occurred where the majority was itself unanimous. The giving of correct judgements by even one other judge was sufficient to eliminate the effect. Since everyday life only rarely presents us with circumstances in which we find ourselves faced with a unanimous majority, it is necessary to present further arguments if one is to argue the generality of the findings of the Asch experiments. The argument favoured by protagonists of the Asch method would be that the method enables us to isolate and analyse the <u>principles</u> underlying social influence processes, even if the experimental setting is quite unlike everyday life.

A further way in which these studies are unusual is that they are based on the naive subject experiencing some degree of conflict in the judgement of the physical world. If we except those with sight or hearing problems from our discussion, the everyday assumption that we all take for granted is that there is constancy of the physical world. I assume that you see what I see, and hear what I hear. On the other hand, I do not assume that your perceptions of social or political events will necessarily match mine. Consequently, one might plausibly expect that social influence processes related to physical judgements would not operate in the same manner as those relevant to social judgements. A crucial series of experiments by Allen (e.g. Allen and Levine, 1968) showed that this was indeed so. Allen and Levine found, just as Asch had, that with physical judgements the addition of one judge who did not go along with the majority eliminated all social influence. On the other hand, they found that when a judgement task based on social opinions was used, the introduction of a dissenter from the majority did not necessarily eliminate the effect of the majority. The effect of the dissenter appeared to vary depending on how close or distant his opinions were from those of the naive subject.

If social influence processes differ in situations involving physical and social judgements, it follows that there needs to be more than one explanation of the process which has so far been loosely termed conformity. Some workers within the Asch tradition had earlier reached the same conclusion. For instance, as early as 1955 Deutsch and Gerard distinguished informational and normative social influence. Informational social influence, later renamed information dependency by Jones and Gerard (1967) occurs in situations of high ambiguity. Lacking any clear indicators of an appropriate response, one uses others as marker posts in deciding what to do. The Sherif study provides a clear instance of this type of influence. Normative social influence, or effect dependency as Jones and Gerard (1967) have it, occurs where there is no necessary ambiguity, but the different judgements or courses of action available will lead to approval or disapproval from significant others. The Asch study has elements of this, but the 'opinions' condition of Allen and Levine (1968) illustrates it more clearly.

The distinction between informational and normative forms of social influence is, of course, reminiscent of the conclusions reached in the previous section that group polarization was a product of information-sharing and social comparison. This convergence is of considerable interest, but in order to evaluate it adequately we must next consider some further limitations of the Asch paradigm. Asch undertook his studies in the USA in the late 1940s, at a time when Senator McCarthy's UnAmerican Activities Committee was exerting a major influence. Asch termed the opposite of conformity as 'independence', and there is a clear undertone to the early studies implying that conformity is a social evil and independence a positive value. The fact that only 35 per cent of Asch's subjects actually conformed would have provided some reassurance that people do have the fortitude to resist unreasonable group pressure. Later authors have argued that this conceptualization oversimplifies what may happen. For instance, Hollander and Willis (1967) point out that the individual's choices are not simply to conform or to be independent. One may also anti-conform, in other words do the opposite of that which one is being pressed to do. In the same vein, Moscovici (1976) argues that the basic flaw in the Asch design is that social influence is presented as an entirely one-way influence process. In other words, Asch sees conformity as a process wherein the majority exercises influence over the minority, and the only options open to the minority are either to accept the influence or to remain independent of it.

While these options may have been the only ones open to the subjects in Asch-type experiments, Moscovici argues for a radically different conceptualization of social influence processes in everyday life. In his view, both minorities and majorities have the possibility of influencing the other. Whether they do so or not will depend not only on their relative numbers, but also on the manner in which they put over their arguments. Moscovici's formulation of social influence processes is still in process of evolution, but the first dimension of social behaviour which he sees as having some potency is its consistency. Moscovici and Faucheux (1972) provide a dramatic reanalysis of some aspects of Asch's data, in which they argue that the majority in Asch's studies achieved its effect not because of the number of judges but because of the consistency of their judgements. They were able to show that the proportion of trials on which Asch's stooges lied or told the truth had a marked effect on how much conformity or independence occurred. Moscovici and Faucheux then go on to report studies in which a minority of two consistent stooges were shown able to influence the opinions of a naive majority in a judgement task concerning the colours of lights.

The influence achieved by this consistent minority is found to persist even after the minority is no longer present, and even when the effects are tested for indirectly rather than directly (Moscovici, 1980). For instance, after majority members have been influenced to perceive as green colours which they previously considered to be blue, they tended, when tested individually afterwards, to perceive red-purple after-images rather than yellow-orange after-images when the 'green' colour was once again presented.

The generality of Asch's findings was earlier criticized on the grounds that they rested too heavily on studies of physical judgements. A number of Moscovici's studies are vulnerable to the same criticism, but Moscovici's co-workers have also extended their work to other types of judgement task. For instance, he cites unpublished work by Mugny, who has studied the effects of a minority on attitudes towards pollution and towards foreigners. His findings are consonant with those concerning physical judgements, but are not wholly satisfactory, since there is no face-to-face interaction between the judges.

There is little doubt that Moscovici's formulation of social influence processes is the most creative and provocative to be published for many years. In his most recent statement (1980), Moscovici delineates two types of social influence, which he terms compliance and conversion. Although similar distinctions have been proposed earlier by other authors, Moscovici's formulation is argued in a more detailed manner. He sees compliance as a process wherein change rests upon the majority's power to influence the minority directly through the use of rewards and sanctions. Conversion, in Moscovici's model is a quite different, indirect process, whereby the minority achieves change in the majority. It occurs through the minority behaving in that manner most likely to convince the majority that the minority view is a valid one. This is done primarily through adopting a consistent position and sticking to it rigidly. Thus, the effectiveness of a minority in achieving influence is seen as a function of the behavioural style of minority members.

Rather in the manner hypothesized by his own theory, Moscovici's adopting of a consistently argued minority critique of research in this field has achieved a certain amount of change in the majority view. Levine (1980) reviews studies showing that a number of investigators have now successfully obtained Moscovici-type minority influence affects in their studies. These have been found in studies of minorities varying in size from one to four. Nemeth, Wachtler and Endicott (1977) found that the impact of minorities of various sizes was a function of how much the majority judged them to be competent and confident in their judgements. More research is required as to which particular aspects of behavioural style are those which convey competence and confidence to others, but whatever they turn out to be, it is clear that Moscovici's conception of minority influence has connections with the process of informational social influence developed by earlier researchers. One way of putting it, would be to say that the majority use the minority as a guide to their judgements under circumstances where the minority's behaviour convinces the majority that it is a reliable source of information. The other form of social influence identified by early researchers - normative social influence - can be assumed to be more strongly found where the majority influences the minority.

Moscovici's critique thus renders more sophisticated earlier analyses by suggesting more precisely the circumstances under which different modes of influence will operate. This work also undermines the arbitrary distinction which social psychologists have maintained for many years between the process of social influence which they refer to as conformity and that which they refer to as leadership. Traditionally, conformity was something that occurred when many individuals influenced one person, whereas leadership was what happened when one person influenced many others, either through having been appointed to do so or by virtue of some emergent qualities. The literature on leadership will now be re-examined in the light of the arguments so far advanced.

LEADERSHIP

It is customary for reviewers to lament the inconclusiveness of research into the process of leadership. This may have something to do with traditional conceptualizations of leadership and of conformity. While conformity is mostly seen as a social ill, leadership is a matter of practical importance. Thus it might be hoped, according to a traditional viewpoint, that research would expose the dangers of conformity and reduce its incidence, but that it would come up with new and more effective methods of leadership and management.

This demand for the practical applicability of the findings of leadership research has had a number of consequences, some positive and some negative. On the positive side, it has ensured that a much larger proportion of studies of leadership have been undertaken outside laboratory settings than is the case for studies reviewed in other sections of this chapter. On the negative side, the much greater variability of non-laboratory research settings has faced leadership researchers with acute problems in obtaining replicable findings. Leadership theories are more stringently tested than the others, and thus the more often found wanting.

Stogdill (1974) provides an encyclopaedic review of several thousand studies of leadership. The review confirms the notion that leadership is best thought of not as a quality or trait of the individual, but as a pattern of behaviour involving both leader and followers. Factor-analytic studies by Stogdill and his associates at Ohio State University in the 1940s and 1950s concluded that the principal dimensions of leadership behaviour could be best described as 'consideration' and as 'initiation of structure in interaction'. A parallel and equally influential differentiation of types of leader was that of Lewin, Lippitt and White (1939), whose principal focus was on the contrast between 'democratic' and 'autocratic' leaders.

Leadership researchers have mostly been interested in examining which types of leadership behaviour are most effective. In order to answer such a question, it is necessary to specify one's criterion of leadership effectiveness. Whilst early researchers tended to assume that effectiveness was a unitary quality, more recently it has become clear that this is not so (Vroom, 1964). A group which is highly productive is not necessarily also highly satisfied with their situation. Whether they are or not, will depend on numerous intervening variables such as the centrality of work in their lives, whether they are hard-working out of choice or coercion, the availability of alternative work, and so forth. Thus, one will only be able to describe a leader as effective in relation to some agreed criterion. A further problem is that even where some association is found between a particular leader behaviour and group performance, it may prove difficult to determine the direction of causation (Smith, 1973). For instance, a foreman may act towards his workers in a warm and friendly fashion, leading them to work hard because they value his praise; but equally, where workers are hard-working, a foreman is more likely to respond in a warm and friendly manner than where they are not. Only through experiments would it be possible to show the direction of causation, if it is indeed the case that one direction does predominate over the other.

Bearing in mind these difficulties of interpretation, we can now review the major approaches. Two main viewpoints continue to be advanced. The first of these sees effective leadership as a process which can be specified in a way applicable to a very wide range of settings. Stogdill (1974) has contributed to this approach, and summarizes the work of himself and others. He reports that both satisfaction and group productivity are related to measures of the leader's consideration and of the leader's initiation of structure. Consideration tends to be more strongly linked to satisfaction, whilst initiation of structure goes more with productivity. The most effective leaders tend to be high on both scales. The strongest current protagonists of this viewpoint are Blake and Mouton (1978, 1981). Blake and Mouton argue that effective leadership is that which simultaneously exhibits high concern for group performance and for the persons in the work group. They term this style of leadership '9,9'. In their view, the fact that previous research has not always been clear cut is because researchers have failed to conceptualize adequately the manner in which the two dimensions of effective leader behaviour interact with one another. For instance, in the Ohio State studies using the Leader Behaviour Description Questionnaire (LBDQ), which comprises the consideration and initiating structure scales, the items on the two scales are quite independent of one another; but, argue Blake and Mouton, the kinds of consideration a leader might show towards a subordinate would vary markedly depending on whether the subordinate was high-performing or low-performing. Since the questionnaires used by most researchers fail to incorporate this interaction between the two dimensions, the theory as advanced by Blake and Mouton remains intriguing but untested, except through the use of Blake and Mouton's own Managerial Grid questionnaire.

The increasing majority of leadership researchers adhere to the second viewpoint, usually termed the contingency approach. The view here is that effective leader behaviour will vary from one situation to another, depending on the qualities of each situation. Even the Ohio State researchers working with the LBDQ have now reformulated their model in terms of a contingency approach (Kerr, Schriesheim, Murphy and Stogdill, 1974). The simplest possible reformulation would be to argue that leaders need to be considerate in some situations and to initiate structure in others. Larson, Hunt and Osborn (1976) obtained data from 14 widely varying organizations, and concluded that a simple generalization of this type was actually a slightly better summary of their findings than the previous specification of consideration plus initiating structure.

The difficulty with findings such as these is that they are rather bland. A theory of the form 'leaders need to do different things in different situations' only becomes interesting when it attempts to say what the leader should do in each specific type of situation. The principal theorist to

attempt this has been Fiedler (1967, 1978). Fiedler distinguishes between leaders whom he terms 'task-centred' and those
whom he terms 'relationship-centred', and examines their
performance in various specified situations. Fiedler's two
leader types clearly have a good deal in common conceptually
with the distinctions reviewed earlier between autocratic and
democratic leaders, and between the initiation of structure by
leaders and consideration. However, all of Fiedler's research
is based on a quite different mode of measuring the leader's
orientation, referred to as LPC (Least Preferred Co-Worker).
Fiedler's leaders are asked to make ratings on semantic differential scales of someone they very much disliked working
with. Those who rate the co-worker particularly negatively are
found to be task-centred, while those who rate the co-worker
less negatively are relationship-centred.

Fiedler then hypothesizes that these two types of leader
will have differential effectiveness in varying situations.
The task-centred leader is expected to do best in situations
which are highly favourable to the leader, and also in situations that are highly unfavourable. Situations which are
intermediate in favourableness will be those in which the
relationship-centred leader will do better. In each case, what
Fiedler means by favourableness of the situation is the
relative ease or difficulty which the leader will have in
influencing followers in a given set of circumstances. He sees
three principal sources of situation favourableness: the
closeness of leader-follower relations, the amount of power
inherent in the leader's position, and the degree of structure
in the group's task.

Fiedler's theory has undergone extensive empirical testing
and attracted a good deal of criticism and debate (Graen,
Alvares, Orris, and Martella, 1970; Miner, 1980). Some of the
criticisms of the theory are substantive, for instance, that
its selection of variables and dimensions is arbitrary and its
predictions are not logically derived. Others are methodological, such as that the evidence which best fits the theory is
that collected before it was formulated, and that the unortho-
dox manner in which it is formulated does not make it clear
how it may validly be tested. The most recent review of findings (Strube and Garcia, 1981) comes down in favour of Fiedler, but so many of the issues raised by earlier critics
remain unresolved that the question to be answered is increasingly not 'Is Fiedler's model correct?' but rather 'Why do the
results favour Fiedler's model?'. This need to rephrase the
research question addressed has been made particularly urgent
by the finding that the behaviour of high and low LPC leaders
is not constant across different types of situation. For

example, Green and Nebeker (1977) found that high LPC leaders were task-centred under highly favourable circumstances, but became more relationship-centred in less favourable circumstances. Thus Fiedler's use of the rather ambiguous LPC measure means that we cannot be sure what attribute it is which is proving to be associated with high performance in different types of situation. Fiedler's initial formulation of the leadership process was the relatively traditional one, whereby a fixed pattern of leader behaviour acts on a situation and achieves a certain effect. Findings such as the Green and Nebeker study indicate that an adequate model of leadership will have to encompass follower-leader influence as well as leader-follower influence. Thus the same type of critique which Moscovici advanced of conformity studies is equally applicable to leadership studies. Those qualities of the situation which affect the situation's favourableness for the leader also affect the situation's favourableness for the follower's possibilities of influencing the leader.

A good illustration of the perils of neglecting this dimension of the leader's situation is provided by Milgram's (1974) classic studies on destructive obedience. These studies appeared to show that simply because the experimenter was established as a legitimately-authorized leader, followers would carry out his instructions, even if this involved the administration of painful and probably dangerous electric shocks. In the standard version of the experiment, 65 per cent of subjects remained wholly obedient. However, Milgram also showed that where other experimental accomplices were also introduced, who refused to accept the experimenter's authority, then only 10 per cent of subjects remained obedient. In other words, when the group context of leadership is eliminated, the leader is pre-eminent. When the group context is restored the leader's influence is once more constrained by the culture of the group.

It is interesting to speculate as to why Milgram's research attracted so much attention and why his findings were seen as having such wide applicability. Most probably their attractiveness lay in their clarity and in the degree to which they resurrected a myth, to which we all subscribe to some degree, that leaders are strong and powerful. The complexity, not to say confusion, of contemporary leadership theory does not have the same appeal.

Some progress towards the formulation of a leadership theory which pays systematic attention to followers as well as leaders has been achieved by House's path-goal theory (House, 1971; House and Dessler, 1974). Path-goal theory argues that leaders are effective in so far as they make it easy for followers to achieve their own goals through doing what the leader wants them to do. The variations in leader behaviour which are considered are primarily those arising from the Ohio State leadership studies. Situational factors considered include followers' personality and task structure, but as with the Fiedler theory, there is no specific rationale for the selection of variables. Once again, the problem is that the manner in which the theory is formulated provides no guidelines as to which attributes of the followers or of the task will be most potent in moderating the leader's influence. Perhaps for this reason, the research findings have been rather inconsistent.

The findings of leadership research can be seen to contrast markedly with those of conformity research. Students of leadership appear to be broadly agreed that the most important dimensions of a leader's behaviour are consideration and the initiation of structure. However, they have failed to make much progress in identifying why this might be so, and consequently cannot say all that much about whether both qualities are always required, or whether a particular balance of the two is required for a given circumstance. Conformity theorists, on the other hand, have attended much more to explanation and much less to the qualities of majorities. The recent work of Moscovici has brought the two fields of research much closer together through attention to the qualities of minorities as sources of influence. It may not have escaped the reader's attention that the leader of a group is a minority, at least in the numerical sense. Is there any further scope for a rapprochement between the two fields?

A leader becomes a leader either through appointment or through emerging from the group. In either case, the process of becoming a leader gives to that person a more extensive range of powers than those enjoyed by Moscovici's minorities. Most leaders have control over some form of resources or sanctions which provide a basis for their ability to influence others. The leader may choose to exert influence through the giving or withdrawal of rewards or sanctions, which Moscovici sees as an attribute of majorities. Alternatively, the leader may exert influence through the provision of frameworks or guidelines for followers' behaviour. This leadership function is more closely analogous to Moscovici's conception of minority influence. The minority, like the leader, can induce change by behaving in a manner which causes others to adopt a new structure of framework for their thinking or their behaviour.

If this connection between the two research fields is validly made, then the distinctive quality of leaders is that they achieve influence both in the manner of majorities and in the manner of minorities. The normative social influence of the majority would be analogous to the consideration dimension of the leader's behaviour. Likewise, the informational social influence of the minority would be analogous to the initiation of structure by the leader. It will take considerable time before it becomes clear whether or not some such reunification of the concepts employed to think about social influence will prove viable. In the closing section of this chapter, attention is given to the manner in which different tasks interact with the social influence processes in a group.

GROUP TASKS

Most groups have some task or external purpose, and such tasks provide the basis for evaluations as to the effectiveness of particular groups. Some tasks may be carried out individually or in groups, whilst others require a group in order that they be carried through at all. In the past, numerous studies have been undertaken comparing individual and group performance on a wide variety of tasks, including learning, problem-solving and decision-making (Davis, 1969). Some difficulty arose in deciding how to compare a group's product with a series of individual products. On many tasks it was found that the group's product was superior to the individual one, but that if account was taken of the number of persons in the group, then the product per person was inferior to individual products.

In practice, there are considerable numbers of tasks in our society which it is not practicable to carry out individually, whether or not that would be the most efficient way. More recent work has focussed on the decrement in performance caused by working in groups, why it occurs and how it may be minimized (Steiner, 1972). Steiner develops a taxonomy of different group tasks and specifies for each a 'prescribed process' which, if followed, would lead to maximal group performance. For example, on a discovery-type problem-solving task (which he terms a 'unitary, conjunctive' task), group performance will be maximal if the group can identify the member with the best solution and put that solution forward as its own. On a task involving the manufacture of a product (a 'divisible task with unspecified subtasks') performance will be optimal where the most skilled member is assigned to each subtask, members are motivated to carry out their tasks and the overall group task is adequately co-ordinated. In most groups, various social influence processes stand in the way of achieving such optimal performance.

Davis and his co-workers (Stasser, Kerr and Davis, 1980; Davis, 1982) have devised mathematical techniques for establishing how in practice a group combines its individual views to form a group product. Working from a knowledge of preferred individual solutions to a problem and of the group's actual decision, various hypothetical decision rules are tested out for goodness of fit to the data. For example, one might compare an equalitarian decision-rule in which all members' views were weighted equally, to a hierarchical one in which views were weighted in proportion to their frequency. More recent developments of this approach attempt to incorporate the manner in which social influence occurs over time rather than momentarily. Studies have been undertaken with mock juries, in which members are asked to record their current verdict every 90 seconds throughout the jury's deliberations. Stasser and his colleagues found that the probability that jurors would change their verdict from guilty to not guilty or vice versa was most closely matched to how large a majority there was for that verdict. They interpreted this as an instance of normative social influence. On the other hand, they found that changes in the degree of certainty a juror felt that the verdict was right was a function of the size of the minority. This was interpreted as a form of informational social influence. This type of mathematical modelling of small group influence process has, thus, now reached the point where it can be used to explore the relative potency of different types of influence. Such modelling is, however, only likely to be useful in the case of decision tasks.

A somewhat different approach to the study of work tasks is that of Hackman and Oldham (1976). These authors devised a procedure known as the Job Diagnostic Survey (JDS), which enables a score to be produced indicating the potential of any particular job for inducing a high performance motivation. Their model assumes that task motivation will be high where the work done is experienced as meaningful, the worker at the task experiences responsibility for the outcome of the work and has knowledge of the actual results of the work. They also acknowledge that differences between individuals will influence the degree of response to a highly motivating task. Hackman and Morris (1975) extend this approach to tasks done in groups. They see the manner in which the processes discussed in this chapter act on a group's task effectiveness as classifiable under three headings:

(1) the level and utilization of member knowledge and skill;
(2) the nature and utilization of task performances and strategies;
(3) the level and co-ordination of members' effort.

While these broad classificatory headings certainly include many of the relevant variables, Hackman and Morris concede that until we have a much clearer view of which types of tasks require which types of organizational structure and influence processes, attempts to enhance group performance will have to rest on diagnoses of each specific situation. They see a usefulness for three types of such attempts, in line with their three headings above: modification of the group's composition, redesign of tasks, and modification of group norms. However, they emphasize that inadequately thought-out interventions may make matters worse rather than better. Job redesign schemes such as job enrichment often fail through inattention to detail, whilst interventions focussed on the interpersonal relationships within a group sometimes neglect task variables.

Groups which concentrate upon their defined task and fail to observe the degree to which the social influence processes within them sabotage group effectiveness, are found all too frequently. They have need of developing technologies such as organization development (French and Bell, 1979; Schmuck and Miles, 1971; Smith, 1980). A particularly vivid delineation of such groups is Janis's (1972) study of 'groupthink'. By analysis of documents, Janis was able to show that under certain circumstances members of important policy-making groups become sufficiently preoccupied by leadership and conformity pressure within their groups that they ignore vital information reaching them from outside. President Kennedy's decision to support the invasion at the Bay of Pigs, Cuba is the principal instance cited. On the information currently available, it appears that the Falklands crisis may prove to have been another.

Studies such as those by Janis serve to underline the tremendous potency for good or ill of social influence processes in powerful groups. Similar effects in more humble groups may have less spectacular effects but remain of interest. This chapter has tried to show how, despite the diverse manner in which studies of social influence have been undertaken in the past few decades, convergences continue to recur in the research findings. Greater awareness has been achieved of the manner in which influence is an outcome of the active confrontation of different tendencies in a group, rather than the passive imposition of influence by one party on another.

Typologies of social influence process such as the division between informational and normative have proved their viability and promise to provide the basis for a more comprehensive understanding of the field than that provided by the earlier, more conventional categories. More attention will be required to the role of group tasks in structuring social interaction if this work is to achieve its promise.

REFERENCES

Allen, V. L. (1965). Situational factors in conformity. In L. Berkowitz (ed.), Advances in Experimental Social Psychology, Vol. 2, 133-175. New York: Academic Press.

Allen, V. L. (1975). Social support for nonconformity. In L. Berkowitz (ed.), Advances in Experimental Social Psychology, Vol. 8, 1-43. New York: Academic Press.

Allen, V. L. and Levine, J. M. (1968). Social support, dissent and conformity. Sociometry, 31, 138-149.

Asch, S. (1951). Effects of group pressure upon the modification and distortion of judgments. In H. Guetzkow (ed.), Groups, leadership and men. Pittsburgh: Carnegie Press.

Blake, R. R. and Mouton, J. S. (1978). The New Managerial Grid. Houston: Gulf.

Blake, R. R. and Mouton, J. S. (1981). Management by grid principles or situationalism: Which? Group and Organization Studies, 6, 439-455.

Brandstatter, H., Davis, J. H. and Stocker-Kreichgauer, G. (1982). Group Decision Making. London: Academic Press.

Brown, R. (1965). Social Psychology. New York: Free Press.

Burnstein, E. and Vinokur, A. (1975). What a person thinks upon learning he has chosen differently from others: nice evidence for the persuasive arguments explanation of choice shifts. Journal of Experimental Social Psychology, 11, 412-426.

Crutchfield, R. S. (1955). Conformity and character. American Psychologist, 10, 195-198.

Davis, J. H. (1969). Group Performance. Reading, Mass: Addison-Wesley.

Davis, J. H. (1982). Social interaction as a combinatorial process in group decision. In H. Brandstatter, J. H. Davis and G. Stocker-Kreichgauer (eds), Group Decision Making. London: Academic Press.

Deutsch, M. and Gerard, H. B. (1955). A study of normative and informational social influences upon individual judgment. Journal of Abnormal and Social Psychology, 51, 629-636.

Festinger, L. (1954). A theory of social comparison processes. Human Relations, 7, 117-140.

Fiedler, F. E. (1967). A Theory of Leadership Effectiveness. New York: McGraw Hill.

Fiedler, F. E. (1978). The contingency model and the dynamics of the leadership process. In L. Berkowitz (ed.), Advances in Experimental Social Psychology, Vol.11, 59-112. New York: Academic Press.

French, W. L. and Bell, C. H. (1979). Organization Development. Second edition. Englewood Cliffs: Prentice Hall.

Graen, G., Alvares, K., Orris, J. B. and Martella, J. A. (1970). Contingency model of leadership effectiveness: antecedent and evidential results. Psychological Bulletin, 74, 285-296.

Green, S. G. and Nebeker, D. M. (1977). The effects of situational factors and leadership style on leader behaviour. Organizational Behavior and Human Performance, 19, 368-377.

Hackman, J. R. and Morris, C. G. (1975). Group tasks, group interaction process and group performance effectiveness: a review and proposed integration. In L. Berkowitz (ed.), Advances in Experimental Social Psychology, Vol. 8, 47-99. New York: Academic Press.

Hackman, J. R. and Oldham, G. R. (1976). Motivation through the design of work: test of a theory. Organizational Behavior and Human Performance, 16, 250-279.

Hollander, E. P. and Willis, R. H. (1967). Some current issues in the psychology of conformity and non-conformity. Psychological Bulletin, 68, 62-76.

House, R. J. (1971). A path-goal theory of leadership effectiveness. Administrative Science Quarterly, 16, 321-338.

House, R. J. and Dessler, G. (1974). The path-goal theory of leadership: some post hoc and a priori tests. In J. G. Hunt and L. L. Larson (eds), Contingency Approaches to Leadership. Carbondale: Southern Illinois University Press.

Janis, I. L. (1972). Victims of Groupthink: a Psychological Study of Foreign-Policy Decisions and Fiascoes. Boston: Houghton-Mifflin.

Jones, E. C. and Gerard, H. B. (1967). Foundations of Social Psychology. New York: Wiley.

Kerr, S., Schriesheim, C., Murphy, C. J. and Stogdill, R. M. (1974). Toward a contingency theory of leadership based upon the consideration and initiating structure literature. Organizational Behavior and Human Performance, 12, 62-82.

Lamm, H. and Myers, D. G. (1978). Group-induced polarization of attitudes and behaviour. In L. Berkowitz (ed.), Advances in Experimental Social Psychology, Vol.11, 145-195. New York: Academic Press.

Larson, L. L., Hunt, J. G. and Osborn, R. N. (1976). The great hi-hi leader behavior myth: a lesson from Occam's razor. Academy of Management Journal, 19, 628-641.

Levine, J. M. (1980). Reaction to opinion deviance in small groups. In P.B. Paulus (ed.), Psychology of Group Influence. Hillsdale: Erlbaum.

Lewin, K., Lippitt, R. and White, R. K. (1939). Patterns of aggressive behaviour in experimentally created social climates. Journal of Social Psychology, 10, 271-301.

Milgram, S. (1974). Obedience to Authority. London: Tavistock.

Miner, J. B. (1980). Theories of Organizational Behavior, Hinsdale, Ill: Dryden.

Moscovici, S. (1976). Social Influence and Social Change. London: Academic Press.

Moscovici, S. (1980). Toward a theory of conversion behavior. In L. Berkowitz (ed.), Advances in Experimental Social Psychology, Vol. 13, 209-239. New York: Academic Press.

Moscovici, S., and Faucheux, C. (1972). Social influence, conformity bias and the study of active minorities. In L. Berkowitz (ed.), Advances in Experimental Social Psychology, Vol.6, 149-202. New York: Academic Press.

Moscovici, S. and Zavalloni, M. (1969). The group as a polarizer of attitudes. Journal of Personality and Social Psychology, 12, 125-135.

Myers, D. G. and Kaplan, M. F. (1976). Group-induced polarization in simulated juries. Personality and Social Psychology Bulletin, 2, 63-66.

Nemeth, C., Wachtler, J. and Endicott, J. (1977). Increasing the size of the minority: some gains and some losses. European Journal of Social Psychology, 7, 15-27.

Schmuck, R. A. and Miles, M. B. (1971). Organization Development in Schools. Palo Alto: National Press Books.

Sherif, M. (1935). A study of some social factors in perception. Archives of Psychology, 27, No. 187.

Smith, P. B. (1973). Groups within Organizations. London: Harper Row.

Smith, P. B. (1980). Small Groups and Personal Change. London: Methuen.

Stasser, G., Kerr, N. L. and Davis, J. H. (1980). Influence processes in decision-making groups. In P. B. Paulus (ed.), Psychology of Group Influence. Hillsdale, N.J.: Erlbaum.

Steiner, I. D. (1972). Group Process and Productivity. New York: Academic Press.

Stogdill, R. M. (1974). Handbook of Leadership. New York: Free Press.

Stoner, J. A. F. (1961). A comparison of individual and group decisions involving risk. MS thesis, Massachussetts Institute of Technology.

Strube, M. J. and Garcia, J. E. (1981). A meta-analytic investigation of Fiedler's contingency model of leadership effectiveness. Psychological Bulletin, 90, 307-321.

Vroom, V. H. (1964). Work and Motivation, New York: Wiley.

Wallach, M. A., Kogan, N. and Bem, D. J. (1962). Group influence on individual risk-taking. Journal of Abnormal and Social Psychology, 65, 75-86.

Zajonc, R. B. (1980). Compresence. In P. B. Paulus (ed.), Psychology of Group Influence. Hillsdale, NJ: Erlbaum.

Chapter 5

PSYCHOLOGY AND CRIME

Jo Borrill

A recent letter in a London evening paper asked why psychologists were not doing sufficient research into crime and were not providing any answers to this 'pervasive problem'. If the writer of the letter had had access to academic journals and official publications, she would have observed that there has been a considerable amount of research into crime, but she would probably find herself confused by the diversity of theories and ideas, the many different attempts to 'treat' or 'modify' criminal behaviour, and the current cynicism about rehabilitative sentencing. The aim of this chapter is to summarize very briefly some of the more influential psychological theories of crime (for a more detailed evaluation of major theories see Feldman, 1977), and to relate these to the changes in emphasis which have taken place within criminology generally. Four topics will then be examined in greater depth as examples of current directions in research and practice: the study of cognitive factors in criminal decision-making, the development of social skills training for offenders, the role of the victim, and the situational approach to crime prevention.

'TRADITIONAL' THEORIES OF CRIME

1. Biology

Perhaps the earliest theories of crime are those which seek to explain criminality in terms of some inborn defect or pathology. Before the development of sophisticated genetic models it was often suggested that criminals possessed certain peculiar types of body build or facial configuration. Although these early studies have been discredited, and later investigations have failed to find any association between body build and offending (McCandless, Persons and Roberts, 1972), the belief in criminal types still persists and may influence the judgements of witnesses, police and juries (Cavior, Hayes and Cavior, 1975; Bull, 1982).

Studies of twins and adopted children have frequently been used in the attempt to measure the relative contribution of heredity and environment to crime (e.g. Christiansen, 1968), though these are fraught with problems of methodology and interpretation. If it were consistently found that monozygotic ('identical') twins were more concordant in their criminality than dizygotic ('fraternal') twins, this could either be interpreted as being the result of their identical genetic endowment or of their more similar social environments and expectations. The main difficulty with adoption studies is the selective placement of children into homes which match their own background; thus any similarity between child and adopted parents may be due either to the social environment they provide or to the matching of adoptive parents to biological parents. For example, Hutchings and Mednick (1974) found that criminality in adopted children was associated with criminality in both biological and adoptive parents, and it is not clear whether this is the result of two independent influences on the child or the result of selective placement. Forde (1978) has argued that the contribution of heredity to crime has been consistently underestimated because researchers have not distinguished between different types of offence and offender; in other words, genetics and environment may contribute differentially to different forms of criminal behaviour.

Genetic factors in aggression were the subject of the controversial XYY studies of the late 1960s and early 1970s. In 1965 it was reported that males with an extra Y chromosome (the XYY syndrome) showed three characteristics: mental retardation, extra tall stature and aggression. Further studies revealed many cases of the XYY syndrome, which had previously been thought to be extremely rare, and a number of American murderers put it forward as a defence. However, the initial interest has waned in the light of conflicting findings. Kahn, Reed, Bates, Coates and Everill (1976) examined a large sample of borstal boys but found no cases of XYY. They proceeded to look at more subtle chromosome abnormalities such as the 'long Y' variant and the 'marginally long Y' but these did not distinguish offenders from non-offenders either, though the 'long Y' borstal boys did score higher on the Jesness delinquency scale than other borstal boys.

A different approach to investigating biological factors in crime is the use of psychophysiological techniques to measure heart rate, muscle tension, skin conductance, etc.

Whereas early work considered arousal levels of delinquents generally, more recent studies have concentrated on violent and sexual offenders (Wadsworth, 1976) and on the mentally abnormal offender (Hinton and O'Neill, 1978). Hinton, O'Neill, Hamilton and Burke (1980) have suggested that psychopathic offenders are in direct contrast to schizophrenics; that is, they have low cortical arousal, strong inhibitory control of internal stimulation, and a consequent lack of imagination. The measures which show this - a low rate of spontaneous electrodermal fluctuation and a long orientating response recovery time - are also said to distinguish between high risk psychopaths and lower risk offenders.

2. Personality

A link between biological and social theories of crime may be found in Eysenck's (1977) theory of criminal personality. Eysenck has claimed that criminals tend to score above average on measures of extraversion (E), neuroticism (N), and psychoticism (P), though different types of offender show different patterns on these three dimensions. Studies have shown that extraverts are more difficult to condition than introverts, and high anxiety also impairs learning, therefore high E and N scorers would be expected to show poor conditioning. By assuming that conscience development depends on classical conditioning (particularly learning to avoid acts which, through punishment, arouse negative feelings), Eysenck argues that criminals fail to become adequately socialized. He has also suggested that increased crime rates are due to a lessening of discipline in society, though this is based on the questionable assumption that official statistics accurately reflect the level of criminal activity.

Eysenck's theory has received considerable criticism (e.g. Hampson, 1982), particularly for his use of questionnaires with people in prison or other institutions. Research suggests that adult male prisoners tend to score higher on N and P than non-prisoners, but high N has also been found to be one of the effects of incarceration (Heskin, Bolton, Smith and Bannister, 1974). There is little support for high E in male prisoners (though Eysenck and Eysenck, 1970, suggested that differences in E should only be expected when groups are matched on N). Women awaiting trial were found to score higher than controls on N and P, but not on E (Barack and Widom, 1978). Self-reported delinquency has been found to be associated with high E and N (Saxby, Norris and Feldman, 1970), though the accuracy of these reports might also vary with personality. The current trend seems to be to look at the interaction between E, N and P rather than at each dimension independently (Allsopp and Feldman, 1975; Marriage, 1977) suggesting that it is a high score on all three which is related to offending.

Theories of personality types have been criticized more generally for paying insufficient attention to specific situational influences (Mischel, 1973). With this in mind, Feldman (1977) has put forward a revised version of Eysenck's theory, suggesting that extreme high scorers will consistently break rules and cause harm to others, extreme low scorers will consistently avoid deviant behaviour except under extreme temptation, but the majority of the population, who are moderate scorers, will vary in their behaviour according to situational influences and constraints.

Another influential personality theory is that of Megargee (1966) who was specifically concerned with abnormally aggressive offenders. He described two types of violent offender: the undercontrolled person, who has a high need for aggression with few controls over its expression, and therefore has a history of frequent but relatively minor assaults, and the overcontrolled type, who has very rigid inhibitions against aggression. In this person anger is rarely expressed, but it builds up until it is eventually released in an extremely aggressive act. The overcontrolled offender is typically described as shy and timid and the offence is seen as 'out of character'.

Some support for Megargee's theory has come from factor-analytic studies of personality using the MMPI (Blackburn, 1975; McGurk, 1978), although the use of this test with criminal populations has been questioned (Dietrich and Berger, 1978). McGurk and McGurk (1979) have suggested that the theory needs revision; in particular, they believe that 'controlled' is a more appropriate term than 'overcontrolled', since this type has also been found in non-violent prisoners. Howells (1981) states that there is little evidence that an aggressive act reduces aggressive drive or that frustrative states exist over long periods of time.

Recent studies have looked at personality differences within groups of offenders to see if different types will require or respond to different forms of treatment. McGurk, McEwan and Graham (1981a) identified four types of young male offenders: anxious, normal, disturbed, and truculent. The anxious group were found to have a considerably lower reconviction rate than the others. Henderson (1982a) identified four types of violent offenders: disturbed/hostile, extravert/hostile, inhibited, and controlled. She concluded that the inhibited group had general difficulties in interpersonal relations, and might benefit from social skills training, whereas the disturbed/hostile group tended to be violent only in very specific situations.

Finally, Yochelson and Samenow (1976) adopted a different approach to the criminal personality. They suggested that criminals possess a unique set of cognitive patterns which are logical but incorrect, according to 'responsible' thinking. These thinking patterns include impulsiveness, manipulativeness, pride, power-orientation and concrete thinking. The theory is essentially descriptive, based on interviews with incarcerated 'hardcore' offenders and does not indicate how these thinking patterns were acquired (see Nietzel, 1979, for a critique).

3. Criminal Families

It has frequently been reported that certain families contain a disproportionate number of offenders. Two themes emerge from the literature on crime and the family: the idea of the family as an agent of socialization, transmitting values and beliefs, and the emphasis on deprived or disturbed families and their association with criminality. Juvenile delinquency has been linked with a variety of childhood disturbances, such as broken homes, 'maternal deprivation', and institutionalization.

However, much of the early work on maternal deprivation has been criticized and the assumptions underlying it - such as the supposed irreversibility of early experience - have been shown to be over-simplistic (see Clarke and Clarke, 1976, for a review of maternal deprivation and crime). Bowlby's influential study of juvenile thieves (Bowlby, 1946) which laid the foundations for this area of research has been criticized on methodological grounds (Feldman, 1977), and it is clear that some of his findings were misinterpreted by later researchers. Separation from parents is more complex than has been assumed, since divorce may be associated with delinquency, whereas separation due to the death of a parent is not (Rutter, 1972). These and other findings suggest that it is the presence of hostile and unhappy family relationships which may lead to deviant behaviour in children. A further complicating factor is that the existence of a broken home or criminal parent may affect the reactions of those involved in the 'labelling' process: a child appearing before a juvenile court who is known to come from a broken or 'bad' home may be more likely to be charged or placed in an institution than a child from a 'respectable' or intact family.

Nevertheless, it is generally accepted that there is a correlation between criminality of parents and children (Osborn and West, 1979), that juvenile delinquency correlates with severe social handicap (Wilson, 1975), and that lax and erratic discipline by parents, combined with the use of severe physical punishment, tends to be associated with delinquency and aggression (Becker, 1964). Wilson (1980) examined three aspects of family life: parental supervision, social handicap and parental criminality. Families were defined as showing lax supervision if they allowed their children to roam the streets, not knowing where they were and with no set rules about coming in at certain times. These families had a delinquency rate seven times higher than that of strict families. The other two factors also correlated with delinquency but less strongly. Even within the same family, there may be differences in attention and supervision; for example, Rahav (1980) found that the highest rates of delinquency were for middle-born children, but this effect was only significant in families of four or more children, where financial resources and attention may be more thinly stretched.

The Cambridge Study of delinquent development has made a 20-year follow-up of working-class boys to see which of them became delinquent and why. The latest report (West, 1982) suggests that delinquency is associated with a number of family variables: low income, large family, parental criminality and 'bad' child rearing (as assessed by social workers). Of particular interest are the factors which may lead to persistent offending: having a father with at least two convictions, a mother or sibling with a criminal record, and being judged as very troublesome by teachers. The study also reports that finding a job or receiving job training may prevent 'high risk' boys from becoming persistent offenders.

4. Learning

Learning theory has provided a useful mechanism for explaining criminal behaviour and has also influenced psychologists' attempts to treat offenders and to design behaviour modification regimes (Nietzel, 1979). Whilst Eysenck sees classical conditioning as the basis of conscience development, others have concentrated on operant conditioning, and the shaping and maintenance of criminal acts through differential reinforcement. Positive reinforcement for criminal activity may come from peer group acceptance, prestige, enhanced self-concept and material gain. Since detection and arrest are only intermittent, criminals may be said to be operating on a partial reinforcement schedule, and such learning is known to be very resistant to extinction.

Social learning theory has placed more emphasis on modelling which plays an important part in both the learning and performance of criminal acts, particularly aggression (Bandura, 1973, 1976). Thus, 'the highest rates of aggressive behaviour are found in environments where aggressive models abound and where aggressiveness is regarded as a highly valued attribute' (Bandura, 1976, p. 203). Models of aggression may be found in the family, the sub-culture, and in symbolic form in films and television. For example, a BBC report (Shaw and Newell, 1972) stated that almost half of the main characters in British television dramatic fiction were involved in violence. There is still disagreement about the extent to which media violence may influence behaviour, since the type of presentation, individual observer differences, and the social climate all play a part. Brody (1977) concluded from an exhaustive review of studies that laboratory research had not convincingly shown that films incite people to physical violence, but Howe (1977) and Belson (1978) argued that there was sufficient evidence for a disinhibiting effect to necessitate action.

Learning theory may help to explain why juvenile offenders do not always go on to become adult criminals, since the pattern of available reinforcement changes as they grow older. If adult reinforcers are inadequate (e.g. lack of job, friends, family) the adolescent pattern of offending may continue (Trasler, 1979). Whilst it provides a very useful mechanism for understanding the acquisition and maintenance of criminal behaviour, learning theory on its own does not fully explain why there are individual differences. To give a complete understanding of crime it may be necessary to combine a learning model with some account of individual personality and also an understanding of the factors affecting a person's encounters with the criminal justice system. Thus, 'the person whose genetic predisposition in combination with a specific learning history, produces a high susceptibility to offending may be pushed into official and progressively more permanent deviance by criminalizing contacts with the legal system' (Nietzel, 1979, p. 115).

The Re-focussing of Criminology

The traditional psychological approaches to crime have been criticized for their limited methodology (e.g. the use of questionnaires, laboratory experiments and simulations) and for their tendency to focus on convicted, incarcerated offenders. Victim surveys (Sparks, Genn and Dodd, 1977) and self-report studies (Gold, 1966) have not only confirmed that there is a large amount of unrecorded crime, but have also shown that official and unofficial criminals differ in personal and social characteristics, so that theories which attempt to explain the attributes of official criminals may present a misleading picture of crime as a whole. The experiences of arrest and imprisonment may themselves lead to changes in perceptions and self-concept which traditional research strategies may fail to uncover.

The growing interest in the process of becoming labelled as criminal or deviant led to an important change in criminology in the 1960s and 1970s, resulting in a new focus on crime as a function of social policy and control. Criminologists became interested in the way laws were created to maintain powerful groups (Goode, 1978). The operation of police discretion, the sociological analysis of court procedures and the factors affecting sentencing were among those topics seen as important, and theories of individual criminality tended to be viewed as old-fashioned and unhelpful.

It has been suggested that psychologists studying crime failed to participate in this change of focus and have continued to research along the traditional lines of 'correctional' criminology (Parker and Giller, 1981). While this would seem to be the case, there has nevertheless been a marked increase of interest in the criminal justice system as part of the psychology and law field. This rapidly developing area is already too large to be reviewed here (see Farrington, Hawkins and Lloyd-Bostock, 1979; Lloyd-Bostock, 1981a, 1981b), but mention must be made of the numerous studies of eyewitness testimony (e.g. Loftus, 1979; Clifford and Bull, 1978; Hollin, 1980), police interrogation (Irving 1981; Irving and Hilgendorf, 1980; Softley, 1980), hypnosis (Gibson, 1982), jury decision-making (Saks and Hastie, 1978; Bridgeman and Marlowe, 1979; Lowenstein, 1980) and the factors affecting arrest (Fisher and Mawby, 1982; Stevens and Willis, 1980). Many of these findings have had important practical implications and have been incorporated into the evidence submitted to such bodies as the Royal Commission on Criminal Procedure.

One consequence of the traditional focus in criminology was the marked neglect of white-collar and female offenders, and this imbalance still exists. For example, virtually all of the major theories of crime discussed above have been based on studies of males, the justification being that official statistics show female crime to be a much smaller problem. Yet self-report studies of delinquency have shown the gap between the sexes to be much smaller than official figures would suggest. Differences in conviction and sentencing may partly account for this discrepancy, though it is misleading to suggest that courts treat female offenders more leniently, since juvenile courts appear to be more severe with female offenders (Mawby, 1977a), particularly where sexual deviance is concerned (Terry, 1970). Smart (1976, 1979) has suggested that there has been a tendency to look for monocausal explanations of female crime, at first concentrating on women as victims of their biological make-up (Lombroso and Ferrero, 1895; Thomas, 1967; Cowie, Cowie and Slater, 1968) and, more recently, blaming the Women's Movement for apparent increase in female crime. Smart points out that similar increases in female crime have occurred during periods of non-liberation, and suggests that the police and courts may have been more affected by changing perceptions of women than many of the women themselves (Smart, 1979). In any case, Thornton and James (1979) provide evidence which refutes the idea that increases in female delinquency are related to the adoption of 'masculine' roles.

AREAS OF DEVELOPING INTEREST

Cognitive Approaches

In the last decade, psychologists have become increasingly interested in the perceptions and cognitions which mediate between personality and behaviour. Studies of crime have begun to examine the way offenders think (see Yochelson and Samenow, 1976), construct reality, and make inferences and attributions. Most of the research has concentrated on violent offenders, since experimental studies have shown that violence may be associated with the attribution of negative events to others rather than to oneself (Dyck and Rule, 1978; Nickel, 1974). Nasby, Hayden and De Paulo (1980) reported that violence in aggressive adolescents was the result of a tendency to infer hostility from social situations, but most studies have looked at aggression in adult psychopathic offenders. Novaco's (1978) model of anger arousal seems to have been particularly influential; he described anger as a combination of physiological arousal and cognitive labelling, determined by external events (frustration, insult, annoyance, etc.), internal cognitive processes (expectations, appraisal, private speech), and behavioural reactions (verbal/physical antagonism, withdrawal, etc.). Each of these influences the others, so that aversive events only cause anger if they are construed in a particular way. Novaco believed that people who have problems in controlling anger need to learn new cognitive coping strategies, and he reports positive results from training subjects in cognitive coping and relaxation skills.

More recently, Howells (1981) has used repertory grids to examine the construct systems of mentally abnormal offenders. He concluded that overcontrolled and undercontrolled offenders differed in their construing, the former tending to blame themselves more and idealize their victims and others. Howell suggests that overcontrolled offenders repress their negative feelings and evaluations of others, but under stress they shift to these 'submerged' hostile cognitions which thus precipitate violence.

There appear to be fewer studies of the perceptions and cognitions of non-violent offenders. Rettig's work in the 1960s examined perceptions of risk, and attempted to ascertain the balance of rewards and costs which would be acceptable to a criminal. He believed that the decision to commit an offence would depend on the perceived expectancy and value of gain, and the subjective probability and severity of punishment (e.g. Rettig and Rawson, 1963). However, Stewart and Hemsley (1979) reported that offenders and non-offenders did not differ in their perceptions of expected gain, though criminals were more likely to say that they would take a risk.

Although the cognitive approach to crime is relatively recent in development, it is likely to have a major influence on future research and practice. Advocates of behaviour therapy and social skills training now include cognitive components in their programmes, and there is a growing interest in attribution judgements, by offenders and by those in the criminal justice system.

Social Skills

One of the interesting developments of the 1970s and 1980s has been the enthusiastic way that the Home Office, police and prison staff have taken up the notion of social skills training as a method of reducing crime. The term 'social skill' can be confusing in the penal context as it has been used to describe various types and levels of intervention, from survival skills (e.g. applying for a job) to role play of offence-related situations (e.g. how to avoid a fight) and the modification of micro-skills (e.g. eye contact, gesture). (See Henderson, 1982b, for example and case studies.)

Social skills training has its roots in social learning theory which sees undesirable or maladaptive behaviour as the result of inappropriate learning, in particular the absence of 'correct' models. Individual, class and cultural differences in social behaviour are important because they affect a person's repertoire of social skills (and consequently his options for avoiding trouble), and because when members of different class and culture interact there is a greater risk of misunderstanding. Deficits of social skill are found in all segments of society but these may be more readily tolerated in persons of greater status and prestige.

There are many ways in which deficits in social skill could have implications for understanding criminal behaviour, particularly offences against the person. An offender may inaccurately perceive another's intent or see violence in any ambiguous situation (Shelley and Toch, 1968). Attribution of blame may be distorted or a person's choice of alternative responses constrained by a limited repertoire or sub-cultural norms. For example, the adolescent boy whose girl-friend is insulted in front of him may choose to pick a fight, not necessarily because he perceives it as a particularly effective strategy but because his sub-culture (and his girl-friend) define physical violence as the only possible response. In other cases, the desirable response may be chosen but performed so unskilfully that it is counterproductive, as with the innocent bystander who, when approached by police on suspicion of involvement in a crime, resists arrest with such aggression that he is finally charged with assault or breach of the peace.

A number of studies have evaluated the effectiveness of social skills training, using the standard practices of modelling, role play and feedback, with young offenders (Spence and Marzillier, 1979, 1981; Kifer, Lewis, Green and Phillips, 1974; Ollendick and Hersen, 1979). The general finding seems to be that changes in target behaviours do occur and are in the desired direction, but they are not always maintained at follow-up (Thelen, Fry, Dollinger and Paul, 1976) and may not generalize to situations outside the training environment. In some cases, improvement in subjects receiving social skills training (SST) has been found to be no greater than in subjects who attended discussion groups, without practice or feedback (Sarason and Ganzer, 1973), though Ollendick and

Hersen reported superior results for SST. Reduced recidivism following SST was reported by McGurk and Newell (1981) but not by Spence and Marzillier (1981).

Social skills training has also been used with violent offenders, often including assertion training for over-controlled offenders who are incapable of expressing anger at a normal level (Foy, Eisler and Pinkston, 1975; Frederiksen, Jenkins, Foy and Eisler, 1976). Howells (1976) reported positive results from a social skills group for violent offenders in a special hospital, and Crawford and Allen (1979) used SST with sex offenders. Burgess, Jewitt, Sandham and Hudson (1980) used SST with sex offenders who were on 'Rule 43' in prison (that is, segregated for their own protection). They claim that considerable improvement in skills occurred, but no independent ratings were made and there was no control group or follow-up.

There are various possible reasons for the mixed results which have emerged from these studies. In some cases, failure to produce change may be due to the use of standard training packages without making a careful analysis of the needs and deficits of the particular client group, a notable exception being Freedman, Rosenthal, Donahue, Schlundt and McFall (1978). A second factor may be the neglect of cognitive components in many early programmes. Trower (1981) has suggested that individuals are prevented from learning from feedback by their own expectations, which become self-fulfilling prophecies. Through behaving in accordance with their erroneous beliefs, they actually confirm their original mistaken perceptions. He believes it is necessary to modify the beliefs that have prevented people from acquiring skills in the normal way, as well as using SST to acquire new verbal and non-verbal skills. However, as yet there is little empirical support for the effectiveness of combining the two techniques (Shepherd, 1980) and they may even be incompatible (Hollin, Huff, Clarkson and Edmondson, 1982).

It should be noted that the majority of these studies have been carried out in institutions which may reinforce incompatible behaviours (Hollin and Henderson, 1981) or prevent the maintenance of cognitive changes such as increased self-esteem and internal locus of control (Spence and Spence, 1980). Future research may need to concentrate on training offenders in the community, in particular on improving their interactions with the police (e.g. Werner, Minkin, Fixsen, Phillips and Wolf, 1975). It is possible that the police, too, might benefit from social skills training, particulary in dealing

Psychology and Crime

with minority groups, as highlighted by the Scarman Report (November, 1981). Although the most important factors influencing police prosecution appear to be age (Fisher and Mawby, 1982), offence type, and previous record (Mawby, 1979), arrest rates do also vary according to sex, race and social class, and therefore some information on cultural and class differences in social behaviour could help police officers to judge their own and others' reactions accurately.

For example, cross-cultural misunderstandings may occur as a result of differences in the pattern of eye contact and gaze. LaFrance and Mayo (1976) videotaped pairs of black and white people in a variety of natural situations and found that black interactants looked significantly less at the other person when listening than white interactants did. This could have important implications, since Baxter and Rozelle (1975) reported that policemen saw gaze as an important cue suggesting witholding of information, deception and guilt.

There have also been references to cultural differences in body movement, gesture and proximity (Argyle, 1967), though Scherer (1974) found that lower class children interacted at closer distances than middle class children, whatever their race. A person who approaches a police officer at a less than 'comfortable' distance may be perceived as threatening, and the police officer's own preferred distance could also be critical. Interestingly, studies of violent prisoners have shown them to have greater 'body buffer zones' than other prisoners (Kinzel, 1970), that is, they are more sensitive to others encroaching on their personal space, especially from behind, though McGurk, Davis and Grehan (1981b) found that this was only the case for violent offenders who scored high on psychoticism.

The American experience, however, has shown that social skills training cannot be expected to solve all the problems of policing a multi-ethnic society. Training in psychology has been used sporadically by American police departments since the 1940s, including role-play and simulation techniques. Most of these programmes have been designed to promote better relations with minority groups, but it has been suggested that many of them are ineffective (Kulis, 1976) and may even harden prejudices (Lifkowitz, 1972). Kulis (1976) has argued that unfair discrimination and abuse by police is most likely to happen when their authority is symbolically defied; thus there is no point in training them to be 'friendly' unless they also learn to retain a sense of control and leadership under stress.

121

Victims

In the 1960s attention was suddenly focussed on victims of crime due to the development of victim compensation schemes in a number of countries. In Britain, an experimental scheme was set up in 1964, but in order to qualify for compensation a victim had to be seen as deserving, and thus the concept of victim precipitation was introduced. The full recognition of victimology as an important area of study came in the 1970s and there has been a growing interest in the role of the victim in the criminal justice system, the psychological effects of being a victim (e.g. Haward, 1981), and the effectiveness of victim support schemes. Nevertheless, our knowledge of victim behaviour and its contribution to criminal events is still limited.

The public stereotype of a victim is often that of a weak, defenceless old lady who is mugged by strangers, but victim surveys have shown this to be inaccurate. The characteristics of victims vary according to the type of offence; but for offences against the person, excluding sexual offences, a fairly consistent pattern emerges as follows: the typical victim of violence is relatively young (Sparks, Genn and Dodd, 1977; Hindenlang, Gottfredson and Garofalo, 1978), and male (Levie, 1979; Lebow, 1976). American studies have reported higher victimization rates for blacks than whites (Levie, 1979), but a British survey found no significant association between race and victimization, apart from the fact that, contrary to popular belief, offender and victim tend to be of the same race (Sparks, Genn and Dodd, 1977). Victimization rates for serious assault are higher for unmarried people than married (Singer, 1980), even when controlled for age effects, and there is a high rate of victimization for the unemployed (Braithwaite and Biles, 1979). Wolfgang (1958) found that victims who in some way precipitated their attack were more likely to have a criminal record than the offenders.

Social and personal characteristics may be reasonable predictors of the victimization rates of groups of people, but they do not account entirely for individual differences within these groups, particularly the phenomenon of 'multiple victimization'. Surveys have shown that the distribution of personal victimization is very skewed, but this cannot apparently be entirely explained by chance factors, by 'contagion' (i.e. one incident increasing the risk of future attacks) or by proneness characteristics (Sparks, Genn and Dodd, 1977). Some measure of the behaviour and attitudes of multiple victims is needed to throw light on this.

Some early information on victim behaviour came from Wolfgang's (1958) study of homicide victims, in which he found that 26 per cent of victims had been the first to use a weapon or physical force, though presumably these figures may be distorted by the fact that the victims were not present to give their version of the incident! Another important factor seems to be the considerable proportion of victims of assault who have been drinking before the attack (e.g. Marek, Widacki and Hanausek, 1974).

A direct test of how a victim's behaviour may influence the outcome of an assault is found in an experimental study by Marques (1979) who investigated the effects of three verbal strategies which a victim might use in trying to resist a violent rape: (i) assertive refusal, (ii) a plea for sympathy, (iii) an attempt to establish a relationship with the rapist. Audiotape descriptions portraying the three strategies in the context of attempted assault were presented to 12 violent rapists, who were asked to report their feelings and attitudes towards the victim.

The results of the study showed that the strategy of assertive refusal, which courts may see as the mark of a genuinely unwilling victim, was counterproductive: it tended to make the rapists more angry and increase the risk of injury. Pleading by the victim succeeded in eliciting sympathy, but produced the highest level of sexual arousal in the rapists, and attempts to establish a relationship had little effect. Offenders' reports indicated that they would be more likely to complete the rape if they were both angry and sexually aroused, but anger was especially likely to result in harm to the victim. This study did not examine any non-verbal signals whereas Ellsworth and Carlsmith (1973) reported that eye contact by the 'victim' to a person delivering electric shocks in an experiment could inhibit aggression and thereby reduce the level of shock, though only if it was applied consistently.

Toch's (1969) analysis of violent men also highlighted the importance of the interaction between victim and offender. For example, the 'self-image promoter' uses violence to demonstrate toughness and status, and invites conflict in order to defend his position. The victim's response to this offender is very important, since 'if they fail to react he concludes that his word is law; if they fight he feels accepted amongst those who settle their differences at High Noon on Main Street'. Other types could also end up as victims themselves, such as the self-image defender who is said to show 'a distinct tendency to choose the wrong opponent and the least effective setting for survival'.

A more recent study by Athens (1980) adopted a similar approach to Toch, but placed more emphasis on the way offenders define situations by taking on the role of the other: a symbolic interactionist approach. Athens suggested that there are four types of interpretations of situations in which violent acts occur:

(1)   the physically defensive interpretation, in which the offender perceives that the victim is going to attack him;

(2)   frustrative: the offender sees the victim as resisting the desired line of action;

(3)   malefic: the offender perceives the victim as deriding or belittling him, and concludes that the victim is a malicious person;

(4)   frustrative/malefic: a combination of the above.

In each case, whether or not the final outcome is violent will depend on whether the person persists in his violent interpretation or whether something, such as a change in the victim's behaviour, causes him to alter his judgement.

Finally, Lejeune (1977) interviewed muggers and concluded that there were two main principles used in selecting victims: those who appeared unlikely to resist (e.g. weak, drunk or scared), and those who looked as if they were worth mugging. However, any personal characteristic or manner which aroused the offender's hostility seemed to increase the risk of victimization, and if victims showed signs of disbelief or resistance this inevitably resulted in increased force or threat.

The Situational Approach

The situational approach to crime is concerned with those factors in the environment which influence peoples' choices, decisions and opportunities to commit offences. These range from the design of buildings and public places, the provision of lighting, and the use of locks and protective paint to the introduction of closed circuit television. The situational approach does not deny the importance of individual and social factors, but its supporters would argue that since indivduals are notoriously difficult to change, crime prevention through environmental design may be more effective.

Much of the original interest in the physical environment and crime came from Newman's highly publicized theory of Defensible Space (Newman, 1972), in which he argued that crime rates will vary according to the extent to which a building or area possesses four characteristics:

(1) Territorial definition of space: the identification of areas or zones which people feel belong to them and will therefore protect (e.g. individual gardens or entrances).
(2) Surveillance: the extent to which residents can see what is happening in public areas, can identify intruders, and can exercise control over activities.
(3) Image: whether the appearance indicates vulnerability or security; e.g. council blocks may easily be recognized as targets.
(4) Milieu: the surrounding area (e.g. parks, roads) must also be safe and secure with adequate surveillance if defensible space is to be created.

The essence of defensible space is that it creates a feeling of group identity and shared responsibility, and enables the potential victim to recognize the potential offender in advance, since no one will choose to commit where they think they will be identified and caught. Much of the interest in defensible space has been in its potential for reducing vandalism, though Newman measured a range of crimes such as theft, mugging and assault.

Newman presented data in support of his theory from 100 housing projects in New York, though he only gave a detailed analysis of two housing estates which differed in their design and their crime rates. Increased height and size of buildings were associated with higher crime rates, and the parts of the buildings which were least protected and had least surveillance (e.g. lifts, stairwells, lobbies) had most crime.

After a period of initial enthusiasm, Newman's theory began to attract criticism on methodological (Bottoms, 1974) and theoretical (Mawby, 1977b) grounds. He subsequently revised his ideas and stated that the social characteristics of the population were stronger predictors of crime rates than design features were, for example, the percentage of families on welfare and the per capita income of residents (Newman, 1976).

British studies have also reported an interaction between social factors and design, with the social factors being stronger predictors of offending. Wilson (1978) examined vandalism in 38 London housing estates and found the most important factor to be the child density; but whereas in the high child density blocks none of her measures of defensible space had any significant relation to vandalism, in the low child density blocks the amount of damage was affected by factors such as size and design. Vandalism in telephone kiosks was found to be highest when they were located near council estates, but in the non-council areas the amount of surveillance from overlooking windows affected the amount of damage (Mayhew, Clarke, Hough and Winchester, 1979). These and other studies led Mayhew (1979) to conclude that 'defensible space has considerable intuitive appeal, but it may have been oversold'.

Nevertheless, there are other situational approaches, less grandiose perhaps, which have been used with some success (see Clarke and Mayhew, 1980, for a series of studies). Hough, Clarke and Mayhew, (1980) outlined eight possible situational measures:

(1) Target hardening: e.g. the introduction of steering column locks on cars led to a reduction in theft, though there was some increase in theft of unprotected cars (Mayhew, Clarke, Sturman and Hough, 1976). Thefts from telephone kiosks have been virtually eliminated by the use of steel cash boxes instead of aluminium;

(2) target removal: e.g. paying employees by cheque to prevent wage robberies;

(3) removing the means to crime: e.g. control of gun sales or other potential weapons;

(4) reducing the pay-off: e.g. marking goods so that if stolen they will be difficult to resell;

(5) formal surveillance: e.g. the introduction of closed circuit television on four underground stations reduced the incidence of theft and robbery (Burrows, 1980);

(6) natural surveillance: e.g. Sturman (1980) found that the amount of vandalism on buses was related to the degree of conductor supervision, which varied according to the design and operation of the bus;

(7) surveillance by employees: e.g. caretakers, lift operators;

(8) environmental management: e.g. creating social cohesion, placement of families.

The major problem facing the situational approach to crime is that of possible displacement of crime to unprotected targets or adjacent areas. There is little evidence for displacement from one crime to another - frustrated vandals are not likely to go off and rob a bank instead - and some very opportunistic crimes would not be expected to show any displacement at all. However, some displacement from protected and unprotected targets is bound to occur as long as there are still cars without locks, houses with open windows, and concrete walls crying out for graffiti. The conclusions reached by the Home Office researchers who have been particularly interested in this kind of work is that 'a certain amount of displacement does not vitiate a preventative measure; so long as the benefits from a reduction in crime exceed the social cost of a measure it can be regarded as a success' (Hough, Clarke and Mayhew, 1980).

CONCLUSIONS

In spite of the limitations of most of the traditional theories discussed above, they are still influential in generating research into the causes of crime. The biological and personality theories seem to appeal to many people, perhaps because they offer a rather comfortable view of crime that blames a hidden aberration for society's problems, even though this line of research is probably more appropriate for the study of mentally abnormal offenders than as an explanation of 'normal' law-breaking.

The family and the social and physical environments appear to be important factors in understanding juvenile delinquency, yet the implications of this are open to dispute: should 'high risk' children be picked out for special intervention or would this lead to undesirable labelling and self-fulfilling prophecies? Learning theory highlights the sources of reinforcement of criminal activity, while studies of declining social conditions and rising unemployment emphasize the lack of alternative routes to excitement and self-esteem.

Where do we go from here? Current developments reflect an increasing interest in the criminal act itself: the cognitive processes involved in decision-making, the environmental cues, the behaviour of victims and police, and the social skills needed to keep out of trouble. Yet the focus of most research is still narrow, concentrating on the official male, working-class offender and ignoring the social and political context within which laws and crimes, are created. Perhaps psychologists need to take more account of the radical view, that the existence of legally-defined criminals is an inevitable consequence of our current social structure.

REFERENCES

Allsopp, J. F. and Feldman, M. P. (1975). Extraversion, neuroticism, psychoticism and antisocial behaviour in school-girls. Social Behaviour and Personality, 2, 184.

Argyle, M. (1967). The Psychology of Interpersonal Behaviour. Harmondsworth: Penguin.

Athens, L. H. (1980). Violent Criminal Acts and Actors - A Symbolic Interactionist Study. London: Routledge & Kegan Paul.

Bandura, A. (1973). Aggression: A social learning analysis. New York: Prentice Hall.

Bandura, A. (1976). Social learning analysis of aggression. In E. Ribes-Inesta and A. Bandura (eds), Analysis of Delinquency and Aggression. Hillsdale, NJ: Lawrence Erlbaum.

Barack, L. I. and Widom, C. S. (1978). Eysenck's theory of criminality applied to women awaiting trial. British Journal of Psychiatry, 133, 452-456.

Baxter, J. C. and Rozelle, R. M. (1975). Nonverbal expression as a function of crowding during a simulated police-citizen encounter. Journal of Personality and Social Psychology, 32, 40-54.

Becker, W. W. C. (1964). Consequences of different kinds of parental discipline. In M. L. Hoffman and L. W. Hoffman (eds), Review Of Child Development Research, Volume I. New York: Russell Sage Foundation.

Belson, W. A. (1978). Television Violence and the Adolescent Boy. Farnborough: Saxon House.

Blackburn, R. (1975). An empirical classification of psychopathic personality. British Journal of Psychiatry, 127, 456-460.

Bottoms, A. E. (1974). Review of 'Defensible Space'. British Journal of Criminology, 14, 203-206.

Bowlby, J. (1946). Forty-four Juvenile Thieves. London: Bailliere, Tindall & Cox.

Braithwaite, J. and Biles, D. (1979). On being unemployed and being a victim of crime. Australian Journal of Social Issues, 14, 192-200.

Bridgeman, D. L. and Marlowe, D. (1979). Jury decision-making: an empirical study based on actual felony trials. Journal of Applied Psychology, 64, 91-98.

Brody, S. (1977). Screen violence and film censorship. Home Office Research Study no. 40. London: HMSO.

Bull, R. (1982). Physical appearance and criminality. Unpublished paper presented at the International Conference on Psychology and Law, Swansea.

Burgess, R., Jewitt, J., Sandham, J. and Hudson, B. L. (1980). Working with sex offenders: a social skills training group. British Journal of Social Work, 10, 133-142.

Burrows, J. (1980). Closed circuit television and crime on the London underground. In R. V. G. Clarke and P. Mayhew (eds), Designing Out Crime. London: HMSO.

Cavior, H. Hayes, S. and Cavior, N. (1975). Physical attractiveness of female offenders. In S. Brodsky (ed.), The Female Offender. London: Sage.

Christiansen, K. O. (1968). Threshold of tolerance in various population groups illustrated by results from Danish criminological twin study. In A. V. S. de-Rueck and R. Porter (eds), The Mentally Abnormal Offender. Boston: Little, Brown.

Clarke, A. M. and Clarke, A. D. B. (1976). Early Experience - Myth and Evidence. London: Open Books.

Clarke, R. V. G. and Mayhew, P. (1980). Designing Out Crime. London: HMSO.

Clifford, B. R. and Bull, R. (1978). The Psychology of Person Identification. London: Routledge & Kegan Paul.

Cowie, J., Cowie, V. and Slater, E. (1968). Delinquency in Girls. London: Heinemann.

Crawford, D. A. and Allen, J. V. (1979). A social skill training programme with sex offenders. In M. Cook and G. Wilson (eds), Love and Attraction. Oxford: Pergamon Press.

Dietrich, S. and Berger, L. (1978). The MMPI and criminology: abuses of application. Journal of Psychiatry and Law, Winter, 453-480.

Dyck, R. J. and Rule, B. G. (1978). Effect on retaliation of causal attributions concerning attack. Journal of Personality and Social Psychology, 36, 521-529.

Ellsworth, P. and Carlsmith, J. M. (1973). Eye contact and gaze aversion in an aggressive encounter. Journal of Personality and Social Psychology, 28, 280-292.

Endler, N. S. (1973). The person versus the situation - a pseudo issue? Journal of Personality, 41, 287-303.

Eysenck, H. J. (1974). Crime and Personality reconsidered. Bulletin of The British Psychological Society, 27, 23.

Eysenck, H. J. (1977). Crime and Personality. London: Routledge & Kegan Paul.

Eysenck, H. J. and Eysenck, S. B. G. (1970). Crime and Personality: an empirical study of the three-factor theory. British Journal of Criminology, 10, 225.

Farrington, D. P., Hawkins, K, Lloyd-Bostock, S. M. (eds) (1979). Psychology, Law and Legal Processes. London: Macmillan.

Feldman, M. P. (1977). Criminal Behaviour: A psychological analysis. Chichester: Wiley.

Fisher, C. J. and Mawby, R. I. (1982). Juvenile delinquency and police discretion in an inner city area. British Journal of Criminology, 22, 63-75.

Forde, R. (1978). Twin studies, inheritance and criminality. British Journal of Criminology, 18, 71-74.

Foy, D. W., Eisler, R. M. and Pinkston, S. G. (1975). Modelled assertion in a case of explosive rage. Journal of Behaviour Therapy and Experimental Psychiatry, 6, 135-137.

Frederiksen, L. W., Jenkins, J. O., Foy, D. W. and Eisler, R. M. (1976). Social skills training in the modification of abusive verbal outbursts in adults. Journal of Applied Behaviour Analysis, 9, 117-125.

Freedman, B. J., Rosenthal, L., Donahue, C., Schlundt, D. G. and McFall, R. M. (1978). A social-behavioural analysis of skills deficits in delinquent and nondelinquent adolescent boys. Journal of Consulting and Clinical Psychology, 46, 1448-1462.

Gibson, H. B. (1982). The use of hypnosis in police investigations. Bulletin of The British Psychological Society, 35, 138-142.

Gold, M. (1966). Undetected criminal behaviour. Journal of Research in Crime and Delinquency, 3, 27-46.

Goode, E. (1978) . Deviant Behaviour: An interactionist approach. Englewood Cliffs, NJ: Prentice-Hall.

Hampson, S. E. (1982). The Construction of Personality an Introduction. London: Routledge & Kegan Paul.

Haward, L. R. C. (1981). Psychological consequences of being a victim of crime. In S. Lloyd-Bostock (ed.), Law and Psychology. Oxford: SSRC Centre for Socio-Legal Studies.

Henderson, M. (1982a). An empirical classification of convicted violent offenders. British Journal of Criminology, 22, 1-20.

Henderson, M. (1982b). Can we prevent violent crimes? New Society, 8 April, 52-53.

Heskin, K. J., Bolton, N., Smith, F. V. and Bannister, P. A. (1974). Psychological correlates of long-term imprisonment. British Journal of Criminology, 14, 150.

Hindenlang, M. J., Gottfredson, M. R. and Garofalo, J. (1978). Victims of Personal Crime: An empirical foundation for a theory of personal victimization. Cambridge, Mass: Ballinger.

Hinton, J. and O'Neill, M. (1978). Pilot study of psychophysiological responses of patients in Broadmoor. British Journal of Social and Clinical Psychology, 17, 103.

Hinton, J., O'Neill, M., Hamilton, S. and Burke, M. (1980). Psychophysiological differentiation between psychopathic and schizophrenic abnormal offenders. British Journal of Social and Clinical Psychology 19. (3).

Hollin, C. (1980). Eyewitness-testimony: nothing but the truth? Police Review, 88 (45.83), 2388-2389.

Hollin, C. and Henderson, M. (1981). The effect of social skills training on incarcerated delinquent adolescents.

International Journal of Behavioural Social Work and Abstracts I., 45-155.

Hollin, C., Huff, G, Clarkson, F. and Edmondson, A. (1982). An evaluation of social skills training with young offenders in a Borstal. Unpublished paper, presented at the International Conference on Psychology and Law, University of Swansea.

Hough, J. M., Clarke, R. V. G. and Mayhew, (1980). Introduction to R. V. G. Clarke and P. Mayhew (eds), Designing Out Crime. London: HMSO.

Howe, M. J. (1977). Television and Children. London: New University Education.

Howells, K. (1976). Interpersonal aggression. International Journal of Criminology and Penology, 4, 319-330.

Howells, K. (1981). Social construing and violent behaviour in mentally abnormal offenders. In J. Hinton (ed.) Dangerousness: Problems of assessment and prediction. London: George Allen & Unwin.

Hutchings, B. and Mednick, S. (1974). Registered criminality in the adoptive and biological parents of registered male adoptees. In R. Fieve, H. Brill and R. Rosenthal (eds), Genetics. Baltimore: Johns Hopkins University Press.

Irving, B. (1980). Police interrogation: a case study of current practice. Royal Commission on Criminal Procedure Research Study No. 2. London: HMSO.

Irving, B. and Hilgendorf, L. (1980). Police interrogation: the psychological approach. Royal Commission on Criminal Procedure Research Study No. 1. London: HMSO.

Kahn, J., Reed, F., Bates, M., Coates, T. and Everitt, B. (1976). A survey of Y chromosome variants and personality in 436 borstal lads and 234 controls. British Journal of Criminology, 16, 233-244.

Kifer, H. E., Lewis, M. A., Green, D. R. and Phillips, E. L. (1974). Training predelinquent girls and their parents to negotiate conflict situations. Journal of Applied Behavioural Analysis, 7, 357-364.

Kinzel, A. F. (1970). Body-buffer zones in violent prisoners. American Journal of Psychiatry, 127, 59-64.

Kulis, J. C. (1976). Police Identity Workshops: Police training in law enforcement. Available from J. C. Kulis, Associate Professor of Psychology, City Colleges of Chicago.

LaFrance, M. and Mayo, C. (1976). Racial differences in gaze behaviour during conversations. Journal of Personality and Social Psychology, 33, 547-552.

Lebow, R. N. (1976). The origins of sectarian assassination: the case of Belfast. Unpublished paper, cited in Fattah,

E. (1979). Some Reflections on the victimology of Terrorism. Terrorism: An International Journal, 3, 81-108.

Lejeune, R. (1977). The management of a mugging. Urban Life, 6, 123-148.

Levie, R. C. (1979). A study of criminal homicide patterns and selected characteristics of offenders in the city of New Orleans 1971-3. Dissertation Abstracts International, 40, (6-A), 3071.

Lifkowitz, J. (1972). Evaluation of a supervisory training program for police sergeants. Personnel Psychology, 25, 95-106.

Lloyd-Bostock, S. (ed.) (1981a). Law and Psychology - papers presented at SSRC Law and Psychology Conferences 1979-80. Oxford, SSRC Centre for Socio-legal Studies.

Lloyd-Bostock, S. (ed.) (1981b). Psychology in Legal Contexts Applications and Limitations. London: Macmillan.

Loftus, E. (1979). Eyewitness testimony. Cambridge, Mass.: Harvard University Press.

Lombroso, C. and Ferrero, W. (1895). The Female Offender. London: Fisher Unwin.

Lowenstein, L. F. (1980). Are juries impartial? Police. February/March, 24-30.

Marek, Z., Widacki, J. and Hanausek, T. (1974). Alcohol as a victimogenic factor of robberies. Forensic Science, 4, 119-123.

Marques, J. K. (1979). The effects of several victim resistance strategies on the sexual arousal and attitudes of violent rapists. Dissertation Abstracts Int. 40 (2-B), 926-927.

Marriage, H. (1977). Personality interaction and criminality: is field dependence involved? Unpublished paper, presented at the BPS Annual Conference, University of Exeter, April 1977.

Mawby, R. I. (1977a). Sexual Discrimination and the Law Probation, 24, 39-43.

Mawby, R. I. (1977b). Defensible Space - a theoretical and empirical appraisal. Urban Studies, 14, 169-179.

Mawby, R. I. (1979). Policing the City. Farnborough: Saxon House.

Mayhew, P. (1979). Defensible space - the current status of a crime prevention theory. The Howard Journal of Penology and Crime Prevention, 18, 150-159.

Mayhew, P., Clarke, R. V. G., Sturman, A. and Hough, J. M. (1976). Home Office Research Study no. 34. London: HMSO.

Mayhew, P., Clarke, R. V. G., Hough, J. M., and Winchester, S. W. C. (1979). Crime in public view. Home Office Research Study no. 49. London: HMSO.

McCachy, C. H. (1976). Deviant Behaviour: crime, conflict and interest groups. New York: Macmillan.

McCandless, B. R., Persons, W. S. and Roberts, A. (1972). Perceived opportunity, delinquency, race and body build among delinquent youth. Journal of Consulting and Clinical Psychology, 38, 281.

McGurk, B. J. (1978). Personality types among normal homicides. British Journal of Criminology, 18, 146-161.

McGurk, B. J., McEwan, A. W., and Graham, F. (1981a). Personality types and recedivism among young delinquents. British Journal of Criminology, 21, 159-165.

McGurk, B. J. and McGurk, R. (1979). Personality types among prisoners and prison officers: an investigation of Megargee's theory of control. British Journal of Criminology, 19, 31-49.

McGurk, B. J., Davis, J. D. and Grehan, J. (1981b). Assaultive behaviour, personality and personal space. Aggressive Behaviour, 7, 317-324.

McGurk, B. J. and Newell, T. C. (1981). Social skills training with a sex offender. Psychological Record, 31, 277-283.

Megargee, E. (1966). Undercontrolled and overcontrolled personality types in extreme antisocial aggression. Psychological Monographs, 80, Whole No. 611.

Mischel, W. (1973). Toward a cognitive social learning reconceptualisation of personality. Psychological Review, 80, 252-283.

Nasby, W., Hayden, B. and DePaulo, B. M. (1980). Attributional bias among aggressive boys to interpret unambiguous social stimuli as displays of hostility. Journal of Abnormal Psychology, 89, 459-468.

Newman, O. (1972). Defensible Space: Crime prevention through urban design. New York: Macmillan.

Newman, O. (1976). Design Guidelines for Creating Defensible Space. National Institute of Law Enforcement and Criminal Justice, US Dept of Justice. Washington, DC: Government Printing Office.

Nickel, T. W. (1974). The attribution of intention as a critical factor in the relation between frustration and aggression. Journal of Personality, 42, 482-492.

Nietzel, M. T. (1979). Crime and its Modification - A Social Learning Perspective. New York: Pergamon Press.

Novaco, R. W. (1978). Anger and coping with stress. In J. P. Foreyt and D. P. Fathjen (eds), Cognitive Behaviour Therapy. New York and London: Plenum Press.

Ollendick, T. H. and Hersen, M. (1979). Social skills training for juvenile delinquents. Behaviour Research and Therapy, 17, 547-554.

Osborn, S. G. and West, D. J. (1979). Conviction records of fathers and sons compared. British Journal of Criminology, 19 (2), 120-133.

Parker, H. and Giller, H. (1981). More and less the same: British delinquency research since the sixties. British Journal of Criminology, 21 (3), 230-245.

Rahav, G. (1980). Birth order and delinquency. British Journal of Criminology, 20 (4), 385.

Rettig, S. and Rawson, H. E. (1963). The risk hypothesis in predictive judgements of unethical behaviour. Journal of Abnormal Social Psychology, 66, 243.

Rutter, M. (1972). Maternal Deprivation Reassessed. London: Harmondsworth, Pelican.

Saks, M. J. and Hastie, R. (1978). Social Psychology in Court. New York: Van Nostrand.

Sarason, I. G. and Ganzer, V. J. (1973). Modelling and group discussion in the rehabilitation of juvenile delinquents. Journal of Counselling Psychology, 20, 442-449.

Saxby, P., Norris, A., Feldman, M. P. (1970). Questionnaire studied self-reported anti-social behaviour and extra-version in adolescents. Unpublished manuscript, Dept of Psychology, University of Birmingham.

Scherer, S. E. (1974). Proxemic behaviour of primary school children as a function of their socioeconomic class and subculture. Journal of Personality and Social Psychology, 29, 800-805.

Shaw, I. S. and Newell, T. S. (1972). Violence in Television: Programme content and viewer perception. London: BBC.

Shelley, E. and Toch, H. H. (1968). The perception of violence as an indictor of adjustment in institutionalised offenders. In H. Toch and H. C. Smith (eds), Social Perception. New York: Van Nostrand.

Shepherd, G. (1980). The treatment of social differences in special environments. In P. Feldman and J. Orford (eds), Psychological Problems: The social context. Chichester: Wiley.

Singer, S. I. (1980). Victims in a subculture: an analysis of the social and criminal background of surveyed victims in the Birth Cohort follow up. Dissertation Abstracts International, 41 (3-A), 1224-5.

Smart, C. (1976). Women, Crime and Criminology - A Feminist Critique. London: Routledge & Kegan Paul.

Smart, C. (1979). The new female criminal - reality or myth? British Journal of Criminology, 19 (I), 50-59.

Softley, P. (1980). Police interrogation - an observational study in four police stations. Home Office Research Study no. 61. London: HMSO.

Sparks, R. E., Genn, H. G. and Dodd, D. J. (1977). Surveying Victims - A Study of the Measurement of Criminal Victimization. Chichester: Wiley.

Spence, A. J. and Spence, S. H. (1980). Cognitive changes associated with social skills training. Behaviour Research and Therapy, 18, 265-272.

Spence, S. H. and Marzillier, J. S. (1979). Social skills training with adolescent male offenders: I - short-term effects. Behaviour Research and Therapy, 17, 7-16.

Spence, S. H. and Marzillier, J. S. (1981). Social skills training with adolescent male offenders: II - short-term, long-term and generalised effects. Behaviour Research and Therapy, 19, 349-368.

Stevens, P. and Willis, L. F. (1980). Race, crime and arrests. Home Office Research Study no. 58. London: HMSO.

Stewart, C. H. M. and Hemsley, D. R. (1979). Risk perception and likelihood of action in criminal offenders. British Journal of Criminology, 19 (2), 105-119.

Sturman, A. (1980). Damage on buses: the effects of supervision. In R. V. G. Clarke and P. Mayhew (eds), Designing Out Crime. London: HMSO.

Terry, R. M. (1970). Discrimination in the handling of juvenile offenders by social control agencies. In P. G. Garabedian and D. C. Gibbons (eds), Becoming Delinquent. Chicago: Aldine.

Thelen, M. H., Fry, R. A., Dollinger, S. J. and Paul, S. C. (1976). Use of videotaped models to improve the interpersonal adjustment of delinquents. Journal of Consulting and Clinical Psychology, 44, 492.

Thomas, W. I. (1967). The Unadjusted Girl. New York: Harper & Row.

Thornton, W. E. and James, J. (1979). Masculinity and Delinquency revisited. British Journal of Criminology, 19 (3), 225-241.

Toch, H. (1969). Violent Men. Chicago: Aldine.

Trasler, G. (1979). Delinquency, recidivism and desistance. British Journal of Criminology, 19, (4), 314-322.

Trower, P. (1981). Social skills disorder. In S. Duck and R. Gilmore (eds), Personal Relationships volume 3: Personal relationships in disorder. London: Academic Press.

Wadsworth, M. E. J. (1976). Delinquency, pulse rates and early emotional deprivation. British Journal of Criminology, 16, 245-256.

Werner, J. S., Minkin, B. L., Fixsen, D. L., Phillips, E. L. and Wolf, M. M. (1975). Intervention package - an analysis to prepare juvenile delinquents for encounters with police officers. Criminal Justice and Behaviour, 2, 55-84.

West, D. J. (1982). Delinquency: Its roots, careers and prospects. London: Heinemann.

Wilson, H. (1975). Juvenile delinquency, parental criminality, and social handicap. British Journal of Criminology, 15, 241-250.

Wilson, H. (1980). Parental supervision: a neglected aspect of delinquency. British Journal of Criminology, 20 (3), 203.

Wilson, S. (1978). Tackling vandalism. Home Office Research Study no. 47. London: HMSO.

Wolfgang, M. E. (1958). Patterns in Criminal Homicide. Philadelphia: University of Pennsylvania Press.

Yochelson, S. and Samenow, S. E. (1976). The Criminal Personality. Volume I: A Profile for Change. New York: Jason Aronson.

Chapter 6

PSYCHOSOMATICS: AN HISTORICAL PERSPECTIVE

Margaret J. Christie

Contributors to this fourth volume of review chapters have been invited to survey their particular field with the help of a few very general references, then to deal more comhensively with a handful of its topics, for a readership which is to some extent at home in psychology's pastures. Contemporary psychosomatics has many varied acres, from clinical interpretations of alexithymia - the inability to describe emotion (Nemiah, Freyberger and Sifneos, 1976) - to psychophysiological investigation of electrodermal activity in states such as relaxation or psychosis (Christie, 1976, 1981a), so the selection of 'a few general references' could be somewhat difficult! Lipowski, Lipsitt and Whybrow (1977), however, edited a comprehensive collection of contributions to an American symposium which reflects a wide range of psychosomatic activity: theoretical, experimental, clinical. A British volume of contributed chapters, edited by Hill (1976), also reflects varied aspects of psychosomatics; the two collections can cover in greater depth and detail much of the material which this chapter, of necessity, treats in a somewhat brief and superficial way. They will, I hope, help to dispel some of the 'confusion nowadays about the subject matter and scope of psychosomatic medicine' (Lipowski, 1977a). Lipowski is a particularly appropriate person to introduce within the context of such confusion, and of its resolution: his overview in Hill's volume does much to 'clear up semantic ambiguities in which this field is shrouded' (Lipowski, 1976), and it provides a definition of psychosomatics which significantly aids our understanding of its diverse elements. Before offering this definition, however, it may be helpful to trace the development of psychosomatics through the present century and up to its contemporary phase, which we can date, somewhat arbitrarily, from the early 1970s.

137

ORIGINS OF PSYCHOSOMATICS

Spaulding (1977) does a particularly thorough review of psychosomatic history, taking us back to HuangTi in the third millenium BC, then forward via Hippocrates, Plato, Galen, Bacon, Cushing towards the present day. Our more modest account begins at the turn of this century, within the era of Freud (1856-1939), Pavlov (1849-1936) and Cannon (1871-1945) after noting with Weiss (1977) that Heinroth introduced the term 'psychosomatic' in 1818 in reaction against 'restricted explanations of physical and psychological events alike to the terms of the exact, or physical, sciences'. In the early decades of the twentieth century there was further reaction, in Germany and Austria, against the mechanistic view of Western medicine then prevailing. After major developments in basic sciences such as microbiology and biochemistry there was a growing emphasis on faulty organ systems and malfunctioning mechanisms, with less evidence of the whole-person approach. Wittkower (1977) recalls the experience of presenting his thesis on the influence of emotions on bodily functions while 'the raucous voices of the Nazis, arousing racial hatred, echoed in the streets of Berlin'. Nazi persecution resulted in the movement of many who had a psychosomatic orientation: Wittkower to London in 1933, Franz Alexander to the United States in 1930. The latter founded there the Chicago Psychoanalytic Institute, generating theoretical notions of psychogenic determinism which eventually, around mid-century, provoked a reaction that 'nearly swept the whole field (of psychosomatics) into oblivion' (Lipowski, 1977a). In the decades before mid-century, psychosomatics appeared to be dominated by psychoanalytic theory, with emphasis on unconscious influences and a heavy dependence on clinical observation which lacked the support of foundational research.

Psychomatic Disorders

During this phase the message was that origins of the psychosomatic disorders - the 'holy seven' of asthma, rheumatoid arthritis, ulcerative colitis, essential hypertension, neurodermatitis, thyrotoxicosis and peptic ulcer - lie in early childhood experience; that unconscious conflicts remain into adulthood as part of a predisposing state which can be reactivated by life events, thus precipitating a 'psychosomatic disorder', the specific nature of which depends on the nature of the conflict. So, for example, peptic ulcer was regarded as the consequence of conflict between dependency and self-sufficiency, between a wish to be fed and cared for and a desire for independence. The current state of the concept of a 'psychosomatic disorder' is comprehensively reviewed by Weiss (1977), who considers the specificity proposition of Alexander, together with the variants of Dunbar, who implicated personality rather than unconscious determinants and, more recently, Graham and his colleagues, who linked acquired attitudes with physiological responses. Weiss concludes that whilst it is possible that there may be a group of illnesses in which a specificity relation is evident, he cannot at present see specificity as an adequate basis on which to structure a category of 'psychosomatic disorder'. Similarly Eastwood (1977), from the viewpoint of psychosocial epidemiology, considers the difficulties inherent in defining 'psychosomatic' disorder and lists four general uses of the term, for:

(1) a physical condition which is specifically stress linked;
(2) a general psychophysiological propensity towards disease, in some 'high risk' individuals;
(3) a term used somewhat loosely to describe physical symptoms which have no known organic basis;
(4) another loose term to indicate that a pre-existing physical condition can be exacerbated by a psychological influence.

Citing the World Health Organization (WHO) Committee on Psychosomatic Disorders (1964), Eastwood argues that the epidemiological approach, which examines the general characteristics of groups, reduces the risk of simplistic statements being made about the psychogenesis of physical disease from the clinical observation or experimental psychophysiology of small numbers. His observation that chronic major physical disorders of contemporary medicine, such as cardiovascular disease, cancer, diabetes or arthritis, all have complicated multifactorial causation is axiomatic in contemporary psychosomatics; and while the WHO Committee suggested that experimental evidence showed psychological stress to be a potent pathogenic factor, Eastwood reminds us of the problems associated with the definition and measurement of this. He concludes, however, that the concept of psychophysiological propensity appears to be useful and that research into high-risk 'vulnerability' is an essential task for the future. We see, then, in the contemporary scene a rejection of those earlier views on specific 'psychosomatic disorders' which could be regarded as an inheritance from the Freudian origins of psychosomatics, but an orientation towards the possibility of non-specific 'stress-induced disorders', which can be seen as a line of development from Cannon (1935), through Selye (1950) and Wolff (1950) to such contemporary tillers of this acre as the Scandinavians Levi (1971) and Frankenhaeuser (1975a), the American Lazarus (1977) and the British Carruthers (1981).

In the contemporary field, however, are those who ask whether 'stress' can, in the psychosomatic context, be unequivocally defined and measured. Writers such as Hinkle (1977) argue most cogently that the concept of 'stress' does not now provide a meaningful scientific description of those organism-environment relationships which, in the increasing complexity of our contemporary society, generate each individual's symbolic threats and challenges which may, via sense organs, central nervous system and neuroendocrine effectors, jeopardize the optimal functioning of the internal environment (Christie, 1975). Thus the preparations for intense physical activity which Cannon described as concomitants of perception of threat may be an inappropriate response to the symbolic threats of modern socioeconomic life: further, with processes of learning, they may be elicited by other stimuli and sustained by the complexities of conditioning which we now know to be far more intricate than was envisaged in Pavlov's day (Levey and Martin, 1981). Hinkle, then, would abandon the concept of 'stress', arguing that relations between social and health variables should be examined only after precise and concrete definition and measurement of the social variable, specification of individual differences in reaction to the social variable, and identification, enumeration and measurement of the health variable.

> That the relation of people to their society and to the people around them can influence the incidence, the prevalence, the cause, and the mortality of diseases seems clear enough. The questions at issue are the questions of when they do so, under what circumstances, by what mechanisms, and to what extent. Precise answers to these questions will not be forthcoming without a great deal of scientific effort (Hinkle, 1977).

If then, the WHO suggestion that 'psychological stress' may be a potent pathogenic factor is valid, there is an urgent need for adequate definition and measurement of this, or for adoption of an alternative variable.

Psychosomatic Medicine

Having traced the present century's development of ideas about 'psychosomatic disorder', and noted the somewhat unsatisfactory nature of the concept, we should bear in mind the suggestion of Weiner (1976) that there is a need to consider possible sub-categories of illness within the psychosomatic context. There is enduring concern with individual differences in psychophysiological response or vulnerability, and contemporary explorations of sub-categories and psychophysiological response are, therefore, reviewed later in this chapter. At this point, however, we need to look at the development of ideas about the nature of 'psychosomatic medicine'. If the existence of psychosomatic disorder is in question, can there be anything which is as specific as psychosomatic medicine? The title of this chapter seems to pussyfoot round a controversy, but an attempt will now be made to take stock of the contemporary scene and to consider the views of those such as Lader (1972) who question the feasibility and value of retaining the term 'psychosomatic medicine'. Returning again to early origins, we can trace effects of influences other than psychoanalytic in the establishment of the journal 'Psychosomatic Medicine' during 1939. Lipowski (1977a) reminds us that its first editorial defined psychsomatic medicine as a study of the interrelation of the psychological and physiological aspects of all normal and abnormal bodily functions: it was both scientific discipline and an approach to medical practice. There was, in this definition, no implication of causal relations, no statements about psychogenesis of somatic disorder. There was also, however, an absence of reference to the environmental factors which are so obvious a feature of contemporary psychosomatics. Lipowski notes that alongside the dominance of psychoanalytic orientations through the earlier decades of the century, there was also experimental and epidemiological research: into correlations between social stimulus situations, subjects' psychological responses to these and correlated changes in physiological function or health status.

Lipsitt (1977) resists the notion that 'psychosomatic medicine' is in any sense a sub-specialty, seeing it as the very core of medicine itself. He describes the establishment of departments of behavioural science within American medical schools and the development of the 'psychosomatic approach' to medicine, which Lipowski (1977b) regards as necessitating study and management of the dynamic interplay between the individual as both person and biological organism, and the social and physical environments. Spaulding (1977) echoes this message, arguing that 'one of the greatest strengths of the good physician is the ability to take an holistic view of patients and their problems'. Krakowski (1977), in his description of consultation and liaison psychiatry defines the former in terms of interpreting the psychosocial aspects of illness and correlating them with the biological medical model, while Reichsman (1977), in a discussion of teaching objectives, regards one of these as the presentation of a 'model of a physician who has a major interest and at least reasonable competence in two areas of medicine - the psychosocial and the physical-physiologic-biochemical'. Lipsitt (1977), while discussing problems associated with teaching of the psychosomatic approach to medicine, notes the need for it to be 'woven into the overall design of the curriculum' and for the need to 'discover new ways to define its body of knowledge'.

The Psychosomatic Approach to Medicine

Lipowski (1976) seems to provide an appropriate definition of its body of knowledge, with the following summary of its three interrelated aspects.

(1) A science of the relations between biological, psychological and social variables as they pertain to human health and disease.
(2) An approach to the practice of medicine that advocates the inclusion of psychosocial factors in the study, prevention, diagnosis and management of all disease.
(3) Clinical activities at the interface of medicine and the behavioural sciences.

What is evident from Lipowski's definition is the marked similarity between his view of psychosomatic medicine and much of what in Britain has been designated as 'Psychology applied to medicine' (Weinman, 1981), or 'Behavioural science in the medical curriculum' (Winefield, 1981). The impetus for this attempt to weave the holistic approach 'into the overall design of the curriculum' was probably the Todd report of 1968, from the Royal Commission on Medical Education. It quoted the General Medical Council's Recommendations as to Basic Medical Education and 'instruction should be given to the study of man as an organism adapting to his social and psychological, no less than to his physical environment'. Todd includes the 'encouragement of an holistic attitude towards patients'. Nowhere, however, in the Todd report, is this

specifically labelled as the 'psychosomatic' approach to medicine, which reflects, perhaps, the fact that 'there is much confusion nowadays about the subject matter and scope of psychosomatic medicine' (Lipowski, 1977a)!
Summarizing this swift description of the century's developments in psychosomatics we can say that its earlier decades saw a reaction against mechanistic medicine, an attempt to foster the holistic approach, the appraisal of emotional and environmental as well as physical aspects, which had, of course, been evident in some physicians, throughout past centuries. We noted that Freud, Pavlov and Cannon stimulated psychosomatic developments but that the psychoanalytic influence seemed to dominate the decades to mid-century, when there was heavy emphasis on clinical observation which lacked the support of foundational research, a focus of attention on the small number of so-called 'psychosomatic diseases' and a tendency to see 'psychosomatic medicine' as a specialty within the broader spectrum of medical activity. During this period, however, the journal of Psychosomatic Medicine was founded and the need for scientific investigation of relations between psychological and physiological aspects of all normal and abnormal bodily functions emphasized. Such investigation had been building up from the foundations of Cannon and the stimulus of Pavlovian research, and came into much greater prominence after mid-century rejection of a narrower concept of psychosomatic medicine.

PSYCHOLOGY IN CONTEMPORARY PSYCHOSOMATICS

The contemporary view is of a psychosomatic approach to all aspects of medical activity. This is reflected in the present day's unprecedented efforts to provide formal training for medical students in the behavioural sciences (Winefield, 1981), in clinical practice and in foundational research into relations between biological, psychological and social variables. Psychologists are evident in all aspects of contemporary teaching, clinical activity and foundational research. Winefield's comprehensive (1981) review of European, Antipodean and North American approaches to teaching behavioural science indicates the range of material offered, whilst in the UK Weinman's successful textbook (1981) demonstrates the ways in which the relevance of fundamental features in contemporary psychology can be presented to medical students. A more obviously psychobiological approach is adopted by Bakal (1979) in his American textbook, whilst an argument for a specifically psychosomatic orientation in pre-clinical teaching was offered by Christie (1978). Psychologists involved in clinical practice are often clinical psychologists: their activities, however, range well beyond the psychiatric into areas such as general practice (Bhagat, Shillitoe and Lewis, 1982), pain control - as evidenced by Pearce in chapter 7 of this volume - and biofeedback control of cardiovascular disorder (Steptoe, 1981). Steptoe, being a psychophysiologist who undertakes, in addition to treatment and teaching, an active research programme in the foundations of psychosomatics, provides a particularly appropriate bridge into our final section: examination of psychophysiology at work in the foundations of psychosomatics (Christie, 1981b).

Psychophysiology and Psychosomatics

In his meditations on psychosocial epidemiology and its relevance for psychosomatics, Cobb (1977) expressed concern about five aspects of work in his field, the first of which was 'the vague use of certain words that are central to our discipline'. Being also concerned about contemporary imprecision, it behoves me to describe psychophysiology before launching enthusiastically into accounts of its applications in the foundations of psychosomatics! Fortunately, the first volume of this Psychology Survey series carried a chapter on psychophysiology from Coles and Gale (1978), which provides a useful introduction to this multi-disciplinary activity, and offers recommendations for further reading in its listing of major volumes published between 1964 and 1977. To this list should be added publications which have appeared in the last five years: several introductory textbooks which recently came from the States (Stern, Ray and Davies, 1980; Hassett, 1978; and Andreassi, 1980), together with an up-to-date and most comprehensive manual of methodology (Martin and Venables, 1980) and a collection of essays from the foundations of psychosomatics, more than half of which are psychophysiological in orientation (Christie and Mellett, 1981). What, then, is psychophysiology? Coles and Gale (1978) and Siddle and Trasler (1981) both note its concern with relations between psychological and behavioural activity; both describe its work with human, rather than infra-human subjects, its range of non-invasive methods for intact subjects and its attempts to ensure that these are minimally disturbed. This can be contrasted with the work of physiological psychologists, and the point made that for the latter the independent variables are usually biological - brain lesions, drug injections and other manipulations of the

physiological state - while psychophysiologists characteristically manipulate the psychological and examine effects on
the dependent variables of physiology and behaviour. Examples
of this strategy include Dixon (1981), who describes changes
in the electrical activity of the brain following the presentation, at intensities below the level of awareness, of
emotionally disturbing material; Carruthers (1981), who
reports the slowing of heart rate in subjects watching the
filmed violence of 'Clockwork Orange'; and a chapter by Cook,
Christie, Gartshore, Stern and Venables (1981) indicates the
value of recording electrical activity of palmar sweat glands
- electrodermal activity - to provide information about physiological consequences of being a human 'executive monkey'.
    These three psychophysiological methods - electro-
encephalography (EEG), electrocardiography (ECG) and electro-
dermatology (EDA) - are probably the most commonly used of
the electrophysiological techniques: biochemical methods for
analyses of body fluids are more recent additions to the
psychophysiologists' laboratory. A simplified schematic
presentation of some psychophysiological indices and their
interrelations can be found in Christie, Little and Gordon
(1980), and a more complex view of these in the chapter of
Christie and Woodman (1980) which surveys the range of biochemical methods having particular relevance for psychophysiologists. Turning from the dependent to the independent variables of psychophysiologists - the psychological states of
their subjects - these can be roughly classified as affective
and cognitive, as involving emotion and information processing. Physiological correlates which are usually recorded in
the latter states are frequently those of the central nervous
system (CNS) obtained by means of the EEG: aspects of this are
described by Coles and Gale (1978), while Siddle and Trasler
(1981) note the recent development of interest in autonomic
nervous systems (ANS) correlates of attention and information
processing. This growing interest centres on the phenomena of
orientating and habituation; Siddle and Trasler (1981) describe these in their chapter and provide several key
references for further reading. They note, however, as do
Coles and Gale (1978), that early psychophysiology was concerned largely with affective states, with the correlates of
emotion. This is an enduring theme of psychophysiology, as it
has been in psychosomatics, and is an obvious point of contact
between foundational research on normal function and its
applicability to medicine.
    Turning, then, from this description of psychophysiology
to the foundations of psychosomatics (which, according to
Lipowski, 1976, are laid by a 'science of the relations

between biological, psychological and social variables as they pertain to human health and disease'), we can begin to consider examples of contributions which psychophysiologists are making. Many such examples are drawn from the Lipowski, Lipsitt and Whybrow (1977) and the Christie and Mellett (1981) collections: they reflect the continuing influences of Freud, Pavlov and Cannon and the psychosomatic themes of earliest aspects, emotion, individual differences and environment. They reflect, also, the bridging function of psychophysiology (Gale, 1979), and its ability to provide that for which Lipowski (1977a) saw a pressing need in contemporary psychosomatics 'an overarching and unifying science of man's psychobiological functioning in ceaseless interaction with his environment' to 'counteract the growing fragmentation of knowledge about man'. Lipowski regarded the investigative and theoretical issues which are addressed in contemporary psychosomatics as being among the urgent concerns of philosophy as well as of science and of all medicine. The theme of psychology developing from its origins in philosophy and physiology towards the scientific examination of organisms interacting with and in their environments - social, physical and internal - has recently been revived (Christie, 1982), alongside the argument that with traditional distinctions between psychophysiology and physiological psychology becoming blurred at the edges, a more useful approach is via the comprehensiveness of psychophysiology's view. There are, to be sure, those who lose the holistic perspective in their enthusiasm for measurement technology, who 'discuss (in what may appear to the outsider as obsessional and excruciating detail) problems of electronic circuitry, electrode preparation and placement, waveform analysis, computer storage of data' (Gale, 1973), or indulge in 'precise and elegant analysis of meaningless data' (Johnson, 1977), but the 'articles of faith' (Martin, 1975) which underpin psychophysiological endeavour reflect its attempt to examine the multifaceted nature of man's interaction with the environment.

The Psychophysiology of Individual Differences in Vulnerability and Stress

What, then, of such psychophysiological endeavour, has special relevance for contemporary psychosomatics? What molecular analyses of mechanisms whereby psyche is translated into soma, what molar activities in the realms of theoretical overview, what bricks and blueprints for the foundations? An appropriate point for departure is David Graham's Presidential Address to the Society for Psychophysiological Research (1971), in which he described psychosomatics as 'clinical psychophysiology'. This is the Graham who was introduced in discussion of the concept of a psychosomatic disorder, but we are more concerned here with the theme of earliest aspects of dysfunction, with what Graham (1971) describes as the 'small physiological steps in the direction of full blown illness', and with psychophysiologists' investigation of these.

Returning once again to Lipowski's first and foundational aspect of psychosomatic activity - its science of relations between the biological, psychological and social variables - this is concerned with human health as well as disease. However, the distinction between these is not wholly clear. Wadsworth and Ingham (1981) describe a fundamental shift in the patterns of contemporary illness; infectious disease, with its swifter time course, having given way to diseases which have less clearly defined onset, longer and more variable duration and less certainty of outcome, shown schematically in figures 3A and 3B of Wadsworth, Butterfield and Blaney (1971). The less clearly defined onset has stimulated the interest of psychophysiologists, as well as social scientists, in the earliest aspect of dysfunction, in the pre-consultation period before health begins to be regarded as disease.

Psychophysiologists look for markers, for indications of abnormal function, which might serve to distinguish individuals who are or may become at risk. An easily appreciated example is that of a subject whose blood pressure rises noticeably when exposed to laboratory stimuli and is slow in returning to the pre-stimulation level. We are inevitably caught up in discussion of individual differences as well as of earliest aspects and can usefully refer to Roessler and Engel (1977) for more detailed treatment of this theme. We are back to a consideration of specificity, and are here concerned with individual-response specificity (IRS) in our example of the subject whose blood pressure rises in the laboratory situation. A variant of this has been regularly demonstrated in hypertensive patients, but now the idiosyncratic response acquires the label of 'symptom specificity': hypertensive patients have been compared with arthritic patients and the latter are seen to respond to laboratory stimuli with increased tension in muscles associated with their diseased joints, in contrast to the blood pressure increase of the hypertensives.

In contrast to IRS there is stimulus-response specificity or stereotypy (SRS), evident if a given stimulus evokes in most subjects a similar physiological response. A possible example of SRS to which we shall return later, is the pattern of physiological change which accompanies perception of an anger-provoking stimulus. Sufficient evidence now exists to suggest that there is a difference between the physiology of fear and that of anger. This appears to be in contrast to the view of Cannon (1929) that such physiological responses were undifferentiated, a view which was supported by Scandinavian workers such as Levi (1972) and Frankenhaeuser (1975b). Roessler and Engel (1977), in their discussion of IRS and SRS, lead readers also into consideration of generalized activation or arousal: this theme was included in the Coles and Gale (1978) chapter and is not pursued further at this point. What should be noted here is Roessler and Engel's (1977) observation that the various forms of IRS probably depend upon previous learning (conditioning) and genetic endowment: they reiterate the fact previously emphasized by Engel (1972) that there is need for longitudinal research to increase our understanding of IRS and of its determinants.

Another approach to the investigation of individual differences in psychophysiological response has been the examination of sub-groups having known differences in their scores on personality inventories. The Eysenck Personality Inventory (EPI), with its scores for extraversion (E) and neuroticism (N), is probably familiar to all readers; Levey and Martin (1981) remind us that Eysenck (1967) regards as orthogonal the two dimensions of extraversion-introversion and neuroticism-stability, which were defined by factor analysis: the physiological bases of these are, respectively, the cortical arousal system mediated by the reticular formation and autonomic activation centred in the limbic system. Introverts are viewed as having more active electrocortical arousal while subjects with high N scores are said to be characterized by more labile autonomic activation. The ego-strength (E_s) dimension of the Minnesota Multiphasic Personality Inventory (MMPI) was used by Roessler and his colleagues through the decade's research which he, as another President of the Society for Psychophysiological Research, reported in the early 1970s (Roessler, 1973). From findings in a number of laboratory studies, in which subjects with differing E_s scores had been exposed to a range of stimuli, Roessler reported that high E_s scores are associated with appropriate degrees of autonomic activation: greater with a greater degree of challenge or stimulus intensity. This appropriate patterning of autonomic activation and de-activation is linked, by Roessler, with the appropriateness of these subjects' perception and interpretation of situations and stimuli: their 'coping' behaviour. In contrast, the low E_s scorers showed invariant autonomic response to challenge or to what Handlon (1962) designated as 'easement': situations in which deactivation, relaxation, stand-down are appropriate. Roessler (1973) attributes this invariant response to an active process of suppression, linked with a distortion of perceptual appraisal of the related stimulus input. One is reminded of Freudian origins, and it is interesting to compare the Roessler (1973) model with the 'perceptual defence' and its physiological correlates which are described by Dixon (1981).

Roessler reported a significant inverse correlation between the Es score of the MMPI and the N score of the EPI. This American finding has been replicated in a British population (described in Cook, Christie, Gartshore, Stern and Venables, 1981). So it may be useful to examine European studies similar to Roessler's, but where the EPI has been used. In looking at these, we are particularly interested in the phenomena of autonomic activation and homeostatic return to the pre-stimulus state, that is, at both response and recovery. Post-challenge recovery has received far, far less attention than what is often designated as the 'stress' response. Some examinations of the recovery from a working week which may be evident after the weekend are described in Christie (1975), whilst investigations of the mid-day meal break and its tranquillizing effects were reported in Christie, Cort and Venables (1976) and Christie and McBrearty (1979a). In all these studies there was evidence of individual differences in recovery being associated with the E and N dimensions of personality. In more molecular examination of laboratory response, Johansson and Frankenhaeuser (1973) and Bull and Nethercott (1972) had suggested that higher N scorers showed slower homeostatic recovery after both psychological and physical challenges. Since the noise-avoidance task used by Stern (1966), for human work similar to the 'executive monkey' studies of Brady and his co-workers, offers the possibility of both psychological and physical stressors, it has been used in several studies to examine autonomic response and recovery in a rest-test-rest paradigm (Cook, Christie, Gartshore, Stern and Venables, 1981), with subjects scored for E, N and E_S. The most obvious findings related to N and E_S: high N or low E_S being associated with less autonomic response to challenge and less efficient homeostatic recovery (or even an increase in autonomic activity reminiscent of the 'executive monkey' study rebound phenomenon) in the post-challenge rest. There was evidence that Roessler's model is valuable for examination of 'coping' and its correlates, and it is tempting, within the psychosomatic context, to leap from laboratory

149

evidence of apparently maladaptive response and recovery to 'general psychophysiological propensity toward disease' and 'psychological stress', which Eastwood (1977) suggested as focal points for research on individual vulnerability. Tempting it is to leap thus, but caution requires us to examine further such aspects as the ecological validity of laboratory-based studies and the concept of 'psychological stress'.

First, it is important to consider whether the conditions of the psychophysiological laboratory are such that data collected there reflect merely the subject's responses to, and in, the experimental environment, and bear no relation to the outside world. The psychophysiological effects of subject-experimenter-situational interaction were reviewed by Christie and Todd (1975). Ways of avoiding the many pitfalls of laboratory-based research have been described by Gale and Baker (1981), and arguments for moving out from laboratory to life presented by Carruthers (1981) and Christie and McBrearty (1981).

From Johnson (1977) comes the much-needed reminder that response in one organ system will influence the activity of others, that such a complexity of feedback mechanisms demands sophisticated monitoring, and that appropriate data analysis is essential. He suggests also that there is need to 'take a multivariate look' at the total organism - at work, at play, in sleep - with 'special emphasis on how the living organism maintains itself at optimal levels in the midst of an on-slaught of exogenous and endogenous disturbances'. Johnson views current instrumentation and methodology as being sufficiently developed to make this feasible, although he believes that the adequacy of theoretical formulations is yet to be tested. The task is even more demanding, though, when one considers the holistic approach of those psychophysiologists who are attempting to measure subjective and behavioural (including analysis of speech content, as by Gottschalk, 1977) as well as physiological variables. Patkai (1977) describes this approach, while Mackay (1980) provides a comprehensive chapter on mood assessment. There remains, however, the need adequately to analyse the data generated from the multivariate look, and the holistic approach: my colleague Spencer Bennett offers his viewpoint in the following paragraph.

There is a growing need in many areas related to psychology (Bennett, Smith and Wedderburn, 1982; Youngman, 1979), including psychosomatics, for a more widespread use of multivariate analysis and techniques. In this chapter, several points and problem areas have been described for which such techniques are eminently suitable. Firstly, a holistic approach emphasizes that the multiple determination of behaviour is rich and varied, including situational, social, biological and personality variables. It is not enough to recognize multiple causation and then proceed to isolate and manipulate the components of such a 'determination vector', as the classical, experimental approach has sought to do, via the techniques of experimental control and randomization. This is because interactions exist, no doubt of great complexity, with each variable modifying and qualifying the others. Secondly, a holistic approach recognizes that on the other side of the equation exists a correspondingly complex 'response vector' or 'pattern' containing a network of varyingly related behavioural and physiological variables. Multivariate techniques are needed to describe and analyse the relationships between such vectors. Thirdly, the fact that determination and response patterns comprise variables which are multidimensional again underlines the need for appropriate analytical techniques. Thus, conceptual clarification and construct explication can both be advanced by such means. Fourthly, there is a need, as this chapter makes clear, to meet the challenge of the complexity described above, not just in the laboratory, but in applied settings. In the latter, classical experimental control and randomization is frequently impossible. Multivariate methods allow control to be exercised statistically, and therefore can be of great value in unravelling relationships in such situations. In addition, the practical value of applied work is often not gauged in terms of statistical significance, but in terms of the strength of relationships, in the sense of prediction precision. Where multiple determination exists, multiple-prediction models are essential if prediction is the most important consideration. Fifthly, the progress of psychosomatics may in part be evaluated in terms of its ability to identify and classify individuals 'at risk'. Discriminant and cluster analyses are techniques that are eminently suitable for such a task where the relevant dimensions of variation are as many and as interrelated as they no doubt are. Use of multivariate techniques is, of course, not new to practically any area of psychology. But their use (and the kind of thinking or theorizing which is associated with them) is not widespread amongst researchers in the more experimental/biological areas, and specifically not in psychosomatics. 'Multivariate thinking' involves conceptualizing relationships between families or patterns of elements, and inhibiting the tendency to go back to thinking of elements in isolation. For instance, a discriminant function analysis may identify a group of individuals 'at risk' in terms of a weighted combination of the three variables, A, B, C. But this can be quite consistent with the observation that in the 'at risk' group predicted by the analysis, individuals can be found who are totally different on any variable taken by itself, or indeed any two variables out of the set. It is the pattern that matters, and the importance of individual variables is subjugated to this pattern.

Turning from problems associated with measurement of response variables to the conceptual chaos associated with the term 'psychological stress', Cobb (1977) expressed concern about the circularity evident in stress-strain reasoning, while that 'most grandly imprecise term in the dictionary of science' (Söderberg, 1967) caused Hinkle (1977) to argue against use of the word 'stress', as we saw at an earlier point. One has sympathy with this view, especially after surveying the range of its meanings described, for example, in Cox's (1978) opening chapter. Attempts are, however, still made to conceptualize 'stress' in terms adequate for research use, especially for use in the foundations of psychosomatics. One such attempt was offered by Christie and McBrearty (1979b) and will be used to structure the remainder of this section on 'psychological stress', drawing in some earlier material on individual differences.

It is customary to launch into consideration of stress with at least a nod towards Selye (1950) as its putative progenitor, and a description of the General Adaptation Syndrome as a non-specific response (in laboratory animals) to a range of damaging or alarming stimuli. Hinkle (1977), however, traces the word to its Latin origins, but describes its seventeenth-century English use for 'hardships, straits, adversity or affliction'. Through the subsequent two centuries the term began to mean force, pressure, strain, etc., exerted upon material, and on a person physically or psychologically. Then, writes Hinkle, it developed the meaning of an object's or individual's resistance to the distorting effect of outside forces and the attempt to return to its earlier state. In nineteenth-century physics and engineering the terms stress, strain and load had quite specific meanings expressable in mathematical terms, a feature which contrasts sharply with the use in biology and medicine. Wolff (1950) discussed 'life stress' and its relations to disease, the WHO implicated 'psychological stress' and the Levi (1971, 1975, 1978) reports of symposia sponsored by this body all carry the same title 'Society, Stress and Disease': everywhere the suggestion that stress and disease are linked, yet everywhere the grand imprecision, and inevitably the questioning of Hinkle about whether stress does denote a variable that can be identified unambiguously, counted, and measured, whether there is a state of stress in the living organism and, if so, whether its identification, measurement and description aids our understanding of how and when disease occurs. Hinkle concludes that the stress concept was heuristically valuable, but is no longer necessary and in some ways is now a hindrance. Part of Hinkle's argument appears to depend on the inappropriateness of Selye's concept for description of human interaction with the social and physical environments, for the reception, perception and interpretation of stimuli, for the processing of information about the challenging, threatening, or supportive aspects of our so-called 'civilized' life. There would appear to be more relevance for a consideration of the 'psychological stress' of contemporary living in Cannon's (1929) account of the psychophysiological preparation for fight or flight - the phenomena of the 'alert' signal - than in Selye's description of survival under siege conditions. Two points, however, could be made: first, that some of Selye (1971) in more recent times has greater relevance for contemporary disorders such as ischaemic heart disease (IHD); and second, that Warburton (1979) has traced links between the psychophysiology of sustained attention (when information processing may be carried out in demanding circumstances) and the neuroendocrine 'stress' responses of an organism challenged by the difficulty of efficiently monitoring sensory input and maintaining a state of optimal electrocortical arousal.

Returning, however, to a conceptualization of stress which is appropriate for the psychophysiological foundations of psychosomatics - to one which draws in elements of our earlier themes such as Cannon and conditioning; perception and personality; adaptiveness of psychophysiological responses and epidemiology; IRS, SRS and activation - we should begin with Cannon, or rather with Bernard and the relative constancy of the internal environment. It can be said that Cannon (1929) contributed to psychosomatics the notion of psychological state as a precursor of physiological preparation for physical activity. The textbook descriptions of emotions associated with fight and flight catalogue autonomic adjustments and metabolic mobilization for the support of active motor function. A contemporary variant of this is the notion of generalized activation, varying in intensity, which we encountered in Coles and Gale (1978) and Roessler and Engel (1977). This psychophysiological response to stimulus or challenge may be detected in a range of electrophysiological and biochemical indices. In much of the literature this is then described as a 'stress' response, and there is concern with the physiological disorder which may be a consequence of 'stress'. Before moving forward from this point we need to note Kimball's (1982) discussion of stress and disease, then exclude from our consideration the phenomena which he regarded as being 'social' and 'psychological' disorder: we are concerned at this point only with physical derangement, and its precursors. Now, when there is generalized activation there may be subjective feelings of distress (Rees, 1975) or strain, but unless this 'psychological stress' is associated with evidence of 'physiological strain' it would seem to be less relevant for the present discussion.

What, then, is 'physiological strain'? It was suggested (Christie, 1975) that this is the state in which homeostatic mechanisms are strained in the maintenance of optimal conditions in the internal environment. Further, that appropriate physiological response to challenge and recovery in easement - as seen, for example, in the low N and high E_s subjects - reduces the risk of developing a 'stressed' system, one where there is physiological strain and in which the optimal conditions of the internal environment are jeopardized. Cobb (1977) maintained that these phenomena were in urgent need of research: his term 'elasticity' excellently describes the flexible and adaptive responses we have described.

It is obvious that we are concerned here with a general activation and have not considered the contribution of IRS, or its determinants, which may well be genetic, the consequence of conditioning, or even of the 'hiving off' of conscious experience which Dixon (1981) discusses while relating subliminal perception to psychosomatic dysfunction. It is obvious, also, that we have yet to consider SRS. That comes later, in the context of cardiovascular disease. At this point, however, we should note the relevance of appropriate perception and interpretation which Roessler's model emphasizes: it is interesting to see these developments from Freud in discussions of perceptual defence, such as those by Dixon or Roessler. (We can note also the increase in attention being paid to measures whereby homeostatic recovery may, perhaps, be hastened by relaxation training, hypnosis, autogenic training, biofeedback ... or whatever. However, as chapter 8 of the present volume deals with some of this material it is not pursued here any further.) In conclusion to this section we must reiterate the message that even if one has demonstrated, in the psychophysiological laboratory, the existence of mal-adaptive response and recovery, and evidence of a stressed system, longitudinal studies and complementary work from psychosocial epidemiology are needed to confirm that the absence of 'elasticity' can indeed be a precursor of disease.

The Psychophysiology of Angry Emotion

We have chosen to examine 'earliest aspects' of physical disorder in the context of precursor 'markers', which it is hoped are detectable by psychophysiological techniques. Other earliest aspects have necessarily had to be omitted, aspects such as intra-uterine (Barrett, 1981) and neonatal (Mills, 1981) experience, and work with children at risk for schizo-phrenia (Venables, 1981). Some discussion of this disorder will be included in the section on environment, but at this point we move from the themes of early aspects and individual differences to some examination of emotion, focussing on fear and anger, and the current status of the suggestion that there is SRS associated with these two states. The early history of this theme - the work of Ax (1953) and Funkenstein (1956) - is probably familiar to readers: for our purposes we can focus on anger and on the suggestion that body fluid levels of the catecholamine nor-adrenaline are increased in angry, hostile, aggressive states. During the two decades following Funken-stein's work in the 1950s there was support, particularly from Scandinavians such as Levi and Frankenhaeuser, for the view that there was not SRS associated with nor-adrenaline output, but that quantity rather than quality - the intensity of emotion - determined whether body fluid levels were increased. Since then, however, work from a number of sources (references to which are available in Christie and Woodman, 1980) suggests again that nor-adrenaline increases are associated with various aspects of aggressive state.

Our particular interest here is in the possible link between this and the development of cardiovascular disorder as, for example, indicated in Carruthers (1981), who describes the work of himself and Taggart - a cardiologist - amid the aggressive competitiveness of racing drivers in circuit condi-tions, and in the conflict of rush-hour traffic! Interest in the aggressive state stemmed from American epidemiological approaches to coronary or ischaemic heart disease (IHD: see

Christie, 1975, for a brief description) which demonstrated that the so-called Type A behaviour pattern was associated with double the risk, in American males, of death from heart disease (see Denolin, 1982: papers by Marmot; Pichot; Kornitzer and co-workers; Rosenman; Haynes and Feinleib; Bernet and co-workers). Two features of Type A behaviour which have particular importance are its extreme time-consciousness and the response of aggressive competitiveness in environmental situations conducive to this. We have, then, the demonstration of links between psychological state and the somatic condition of cardiovascular pathology, but a need to demonstrate the neuroendocrine and metabolic mechanisms whereby psyche is translated into soma. Carruthers and Taggart focussed on the increased production of nor-adrenaline, which not only has the effect of raising blood pressure - and hypertension is a known risk factor for IHD - but is also associated with raised levels of blood fats, even in fasting subjects.

The putative link between dietary fat - specifically the saturated animal fats - and IHD (via the development of atherosclerosis) is familiar to all who see Flora, and similar, advertisements: but Carruthers (1974) crisply comments that 'it's not what you eat, but what eats you ...!'. What must be emphasized, however, is that IHD is the result of interaction between a range of predisposing and precipitating factors - such as raised blood pressure, smoking, serum cholesterol, obesity - as well as the possible involvement of the psychosocial aspects emphasized by Carruthers (1974, 1981) and by Marmot (1981). The latter's approach is characterized by an epidemiologist's attention to the sociocultural environment, which we will touch on in the final section. Meanwhile, we should give some attention to the emphasis laid by psychophysiologists such as Obrist (1981), Brener (1982) and Edelberg (1973) on the close links, in our biological make-up, between psychological state and preparation for action. Many psychophysiologists have commented in their various ways on the fact that we are organisms hard-wired for motor response to signals from the psyche, and that this 'stone age' mismatch between psyche and soma may be a precursor of physical disorder. As Levey and Martin (1981) write, 'we deal with an organism equipped with a number of primitive subcortical mechanisms designed to ensure survival in the jungle, and a highly differentiated cortex which is nevertheless unable to inform the subcortex that we no longer live there'.

Obrist and Brener focus on the close links between cardiac and vascular function and on the provision of metabolic back-up, such as increased oxygen, for intense physical activity. Local metabolic signals can influence vascular activity, ensuring reduction in function when local metabolic conditions indicate that, for example, reduced physical activity is reducing the amount of oxygen needed for muscle cells. Meanwhile, however, in our inactive 'civilized' living, symbolic threat - be it from the exam paper, the aggressive colleague or the overdraft - may be ensuring that neural signals stimulate heart activity and that the two systems, the cardiac and the vascular, are receiving apparently discrepant information, and functioning in a discordant manner. Again, the longitudinal study of individuals who can be monitored in 'real-life' conditions is an essential route for testing this psychosomatic hypothesis. It is one which appears to have undoubted heuristic value and is an intriguing example of Cannon's enduring influence on the field.

Psychophysiology and Environments

Lastly, the most recent addition to the themes of psychosomatics: that of environment. Lipowski (1977a) observed that when the journal Psychosomatic Medicine was launched in 1939 there was no evidence of interest in this, and Kimball (1970), in his review of conceptual developments, comments on the 'shift from concern with intrapsychic events and disease to emphasis on the environments in which illness occurs'. This is evident, for example, in Marmot's (1981) description of epidemiological approaches to the origins of cardiovascular disorder, approaches which range from comparisons of Japanese migrants in Hawaii and San Francisco to the longitudinal study of British civil servants (Marmot, Rose, Shipley and Hamilton, 1978). There has also been development of concern with the environments in which illness is treated: Gordon (1981) provides a comprehensive review of this area as does Moos (1977), who notes the problems inherent in measuring the psychosocial environment and its specific features. The effects of the psychological environment on the physiological, dependent variables, have been examined by a range of workers: we earlier saw the interest in psychophysiological laboratory environments and to this we can now add the Leiderman and Shapiro volume of 1965 which seemed to be the prelude to the development of 'social psychophysiology' reviewed by Shapiro and Schwartz (1970), Schwartz and Shapiro (1973), and to the work reviewed in the more recent chapters of Christie and Todd (1975), and Gale and Baker (1981).

One feature which is of interest in contemporary psychosomatics is the effect, on schizophrenic patients who are living at home and treated with maintenance phenothiazines, of the emotional quality of this particularly potent psychosocial environment. It is of particular interest because it points us towards those characteristics of schizophrenia which suggest its relevance as a 'psychosomatic' topic, and because it offers an opportunity of introducing some consideration of psychotropic drugs and their use in a psychosomatic context. Leff and Tarrier (1981) describe the gulf between genetic and environmental theories of schizophrenia and the psychosomatic bridge between these offered by their work in the Social Psychiatry Unit at the Institute of Psychiatry, London. As recent findings suggest that the most generous estimate of the genetic contribution is no more than 70 per cent there is, they argue, room for environmental influences to operate. The results of earlier drug trials - which had involved life events questionnaires (Brown and Birley, 1968) and examination of these events in relation to schizophrenic patients on maintenance therapy - suggested that phenothiazines protect patients against the onslaughts of everyday life, but that in some of them, significant life events had broken through the protection, precipitating relapse (Brown, Birley and Wing, 1972). The factor which, it was believed, offered the protection to schizophrenic patients who had experienced the same number of significant life events but did not relapse, was the emotional climate of the home: a low-key atmosphere offering protection against relapse.

In the high-keyed emotional atmosphere, however, its deleterious influence was significantly reduced if the patient could reduce social contact with relatives to something less than around 35 hours per week. In this case, the low-key atmosphere of the home was beneficial to the patient: in relation to beneficial environments and heart disease, Marmot (1981) has reviewed European evidence for the protective effect of a supportive spouse and has suggested that the Japanese culture has protective features. Psychophysiology has contributed to examination of the physiological responses of schizophrenic patients to the key relatives in the home environment, but despite Bovard's (1959) review of the protective effects of social support in situations capable of generating sympathetic activation, there is still a dearth of theoretical or empirical material from psychophysiology to further productive research into protective environments. It does seem evident that there is more concern with dysphoric than with euphoric states (Stern, Farr and Ray, 1975), with anxiety rather than tranquillity (Wenger, 1966), yet a contribution to the psychophysiology of supportive phenomena may come via the investigation of quasi-mystical and similar states, reviewed in chapter 8.

Meanwhile, we can continue to collect evidence about the deleterious effects of environments from Ostfeld and D'Atri's (1977) review, which covers 'urban stress', crowding, information overload, noise, driving, and so on. A more specific and growing concern with deleterious aspects of the working environment is being expressed in Europe: some features of this concern were reviewed by Christie and Cullen (in press) under the label of 'industrial psychosomatics', covering such themes as the effects of shiftworking; the changing nature of industrial activity in which there is a replacement of physical action and human interaction by solitary monitoring in a state of continued inertness; and the importance of having control over one's activities. Data from a longitudinal study of nearly 20,000 British civil servants, mentioned earlier, showed that the lower the occupational grade the greater the risk of heart disease. The differences could not be accounted for in terms of traditional risk factors, and they showed an inversion of the trends reported in earlier decades of the century. Such phenomena encourage the investigation of 'occupational stress'; a selection of its topics is evident in Mackay and Cox (1979).

SUMMARY AND CONCLUSIONS

We have rambled far round the psychosomatic field: or perhaps it has been a swift gallop on a succession of the writer's hobby horses! What, then, can be said to summarize the characteristics of contemporary psychosomatics? First, that in the words of Crisp (1975), 'the notion that disease arises from the complex interplay of multiple factors over the years, existing and arising with the environment and the individual's make-up, appeals mostly to those of a divergent turn of mind and perhaps also to those most prepared to tolerate a degree of uncertainty'. There are undoubtedly degrees of uncertainty tolerated within contemporary psychosomatics and it is an eclectic area of activity which is accepting of all comers: from research; clinical and teaching activities; from the behavioural and life sciences; from medicine and surgery; with orientations developed via Freud, Pavlov and Cannon. Moving, however, to the first of Lipowski's aspects - the scientific foundations which have been the central theme of this chapter - there is less scope for toleration of ambiguity, for confusions of conceptualization: if science is, as Lord Kelvin (1889) has claimed, measurement, one must have a clear idea of that which one measures. While psychophysiologists now possess an impressive array of measuring devices for monitoring an impressive range of physiological functions, their attention could usefully be turned from bricks to blueprints, from the production of discrete bits of data to the generation of heuristic models for psychosomatics.

There are exceptions, of course. Obrist's (1981) view of cardiac-vascular mismatch has obvious value and relevance, but there are few attempts to conceptualize adequately a 'stressed system' in terms which could provide for the follow-through of a longitudinal study, tracing high risk response to development of disorder. One aspect of the stressed system may well be an absence of 'elasticity', and all too often the opportunity of examining this is lost when response to - but not recovery from - challenge is measured. Further, there is an obvious need for adequate analysis of the data collected in a holistic approach to individual differences in vulnerability: if one has, for example, circadian records of 'real life' response on several channels of Medilog tape and subjective reports as well as recorded indices of behaviour, what is the appropriate way of assessing the significance of such a compilation?

Returning from Bennett's approach to the problems of data analysis and moving to the notion of 'psychosomatic disorders', we have seen the apparent demise of 'psychosomatic medicine', and the increase in enthusiasm for a 'psychosomatic approach' to medicine. However, there is evidence of an enduring unwillingness wholly to relinquish the idea of specifically 'psychosomatic' disorders, disorders in which the psychological aspects of aetiology are particularly evident. Weiner is outstanding in the field of psychosomatic activity and currently editor of Psychosomatic Medicine. An earlier editorial (Weiner, 1976) indicates his views regarding the need to reappraise the concept of a 'psychosomatic' disorder. There may indeed, as he suggests, be sub-categories of patients who can be classified in terms of a 'psychosomatic' aetiology. The earlier approaches via psychoanalytic routes may now be unacceptable, but the suggestion of Dixon (1981), for example, that those individuals in whom perceptual defence is associated with an 'unconscious' somatic response, has undoubted mileage. Another aspect of our 'unconscious' activity is the complexity of conditioned response which can be established and maintained, as Levey and Martin (1981) described. That there are individual differences in conditionability should set us searching also along this route towards vulnerability, towards a possible sub-category, reflecting an inheritance from Pavlov. Lastly, from origins in Cannon, and the focus on mobilization for action evident in muscle, in metabolism, in cardiovascular adjustments, comes the question of whether our primitive programming for fight and flight is a maladaptive response to our largely symbolic contemporary threats which are not normally met with intense activity. Individual vulnerability for development of this type of dysfunction remains as an area to which research attention could be directed. An ideal programme of investigation would involve longitudinal examination, with psychophysiological measurement of high risk individuals: lacking, perhaps, the elasticity of Cobb (1977), and having the low E_s of Roessler (1973)? Epidemiological approaches would complement laboratory and field examination, and eventually one might be able to assess the significance of the suggestion that the stone-age response, stimulated by competitive aspects of the Western environment, is the source of a 'psychosomatic' disorder.

REFERENCES

Andreassi, J. L. (1980). Psychophysiology: Human behavior and physiological response. New York: Oxford University Press.

Ax, A. (1953). The physiological differentiation between fear and anger in humans. Psychosomatic Medicine, 5, 433-442.

Bakal, D. H. (1979). Psychology and Medicine: Psychobiological dimensions of health and illness. London: Tavistock.

Barrett, J. H. W. (1981). Intra-uterine experience and its long-term outcome. In M. J. Christie and P. G. Mellett (eds), Foundations of Psychosomatics. Chichester: Wiley.

Bennett, S. and Bowers, D. (1976). An Introduction to Multivariate Techniques for Social and Behavioural Sciences. London: MacMillan.

Bennett, S., Smith, P. A. and Wedderburn, A. A. I. (1982). Towards a synthesis of research findings for applications to shiftworkers. Proceedings of the 6th International Symposium on Night- and Shift-Work. Kyoto, Japan.

Bhagat, R., Shillitoe, R. and Lewis, A. (1982). We can save time by sitting with patients. General Practitioner, 24, September, 68.

Bovard, E. W. (1959). The effects of social stimuli on the response to stress. Psychological Review, 66, 267-277.

Brady, J. V., Porter, R. W., Conrad, O. and Mason, J. W. (1958). Avoidance behaviour and the development of gastroduodenal ulcers. Journal of the Experimental Analysis of Behaviour, 1, 69-72.

Brener, J. M. (1982). Excessive cardiac activity. Bulletin of The British Psychological Society, 35, A21-A22.

Brown, G. W. and Birley, J. L. T. (1968). Crises and life changes and the onset of schizophrenia. Journal of Health and Social Behaviour, 9, 203-214.

Brown, G. W., Birley, J. L. T. and Wing, J. K. (1972). Influence of family life on the course of schizophrenic disorders: a replication. British Journal of Psychiatry, 121, 241-258.

Bull, R. H. C. and Nethercott, R. E. (1972). Physiological recovery and personality. British Journal of Clinical Psychology, 11, 297.

Cannon, W. B. (1929). Bodily Changes in Pain, Hunger, Fear and Rage (2nd edn). New York: Appleton-Century-Crofts.

Carruthers, M. (1974). The Western Way of Death. London: Davis-Poynter.

Carruthers, M. (1981). Field studies: emotion and -blockade. In M. J. Christie and P. G. Mellett (eds), Foundations of Psychosomatics. Chichester: Wiley.

Christie, M. J. (1975). The psychosocial environment and precursors of disease. In P. H. Venables and M. J. Christie (eds), Research in Psychophysiology. London: Wiley.

Christie, M. J. (1976). Electrodermal activity. In O. W. Hill (ed.), Modern Trends in Psychosomatic Medicine. London: Butterworths.

Christie, M. J. (1978). Bodies and minds revisited. Bulletin of The British Psychological Society, 31, 355-357.

Christie, M. J. (1981a). Electrodermal activity in the 1980s: a review. Journal of the Royal Society of Medicine, 74, 616-622.

Christie, M. J. (1981b). Foundations of psychosomatics. In M. J. Christie and P. G. Mellett (eds), Foundations of Psychosomatics. Chichester: Wiley.

Christie, M. J. (1982). Psychophysiology at work. Inaugural lecture, University of Bradford.

Christie, M. J., Cort, J. and Venables, P. H. (1976). Individual differences in post-prandial state: exploration with palmar skin potentials. Journal of Psychosomatic Research, 20, 501-508.

Christie, M. J. and Cullen, J. H. In A. Krakowski (ed.), Psychosomatic Medicine. In press.

Christie, M. J., Little, B. C. and Gordon, A. M. (1980). Peripheral indices of depressive states. In H. M. Van Praag, M. H. Lader, O. J. Rafaelsen and E. J. Sachar (eds), Handbook of Biological Psychiatry, Part II, Brain mechanisms and abnormal behaviour: psychophysiology. New York: Marcel Dekker.

Christie, M. J. and McBrearty, E. M. (1979a). Psychophysiological investigations of post lunch state in male and female subjects. Ergonomics, 22, 307-323.

Christie, M. J. and McBrearty, E. M. (1979b). Stress - response and recovery. In C. Mackay and T. Cox (eds), Response to Stress: Occupational aspects. Guildford: IPC.

Christie, M. J. and McBrearty, E. M. (1981). The laboratory environment, psychophysiology and psychosomatics. In G. KoptagelIlal and O. Tuncer (eds), Proceedings of the 13th European Conference on Psychosomatic Research. Istanbul: University Press.

Christie, M. J. and Mellett, P. G. (eds) (1981). Foundations of Psychosomatics. Chichester: Wiley.

Christie, M. J. and Todd, J. A. (1975). Experimenter-subject-situational interactions. In P. H. Venables and M. J. Christie (eds), Research in Psychophysiology. London: Wiley.

Christie, M. J. and Woodman, D. D. (1980). Biochemical methods. In I. Martin and P. H. Venables (eds), Psychophysiological Techniques. Chichester: Wiley.

Cobb, S. (1977). Epilogue: mediations on psychosomatic medicine. In Z. J. Lipowski, D. R. Lipsitt and P. C. Whybrow (eds), Psychsomatic Medicine: Current trends and clinical applications. New York: Oxford University Press.

Coles, M. G. H. and Gale, A. (1978). Psychophysiology. In B. M. Foss (ed.), Psychology Survey No. 1. London: George Allen & Unwin.

Cook, E., Christie, M. J., Gartshore, S., Stern, R. and Venables, P. H. (1981). After the 'executive monkey'. In M. J. Christie and P. G. Mellett (eds), Foundations of Psychosomatics. Chichester: Wiley.

Cox, T. (1978). Stress. London: Macmillan.

Crisp, A. H. (1975). Psychosomatic research today: a clinician's overview. International Journal of Psychiatry in Medicine, 6, 159-160.

Denolin, H. (ed.) (1982). Psychological Problems Before and After Myocardial Infarction. Advances in Cardiology, 29. Basel: Karger.

Dixon, N. F. (1981). Psychosomatic disorder: a special case of subliminal perception. In M. J. Christie and P. G. Mellett (eds), Foundations of Psychosomatics. Chichester: Wiley.

Eastwood, M. R. (1977). Epidemiological studies in psychosomatic medicine. In Z. J. Lipowski, D. R. Lipsitt and P. C. Whybrow (eds), Psychosomatic Medicine: Current trends and clinical applications. New York: Oxford University Press.

Edelberg, R. (1973). Mechanisms of electrodermal adaptations for locomotion, manipulation or defence. In E. Stellar and J. M. Sprague (eds), Progress in Physiological Psychology, 6. New York: Academic Press.

Engel, B. T. (1972). Response specificity. In N. S. Greenfield and R. A. Sternbach (eds), Handbook of Psychophysiology. New York: Holt, Rinehart & Winston.

Eysenck, H. J. (1967). The Biological Basis of Personality. Springfield, Ill.: Charles C. Thomas.

Frankenhaeuser, M. (1975a). Sympathetic-adrenomedullary activity, behaviour and the psychosocial environment. In P. H. Venables and M. J. Christie (eds), Research in Psychophysiology. London: Wiley.

Frankenhaeuser, M. (1975b). Experimental approaches to the study of catecholamines and emotion. In L. Levi (ed.), Emotions, their Parameters and Measurement. New York: Raven Press.

Funkenstein, D. H. (1956). Norepinephrine-like and epinephrine-like substances in relation to human behaviour Journal of Nervous and Mental Diseases, 124, 58-65.

Gale, A. (1973). The psychophysiology of individual differences: studies of extraversion and the EEG. In P. Kline (ed.), New Approaches in Psychological Measurement. London: Wiley.

Gale, A. (1979). Psychophysiology: a bridge between disciplines. Inaugural lecture, University of Southampton.

Gale, A. and Baker, S. (1981). In vitro? Some effects of laboratory environments, with particular reference to the psychophysiology experiment. In M. J. Christie and P. G. Mellett (eds), Foundations of Psychosomatics. Chichester: Wiley.

Gordon, A. (1981). The treatment environment. In M. J. Christie and P. G. Mellett (eds), Foundations of Psychosomatics. Chichester: Wiley.

Gottschalk, L. A. (1977). Quantification and psychological indicators of emotions: the content analysis of speech and other objective measures of psychological states. In Z. J.

Lipowski, D. R. Lipsitt and P. C. Whybrow (eds), Psychosomatic Medicine: Current trends and clinical applications. New York: Oxford University Press.

Graham, D. T. (1971). Psychophysiology and medicine. Psychophysiology, 8, 121-131.

Handlon, J. H. (1962). Hormonal activity and individual responses to stresses and easements in everyday living. In R.
Roessler and N. S. Greenfield (eds), Physiological Correlates of Psychological Disorder. Madison: University of
Wisconsin Press.

Hassett, J. (1978). A Primer of Psychophysiology. San Francisco: W. H. Freeman.

Hill, O. W. (1976). Modern Trends in Psychosomatic Medicine,
No. 3. London: Butterworths.

Hinkle, L. E., Jr (1977). The concept of 'stress' in the
biological and social sciences. In Z. J. Lipowski, D. R.
Lipsitt and P. C. Whybrow (eds), Psychosomatic Medicine:
Current trends and clinical applications. New York: Oxford
University Press.

Johansson, G. and Frankenhaeuser, M. (1973). Temporal factors
in sympathoadrenomedullary activity following acute behavioural activation. Biological Psychology, 1, 53-73.

Johnson, L. C. (1977). Psychophysiological research: aims and
methods. In Z. J. Lipowski, D. R. Lipsitt and P. C. Whybrow (eds), Psychosomatic Medicine: Current trends and
clinical applications. New York: Oxford University Press.

Kelvin, William Thomson, Baron (1889). Popular Lectures and
Addresses. London: Macmillan.

Kimball, C. P. (1970). Conceptual developments in psychosomatic medicine: 1939-1969. Annals of Internal Medicine,
73, 307-316.

Kimball, C. P. (1982). Stress and psychosomatic illness.
Journal of Psychosomatic Research, 26, 63-71.

Krakowski, A. J. (1977). Consultation-liaison psychiatry: a
psychosomatic service in the general hospital. In Z. J.
Lipowski, D. R. Lipsitt and P. C. Whybrow (eds), Psychosomatic Medicine: Current trends and clinical applications.
New York: Oxford University Press.

Lader, M. (1972). Psychophysiological research and psychosomatic medicine. In R. Porter and J. Knight (eds), Physiology, Emotion and Psychosomatic Illness. Ciba Foundation
Symposium 8 (new series). Amsterdam: Associated Scientific
Publishers.

Lazarus, R. (1977). Psychological stress and coping in adaptation and illness. In Z. J. Lipowski, D. R. Lipsitt and P.

C. Whybrow (eds), Psychosomatic Medicine: Current trends and clinical applications. New York: Oxford University Press.

Leff, J. and Tarrier, N. (1981). The home environment of schizophrenic patients and their response to treatment. In M. J. Christie and P. G. Mellett (eds), Foundations of Psychosomatics. Chichester: Wiley.

Leiderman, P. H. and Shapiro, D. (1965). Psychobiological Approaches to Social Behaviour. London: Tavistock.

Levey, A. B. and Martin, I. (1981). The relevance of classical conditioning to psychosomatic disorder. In M. J. Christie and P. G. Mellett (eds), Foundations of Psychosomatics. Chichester: Wiley.

Levi, L. (ed.) (1971). Society, Stress and Disease. Volume 1: The Psychosocial Environment and Psychosomatic Disease. London: Oxford University Press.

Levi, L. (1972). Stress and Distress in Response to Psycho-social Stimuli. Oxford: Pergamon.

Levi, L. (ed.) (1975). Society, Stress and Disease. Volume 2: Childhood and Adolescence. Oxford: Oxford University Press.

Levi, L. (ed.) (1978). Society, Stress and Disease. Volume 3: The Productive and Reproductive Age - Male/Female Roles and Relationships. Oxford: Oxford University Press.

Lipowski, Z. J. (1976). Psychosomatic medicine: an overview. In O. W. Hill (ed.), Modern Trends in Psychosomatic Medicine, No. 3. London: Butterworths.

Lipowski, Z. J. (1977a). Psychosomatic medicine: a science, movement, or point of view? In Z. J. Lipowski, D. R. Lipsitt and P. C. Whybrow (eds), Psychosomatic Medicine: Current trends and clinical applications. New York: Oxford University Press.

Lipowski, Z. J. (1977b). Physical illness and psychopathology. In Z. J. Lipowski, D. R. Lipsitt and P. C. Whybrow (eds), Psychosomatic Medicine: Current trends and clinical applications. New York: Oxford University Press.

Lipowski, Z. J., Lipsitt, D. R. and Whybrow, P. C. (eds) (1977). Psychosomatic Medicine: Current trends and clinical applications. New York: Oxford University Press.

Lipsitt, D. R. (1977). Some problems in the teaching of psychosomatic medicine. In Z. J. Lipowski, D. R. Lipsitt and P. C. Whybrow (eds), Psychosomatic Medicine: Current trends and clinical applications. New York: Oxford University Press.

Mackay, C. J. (1980). The measurement of mood and psycho-physiological activity using self-report techniques. In I.

Martin and P. H. Venables (eds), Techniques of Psycho-physiology. Chichester: Wiley.

Mackay, C. J. and Cox, T. (eds) (1979). Responses to Stress: Occupational aspects. Guildford: IPC.

Marmot, M. (1981). Culture and illness: epidemiological evidence. In M. J. Christie and P. G. Mellett (eds), Foundations of Psychosomatics. Chichester: Wiley.

Marmot, M. G., Rose, G., Shipley, M. and Hamilton, P. J. S. (1978). Employment grade and CHD in British civil servants. Journal of Epidemiology and Community Health, 32, 244-249.

Martin, I. (1975). Changing articles of faith. Paper to Psychophysiology Society, London.

Martin, I. and Venables, P. H. (eds) (1980). Techniques of Psychophysiology. Chichester: Wiley.

Mills, M. (1981). Individual differences in the first week of life. In M. J. Christie and P. G. Mellett (eds), Foundations of Psychosomatics. Chichester: Wiley.

Moos, R. J. (1977). Determinants of physiological response to symbolic stimuli: the role of the social environment. In Z. J. Lipowski, D. R. Lipsitt and P. C. Whybrow (eds), Psychosomatic Medicine: Current trends and clinical applications. New York: Oxford University Press.

Nemiah, J. C., Freyberger, H. and Sifneos, P. E. (1976). Alexithymia: a view of the psychosomatic process. In O. W. Hill (ed.), Modern Trends in Psychosomatic Medicine, No. 3. London: Butterworths.

Obrist, P. A. (1981). Cardiovascular Psychophysiology. New York: Plenum Press.

Ostfeld, A. M. and D'Atri, D. A. (1977). Psychophysiological responses to the urban environment. In Z. J. Lipowski, D. R. Lipsitt and P. C. Whybrow (eds), Psychosomatic Medicine: Current trends and clinical applications. New York: Oxford University Press.

Patkai, P. (1977). Laboratory studies of psychological stress. In Z. J. Lipowski, D. R. Lipsitt and P. C. Whybrow (eds), Psychosomatic Medicine: Current trends and clinical applications. New York: Oxford University Press.

Rees, W. L. (1975). Stress, distress and disease. British Journal of Psychiatry, 128, 3-18.

Reichsman, F. (1977). Teaching psychosomatic medicine to medical students. In Z. J. Lipowski, D. R. Lipsitt and P. C. Whybrow (eds), Psychosomatic Medicine: Current trends and clinical applications. New York: Oxford University Press.

Roessler, R. (1973). Personality, physiology and performance. Psychophysiology, 10, 315-327.

Roessler, R. and Engel, B. T. (1977). The current status of the concepts of physiological response specificity and activation. In Z. J. Lipowski, D. R. Lipsitt and P. C. Whybrow (eds), Psychosomatic Medicine: Current trends and clinical applications. New York: Oxford University Press.

Royal Commission on Education (1968). 1965-68 Report. London: HMSO.

Schwartz, G. E. and Shapiro, D. (1973). Social psychophysiology. In W. F. Prokasy and D. C. Raskin (eds), Electrodermal Activity in Psychological Research. New York: Academic Press.

Selye, H. (1950). Stress. Montreal: Acta Inc.

Selye, H. (1971). The evolution of the stress concept - stress and cardiovascular disease. In L. Levi (ed.), Society, Stress and Disease, Volume 1: The Psychosocial Environment and Psychosomatic Disease. London: Oxford University Press.

Shapiro, D. and Schwartz, G. E. (1970). Psychophysiological contributions to social psychology. Annual Review of Psychology, 21, 87-112.

Siddle, D. A. T. and Trasler, G. B. (1981). The psychophysiology of psychopathic behaviour. In M. J. Christie and P. G. Mellett (eds), Foundations of Psychosomatics. Chichester: Wiley.

Söderberg, U. (1967). Neurophysiological aspects of stress. In L. Levi (ed.), Emotional Stress. Basel: S. Karger.

Spaulding, W. B. (1977). The psychosomatic approach to the practice of medicine. In Z. J. Lipowski, D. R. Lipsitt and P. C. Whybrow (eds), Psychosomatic Medicine: Current trends and clinical applications. New York: Oxford University Press.

Steptoe, A. (1981). Psychological Factors in Cardiovascular Disorders. London: Academic Press.

Stern, R. M. (1966). A re-examination of the effects of response-contingent aversive tones on gastrointestinal activity. Psychophysiology, 2, 217-223.

Stern, R. M., Farr, J-A. H. and Ray, W. J. (1975). Pleasure. In P. H. Venables and M. J. Christie (eds), Research in Psychophysiology. London: Wiley.

Stern, R. M., Ray, W. J. and Davis, C. M. (1980). An Introduction to Psychophysiological Recording. New York: Oxford University Press.

Venables, P. H. (1981). Studies of children at high risk for schizophrenia. In M. J. Christie and P. G. Mellett (eds), Foundations of Psychosomatics. Chichester: Wiley.

Wadsworth, M., Butterfield, W. J. H. and Blaney, R. (1971). Health and Sickness: The choice of treatment. London: Tavistock.

Wadsworth, M. and Ingham, J. (1981). How society defines sickness: illness behaviour and consultation. In M. J. Christie and P. G. Mellett (eds), Foundations of Psychosomatics. Chichester: Wiley.

Warburton, D. M. (1979). Physiological aspects of information processing and stress. In V. Hamilton and D. M. Warburton (eds), Human Stress and Cognition: An information processing approach. Chichester: Wiley.

Weiner, H. (1976). The heterogeneity of 'psychosomatic disease'. Psychosomatic Medicine, 38, 371-372.

Weinman, J. (1981). An Outline of Psychology as Applied to Medicine. Bristol: John Wright & Sons.

Weiss, J. H. (1977). The current state of the concept of a psychosomatic disorder. In Z. J. Lipowski, D. R. Lipsitt and P. C. Whybrow (eds), Psychosomatic Medicine: Current trends and clinical applications. New York: Oxford University Press.

Wenger, M. A. (1966). Studies of autonomic balance: a summary. Psychophysiology, 2, 173-186.

Winefield, H. R. (1981). Behavioural science in the medical curriculum: why and how. In M. J. Christie and P. G. Mellett (eds), Foundations of Psychosomatics. Chichester: Wiley.

Wittkower, E. D. (1977). Historical perspective of contemporary psychosomatic medicine. In Z. J. Lipowski, D. R. Lipsitt and P. C. Whybrow (eds), Psychosomatic Medicine: Current trends and clinical applications. New York: Oxford University Press.

Wolff, H. (1950). Life stress and bodily disease. Research Publications of the Association for Study of Nervous and Mental Diseases, 29, 1135.

World Health Organisation (1964). Psychosomatic Disorders. World Health Organisation Technical Report Service No. 275.

Youngman, M. B. (1979). Analysing Social and Educational Research Data. London: McGraw-Hill.

Chapter 7

PAIN

Shirley Pearce

INTRODUCTION

Pain is an experience of which many people have first-hand knowledge. Indeed, most people think they know what pain is, and yet from a scientific point of view it is a state about which relatively little is known. It has been hard for researchers to agree upon a definition of pain and harder still to develop a theory that accounts for all the different observations that have been made. Psychological influences on pain have only recently been considered important enough to investigate systematically. This is surprising since most people can recall times when psychological variables seem to have influenced the intensity of their own pain experience. A headache, for example, may be much less troublesome when one's attention is distracted by an engrossing film than when sitting in a tedious lecture or studying for exams. Personality and cultural variables, mood, feelings of control and social influences have all been suggested to affect pain. This chapter aims to cover some of these topics and describe the contributions that psychologists are beginning to make to the treatment of pain. First of all, however, the major theories of pain will be described and the important problems of measurement in this area will be discussed.

THEORIES OF PAIN

The specificity model of pain, arising largely from the work of early physiologists and anatomists, views pain as a sensation caused by activity in peripheral pain receptors, known as nociceptors. This activity occurs as a result of tissue damage, and is transmitted along specific neural pathways to a central brain area responsible for the perception of pain. The intensity of the unpleasant sensation is considered to be directly related to the extent of the tissue damage. There is

170

now considerable evidence that a variety of psychological factors can intervene to affect the relationship between the extent of tissue damage and the subjective intensity of pain. This, in conjunction with certain physiological and surgical observations, has led to a general rejection of the specificity model. Despite this rejection at a theoretical level, however, the specificity model continues to dominate much medical practice.

An opposing theory of pain is known as the pattern theory, e.g. Crue and Carregal (1975). This rejects the idea of pain as a primary sensory modality and proposes that the perception of pain is based on stimulus intensity and central summation mechanisms rather than specific pain receptors and pain pathways. Despite some evidence for both spatial and temporal patterning, this theory has also been rejected since it does not fit with the evidence of physiological specialization.

The recognition that both specificity and pattern theories are inadequate led Melzack and Wall (1965) to propose the gate control theory of pain. This essentially provided an anatomical basis for the view that sensory input could be modulated by certain physiological and psychological processes. Input from the peripheral nociceptors is thought to pass through a neural 'gate' in the spinal cord before being transmitted to the brain. This 'gate' may be opened or closed according to the relative activity in small and large afferent fibres as well as the activity in fibres descending from the brain. The theory is described at length in a number of places (Melzack, 1973; Wall, 1976) and will not be discussed in detail here. The theory has been the subject of considerable controversy and although neurophysiological studies (Franz and Iggo, 1968; Dyck, Lambert and O'Brien, 1976) have not always confirmed the existence of some of the proposed mechanisms, the basic concept of input modulation is widely accepted and the gate-control theory is viewed as one of the most important theoretical advances in recent pain research.

Another major advance in pain research has been the discovery of certain areas of the midbrain, stimulation of which has been shown to produce analgesia (Reynolds, 1969; Liebeskind and Paul, 1977). This stimulation produced analgesia (SPA) and has led to considerable interest in the role of naturally produced opiate substances known as endorphins. These endorphins produced by SPA have been shown to block behavioural responses even to intense pain stimulation in many different animal species. They provide a potential explanation for the way psychological variables such as anxiety and expectations can affect pain perception, since different

171

psychological states might either trigger or suppress the release of endorphins and hence influence the intensity of the pain experienced (Sherman and Liebeskind, 1979).

Since a theory of pain as a sensation has become untenable, models have been proposed which view pain as a multi-dimensional experience. Melzack (1973) distinguishes between the sensory and affective components of the subjective experience of pain. Other views have included activity in physiological and behavioural systems as part of the experience of pain. The following diagramatic representation of pain is adapted from Fordyce (1978):

Nociception .... PHYSIOLOGICAL
↓
Sensation ....⎫
↓   ⎬ SUBJECTIVE
Negative Affective Response ....⎭
↓
Pain Behaviours .... BEHAVIOURAL

Activity in the physiological system (pain receptors and nociceptive pathways) is perceived at a subjective level both as a sensation (burning, pricking) and as an unpleasant feeling or affect (distress, discomfort). This negative affective response, as it has been called, stimulates pain behaviours (wincing, taking pills) which are aimed at communicating the pain experience to those around and at reducing the intensity of the pain experience.

Such a model allows the notion of a linear relationship between noxious stimulation and pain intensity to be discarded. The further away from the level of nociception, the more other factors besides the level of physiological activity are likely to become implicated in the pain experience. For example, social and cultural variables are likely to influence pain behaviours more than activity in the nociceptive fibres. Hence the concordance between these three systems, physiological, subjective and behavioural, may vary. Similar models have been produced by psychologists to explain fear and anxiety (Rachman, 1976; Hugdahl, 1981) and it is possible that the sorts of variables shown to affect concordance between the systems in anxiety states may also apply to pain. For example, Rachman and Hodgson (1974) suggest that fear reduction techniques aimed primarily at the subjective experience of anxiety, e.g. imaginal desensitization, may effect a greater reduction in subjective distress than in measures of behavioural avoidance, so that the patient may report less distress but still continue avoiding the feared object. In pain states, particularly chronic pain, analgesic medication and attempts to reduce the distress of the pain experience may have little effect on the pain behaviours such as taking it easy or walking with a stick.

Before discussing the variety of psychological factors that have been shown to affect the overall pain experience and influence the concordance between the three systems, the problems involved in the measurement of pain will be discussed.

THE MEASUREMENT OF PAIN

Research on pain can be broadly divided into two areas, namely investigations of experimental and clinical pain states. These two areas of research are often amalgamated and general conclusions made about pain phenomena. This is a dangerous tendency as the two states are often very different and extrapolations from research on experimental pain to clinical pain may be very misleading. Indeed, much debate has surrounded the value of any research on experimentally induced pain (e.g. Proccaci, Zappi and Maresca, 1979). The differences in the two states become clear when considering the measurement of pain. In experimental pain studies the investigator is always able to specify the pain stimulus in some quantifiable terms, e.g. level of electrical stimulation or radiant heat. Clearly, in clinical pain states the pain stimulus cannot be so easily defined or measured even if it is identifiable. Hence, in clinical pain states there is no objective criterion against which to compare subjective reports or level of pain behaviours. The measurement issues and attempts to quantify pain in each of the two states will be discussed separately.

EXPERIMENTAL PAIN MEASUREMENT

Early psychophysical approaches to the measurement of experimental pain began with Von Frey in 1894 (see Boring, 1942) but it was not until Hardy, Wolff and Goodell (1952) that measurement became more systematic. A number of types of aversive stimulation have been used: heat, cold, electrical stimulation, pressure and ischaemic methods (use of tourniquet). A number of pain response parameters have been investigated of which pain threshold, the just noticeable difference (JND) and the pain tolerance level are the most important. The concepts are discussed at length by Wolff (1978) and will only be briefly outlined here.

Pain Threshold

This is the term used to refer to the level of stimulation at which the subject just begins to feel pain in an ascending trial or at which pain just disappears in a descending trial. Considerable debate has surrounded the existence of an absolute pain threshold for each individual and early studies of the reliability and validity of the measure showed not only that pain threshold could be affected by psychological and physical factors such as anxiety, type of instructions, and drugs, but also that low correlations exist between pain thresholds assessed in different stimulus modalities (Wolff and Jarvik, 1963; Davidson and McDougall, 1969).

The Just Noticeable Difference (JND)

The JND is the smallest interval between two stimuli which can be discriminated. This measure was the basis of Hardy, Wolff and Goodell's (1952) attempt to develop a scale based on the experimental measurement of pain for use in the assessment of clinical pain. The intervals along this 'Dol' scale were based on JNDs ranging from no pain to pain tolerance for radiant heat stimulation. One Dol was defined as two JNDs. Patients with clinical pain were asked to use the Dol scale to compare the intensity of their own pain with that of the experimental radiant heat. In practice, it has proved to be of minimal value since the task involves too many categories, or Dols, to be used easily (Wolff, 1978).

Pain Tolerance

This is defined as the highest level of pain that the subject is able to bear. It may be measured in terms of the intensity of the stimulus or its duration. Early studies found that pain tolerance levels could be measured reliably (Clark and Bindra, 1956; Wolff and Jarvik, 1963; Davidson and McDougall, 1969). More recent research, however, has indicated that when different types of painful stimuli (e.g. heat and shock) are applied to the same individual only low correlations between tolerance levels are found (Davidson and McDougall, 1969). As will be seen later, pain tolerance levels can be influenced by many psychological variables.

Signal Detection Approaches to Pain Measurement (SDT)

Signal detection theory has had a major impact on pain research. A full description of SDT will not be given here, but the method and the issues surrounding its application to pain are detailed in a number of reviews (e.g. Chapman, 1977; Rollman, 1977). Essentially, the method uses information about the variability of verbal report to separate responses into two parameters. The first, known as d', or discriminability, is a measure of the ability to discriminate one stimulus from another and is assumed to be a measure of the sensitivity of the sensory mechanisms. The second parameter, often called the response criterion, or β, is assumed to reflect the likelihood that an individual will use certain verbal labels to describe a perceptual event. In applying SDT methods to pain research, d' has been interpreted as a pure measure of pain sensitivity while β has been seen as a measure of psychological factors influencing the subject's willingness to label the sensation as pain. This distinction has been supported by studies which show that <u>physiological</u> manipulations tend to alter d' only, while <u>psychological</u> manipulations tend to alter the response criterion. However, not all studies have found these results. This has led critics such as Rollman (1977) to suggest that it is an inappropriate methodology for the measurement of pain. The situation remains unresolved, but as Gracely (1980) concludes, SDT has had an important effect in attempting to separate different components of pain and in making an explicit attempt to assess the sorts of factors that influence pain reports.

MEASUREMENT OF CLINICAL PAIN

Despite the widespread application of psychophysical methods to the measurement of experimentally induced pain, these methods have had relatively little to contribute to the measurement of clinical pain. The aims of measuring clinical pain are rather different from those involved in the measurement of experimental pain and are usually either to aid iagnosis or to assess change in the pain over time, in order, for example, to assess the efficacy of a particular treatment.

Approaches to measuring the physiological, subjective and behavioural components of pain will be dealt with one at a time.

Measurement of the Physiological Component

Although physiological recordings have often been used in experimental studies of pain, e.g. cortical evoked responses (Chapman, Chen and Harkins, 1979), they have rarely been used to complement assessment of pain states. An exception to this is a pain state where one particular physiological variable has been implicated as a causal factor in the pain problem. For example, in tension headache the pain has always been assumed to be due to raised EMG levels (Friedman, 1962). Although some studies have found an association between EMG levels (physiological component) and pain intensity (subjective component), an increasing number of reports suggest that there is a rather poor correlation between pain and EMG levels (Philips, 1977; Pearce and Morley, 1981). Such a lack of concordance between pain components, i.e. physiological and subjective, does not mean that physiological variables should not be assessed, but rather that the reason for measuring them should not be primarily for diagnostic purposes as it has tended to be in the past. Instead, physiological measures should be seen as one of several measures of value in assessing changes in the pain.

Measurement of the Subjective Component

The measurement of the sensation and affective components of pain will be considered together as they are both affected by similar problems of measurement in that they are dependent on subjective report. Some people (e.g. Fordyce, 1978) view the problems of assessing subjective report as insurmountable and rely only on behavioural measures of pain and activity in order to assess a patient's pain. However, this view is not shared by all and there have been a wide range of approaches to the assessment of the subjective components of pain.

Rating scales

Numerous kinds of rating scales have been used. These can be broadly divided into Visual Analogue Scales (VAS) and Verbal Rating Scales (VRS).

e.g. VAS /_____/
       No pain   Unbearable pain

The line may be either vertical or horizontal and the patients' task is to place a mark on the line to represent the point on the scale that best describes the intensity of their pain.

VRS   1   2   3   4   5
       No pain   Mild   Moderate Severe Unbearable

Here patients are asked to say which category best describes their pain.

Attempts to assess the reliability and validity of VAS and VRS generally show a high correlation between scores obtained by the two types of scale (Woodforde and Merskey, 1972a; Downie, Leatham, Rhind, Wright, Branco and Anderson, 1978), although Scott and Huskisson (1976) showed that the VAS produced a more uniform distribution of scores. Problems arise, however, when measuring change over time. Scott and Huskisson (1979) advocated making previous ratings available to patients so that they may compare their current pain with their ratings on previous occasions. This produced bigger differences between past and present ratings than when patients were denied access to their previous ratings. Johnson and Rice (1974) attempted to improve the reliability of their scales by asking for separate judgements for sensory and affective aspects of pain. The value of making separate judgements in this way can be seen from studies showing differential effects of narcotics and minor tranquillizing drugs on different subjective aspects of pain. Gracely, Dubner and McGrath (1979) showed that Fetanyl, a narcotic, produced reductions in ratings of sensory intensity after tooth pulp stimulation. However, Diazepam, a minor tranquillizer, produced no change on the sensory rating scale but caused reductions in the unpleasantness ratings. Fetanyl actually caused increased ratings of unpleasantness. Clearly, reliance on single scales might distort the conclusions of otherwise well-designed studies.

VAS and VRS are often incorporated into diary cards to assess change in pain over time. This method has been widely used in the investigation of headaches (Budzinski, Stoyva, Adler and Mullaney, 1973; Collins and Martin, 1980; Philips and Hunter, 1981). One of the problems with this approach is ensuring that the patients remember to fill them in each day and hence prevent the diaries being completed retrospectively (Epstein and Abel, 1977). Andrasik and Holroyd (1980) compared diary records with headache questionnaires. Data collected by diary cards showed minimal correspondence with the questionnaire results, with lower reporting of both frequency and intensity on the questionnaire. They conclude that daily records may be less subject to distortions than questionnaire methods.

Questionnaires

Despite the problems of memory distortion in questionnaire methods, there are considerable advantages to having a questionnaire which can be administered on a single occasion to gain information about various different aspects of pain.

The McGill Pain Questionnaire (MPQ: Melzack, 1975) is one of the best-known and most widely-used pain questionnaires. It consists of a list of 78 adjectives (e.g. pounding, tearing, burning, etc.) arranged into 20 groups, each group reflecting slightly different aspects or qualities of pain. Subjects are asked to indicate which words describe their pain and the questionnaire may be scored in a number of ways to derive either a score reflecting the intensity of the words checked or just the total number of words checked. The words and the organization of the questionnaire were derived from a study by Melzack and Torgerson (1971) which showed agreement between patients, students and physicians in terms of the meaning attached to pain adjectives. Its value is that it allows patients to describe their subjective experience of pain on a number of dimensions. Hence, it may overcome some of the problems described previously which derive from relying on a unidimensional rating scale.

The MPQ has become widely used in investigations of both clinical pain (Rybstein Blinchik, 1979; Philips and Hunter, 1981) and experimental pain (Crockett, Prkachin and Craig, 1977; Klepac, Dowline and Hauge, 1981). The reliability of the adjective grouping has been assessed by Reading, Everitt and Sledmere (1982), who confirmed a clear distinction between the sensory and affective word groups, but questioned the assumption that adjectives in each of the groups could be ordered along a single intensity dimension. A further problem with the MPQ is that there are a great deal more adjectives on the questionnaire that describe the sensory qualities of pain than the affective qualities. This predisposes the questionnaire to more effective measurement of the sensory than the affective component of pain.

In conclusion, the MPQ is widely used and of considerable face validity. However, its internal structure and methods of scoring deserve further attention; more particularly, considering its widespread use with chronic pain populations, attention might be directed towards attempting to include more affective descriptors to balance the present over-representation of sensory words.

Measurement of the Behavioural Component

Pain behaviours are probably the most objective and quantifiable aspects of the pain experience, and hence should be subject to fewer measurement problems. Frederickson, Lynd and Ross (1978) distinguish three categories of pain behaviours: (i) somatic interventions, such as taking medication, receiving nerve blocks; (ii) impaired functioning, decreased mobility, avoidance of social/work activities; (iii) pain complaints, moaning, facial grimaces, etc.

Pain behaviours may be measured by direct observation, e.g. nurse observations of the number of hours per day the patient is up and walking about rather than sitting or lying in bed, or by patient records, e.g. of the number of pills taken each day.

Some attempts have been made to develop questionnaires which although not directly assessing pain behaviours, do attempt to estimate the level of disruption the pain is causing in the patient's everyday life. The Sickness Impact Profile (Pollard, Bobbitt, Bergner, Martin and Gilson, 1976) is an example of such a questionnaire; although relatively little research has yet been done on this instrument, it is used to assess improvement in a number of American pain clinics.

ACUTE AND CHRONIC PAIN

In discussing measurement issues, a distinction has been made between experimentally induced pain and clinical pain states. A further distinction should also be made between acute and chronic pain. Sternbach (1978) and Fordyce (1978) have argued that both the experimental and clinical literature support the view that acute pain, i.e. pain of recent onset, is typically associated with increased anxiety and autonomic arousal. Chronic pain, usually defined as pain of at least six months' duration, is a condition in which the pain has persisted beyond any 'warning' value it may initially have had. Clinical observations (Sternbach, 1978) suggest that autonomic responses have habituated, and behaviours similar to those observed in depression may emerge, e.g. sleep disturbance, appetite changes, irritability, etc. Fordyce (1978) suggests that as chronicity advances, the nature of the pain problem changes in that pain behaviours become established as a regular component of the individual's behavioural repertoire, and hence are more likely to come under environmental or operant control. This means that, irrespective of the supposed <u>cause</u> of the pain (i.e. whether or not organic pathology has been discovered), any treatment intervention must consider producing change at the behavioural level as well as at a physiological level. This issue will be returned to in the section on psychological approaches to treatment, but the view that different processes may be involved in acute and chronic pain should be borne in mind when considering the subsequent discussion of the influence of psychological factors on pain perception.

PSYCHOLOGICAL FACTORS AND PAIN PERCEPTION

Personality

Several studies have shown that personality variables affect both subjective and behavioural components of pain. While neuroticism has been shown to relate to pain severity ratings for both clinically and experimentally induced pain (Eysenck, 1961; Lynn and Eysenck, 1961; Pilling, Brannick and Swenson, 1967; Bond and Pearson, 1969; Bond, 1971, 1973), extraversion has been linked with complaint behaviour. Bond and Pearson (1969) reported that in a group of women with advanced cancer of the cervix, all of whom had high neuroticism scores, those with high extraversion scores were more likely to complain of pain, despite the fact that the introverts actually showed higher subjective ratings of pain on analogue scales. Barnes (1975) discussed these findings in relation to the apparently contradictory experimental studies which show that extraverts generally have higher levels of pain tolerance than introverts and might therefore be expected to bear more pain in a clinical situation. However, by viewing pain as a multidimensional experience with potential desynchrony between the systems, such apparent discrepancies can be understood. Philips (1976) showed that although personality measures were not useful in distinguishing between headache sufferers and the general population, within the headache group neuroticism correlated with measures of pain severity whilst extraversion correlated with levels of medication intake, i.e. a behavioural component of pain.

It seems then, that personality variables may be involved in determining the overall nature of an individual's response to pain. This has led to considerable speculation about the role of personality variables in the development of chronic pain in patients for whom no organic pathology can be found. A number of studies have suggested that patients with chronic pain have different personality profiles from non-pain populations (Woodforde and Merskey, 1972b; Bond, 1973; Sternbach, 1974). This led to the notion of the 'psychogenic pain personality', i.e. a personality type which is more likely to recover slowly from physical trauma or develop painful conditions in the absence of physical pathology. This view is supported by studies which show chronic pain patients to have abnormal profiles on the MMPI. The most commonly reported MMPI profile for chronic pain patients is that of elevated hypochondriasis, depression and hysteria scores, with hypochondriasis and hysteria scores being greater than the depression scores (Sternbach, 1974). This personality profile has come to be called the 'conversion profile' and people with this personality structure are seen as responding to anxiety and conflicts not by becoming depressed but by experiencing pain, i.e. they 'convert' their anxiety into a physical symptom.

Engel (1959) has written extensively on the psychoanalytic theory of chronic pain and views pain as the individual's way of dealing with guilt. Engel suggests that the pain-prone individual has a history of using pain as punishment, is constitutionally gloomy, pessimistic and guilt ridden. A major problem with such psychodynamic theories of personality and psychopathology is that it is extremely hard to quantify and measure many of the processes involved and hence test the theory.

In general, the fact that (i) a number of studies have failed to reproduce reliably the 'conversion' findings, and (ii) similar personality profiles have been observed in pain patients irrespective of whether or not organic pathology has been observed, has led to a certain disenchantment with the notion of the psychogenic pain personality. The other theoretical position relating personality variables to pain complaint is that changes in personality occur as a result of suffering pain for extended periods and occurs whether or not organic pathology is observed. This view is supported by the findings of Sternbach and Timmermans (1975) who showed that personality variables as measured by the MMPI returned nearer

181

to normal when chronic pain patients become free from their pain.

The chicken and egg problem of the role of personality variables in relation to chronic pain may only be answered by a prospective study following patients for some time after a potentially pain-inducing situation, e.g. road traffic accident, and looking at differences between those who do and those who do not develop chronic pain states. However, there would certainly also be a place for more studies such as that of Sternbach and Timmermans (1975) where personality variables of patients experiencing pain relief are closely investigated.

Cultural Influences on Pain Perception

Melzack (1973) outlines a number of cultural rituals involving pain which would be considered bizarre in western cultural terms. He provides the example of the Indian hook-hanging ritual in which a young man is chosen each year to hang from a moveable scaffold by large hooks inserted into his back. He is then waved over the crops and his function is to bless the crops and ensure a good harvest. To observers, he appears to be in a sort of trance and to experience minimal discomfort. Furthermore, the injuries to his back are usually relatively slight and heal much more quickly than would be expected of similar insult caused by other means, e.g. a car accident. It would appear that considerable honour is attached to being chosen to bless the crops and that this alters the meaning of the trauma and hence somehow reduces its physiological and psychological effects. Beecher (1956) has also suggested that the meaning of the situation can influence pain experience. He reported that soldiers injured on the battlefield typically failed to complain of pain or request medication, while civilians with similar trauma induced by surgery reported considerably more pain and discomfort. If the meaning of the situation can induce temporary changes in pain response in people of any cultural background, then painful cultural rituals can be explained without invoking hypotheses about general differences in pain responsiveness across cultures.

Nevertheless, studies of experimental pain have suggested cultural differences in threshold and tolerance. Chapman and Jones, as early as 1944, used radiant heat to assess pain threshold and tolerance in groups of different cultural descent not fully assimilated into US culture, namely South American negros, Ukranians, Jews and Northern Europeans. They found considerable differences between the groups, with the negro group perceiving pain at the lowest level and showing tolerance points close to the pain thresholds of the Northern Europeans. Similar findings were reported by Sternbach and Tursky (1965). Lambert, Libman and Poser (1960) also showed that individuals from one cultural group could be induced to increase their pain tolerance significantly if informed that their cultural group generally had lower pain tolerance than another cultural group. Weisenberg (1977) has suggested that these studies may be explained not in terms of constitutional differences between the cultural groups but as artefacts of the testing situation and as a consequence of the expectations of cultural performance held by both experimenter and subjects. He suggests that black subjects tested by white experimenters may show lower pain tolerance as a consequence of mutual expectations of the lower performance of blacks. Although such an explanation is unlikely to account for all the cultural variations in pain threshold and tolerance observed in experimental studies, the interaction between experimenter and subject in these experiments deserves further attention.

Not all experimental studies have found the clear cultural differences that were observed in the early studies (Merskey and Spear, 1964). Furthermore, the few clinical studies of subjective distress and pain suggest that the differences between cultures may be relatively small. Flannery, Sos and McGovern (1981) looked at pain ratings at episiotomy (incision of the perineum during labour to prevent excessive tearing) in five different ethnic groups: Black, Italian, Jewish, Irish and Anglo-Saxon. They found no difference in pain ratings between any of the cultural groups. It should be noted that this study was concerned only with the measurement of the subjective component of the pain experience and hence may not have detected cultural variations in pain behaviour. Considerable differences have been observed across cultures in the ways in which people respond to symptoms, not just pain, and hence if Flannery had been able to follow up these different cultural groups in the post-natal period at home and back in their own cultural environment, differences in pain behaviours might well have appeared. Cultural differences in pain behaviour were first reported by Zborowski (1969) in his now classic study. He showed that both Jewish Americans and those of Italian descent complained more about their pain than did an 'Old American' group. However, whereas the Italian group stopped complaining about their pain after the disorder had been treated, the Jewish group tended to continue to express concern about the pain in case it were to jeopardize their future health.

Social Influences on Pain

Craig (1978) outlines a number of studies that demonstrate that the behaviour of other individuals can influence both subjective and behavioural components of pain. Craig and Weiss (1971) examined the effect of exposure to tolerant and intolerant social models on verbal reports of pain to electrical stimulation. Subjects believed the model was receiving the same level of stimulation as themselves. When the model was apparently not experiencing much pain the subject was willing to endure significantly higher levels of electrical stimulation than when the model was apparently experiencing a great deal of pain. Later studies showed that the naive subjects could be induced to report painful stimulation for levels of electrical shock which under normal conditions are described merely as tingling (Craig and Weiss, 1972; Craig, Best and Ward, 1975). At a theoretical level it is important to ascertain whether this effect of social influence occurs at a subjective or a behavioural level, or both. Does the behaviour of others alter the subjective intensity of the electrical stimulation (make it seem less painful) or does it simply put a social constraint on pain behaviour, so that the same intensity of pain is perceived but the subject does not report it as unbearable until he/she feels it is socially acceptable to do so? A number of studies suggest that the former explanation may be correct. Craig and Neidermayer (1974) showed that groups of subjects who differed in their pain reports in a manner consistent with the model's behaviour (either tolerant or intolerant) could not be distinguished on the basis of concurrent physiological recordings of skin conductance or heart rate during electrical stimulation. The subjects who were induced by social factors to tolerate higher levels of pain did not appear to be any more physiologically aroused than those with lower tolerance. If they were suppressing pain behaviours, higher levels of physiological arousal might have been expected. Craig (1978) suggests that the effect of the model is to produce a fundamental change in the affective qualities of the pain. Social influences are also likely to play a part in the response to clinical pain and have been implicated as causal factors in the development of chronic pain. For example, Apley (1975) showed that parents and sibs of children with recurrent abdominal pain were six times more likely to complain of pain themselves than were the parents of control children.

Social influences are likely to be important in many clinical situations. Hospital wards and out-patient clinics are places where patients are frequently seen in pain. Little is known as yet about the effect of one patient's pain behaviour on the subjective distress of other patients on the ward. Similarly, the influence of an observer's presence (e.g. medical student or patient's relative) during a painful procedure (e.g. injection, examination in casualty) deserves investigation.

Predictability and Control

A number of studies have shown a relationship between the extent to which an individual believes he has control over the aversive stimulus and the intensity of experimental pain induced. Thompson (1981) reviews the studies and concludes that behavioural control (which Averill, 1973, defined as the belief that one has a behavioural response available that can reduce the aversiveness of an event, e.g. turning off the shock) increases pain tolerance levels (Bowers, 1968; Staub, Tursky and Schwartz, 1971; Kanfer and Seider, 1973). It is unclear whether this belief of control is effective in reducing the perceived intensity of the shock or whether it acts to increase behavioural endurance. Studies looking at self-report and control are equivocal with some reporting no effect (Pervin, 1963; Averill and Rosen, 1972) and others finding a reduction in perceived intensity (Staub, Tursky and Schwartz, 1971). Similar inconsistent results have been found in studies of perceived control and stress; for example, Geer, Davison and Gatchel (1970) showed that behavioural control reduced arousal prior to shock, although it was unclear whether it had any effect on the level of arousal at the time of impact.

It has also been suggested that cognitive control increases pain tolerance. Cognitive control is defined as the belief that one has a cognitive strategy that will reduce the aversiveness of an event. Thompson (1981) concludes that the evidence suggests that cognitive control may be effective in reducing not only anticipatory anxiety, but also the perceived intensity of the stimulus at the time of impact. Most attempts to explain this effect include reduction in anxiety as a mediating variable, i.e. by some means, the belief in a cognitive control strategy acts to reduce anxiety and hence reduces subjective pain intensity. The potential value of teaching cognitive strategies to pain patients to help reduce their distress is discussed in a later section.

Effects of Anxiety on Pain

It is frequently stated that anxiety and pain are related, such that the greater the anxiety the greater the subjective distress of the pain. However, the evidence for this is largely indirect, e.g. from studies such as those on predictability and control described above. Studies of the relationship between psychiatric disorders and pain have also been used to support the relationship. Spear (1967) found that pain as a symptom among psychiatric patients appeared with highest incidence in patients diagnosed as suffering from anxiety states. Merskey (1965a, 1965b) also showed an association between pain and neurotic disorders. However, pain and depression have frequently been linked in other studies. Pilowsky and Bassett (1982) looked at state and trait anxiety in depressed and chronic pain patients and found that on both measures the depressed group showed significantly higher anxiety scores, which would argue against an association between pain and anxiety in chronic pain patients. In general, this question has received rather little direct attention and there are few methodologically adequate studies in this area. This is partly due to the fact that the term anxiety may be used to refer to either personality traits or state variables. Care must be taken not to make generalizations from studies measuring trait anxiety (as many of the psychiatric studies have done) to make conclusions about the role of state anxiety and pain. Similarly, findings from studies of anxiety and chronic pain states should not be used to make conclusions about the relationship between anxiety and acute pain, either of experimental or clinical origin.

Generally, the conclusions seem to be clearest for the effect of state anxiety on acute pain states; for example, Frid, Singer and Rana (1979) looked at state anxiety and tolerance time to ischaemic pain. They found state anxiety, measured immediately prior to testing, showed a significant negative correlation with pain tolerance.

Recently, considerable interest has developed in the role of acute stress and pain perception. Much evidence has been amassed from animal studies to show that under conditions of extreme stress animals do not show their normal responses to pain stimuli. This analgesic effect has been termed stress induced analgesia and is probably mediated by the release of endorphins, since it has been shown to be blocked by the opiate antagonist, naloxone (Grevert and Goldstein, 1977; Madden, Akil, Patrick and Barchas, 1977).

Acute stress and state anxiety would seem then to have opposite effects on pain perception. This issue is discussed and reviewed by Bolles and Fanselow (1980) who put forward a model of pain and fear which attempts to incorporate and explain these findings.

Suggestion, Expectations and Pain

Much of the information about the role of suggestion and expectancies in pain perception has been derived from research on placebo responses. A placebo is defined as a substance or procedure administered with suggestions that it will modify a symptom or sensation but which, unknown to its recipient, has no specific pharmacological impact on the reaction concerned.

The effect of placebo medication on pain has been well documented. Beecher (1972) showed that 35 per cent of patients received pain relief with placebo. Early psychological explanations for placebo phenomena focussed on the characteristics of the patient that responded. In fact, studies that have looked at, for example, intelligence, suggestibility and numerous personality variables, have failed to find the 'placebo responder' (Evans, 1974; Shapiro and Morris, 1978). What they found was that subjects' responses vary considerably across time and across situations. It is generally agreed now that there is no absolute level of placebo response, and the nature and strength of the response varies according to a number of situational variables (Ross and Olsen, 1982).

The most likely explanation for placebo responses is that subjects' expectations are influencing the response. Precisely how these expectations produce change is unclear. Perhaps the most feasible explanation, which is particularly relevant for pain, is that the placebo acts to reduce anxiety because the patient is reassured that something is being done.

Placebo responses are not limited to drug effects. Studies of audio analgesia (Gardner and Licklider, 1959) show that music and white noise can be effective in suppressing dental pain. Melzack (1973) describes the way audio analgesia became popular with dentists, some of whom subsequently found it quite ineffective. Melzack and Weiss (1963) showed that auditory stimulation <u>per se</u> did not suppress cold pressor pain, and that it was the level of suggestion of effectiveness that predicted subjects' responses by determining whether the subjects were willing to use the noise in an active fashion to distract themselves from the pain.

PSYCHOLOGICAL APPROACHES TO THE MANAGEMENT OF PAIN

The growing acceptance that psychological factors influence pain perception has led to interest in the application of psychological treatment approaches to the management of both acute and chronic pain. This section outlines the main approaches that have received attention.

Relaxation

As might be expected from the observations that anxiety exacerbates pain perception, relaxation has been used as a strategy to increase pain tolerance. Experimental studies show promising results. Bobey and Davidson (1970) compared four 'treatment' conditions for women subjects exposed to radiant heat and pressure algometer pain. The four groups were: relaxation, increased anxiety (showing subjects tapes of women screaming), cognitive rehearsal of pain and a no-intervention group as a control. The relaxation group showed the highest tolerance scores while the control group had the least. Interestingly, the 'increased anxiety' group showed better results than the control, possibly because the tapes acted as a distracting influence rather than a source of anxiety.

More recently, Clum, Luscomb and Scott (1982) looked at the relative effects of relaxation training, relaxation instructions and an attention redirection technique. He found that relaxation training (Bernstein and Borkovec, 1973), but not relaxation instructions alone, was successful in reducing verbal ratings of pain as measured by a cross modality matching technique (squeezing a hand dynamometer to the same level of pain as experienced by the pain stimulus: ischaemic pain produced by a blood pressure cuff). The attention redirection technique produced no change in pain ratings from the baseline condition but produced a decrease in pain sensation as measured by the cross modality matching. This raises the possibility that different types of psychological interventions all aimed at the subjective component of pain may act by different mechanisms, i.e. relaxation may reduce the affective component whilst attention redirection may affect the sensory component.

Clinical applications of relaxation techniques include the development of imaginal desensitization programmes to overcoming pain and anxiety at menstruation. Tasto and Chesney (1974) and Chesney and Tasto (1975) have shown that relaxation and imaginal desensitization to events surrounding menstruation are more effective than a discussion group or a no-treatment control in reducing symptom distress for women with spasmodic but not congestive dysmennorrhea (Dalton, 1969). For a review of studies in this area see Denney and Gerrard (1981).

There are potentially many other pain situations where a relaxation approach might help to reduce distress, particularly those where anxiety levels are typically high, e.g. dental pain and minor surgical operation. To date, however, relaxation training has been mainly used for chronic pain conditions. The rationale for its use in chronic pain is not to reduce anxiety but to reduce the level of EMG activity in muscles thought to be causing the pain. In other words, the aim is to effect a reduction in the physiological component of the pain. Hence, relaxation has been used primarily for tension headaches and myofascial pain dysfunctions. Turner and Chapman (1982a) conclude that relaxation can be effective for such disorders, although it is unclear whether it acts primarily by causing a reduction in EMG.

Biofeedback

Closely related to relaxation approaches, are attempts to use biofeedback procedures to bring about a reduction in the physiological component of the pain. Again, these procedures have been most widely applied to chronic pain conditions. Four types of biofeedback have been used:

(1) EEG (electroencephalographic) feedback. This is in its infancy, and as yet there have been no well-controlled trials of its use. However, there is some suggestion that training patients to produce alpha waves may delay the onset of migraine headaches (Gannon and Sternbach, 1971).

(2) Skin temperature biofeedback. This is used with migraine patients to teach them to increase their finger temperature on the assumption that migraine pain is due to

excessive cranial vascular activity and that increasing peripheral blood flow will decrease cranial activity. Although a number of studies have shown finger temperature feedback can reduce migraine frequency (Johnson and Turin, 1975; Adler and Adler, 1976), more recent studies have questioned whether this is a specific effect of the feedback (Mullinix, Norton, Hack and Fishman, 1978).

(3) Blood volume pulse feedback (BVP). Reductions in cranial artery activity have also been attempted by BVP feedback with positive results (Bild and Adams, 1980).

(4) Electromyographic biofeedback (EMG). Many studies have been conducted using EMG biofeedback for headache. Most show that this approach can be effective in reducing both headache frequency and intensity. However, it now seems unlikely that this is a specific effect since reductions in headache do not always correspond closely with similar reductions in frontalis EMG (Cox, Freundlich and Meyer, 1975; Epstein, Abel, Collins, Parker and Cinciripini, 1978). Furthermore, Turner and Chapman (1982a) conclude that for tension headache, EMG biofeedback has not been shown to be any more effective than relaxation alone (Haynes, Griffin, Mooney and Parise, 1975; Chesney and Shelton, 1976).

Cognitive Methods of Pain Control

Cognitive methods are those which attempt to modify thought processes in order to attenuate pain. The underlying assumption is that a person's cognitions or appraisal of his environment are crucial determinants of his experience. Hence, cognitive methods aim directly at the subjective component of the pain by attempting to alter cognitions from negative to positive, thereby making the pain less unpleasant. Indeed, there is some evidence that chronic pain patients do make cognitive errors about their pain (Lefebvre, 1981). Cognitive methods involve: (i) providing information about a coming aversive event; (ii) teaching patients to identify maladaptive responses to stress-provoking situations; (iii) teaching patients to use specific cognitive coping strategies. Meichenbaum and Turk (1976) showed that teaching cognitive strategies by a method they called 'stress inoculation' was effective in increasing experimental pain thresholds and tolerance.

Cognitive methods have only recently been applied to clinical pain problems but the results are encouraging and are reviewed by Tan (1982) and Turner and Chapman (1982b). An example of a cognitive treatment for chronic headache is provided by Rybstein Blinchik (1979), who found that patients instructed to reinterpret their pain experience (e.g. relabel it as numbness/ticklishness) obtained lower scores on the Melzack Pain Questionnaire and had lower pain intensity ratings than did an 'irrelevant reinterpretation' group (instructed to think about something different) or a no-treatment control group. However, no follow-up data are provided so long-term effectiveness cannot be assessed. In practice, cognitive methods are often linked to a behavioural procedure, e.g. relaxation or biofeedback. An example of this for acute clinical pain is the work that has been done on psychological preparation for surgery.

Preparation for Surgery

Egbert, Battit, Welch and Bartlett (1964), in a now classic study, showed that relatively minimal interventions prior to surgery could improve post-operative outcome, both in terms of levels of medication required (and hence, it was presumed, post-operative pain and discomfort) and length of hospital admission. More recently, Hayward (1975) gave patients information about hospital routines, pre-operative preparation and information about what pain and discomfort to expect following surgery as well as relaxation exercises. It was found that prepared patients required fewer analgesics and were more quickly free of post-operative pain. Experimental support for the view that information can reduce distress is provided by Johnson (1973), who reports that subjects who received information about the sensations associated with ischaemic pain showed lower pain distress ratings on stimulation than did subjects who received procedural information only. He concluded that information was of value if it increased the correspondence between the expected sensations and those that are eventually perceived.

In a clinical situation, he showed that patients undergoing endoscopy provided with a tape explaining the sensations they were likely to experience showed lower heart rates than those given only procedural information. Unfortunately, ratings of pain per se were not recorded (Johnson and Leventhal, 1974). Other studies have failed to show clear benefits of such preparation (e.g. Langer, Janis and Wolfer, 1975). It is probably unwise to expect any general conclusions to emerge from studies such as these where the outcome is likely to be affected by so many other powerful variables besides the precise nature of the content of the preparation package. For example, hospital ward organization with all its powerful social influences may be a more important variable than relaxation instruction or information prior to surgery. There is also some evidence that increasing information prior to surgery may be detrimental to some patients. Individuals' coping styles have been implicated as a factor that may determine whether prior information is advantageous or deleterious. Andrew (1970) concluded that patients who generally tried to avoid threat, 'deniers' or 'avoiders', tended to react adversely to the experimental intervention.

In view of the complexity of the clinical situation in trying to assess the role of coping styles and preparation for surgery, future research might benefit from looking at the interaction between coping style, the nature of the preparation and pain tolerance in the more easily manipulable experimental pain situation.

Hypnosis

Although it has been used for many years as an 'analgesic', the mode of action of hypnosis is far from understood. Hilgard (1975) states that the critical components are (i) mental relaxation, (ii) a narrowing of concentration, and (iii) heightened suggestibility. A number of studies have shown hypnosis to be effective in increasing threshold and tolerance for experimental pain (Greene and Reyher, 1972) and reducing pain in chronic pain conditions (Sacerdote, 1970). However, the studies are on the whole methodologically very weak and it is unclear whether hypnosis has any specific effect in pain reduction.

Operant Methods

The use of operant methods for the management of chronic pain stems largely from the work of Fordyce, Fowler, Lehmann, Delatour, Sand and Treischmann (1973) and Fordyce (1978). Fordyce's view of chronic pain has been outlined earlier and the aim of his treatment methods is to reduce 'pain' behaviours by withdrawing reinforcers (e.g. social attention), and increasing 'well' behaviours.

Intensive operant programmes are conducted on an inpatient basis. Family members and hospital staff are instructed to ignore pain behaviours and praise healthy behaviours.

In addition, careful physical rehabilitation programmes involving graded exercises are introduced. Considerable social reinforcement is provided for successful completion of the daily exercise quota. Medication intake is reduced by providing a 'pain cocktail' at fixed time intervals rather than on a 'take it as you need it' basis which Fordyce conceptualizes in learning theory terms as potentially reinforcing pain reports. The active ingredients of the pain cocktail are gradually reduced until the patient is only consuming the inert vehicle.

Since Fordyce questions the validity of assessing the subjective component of pain (pain intensity measures), he evaluates the programme in terms of the patients' activity levels. Both Fordyce, Fowler, Lehmann, Delatour, Sand and Treishmann (1973) and Roberts and Reinhardt (1980) have shown that severely disabled pain patients can show significant increases in activity as a result of such an approach. However, these studies are uncontrolled and hence no conclusions can be drawn about which of the many components of the treatment programme are effective.

CONCLUDING REMARKS

This chapter has attempted to provide an introduction to psychological studies of pain. It is clear that in general terms the importance of psychological factors in the experience of pain can no longer be disputed. However, there are still many unanswered questions about the nature and mode of action of specific psychological variables and their interaction with physical variables in clinical pain. In some of the areas discussed the standard of research has not matched that in other areas of psychology. An example of this is provided by the studies evaluating psychological treatments for pain which are frequently poorly conducted, often being uncontrolled and with poor follow-up data. This is in marked contrast to the psychotherapy outcome studies for psychological disorders which have become methodologically quite sophisticated (Bergin and Lambert, 1978).

It is hoped that future research in pain will be more closely linked to developments in other related areas of psychology. It would also be advantageous for psychologists concerned with pain to work more closely with other related disciplines, e.g. physiology and biochemistry, so that evelopments in other disciplines may be integrated more easily.

REFERENCES

Adler, C. S. and Adler, S. M. (1976). Biofeedback therapy for the treatment of headaches: a five year follow-up. Headache, 16, 189-191.

Andrasik, F. and Holroyd, K. A. (1980). Reliability and concurrent validity of headache questionnaire data. Headache, 20, 44-46.

Andrew, J. M. (1970). Recovery from surgery, with and without preparatory instruction, for three different coping styles. Journal of Personality and Social Psychology, 15, 223-226.

Apley, J. (1975). The Child with Abdominal Pains. Oxford: Blackwell Scientific Publications.

Averill, J. R. (1973). Personal control over aversive stimuli and its relationship to stress. Psychological Bulletin, 80, 286-303.

Averill, J. R. and Rosen, M. (1972). Vigilant and non-vigilant coping strategies and psychophysiological stress reactions during the anticipation of electric shock. Journal of Personality and Social Psychology, 23, 128-141.

Barnes, G. E. (1975). Extraversion and pain. British Journal of Social and Clinical Psychology, 14, 303-308.

Beecher, H. K. (1956). Relationship of significance of wound to the pain experienced. Journal of the American Medical Association, 161, 1609-1613.

Beecher, H. K. (1972). The placebo effect as a non-specific force surrounding disease and the treatment of disease. In R. Janzen and W. D. Keidel (eds), Pain: Basic principles, pharmacology, therapy. Stuttgart: Georg Thieme.

Bergin, A. E. and Lambert, M. J. (1978). The evaluation of therapeutic outcomes. In S. L. Garfield and A. E. Bergin (eds), Handbook of Psychotherapy and Behaviour Change: An empirical analysis, 2nd edn. New York: Wiley.

Bernstein, D. A. and Borkovec, T. D. (1973). Progressive Relaxation Training. Champaign, Ill.: Research Press.

Bild, R. and Adams, H. (1980). Modifications of migraine headaches by cephalic blood volume pulse and E.M.G. biofeedback. Journal of Consulting Clinical Psychology, 48, 51-57.

Bobey, M. J. and Davidson, P. O. (1970). Psychological factors affecting pain tolerance. Journal of Psychosomatic Research, 14, 371-376.

Bolles, R. C. and Fanselow, M. S. (1980). A perceptual-defensive-recuperative model of fear and pain. The Behavioural and Brain Sciences, 3, 291-323.

Bond, M. R. (1971). The relation of pain to the Eysenck Personality Inventory, Cornell Medical Index and Whitely Index of Hypochondriasis. British Journal of Psychiatry, 119, 671-678.

Bond, M. R. (1973). Personality studies in patients with pain secondary to organic disease. Journal of Psychosomatics, 17, 251-263.

Bond, M. R. and Pearson, I. B. (1969). Psychological aspects of women with advanced cancer of the cervix. Journal of Psychosomatic Research, 13, 13-19.

Boring, E. G. (1942). Sensation and Perception in the History of Experimental Psychology. New York: Appleton-Century-Crofts.

Bowers, K. S. (1968). Pain, anxiety and perceived control. Journal of Consulting and Clinical Psychology, 32, 596-602.

Budzinski, T. H., Stoyva, J. M., Adler, C. S. and Mullaney, D. J. (1973). E.M.G. biofeedback and tension headache: a controlled outcome study. Psychosomatic Medicine, 35, 484-496.

Chapman, C. R. (1977). Sensory decision theory methods in pain research: a reply to Rollman. Pain, 3, 295-305.

Chapman, C. R., Chen, A. C. N. and Harkins, S. W. (1979). Brain evoked potentials as correlates of laboratory pain: a review and perspective. In J. J. Bonica and D. Albe-Fessard (eds), Advances in Pain Research and Therapy, Vol. 3. New York: Raven Press.

Chapman, W. P. and Jones, C. M. (1944). Variations in cutaneous and visceral pain sensitivity in normal subjects. Journal of Clinical Investigation, 23, 81-91.

Chesney, M. A. and Shelton, J. L. (1976). A comparison of muscle relaxation and electromyogram biofeedback treatments for muscle contraction headache. Journal of Behaviour Therapy and Experimental Psychiatry, 7, 221-225.

Chesney, M. and Tasto, D. (1975). The effectiveness of behaviour modification with spasmodic and congestive dysmenorrhea. Behaviour Research and Therapy, 13, 245-253.

Clark, J. W. and Bindra, D. (1956). Individual differences in pain thresholds. Canadian Journal of Psychology, 10, 69-76.

Clum, G. A., Luscomb, R. L. and Scott, L. (1982). Relaxation training and cognitive redirection strategies in the treatment of acute pain. Pain, 12, 175-183.

Collins, F. L. and Martin, J. E. (1980). Assessing self report of pain: a comparison of two recording processes. Journal of Behavioural Assessment, 2, 55-63.

Cox, D. J., Freundlich, A. and Meyer, R. G. (1975). Differential effectiveness of electromyographic feedback, verbal relaxation instructions and medication placebo with tension headaches. Journal of Consulting and Clinical Psychology, 43, 892-898.

Craig, K. D. (1978). Social modelling influences on pain. In R. A. Sternbach (ed.), The Psychology of Pain. New York: Raven Press.

Craig, K. D., Best, H. and Ward, L. M. (1975). Social modelling influences on psychophysical judgements of electrical stimulation. Journal of Abnormal Psychology, 84, 366-373.

Craig, K. D. and Neidermayer, H. (1974). Autonomic correlates of pain thresholds influenced by social modelling. Journal of Personality and Social Psychology, 29, 246-252.

Craig, K. D. and Weiss, S. M. (1971). Vicarious influences on pain threshold determinations. Journal of Personality and Social Psychology, 19, 53-59.

Craig, K. D. and Weiss, S. M. (1972). Verbal reports of pain without noxious stimulation. Perceptual and Motor Skills, 34, 943-948.

Crockett, D. J., Prkachin, K. M. and Craig, K. D. (1977). Factors of the language of pain in patient and normal volunteer groups. Pain, 4, 175-182.

Crue, B. L. and Carregal, E. J. A. (1975). Pain begins in the dorsal horn - with a proposed classification of the primary senses. In B. L. Crue (ed.), Pain: Research and Treatment. New York: Academic Press.

Dalton, K. (1969). The Menstrual Cycle. New York: Pantheon Books.

Davidson, P. O. and McDougall, C. E. (1969). The generality of pain tolerance. Journal of Psychosomatic Research, 13, 83-89.

Denney, D. R. and Gerrard, M. (1981). Behavioural treatments of primary dysmenorrhea: a review. Behaviour Research and Therapy, 19, 303-312.

Downie, W. W., Leatham, P. A., Rhind, V. M., Wright, V., Branco, J. A. and Anderson, J. A. (1978). Studies with pain rating scales. Annals of Rheumatic Disease, 37, 378-381.

Dyck, P. J., Lambert, E. H. and O'Brien, P. (1976). Pain in peripheral neuropathy related to size and rate of fibre degeneration. In M. Weisenberg and B. Tursky (eds), Pain: Therapeutic approaches and research frontiers. New York: Plenum Press.

Egbert, L. D., Battit, G. E., Welch, C. E. and Bartlett, M. D. (1964). Reduction of postoperative pain by encouragement and instruction of patients. The New England Journal of Medicine, 270, 825-827.

Engel, G. L. (1959). 'Psychogenic' pain and the pain prone patient. American Journal of Medicine, 26, 899-918.

Epstein, L. H. and Abel, G. C. (1977). Analysis of biofeedback training effects for tension headache patients. Behaviour Therapy, 8, 37-47.

Epstein, L. H., Abel, G. C., Collins, F., Parker, L. and Cinciripini, P. M. (1978). The relationship between frontalis muscle activity and self reports of headache pain. Behaviour Research and Therapy, 16, 153-160.

Evans, F. J. (1974). The placebo response in pain reduction. Advances in Neurology, 4, 289-296.

Eysenck, S. B. G. (1961). Personality and pain assessment in childbirth of married and unmarried mothers. Journal of Mental Science, 107, 417-430.

Flannery, R. B., Sos, J. and McGovern, P. (1981). Ethnicity as a factor in the expression of pain. Psychosomatics, 22, 39-50.

Fordyce, W. E. (1978). Learning processes in pain. In R. A. Sternbach (ed.), The Psychology of Pain. New York: Raven Press.

Fordyce, W. E., Fowler, R. S., Lehmann, J. F., Delatour, B. J., Sand, P. L. and Treischmann, R. B. (1973). Operant conditioning in the treatment of chronic pain. Archives of Physical Medicine and Rehabilitation, 54, 399-408.

Franz, D. N. and Iggo, A. (1968). Dorsal root potentials and ventral root reflexes evoked by nonmyelinated fibres. Science, 162, 1140-1142.

Frederickson, L. W., Lynd, R. S. and Ross, J. (1978). Methodology in the measurement of pain. Behavioural Therapy, 9, 486-488.

Frid, M., Singer, G. and Rana, C. (1979). Interactions between personal expectations and naloxone: effects on tolerance to ischaemic pain. Psychopharmacology, 65, 225-231.

Friedman, A. P. (1962). Ad hoc committee on classification of headache. Journal of the American Medical Association, 179, 717-718.

Gannon, L. and Sternbach, R. A. (1971). Alpha enhancement as a treatment for pain: a case study. Journal of Behaviour Therapy and Experimental Psychiatry, 2, 209-213.

Gardner, W. J. and Licklider, J. C. R. (1959). Auditory analgesia in dental operations. Journal of the American Dental Association, 59, 1144.

Geer, J. H., Davison, G. C. and Gatchel, R. I. (1970). Reduction of stress in humans through nonveridical perceived control of aversive stimulation. Journal of Personality and Social Psychology, 16, 731-738.

Gracely, R. H. (1980). Pain measurement in man. In L. Ng and J. J. Bonica (eds), Pain, Discomfort and Humanitarian Care. Amsterdam: Elsevier/North Holland.

Gracely, R. H., Dubner, R. and McGrath, P. A. (1979). Narcotic analgesia: Fentanyl reduces the intensity but not the unpleasantness of painful tooth pulp sensations. Science, 203, 1261-1263.

Greene, R. and Reyher, J. (1972). Pain tolerance in hypnotic analgesia and imagination states. Journal of Abnormal Psychology, 79, 29-38.

Grevert, P. and Goldstein, A. (1977). Some effects of naloxone on behaviour in the mouse. Psychopharmacology, 53, 111-113.

Hardy, J. D., Wolff, H. G. and Goodell, H. (1952). Pain Sensations and Reactions. New York: Hafner.

Haynes, S., Griffin, P., Mooney, D. and Parise, M. (1975). Electromyographic biofeedback and relaxation instructions in the treatment of muscle contraction headaches. Behaviour Therapy, 6, 672-678.

Hayward, J. C. (1975). Information: A prescription against pain. London: Royal College of Nursing.

Hilgard, E. R. (1975). The alleviation of pain by hypnosis. Pain, 1, 213-231.

Hugdahl, K. (1981). Three systems model of fear and emotion. Behaviour Research and Therapy, 19, 75.

Johnson, J. E. (1973). The effects of accurate expectations about sensations on the sensory and distress components of pain. Journal of Personality and Social Psychology, 27, 261-275.

Johnson, J. E. and Leventhal, H. (1974). Effects of accurate expectations and behavioural instructions on reactions during a noxious medical examination. Journal of Personality and Social Psychology, 29, 710-718.

Johnson, J. E. and Rice, V. H. (1974). Sensory and distress components of pain. Nursing Research, 23, 203-209.

Johnson, W. G. and Turin, A. (1975). Biofeedback treatment of migraine headache: a systematic case study. Behaviour Therapy, 6, 394-397.

Kanfer, F. and Seider, M. L. (1973). Self-control: factors enhancing tolerance of noxious stimulation. Journal of Personality and Social Psychology, 25, 231.

Klepac, R. K., Dowline, J. and Hauge, G. (1981). Sensitivity of the McGill Pain Questionnaire to intensity and quality of laboratory pain. Pain, 10, 199-207.

Lambert, W. E., Libman, E. and Poser, E. G. (1960). The effect of increased salience of a membership group on pain tolerance. Journal of Personality, 28, 350.

Langer, E. L., Janis, I. L. and Wolfer, J. A. (1975). Reduction of psychological stress in surgical patients. Journal of Experimental Social Psychology, 11, 155-165.

Lefebvre, M. F. (1981). Cognitive distortion and cognitive errors in depressed psychiatric and low back pain patients. Journal of Consulting and Clinical Psychology, 49, 517-525.

Liebeskind, J. M. and Paul, L. A. (1977). Psychological and physiological mechanisms of pain. Annual Review of Psychology, 28, 41-60.

Lynn, R. and Eysenck, H. J. (1961). Tolerance for pain, extraversion and neuroticism. Perceptual and Motor Skills, 12, 161-162.

Madden, J., Akil, H., Patrick, R. L. and Barchas, J. D. (1977). Stress-induced parallel changes in central opiod levels and pain responsiveness in the rat. Nature, 265, 358-360.

Meichenbaum, D. and Turk, D. (1976). The cognitive-behavioural management of anxiety, anger and pain. In P. O. Davidson (ed.), The Behavioural Management of Anxiety, Depression and Pain. New York: Brunner/Mazel.

Melzack, R. (1973). The Puzzle of Pain. New York: Basic Books.

Melzack, R. (1975). The McGill Pain Questionnaire: major properties and scoring methods. Pain, 1, 275-299.

Melzack, R. and Torgerson, W. S. (1971). On the language of pain. Anesthesiology, 34, 50-59.

Melzack, R. and Wall, P. D. (1965). Pain mechanisms: a new theory. Science, 150, 971-979.

Melzack, R. and Weiss, A. Z. (1963). Strategies for controlling pain: contributions of auditory stimulation and suggestion. Experimental Neurology, 8, 239.

Merskey, H. (1965a). The characteristics of persistent pain in psychological illness. Journal of Psychosomatic Research, 9, 291-298.

Merskey, H. (1965b). Psychiatric patients with persistent pain. Journal of Psychosomatic Research, 9, 299-309.

Merskey, H. and Spear, F. G. (1964). The reliability of the pressure algometer. British Journal of Clinical Psychology, 3, 130-136.

Mullinix, J. M., Norton, B. J., Hack, S. and Fishman, F. A. (1978). Skin temperature biofeedback and migraine. Headache, 17, 242-244.

Pearce, S. and Morley, S. (1981). An experimental investigation of pain production in headache patients. British Journal of Clinical Psychology, 20, 275-281.

Pervin, L. A. (1963). The need to predict and control under conditions of threat. Journal of Personality, 31, 570-587.

Philips, C. (1976). Headache and personality. Journal of Psychosomatic Research, 20, 535-542.

Philips, C. (1977). A psychological analysis of tension headache. In S. Rachman (ed.), Contributions to Medical Psychology, Volume 1. Oxford: Pergamon.

Philips, C. and Hunter, M. (1981). Pain behaviour in headache sufferers. Behaviour Analysis and Modification, 4, 257-266.

Pilling, L. F., Brannick, T. L. and Swenson, W. M. (1967). Psychological characteristics of psychiatric patients having pain as a presenting symptom. Canadian Medical Association Journal, 97, 387-394.

Pilowsky, I. and Bassett, D. (1982). Pain and depression. British Journal of Psychiatry, 141, 30-36.

Pollard, W. E., Bobbitt, R. A., Bergner, M., Martin, D. P. and Gilson, B. S. (1976). The Sickness Impact Profile: reliability of a health status measure. Medical Care, 14, 146-155.

Procacci, P., Zappi, M. and Maresca, M. (1979). Experimental pain in man. Pain, 6, 123-140.

Rachman, S. (1976). The passing of the two stage theory of fear and avoidance: fresh possibilities. Behaviour Research and Therapy, 14, 123-131.

Rachman, S. and Hodgson, R. (1974). Synchrony and desynchrony in fear and avoidance. Behaviour Research and Therapy, 12, 311-326.

Reading, A. (1982). Testing pain mechanisms in persons in pain. In P. D. Wall and R. Melzack (eds), Textbook of Pain. London: Churchill Livingstone.

Reading, A. E., Everitt, B. S. and Sledmere, C. M. (1982). The McGill Pain Questionnaire: a replication of its construction. British Journal of Clinical Psychology, (in press).

Reynolds, D. V. (1969). Surgery in the rat during electrical analgesia induced by focal brain stimulation. Science, 164, 444-445.

Roberts, A. H. and Reinhardt, L. (1980). The behavioural management of chronic pain: long-term follow-up with comparison groups. Pain, 8, 151-162.

Rollman, G. B. (1977). Signal detection theory measurement of pain: a review and critique. Pain, 3, 187-211.

Ross, M. and Olsen, J. M. (1982). Placebo effects in medical research and practice. In J. R. Eiser (ed.), Social Psychology and Behavioural Medicine. London: Wiley.

Rybstein Blinchik, E. (1979). Effects of different cognitive strategies on chronic pain experience. Journal of Behavioural Medicine, 2, 92-101.

Sacerdote, P. (1970). Theory and practice of pain control in malignancy and other protracted or recurring painful illnesses. International Journal of Clinical Experimental Hypnosis, 18, 160-180.

Scott, J. and Huskisson, E. C. (1976). Graphic representation of pain. Pain, 2, 175-184.

Scott, J. and Huskisson, E. C. (1979). Accuracy of subjective measurements made with or without previous scores: an important source of error in serial measurement. Annals of Rheumatic Disease, 38, 558-559.

Shapiro, A. K. and Morris, L. A. (1978). The placebo effect in medical and psychological therapies. In S. L. Garfield and A. E. Bergin (eds), Handbook of Psychotherapy and Behaviour Change: An empirical analysis (2nd edn). New York: Wiley.

Sherman, J. E. and Liebeskind, J. C. (1979). An endorphinergic centrifugal substrate of pain modulation: recent findings, current concepts and complexities. Proceedings of the Association for Research in Nervous and Mental Diseases. New York: Reven Press.

Spear, F. G. (1967). Pain in psychiatric patients. Journal of Psychosomatic Research, 11, 187-193.

Staub, E., Tursky, B. and Schwartz, G. E. (1971). Self control and predictability: their effects on reactions to aversive stimulation. Journal of Personality and Social Psychology, 18, 157-162.

Sternbach, R. A. (1974). Pain Patients: Traits and treatments. New York: Academic Press.

Sternbach, R. A. (1978). Clinical aspects of pain. In R. A. Sternbach (ed.), The Psychology of Pain. New York: Raven Press.

Sternbach, R. A. and Timmermans, G. (1975). Personality changes associated with reduction of pain. Pain, 1, 177-181.

Sternbach, R. A. and Tursky, B. (1965). Ethnic differences among housewives in psychophysical and skin potential responses to electric shock. Psychophysiology, 1, 241-246.

Tan, S. (1982). Cognitive and cognitive-behavioural methods for pain control: a selective review. Pain, 12, 201-228.

Tasto, D. L. and Chesney, M. A. (1974). Muscle relaxation therapy for primary dysmenorrhea. Behaviour Therapy, 5, 668-672.

Thompson, S. C. (1981). Will it hurt less if I can control it? A complex answer to a simple question. Psychological Bulletin, 90, 89-101.

Turner, J. A. and Chapman, C. R. (1982a). Psychological interventions for chronic pain: a critical review. I. Relaxation training and biofeedback. Pain, 12, 1-21.

Turner, J. A. and Chapman, C. R. (1982b). Psychological interventions for chronic pain: a critical review. II. Operant conditioning, hypnosis and cognitive-behavioural therapy. Pain, 12, 23-46.

Wall, P. D. (1976). Modulation of pain by non-painful events. In J. J. Bonica and D. Albe-Fessard (eds), Advances in Pain Research and Therapy, Volume 1. New York: Raven Press.

Weisenberg, M. (1977). Pain and pain control. Psychological Bulletin, 84, 1008-1044.

Wolff, B. B. (1978). Behavioural measurement of human pain. In R. A. Sternbach (ed.), The Psychology of Pain. New York: Raven Press.

Wolff, B. B. and Jarvik, M. E. (1963). Variations in cutaneous and deep pain sensitivity. Canadian Journal of Psychology, 17, 37-44.

Woodforde, J. M. and Merskey, H. (1972a). Some relationships between subjective measures of pain. Journal of Psychosomatic Research, 16, 173-178.

Woodforde, J. M. and Merskey, H. (1972b). Personality traits of patients with chronic pain. Journal of Psychosomatic Research, 16, 167-172.

Zborowski, M. (1969). People in Pain. San Francisco: Jossey-Bass.

Chapter 8

SOME ASPECTS OF THE PHYSIOLOGY
OF THE MYSTICAL EXPERIENCE

P. B. C. Fenwick

Bucke, the Canadian psychiatrist who lived at the turn of the century, in his book 'Cosmic Consciousness' was one of the first Western scientists to attempt to define mystical experience or the cosmic sense as he called it. In his book he only deals with a very restricted range of experiences, namely those in which the individual loses his personal sense of 'I' and comes to view the world from the point of view of the Universal. Thus the experiences that he quotes are very wide and are experienced by very rare people, mainly those with a religious or philosophical training, e.g. saints, mystics or religious devotees.

An example follows:

Now came a period of rapture so intense that the universe stood still as if amazed at the unutterable majesty of the spectacle: only one in all the infinite universe. The All-caring, the Perfect One, the Perfect Wisdom, truth, love and purity! And with the rapture came insight. In that same wonderful moment of what might be called supernal bliss, came illumination. I saw with intense inward vision the atoms or molecules of which seemingly the universe is composed - I know not whether material or spiritual - rearranging themselves as the cosmos passed from order to order. What joy when I saw there was no break in the chain - not a link left out - every thing in its place and time. Worlds, systems all blended in one harmonious world Universal synonymous with Universal Love.

Bucke lists nine major features which have been used as a basis by subsequent authors to categorize the elements of the experience. Deikman (1966) has reduced these to five main features:

(1)   the intense realness of the experience;
(2)   unusual sensations;

(3) feelings of unity;
(4) ineffability or the inability to speak about the experience, usually because words are not available to describe it;
(5) trans-sensate phenomena.

Quite clearly, for an experience to have all these features at once it must be very powerful indeed.

These five features are described as follows. First, realness: the realness is such that the experiencer is overcome by the validity and meaning of the experience. It is this feeling which is its own justification: it must be true, because it feels true. Feelings of intense realness are common in drug experience, particularly in the wider experiences of LSD. The primary delusions of an acute paranoid psychosis are also examples of the same sudden feeling of intense realness occurring in a setting of clear consciousness: it comes with the conviction of absolute truth.

Next, unity, the feeling that the experiencer has seen through to the fundamental nature of the universe and that he and it are united. This feeling, combined with the feeling of realness leads to an absolute certainty that the very depths of the universe have been perceived and understood. Realness and unity combine to form the cornerstone of insight and artistic creation. Both these features of the mystical experience are reported to some degree with nitrous oxide and other drugs. An example of a nitrous oxide experience:

> The ego and its objects, the meum and the tuum, are one. Now this, only a thousandfold enhanced, was the effect upon me of the gas: and its first result was to make peal through me with unutterable power the conviction that Hegelism was true after all, and that the deepest convictions of my intellect hitherto were wrong. Whatever idea of representation occurred to the mind was seized by the same logical forceps, and served to illustrate the same truth; and that truth was that every opposition, among whatsoever things, vanishes in a higher unity in which it is based; that all contradictions, so-called, are but differences; that all differences are of degree; that all degrees are of a common kind; that unbroken continuity is of the essence of being; and that we are literally in the midst of an infinite, to perceive the existence of which is the utmost we can attain (William James, 1882).

Third, the feelings are 'ineffable', i.e. literally cannot be spoken about, because there are no words to describe the experience. All sensory experience would fall into this category if language did not contain terms to describe elements of the sensations. As soon as some new or unusual element is experienced, then it becomes ineffable. This is common, for example, in people with epilepsy who say they have a funny feeling they cannot describe before the onset of an attack; no amount of questioning can elicit the particular feeling, as there are no words to express it.

Fourth, trans-sensate experiences are experiences which are thought to be different from those of the five senses, an insight and communication with other aspects of nature not normally available to us.

Fifth, unusual percepts, e.g. the perception of reality in a different way, as if the mystic were seeing through to a new aspect of underlying reality. This perception comes through the normal channels of perception.

After an examination of the experience of mystical consciousness expressed by a subject undergoing a drug experience, Pahnke (1963) defined nine interrelated categories. These categories overlap Deikman's, but also extend them. Pahnke and Richards, in an article in 1966, illustrate this with excerpts from drug experiences as follows:

I   Unity. I found myself greatly in agreement or mumbling 'Of course, it has always been this way' over and over again, as the panorama of my life seemed to be swept up by this unifying and eternal principle ...

II   Objectivity and Reality shown by (1) insightful knowledge or illumination and (2) authoritativeness or the certainty from the experiences that such knowledge is truly or ultimately real in contrast to the feeling that the experience is a subjective delusion ...

III   Transcendence of Space and Time. In this state of consciousness, space and time are generally meaningless concepts, although one may feel one can look back on the totality of history from this transcendental perspective ...

IV   Sense of Sacredness. Sacredness is here defined as a non-rational, intuitive, hushed, palpitant response in the presence of inspiring realities. It is that which a person feels to be of special value and capable of being profaned ...

V   Deeply Felt Positive Mood. This category focuses upon the feelings of joy, blessedness, and peace inherent in mystical consciousness. It may be ebullient or quiet ...

VI   Paradoxicality. This category reflects the manner in which significant aspects of mystical consciousness are felt by the experiencer to be true in spite of the fact that they violate the laws of Aristotelian logic. For example, the subject claims to have died or ceased to exist, yet obviously continues to exist and even writes about his experience ...

VII   Alleged Ineffability. When such a subject attempts to communicate mystical consciousness verbally to another person, he usually claims that the available linguistic symbols - if not the structure of language itself - are inadequate to contain or even accurately reflect such experience ...

VIII   Transiency. This category refers to the temporary duration of mystical consciousness, in contrast to the relative permanence of the usual experience ... The characteristics of transiency indicate that the mystical state of consciousness is not sustained indefinitely and marks one of the important differences between it and psychosis.

IX   Positive Changes in Attitudes and/or Behaviour. Persons who have experienced the contents of the eight categories discussed above are also known to report concomitant changes in attitudes (1) towards themselves (2) towards others (3) towards life and (4) towards mystical consciousness itself.

All the features described above are quoted widely in mystical literature; but what is clear is that they are not in any way only limited to the rare mystical experience, but can be construed to be part of everyday experience and, as such, are also included in pathological states such as the psychoses.

The question, then, is how common are these states? Very little evidence exists concerning very wide mystical states, although there are many studies of mystical or religious experience. Hay, in his book 'Exploring Inner Space' (1982) reviews the early literature on religious experience. Early religious experience studies (Gloch and Stark, 1965) showed that over 45 per cent of Protestants and 43 per cent of Roman Catholics had had 'a feeling that you were somehow in the presence of God'. Gallup surveys in the United States by Back and Bourque in 1963, 1966 and 1967 showed that $20\frac{1}{2}$ per cent, 32 per cent and 44 per cent, respectively, had had a 'religious or mystical experience', the percentage increasing as the decade advanced, presumably due to the hippie movement allowing people to express their mystical experiences more freely. However, by 1978, the Princeton Religion Research Center found, in answer to a similar question, that the positive response was down to 35 per cent, possibly a reflection of a waning of popular interest in the mystical. In Britain, David Hay organized a NOP survey in 1976 asking a similar question and found a similar rate of reply: about 36 per cent gave positive responses. Of interest is the finding that although about a third of all people have had the experience, only 18 per cent have had it more than twice and only 8 per cent 'often' and more. There was no correlation with age, but positive replies were commonest in those whose education went beyond 20, e.g. the more articulate university graduates. There was also, interestingly, a sex difference; 41 per cent of women gave positive replies against 31 per cent of men. Fifty-one per cent said it lasted for between seconds to minutes and 74 per cent that it lasted less than a day.

If mystical experience is so common, then it is logical to assume that there must be a brain mechanism which allows the expression of the experience. The question then is, what mechanism?

Mystical states are seen with disorders of mood, psychotic illnesses and in some forms of epilepsy. I will deal mainly with the last category.

EPILEPSY AND MYSTICAL STATES

Epilepsy was in early Grecian and Roman times known as the sacred disease, despite a strong condemnation of the term by Galen. It was not, however, until this century that specific evidence for its association with mystical experience became available. This was started in the middle of the last century by Dostoevsky when, in his book 'The Idiot', he gave this speech to Prince Mishkin:

> He was thinking incidentally that there was a moment or two in his epileptic condition, almost before the fit itself (if it occurred during his waking hours), when

suddenly amid the sadness, spiritual darkness, and depression, his brain seemed to catch fire at brief moments, and with an extraordinary momentum his vital forces were strained to the utmost all at once ... All his agitation, all his doubts, and worries seemed composed in a twinkling, culminating in a great calm, full of serene and harmonious joy and hope, full of understanding and the knowledge of the final cause.

There is no doubt about the quality of this experience and that it fits perfectly into the description of a true mystical experience. It will be remembered that Fydor Mikhailovitch Dostoevsky himself suffered from epilepsy, and this speech of Prince Mishkin's has been interpreted by most authorities as representing the aura which occurred at the onset of Dostoevsky's attack. This view was encouraged by Dostoevsky's great friend Strakhov and his acquaintance, the mathematician Sofya Kovelevskaya, who reported in their memoirs that Dostoevsky had told them such a story. Dostoevsky was said to have had temporal lobe epilepsy and his ecstatic aura was part of a complex partial seizure. Considerable doubt has now crept into this very attractive account, and this I shall consider later.

How common, then, are these positive experiences as part of the epileptic aura? They are very rare: in Gowers' (1881) study of 505 epileptic auras, only 3 per cent were said to be emotional and none positive. In the Lennox (1960) study of 1,017 auras, only nine were said to be pleasant (0.9 per cent) and of these 'only a few showed positive pleasure'. Penfield and Kristiansen (1951) cite only one case with an aura of a pleasant sensation followed by an epigastric feeling of discomfort. Until 1980 no cases of temporal lobe epilepsy (TLE) and an ecstatic aura had been reported. Despite this, ecstatic states were frequently attributed in the literature to TLE (Gastaut, 1954; Ionasescu, 1957; Chavany, 1958; Alajouanine, 1973) and, as Gastaut (1978) explains, this was because people expected ecstatic states to be present, even though they were not reported.

However, Slater and Beard (1963) in their foundation paper on the interictal psychoses of epilepsy mention religious conversion experiences and ecstatic states as being common in their group of patients with temporal lobe epilepsy. They also pointed out that the religious conversion experiences, psychosis and temporal lobe epilepsy, were all linked. It was this which led to temporal lobe epilepsy and religious (mystical) experience coming to be even more closely associated. Slater and Beard's paper was written before the possibility that left- and right-sided temporal lobe lesions might lead to different aura contents or to different forms of psychosis had been clearly recognized. So, in that paper, the authors make no mention of whether they consider the right or left temporal lobe to be more involved.

MYSTICS, SAINTS AND TLE

Dewhurst and Beard (1970), in an excellent paper, looked specifically at those cases of temporal lobe epilepsy collected from the Maudsley and Queen Square Hospitals that showed religious conversion. The conversion usually came suddenly and was not always related to a mystical aura; of more interest, the majority of their cases had previously had a psychotic illness. It was thus difficult to know whether the experience was related to their epilepsy or their psychosis. It is just worth noting that both the Slater and Beard studies and the Dewhurst and Beard studies had several patients in common and so were not totally independent. The desire to explain the mystical in terms of the physical is nowhere more apparent than in the epilepsy literature. Temporal lobe epilepsy is the obvious place to look.

Many authors, among them the above, have drawn attention to the relationship between the mystical experience of some of the saints and reported alteration in their consciousness and behaviour. In many cases, changes of behaviour accompanied by an alteration in consciousness could be interpreted as being epileptic in nature. Dewhurst and Beard mention that St Catherine dei Ricci (1522-1590) had frequent hallucinations and stigmata. She lost consciousness regularly at weekly intervals, being 'out' from noon on Thursday until 4 p.m. the next day. These could have been epileptic, although I suspect some were possibly hysterical.

St Therese of Lisieux (1873-1897) had a series of mystical experiences when she was nine years old. They started with attacks of violent trembling, such that she thought she was going to die. Later, she had frightening hallucinations leading to a mystical experience and complete conversion when she was aged 14. These experiences could possibly be attributed to temporal lobe epilepsy. Dewhurst and Beard quote from Leuba (1925) as saying

These other Christian mystics also suffered from abnormal mental states which he tentatively diagnosed as hysteria, although their symptoms equally well suggest temporal lobe epilepsy. They were St Catherine of Genoa (1447-1510), Mme

Guyon (1648-1717) and St Margarite Marie (1647-1690). These mystics had periodic attacks which include the following symptoms: sensations of extremes of heat and cold, trembling of the whole body, transient aphasia, automatisms, passivity feelings, hyperaesthesiae, childish regression, dissociation, somnambulism, transient paresis, increased suggestibility and inability to open the eyes.

Bryant (1953) likes to include St Paul on the list, because of his sudden religious conversion on the way to Damascus with photism, paralysis, transient blindness and confusion. He goes on to suggest that St Paul's 'thorn in the flesh' could have been epilepsy. Bryant is also an enthusiast about genius and epilepsy. In his book, which should be read, he quotes the following people as having both genius, epilepsy and some mystical experience: Buddha, Socrates, Caligula, St Cecilia, Boehme, Pascal, George Fox, Napoleon, Caesar, Alexander, Mohammed, St Paul and Van Gogh, Peter I (the Great), Swedenborg, William Pitt, Paul I (of Russia), Byron and Swinburne, but not everyone agrees.

It is important to keep in mind that, despite the wide ranging of epileptologists throughout the world's mystical literature, very few true examples of the ecstatic aura and the temporal lobe fit had been reported in the world's scientific literature prior to 1980. If, then, epilepsy, and temporal lobe epilepsy in particular, can be one source of the mystical experience, is there any evidence that mystical experience occurs more with dominant or non-dominant temporal lobe lesions?

MYSTICAL EXPERIENCE, TLE AND INTERICTAL PERSONALITY

If the ecstatic aura was rare, ideas about the relationship of mystical states and religious ideas in patients with TLE were very common. Personality profiles suggested that religious inclination and mystical states were common in TLE; but, of even more interest, there was the suggestion that these experiences may be more common if the lesion is in one temporal lobe rather than the other.

However, confusion with regard to terminology rages unchecked through the literature. Religiosity, religious interest, mystical states and ecstatic states are frequently used as synonyms or left undefined. Unfortunately, this situation still remains.

That temporal lobe epilepsy has been related to specific disorders of the personality has been known and widely reported since the 1950s. A comprehensive early review is that of Tizard (1962), and a later one more specifically related to temporal lobe epilepsy is that of Fenton (1981). The figures quoted in studies concerned with TLE and psychiatric handicap reveal that about 50 per cent of patients with TLE show some form of psychiatric disorder. Generally, they were either aggressiveness, adhesiveness or alterations in either the emotional or volitional spheres. Religious interests and mystical experience were usually added, but did not become a major part of the TLE literature until the mid-1970s. Then David Bear (1979) put forward in 1975 his theory of limbic hyperconnection. He suggested that TLE was a reverse Kluver and Bucy (1939) syndrome. It will be remembered that Kluver and Bucy removed both temporal lobes of monkeys. They found that these monkeys lost their aggressive qualities, showed hyperphagia, losing their discrimination in what they ate, showed hypersexuality, losing their discrimination in their sexual objects, and extensively explored their environment: hypermetamorphosis.

In the sensory-limbic hyperconnection syndrome, Bear suggested:

> our analysis of the psychological changes occurring interictally in temporal lobe epilepsy emphasized extensive and progressive investment of stimulus complexes with intense affective significance. It was suggested that this phenomenon is produced anatomically by the formation of new, extensive and excessive sensory (or polysensory) limbic bonds.

Thus he suggests that one effect of TLE is to add excessive meaning to the world of the temporal lobe epileptic by the mechanism described above. This leads the epileptic to invest with meaning simple everyday life events. Religiosity is defined as: I have some very unusual religious experiences. This adds an emotional tone to ordinary everyday events, which then become charged with religious meaning.

Bear and Fedio (1977) in a subsequent paper looked at this idea formally, with a comparison between patients with TLE and two other control groups. They formed their own questionnaire and obtained ratings from both patients and their near relatives. They found that:

> right temporal foci led to external emotive or behavioural manifestations: anger, sadness, elation,

circumstantiality, viscosity and hypermoralism. By contrast, left hemisphere patients had ruminative intellectual tendencies: <u>religiosity</u>, philosophical interests, and sense of personal destiny.

This finding was important as it could indicate possibly that the left temporal lobe was involved with the mystical experience, or it may be that it was simply a reflection of interest in religious subjects, the experience only arising from the right side. They point out that 'thus experienced, objects and events shot through with affective colouration engenders a typically religious world view'.

Waxman and Geschwind (1975) were also concerned with a temporal lobe syndrome in which alterations in sexual behaviour, religiosity and compulsive writing were seen. Their explanation is in the same vein as that of Bear, an interictal temporal lobe syndrome. Geschwind (1979) is also a supporter of this view.

This idea, although attractive and providing a physiological explanation for enhanced mystical states, is not looking as strong as previously. Two recent papers controlling for brain damage, psychiatric morbidity and epilepsy have not found the same temporal lobe personality, although minor changes are still there.

Mungas (1982) compared patients with TLE and psychiatric illness against control groups of brain-damaged psychiatric patients and just psychiatric patients. On the Bear and Fedio questionnaire no differences were found. Then in a second study, he looked at the above groups plus a group of patients with movement disorders and a group of normal volunteers. His finding was that a very large part of the variance of the trait scores can be accounted for by psychiatric illness. Thus it looks as if the correlation is via psychiatric morbidity, which is high in patients with TLE rather than with a specific temporal lobe epileptic interictal personality profile.

Bear, Levin, Blumer, Chetham and Ryder (1982), using character disorders, affective disorders and schizophrenic control groups, found that there was no difference in religiosity between the schizophrenic and the temporal lobe epilepsy group. This finding again indicates that it may be the common link of psychosis in temporal lobe populations that leads to the apparent features of religiosity in the groups. It must also be remembered that mystical experience has only been found in the temporal lobe populations that were, or had been, psychotic. This suggests again that the link is via psychosis and not the TLE. Looking in more detail at their results, the difference in religiosity between the temporal lobe group and the control groups was greatest for the character disorders and had vanished for the psychotic schizophrenic group, again suggesting it was psychosis which was important. They also found a difference between the temporal lobe epileptics and a group of generalized epileptics on the dimension of religiosity, but, as this generalized group probably did not contain patients with a history of psychosis, while the temporal lobe group most probably did, the difference can again be explained.

MYSTICAL EXPERIENCE: GENERALIZED AND TEMPORAL LOBE EPILEPTICS

Sensky and Fenwick (1982) were interested in this point, and examined a population of temporal lobe epileptics and compared them with a population of patients with generalized epilepsy. Subjects were taken from the Maudsley Hospital Epilepsy Clinic. The groups were compared with national samples of the general population obtained from other studies.

Mystical states were assessed by questionnaire: the questions included: 'Did your faith come gradually or was there a point at which you suddenly "saw the light"?' and 'Have you ever felt at one with the universe and in touch with the universal?' Reported experiences were discounted as psychotic if the case notes indicated that they were not isolated phenomena, but formed part of a wider range of symptoms diagnosed as psychotic.

There was a 76 per cent response rate. Of the 55 respondents, 28 were male and 27 female. Fourteen patients had generalized epilepsy (26 per cent) and 30 (56 per cent) had a diagnosis of TLE. Of the TLE, 16 had dominant foci, seven nondominant and seven bilateral. The results are shown in table 1.

These results show that our subjects with TLE are not more inclined towards religion than those with generalized epilepsy, nor did they report more frequently a belief in, or an experience of, mystical or psychic states. Of more importance, the epileptics under-report mystical and psychic states compared to the general population. This finding would seem to be at variance with the American workers who find religiosity over-represented in their temporal lobe epileptics (why don't they compare the generalized groups with the other control groups?). It does suggest that the term 'religiosity' may not be travelling across the Atlantic very easily and that part of the confusion is a confusion of definition.

Sensky, in an excellent article (in press), points out some of the confusion that reigns with regard to terminology. He asks if the Americans are discussing 'religious inclination' rather than religiosity. He raises the question of the relationship of 'mystical delusional experience' occurring in the context of schizophreniform psychosis and religiosity. He also draws attention to Slater and Beard's original definition of religiosity as the meaningless interlarding of conversation with sanctimonious religiose phrases. This is a far cry from Bear, Levin, Blumer, Chetham and Ryder's paper (1982), in which they define religiosity as 'holding deep religious beliefs, often idiosyncratic, multiple conversions, cosmic consciousness'.

ICTAL MYSTICAL EXPERIENCE

So the case, as far as the interictal picture and epilepsy is concerned, must remain unproved, but what of ictal episodes? As mentioned above, ictal ecstatic episodes are also very rare or non-existent outside the schizophreniform psychoses of epilepsy, apart from the case of Dostoevsky. A paper by Gastaut (1978) suggests that there is considerable doubt even about this. He suggests that Dostoevsky suffered from idiopathic grand mal epilepsy and not temporal lobe epilepsy. The reasons Gastaut gives are:

(1) a family history of epilepsy: one of his sons died of status epilepticus;
(2) no evidence of brain damage;
(3) his fits were generalized from the start: a cry, then he fell unconscious and jerked, and afterwards was confused;
(4) there is no satisfactory evidence for partial complex seisures;
(5) nowhere in his diaries did Dostoevsky himself describe such auras, although he described his seizures in detail.

Gastaut goes on to analyse why the ecstatic aura came to be regarded as true in medical circles. It fulfilled a need, making the idea of emotional auras symmetrical: not only were emotional auras negative, which is common, leading to feelings of anxiety and fear of death, but also they should be positive, leading to feelings of joy and ecstasy. Dostoevsky provided the missing positive half.

This situation would have been understandable, and neat and tidy, had not Cirignotta, Cicogna and Lugharesi (1980)

Table 1 Reported belief in, and experience of, mystical and other psychic phenomena according to diagnosis

% of respondents

	TLE	Generalized epilepsy	General population* controls
	(N=30)	(N=16)	(N=1865)
Religious	56	72	57
Mystical experience			
Sudden gaining of faith	40	62	42
In touch with universe	12	33	19
Other psychic states			
Belief in	54	100	65
Experience of	4	36	20

* Data from Hay and Morisy (1978) based as a specified sample of the UK population

published a report of a patient with an ecstatic aura and right-sided temporal lobe fits and pictures of an EEG during a fit to prove it. In their paper, they said:

> Seizures generally come on when he is relaxed or drowsy. The subjective symptoms are defined by the patient himself as 'indescribable', words seeming to him inadequate to express what he perceives in those instants. However, he says that the pleasure he feels is so intense that he

cannot find its match in reality. Qualitatively, these sensations can only be compared with those evoked by music. All disagreeable feelings, emotions, and thoughts are absent during the attacks. His mind, his whole being is pervaded by a sense of total bliss. All attention to his surroundings is suspended: he almost feels as if this estrangement from the environment were a sine qua non for the onset of seizures. He insists that the comparable pleasure is that conveyed by music. Sexual pleasure is completely different: once he happened to have an attack during sexual intercourse, which he carried on mechanically, being totally absorbed in his utterly mental enjoyment.

Thus the question is again left open, with the suggestion that the temporal lobes and, possibly, the right temporal lobe are involved in the mystical experience.

PSYCHIC SENSITIVES AND THE MYSTICAL EXPERIENCE

In a study of psychic sensitives, Fenwick, Galliano, Coate, Rippere and Brown (1983) asked about the occurrence of mystical experience. The study was set up to investigate psychic sensitivity and to see how this related to brain function. Anecdotally, head injury has been linked with the onset of psychic powers. There is a frequently quoted case of a Dutchman who fell off a ladder and, on regaining consciousness in hospital, found that he could read the minds telepathically of his doctors and nurses. Nelson (1970) found temporal lobe EEG abnormalities in 10 out of 12 mediums, suggesting an abnormality of temporal lobe function. Neppe (1980) describes a significant similarity between temporal lobe epileptic symptoms and subjective paranormal experiences. A definite hemisphere asymmetry, with the non-dominant hemisphere being important in these experiences has been suggested by Andrew (1975), Braud and Braud (1975) and Broughton (1975).

Twenty psychic sensitives were allocated to the study by the College of Psychic Studies, but only 17 could take part. Seventeen age- and sex-matched controls were obtained from local church congregations: they had to have attended church weekly throughout the preceding year. Each subject was given a long interview by one of the study's psychologists, enquiring about medical data, head injuries, periods of unconsciousness, mystical and psychical experiences. Each subject was then given the shortened WAIS test, the Weschler Logical Memory test (left temporal lobe functioning) and Benton's Visual Retention test (right hemisphere and right temporal).

Significant mystical experience was statistically significantly more common among the sensitives (15-88 per cent), but it was also surprisingly common among the controls (8-47 per cent). Other differences were also seen between the groups, the sensitives being rather more fragile than the controls. The sensitives were significantly single more often: they had significantly more serious illnesses, head injuries, being knocked unconscious, having had blackouts, and had consulted a psychiatrist significantly more frequently. As far as the tests were concerned, the shortened WAIS showed a significantly different verbal IQ between the groups: 129 (SD 12.1) for the sensitives and 139 (SD 5.5) for the controls. There was no difference in performance IQ, both means 118. No significant differences were found for any of the other tests, so the groups were then combined. There were no left hemisphere abnormalities for either group, although both right hemisphere and right temporal abnormalities were found.

The positive associations with right temporal lobe impairment and right hemisphere impairment are shown in table 3 below and, as can be seen, this adds no support to the idea of right temporal lateralization for mystical experience.

However, when head injury is looked at, then a relationship with mystical experience is just found (see table 4).

It is of interest in this study that two subjects, one control and one sensitive, who had moderately severe head injuries with Rey Osterreith scores of nearly zero, after the injury had very wide mystical experiences. This adds support to studies which suggest that the right hemisphere and particularly the right temporal lobe, may be impaired in some subjects who have mystical experiences, but it also suggests that mystical experience can occur in those without any right hemisphere impairment.

MYSTICAL EXPERIENCE AND BRAIN FUNCTION

If we can accept that the right temporal area of the brain is to some extent involved with the mystical experience, can we, by present knowledge of right temporal functioning, explain any or all of the characteristics of the mystical experience? Taking Pahnke's (1963) criteria, both (I) the feeling of unity and (II) objectivity and reality can be explained by altered right temporal functioning. It could be argued that in the same way that the aura of a right temporal seizure can contain the feeling of certainty or familiarity (déjà vu is a non-dominant temporal lobe aura), so the right temporal lobe may, in the mystical experience, suddenly add meaning and harmony to the experience. The sense of sacredness (IV) can be explained in a similar manner as the addition of positive meaning to the outside world. The transcendence of space and time (III) could be explained by the distortion of the time sense which usually occurs in a temporal lobe aura, as if 30 seconds lasts for hours. Linked with this is the idea of transience (VIII) as if the functioning was changed only temporarily before returning to its previous state. The deeply felt positive mood (V) fits in well with the right temporal discharge described above. Paradoxicality and ineffability (VI and VII) are the hallmarks of the temporal aura. The self frequently feels itself alienated, split or fragmented during the temporal lobe aura, while the quality of the experience is such that it cannot (even if it can be remembered) be communicated in words. There are no words to describe such feelings. As for IX, a positive change in attitude, this is part of the way people respond after a powerful experience of any kind, mystical or frightening, and no special brain area is involved.

Thus, the mystical experience can be seen to draw heavily on components of right temporal functioning, and the three-dimensional and spatial quality of the experience gives additional weight to the possible localization. The insights which are obtained in the mystical experience are usually symbolic and frequently contain a spatial element: again, both these elements can be seen to be right sided. It must be said, however, that the true experience is greater than all these elements and must involve many different brain areas.

CONCLUSION

Much is yet to be known about the frequency, genesis and character of mystical experiences. Very little progress will be made until a precisely defined terminology has been agreed and is in use with workers in the field. Researchers in the medical field and particularly those in the United States would do well to bear in mind the religious and mystical experiences literature before designing their own questionnaires.

Despite a very confused field, some clues can be gleaned. Mystical experience of a simple kind is very common, with at least a third of the population having experienced at least

Table 2. The medical history of the sensitives and the control group is shown with the significance of the differences between them, using a chi square test.

	Sensitives	Controls	Significance chi square
Normal birth	17 (100%)	16 (94%)	NS
Serious operations	8 (47%)	8 (47%)	NS
Serious illnesses	8 (47%)	1 (6%)	0.05
Serious head injury	10 (59%)	2 (12%)	0.01
Time unconscious:			
approx. 1 hour	3	0	–
approx. 2 hours	2	0	–
Knocked out	8 (47%)	2 (12%)	0.05
Blackouts	7 (41%)	1 (6%)	0.04
Epilepsy	0	0	–
Migraine	9 (53%)	4 (24%)	NS
Prolonged medication	6 (35%)	2 (12%)	NS
Consulted psychiatrist	7 (41%)	1 (6%)	0.04
Handedness R.	16 (94%)	15 (88%)	NS

Table 3. R. Temporal lobe impairment: positive associations.

Item	(N=34)	With	Without	Significance chi square
Precognition		9 (27%)	4 (12%)	0.04
Clairaudience		8 (24%)	3 (9%)	0.05
Telepathy		11 (33%)	7 (21%)	0.07 (NS)
Work with a psychic helper	(N=18)	7 (39%)	4 (22%)	0.01 (Fishers (test)
Have a psychic guide		11 (33%)	6 (18%)	0.05

R. hemisphere impairment - position in physical space of helper R(X^2 sig. 0.04)

Table 4.

Combined groups (N=34)

Item	With (12)	Without (22)	Significance chi square
Precognition	8 (24%)	5 (15%)	0.03
Clairaudience	7 (21%)	4 (12%)	0.04
Has a psychic 'guide'	11 (32%)	1 (3%)	0.002
Sense 'guide' in physical space	9 (27%)	3 (9%)	0.04
Mystical experience	11 (32%)	1 (3%)	0.06 (NS)
Clairvoyance	10 (29%)	9 (27%)	0.04
Telepathy	8 (24%)	4 (12%)	NS
Clairsentience	8 (24%)	4 (12%)	NS
Healing	5 (15%)	7 (21%)	NS
Mediumship	5 (15%)	17 (50%)	NS

one episode. Wider experiences are much rarer. The right temporal lobe does seem to have some part to play in the genesis of the experience, while the left temporal lobe may be involved with a rather more formal interest in, and discussion of, mystical ideas. It is, however, too early yet, if indeed it will ever be possible, to point to a brain area and say it is through here that we come into contact with the universe and see the very nature of creation.

REFERENCES

Alajouanine, T. (1973). Litterature et epilepsie. In Cahiers de l'Herne, No. 24: Dostoievski. Paris: Editions de L'Herne.

Andrew, K. (1975). Psychokinetic influences on an electro-mechanical random number generator during evocation of 'left-hemispheric' vs 'right-hemispheric' functioning. In J. D. Morris, W. G. Roll and R. L. Morris (eds), Research in Parapsychology. Metuchen, NJ: Scarecrow Press.

Back, K. and Bourque, L. B. (1970). Can feelings be enumerated? Behavioural Science, 15, 487-496.

Bear, D. M. and Fedio, P. (1977). Quantitative analysis of interictal behaviour in temporal lobe epilepsy. Archives of Neurology, 34, 454-467.

Bear, D. (1979). Temporal lobe epilepsy - a syndrome of sensory-limbic hyperconnection. Cortex, 15, 357-384.

Bear, D., Levin, K., Blumer, D., Chetham, D. and Ryder, J. (1982). Interictal behaviour in hospitalized temporal lobe epileptics: relationship to idiopathic psychiatric syndromes. Journal of Neurology, Neurosurgery and Psychiatry, 45, 481-488.

Braud, W. G. and Braud, L. W. (1975). The psi-conducive syndrome: 3-response GESP performance following evocation of 'left-hemispheric' v 'right-hemispheric functioning. In J. D. Morris, W. G. Roll and R. L. Morris (eds), Research in Parapsychology. Metuchen, NJ: Scarecrow Press.

Broughton, R. S. (1975). Brain hemisphere specialisation and its possible effects on ESP performance. In J. D. Morris, W. G. Roll and R. L. Morris (eds), Research in Parapsychology. Metuchen, NJ: Scarecrow Press.

Bryant, J. E. (1953). Genius and Epilepsy. Brief sketches of great men who had both. Concord, Mass.: Ye Old Depot Press.

Bucke, R. (1961). Cosmic Consciousness: A study in the evolution of the human mind. New Hyde Park, NY: University Books.

Chavany, J. A. (1958). Epilepsie: Etude clinique, diagnostique, physiopathogenique et therapeutique. Paris: Masson.

Cirignotta, F., Cicogna, P. and Lugharesi, E. (1980). Epileptic seizures during card games and draughts. Epilepsia, 21, 137-140.

Deikman, A. (1966). Implication of experimentally induced contemplative meditation. Journal of Nervous and Mental Disorders, 142, 101-116.

Dewhurst, K. and Beard, A. W. (1970). Sudden religious conversions in temporal lobe epilepsy. British Journal of Psychiatry, 117, 497-507.

Fenton, G. W. (1981). Personality and behaviour disorders in adults with epilepsy. In E. H. Reynolds and M. R. Trimble (eds), Epilepsy and Psychiatry. London: Churchill Livingstone.

Fenwick, P. B. C., Galliano, S., Coate, M. A., Rippere, V. and Brown, D. Mediums, psychic gifts, psychic sensitivity and brain pathology. Submitted to the Journal of Nervous and Mental Diseases. (Preprints available from author.)

Gastaut, H. (ed.) (1954). The Epilepsies. Springfield, Ill.: Charles C. Thomas.

Gastaut, H. (1978). Fjodor Dostoevsky's involuntary contribution to the symptomatology and prognosis of epilepsy. Epilepsia, 19, 186-201.

Geschwind, N. (1979). Behavioural changes in temporal lobe epilepsy. Psychological Medicine, 9, 217-219.

Gloch, C. Y. and Stark, R. (1965). Religion and Society in Tension. Chicago: Rand McNally.

Gowers, W. R. (1881). Epilepsy and Other Chronic Consulsive Diseases. London: Churchill.

Hay, D. (1979). Religious experience amongst a group of post graduate students: a qualitative study. Journal for the Scientific Study of Religion, 18, 164-182.

Hay, D. (1982). Exploring Inner Space: Is God still possible in the twentieth century? Harmondsworth: Penguin.

Hay, D. and Morisy, A. (1978). Reports of ecstatic, paranormal or religious experience in Great Britain and the United States - a comparison of trends. Journal for the Scientific Study of Religion, 17, 255-268.

Ionasescu, V. (1957). Epilepsia Temporala. Bucharest: Editura Medicala.

James, W. (1882). Subjective effects of nitrous oxide. Mind, 7, 186-208. Reprinted in C. T. Tart (ed.) (1969), Altered States of Consciousness. New York: Wiley.

Kluver, H. and Bucy, P. C. (1939). Preliminary analysis of functions of the temporal lobes in man. Archives of Neurology and Psychiatry, 42, 979-1000.

Lennox, W. (1960). Epilepsy and Related Disorders, Volume 1. London: Churchill.

Leuba, J. H. (1925). The Psychology of Religious Mystics. London: Kegan Paul.

Mungas, D. (1982). Interictal behaviour abnormality in temporal lobe epilepsy: a specific syndrome or non specific psychopathology. Archives of General Psychiatry, 39, 108-111.

Nelson, G. K. (1970). Preliminary study of the electro-encephalographs of mediums. Parapsychologica IV, 9, 30-35.

Neppe, V. H. (1980). Subjective paranormal experience and temporal lobe symptomatology. Parapsychological Journal of South Africa, 1:2, 78-98.

Pahnke, W. (1963). Drugs and mysticism: an analysis of the relationship between psychedelic drugs and the mystical consciousness. Unpublished thesis, Harvard University, Cambridge, Mass.

Pahnke, W. and Richards, W. A. (1966). Implications of LSD and experimental mysticism. Journal of Religion and Health,

5, 175-208. Reprinted in C. T. Tart (ed.), Altered States of Consciousness. New York: Wiley.

Penfield, W. and Kristiansen, K. (1951). Epileptic Seizure Patterns. Springfield, Ill.: Charles C. Thomas.

Princeton Religion Research Center (1978). The Unchু ed American. Princeton, NJ: Princeton Religion Research Center and the Gallup Organisation.

Sensky, T. and Fenwick, P. B. C. Religiosity, mⁿstical experience and epilepsy. In F. Clifford Rose (ed.), Progress in Epilepsy. In press.

Slater, E. and Beard, A. W. (1963). The schizophrenia-like psychoses of epilepsy. 1. Psychiatric aspects. British Journal of Psychiatry, 109, 95-150.

Tizard, B. (1962). The personality of epileptics: a discussion of the evidence. Psychological Bulletin, 59, 196.

Waxman, S. G. and Geschwind, N. (1975). The interictal behaviour syndrome of temporal lobe epilepsy. Archives of General Psychiatry, 32, 1580-1586.

Acknowledgement

My thanks are due to Mrs A. Wyer and Mrs P. Place for their kind help and organization in preparing the manuscript.

Chapter 9

HUMAN SOCIOBIOLOGY

Peter K. Smith

The last two decades have seen a renewed impetus to the application of evolutionary theory to animal social behaviour. Wilson's monumental book, 'Sociobiology: The new synthesis' (1975) was instrumental in bringing this body of theory and data to the attention of social scientists generally, and the last chapter specifically attempted to extrapolate from mammalian and primate sociobiology to the understanding of human behaviour. The claims of human sociobiology continue to be hotly contested in psychology and other social science disciplines.

WHAT IS SOCIOBIOLOGY?

Sociobiology aims to provide a systematic account of the evolution of behaviour, and especially social behaviour, in relation to genetic advantage and biological fitness. Within the phylogenetic constraints and possibilities of a particular species, behaviour should evolve so that, in general, when in their natural environment, individuals should act to maximize their inclusive fitness. Inclusive fitness refers to the number of descendants left in future generations, including those of relatives as well as direct descendants. Ultimately, biological fitness refers to gene frequencies; if animals are seen as having behaviour controlled by genes, then successful genes will be those which induce behaviour leading to their own replication in future organisms.

   This emphasis on selection of genes is in distinction to earlier ideas that behaviour was selected for the benefit of a group of animals, or a whole species. Rather, the social behaviour of animals is seen as a complex mixture of selfishness and altruism. Much behaviour may be to the benefit of an individual (and hence its genes); some behaviour will be mutual y beneficial to the animal performing it and the recipient. Some behaviours may manipulate or exploit others. Some behaviours will be 'genuinely' altruistic at the individual level, being to the net benefit of another individual; most notably if the other individual is related (kin altruism), also possibly if reciprocation is expected later (reciprocal altruism), or if the donor individual is coerced into being altruistic.

The development of sociobiological theory has produced a framework for explaining such phenomena as mating systems, aggression and territoriality, co-operation, and parental care, in terms of the costs and benefits of certain behavioural strategies to the individual. The concept of the 'evolutionarily stable strategy' (Maynard Smith, 1982) takes account of the behaviour of other animals in calculating the optimal strategy of one individual. Some of the theoretical developments are closely similar to parts of economic theory, and this is especially true of optimal foraging theory, which predicts an individual's feeding patterns in particular resource distributions. At first glance a purely individual matter, in practice the feeding behaviour of other conspecifics will clearly be important. The term 'behavioural ecology', which some researchers now prefer to sociobiology, can be used to refer to all these areas in which evolutionary theory, in the guise of cost/benefit analysis of behaviour in terms of inclusive fitness, is applied to an animal in a particular ecological situation.

The application of such theories to animal behaviour is not widely in dispute, although within the framework of the theory there is considerable controversy over certain points, for example, the relative importance of kin selection. Recent publications relevant to the general areas of sociobiology and behavioural ecology are Markl (1980), Krebs and Davies (1981), and King's College Sociobiology Group (1982).

PUBLICATIONS IN HUMAN SOCIOBIOLOGY

Human sociobiology claims that, by arguments of evolutionary continuity, the principles of animal sociobiology can be applied, at least to some extent, to the study of human behaviour. This was argued in full by Wilson (1978) in 'On Human Nature', developing the last chapter of his 1975 book. Similar expositions of human sociobiology are Daniel Freedman's 'Human Sociobiology' (1979), Richard Alexander's 'Darwinism and Human Affairs' (1980) and David Barash's 'The Whisperings Within' (1981). The weightiest collection of empirical studies is edited by Napoleon Chagnon and William Irons, 'Evolutionary

Biology and Human Behaviour: An Anthropological Perspective'
(1979). The theoretical link between biological and cultural
evolution has been furthest developed by Charles Lumsden and
E. O. Wilson in 'Genes, minds and culture' (1981). A scientific journal specifically devoted to the area, Ethology and
Sociobiology, is completing its third volume, and the International Society for Human Ethology publishes the Human Ethology Newsletter. Other journals which frequently publish
articles relevant to human sociobiology include The Behavioural and Brain Sciences, Current Anthropology, American
Anthropologist, and Journal of Human Evolution.

Generally, favourable reviews or collections are provided
by Gregory, Silvers and Sutch (1978), Ruse (1979), and Barlow
and Silverberg (1980). More critical books are Sahlins (1976),
Harris (1979), Midgley (1979), and Montagu (1980). Wind (1981)
reviews 15 books on human sociobiology.

WHAT HAS HUMAN SOCIOBIOLOGY TRIED TO EXPLAIN?

As some of the above publications will indicate, much of the
impact of human sociobiology so far has been on anthropology.
Because of the way the study of human behaviour has come to be
partialled out among social science disciplines, the study of
human mating patterns, resource allocations, warfare, infanticide and kin-related behaviour in different societies has been
the province of anthropologists rather than psychologists.
Much of this work has utilized the data on 186 pre-industrial
societies compiled by Murdock and White in 1969 as a standard
cross-cultural sample. Other areas in which sociobiological
theorizing is well-developed, such as parent-offspring relationships, sex differences, and the conditions for altruistic
behaviour, are more the traditional province of psychologists.
However, I shall not pursue what are essentially irrelevant
interdisciplinary boundaries, but rather review some of the
main areas of human behaviour where human sociobiology has had
an appreciable application.

MARRIAGE PATTERNS AND SEX DIFFERENCES IN REPRODUCTIVE SUCCESS

In mammals, there is a biological asymmetry in the investment
mothers and fathers need to make in offspring. A mother necessarily invests a great deal of time and energy in bearing and

suckling an infant: a father need make no more effort than one copulation. Thus, generally, in mammals, females are more choosy than males about mating; and males have a greater variance in reproductive success. Such differences are strong in polygamous species, but less strong in a relatively few monogamous species of mammals in a number of which males do play a considerable part in rearing their offspring.

Depending on how exactly the calculations are done, some 76-85 per cent of human societies are polygynous, and some 15-23 per cent monogamous (though the latter of course include the numerically predominant industrial societies). In polygynous societies, males do have greater variance in reproductive success, as shown empirically for the Turkmen by Irons (1979) and Yanomamo by Chagnon (1979). For example, in one Yanomamo village, the most fertile male fathered 43 children, the most fertile female 14 children (conversely some males will father no children, but almost all females will mother several).

Monogamy is relatively common in hunter-gatherer societies on the one hand, and industrial societies on the other, in both of which fathers can play an important role in looking after children. Polygyny is relatively common in agricultural societies, where males can compete in the accumulation of wealth (e.g. cattle) and successful males can buy a number of brides (van den Berghe, 1979). As expected, polyandry is very rare in human societies (about 0.6 per cent of total). If two or more males are married to one female, then one of the males is likely to be investing in offspring who are not his own. When polyandry does occur, it is often fraternal, so the male is then investing in nephews and nieces.

Symons (1979, 1980; see also Hrdy, 1979a) has developed a sociobiological approach to a variety of sex differences in human physiology and behaviour. Greater sexual competitiveness among males is seen as a cause of the slight to moderate sexual dimorphism in humans, a greater desire for sexual variety and greater ease of sexual arousal in men than women, and greater male than female jealousy over adultery. Symons argues that men tend to be evaluated as possible partners primarily in terms of status, women primarily in terms of age and attractiveness, these being different indicators of their potential reproductive success. The asymmetry in sexual jealousy has been considered further by Daly, Wilson and Weghorst (1982), and the relationship between sexual dimorphism and marriage systems by Alexander, Hoogland, Howard, Noonan and Sherman (1979).

KINSHIP TERMINOLOGIES, PROPERTY INHERITANCE AND PATERNITY CERTAINTY

Kinship is of great importance in sociobiological theory, and animals may use behavioural co-variates of kinship, such as familiarity or co-rearing, to influence their behaviour appropriately. In principle, humans could use a more exact and conscious classification of kin to similar effect. Fox (1979) indeed regards the universality of kinship classification as having such functions, notably to regulate altruistic behaviour and choice of marriage partners (see next two sections).

One set of difficulties with this view is that kinship terminologies and prescriptions often do not very accurately reflect actual genetic relatedness. For example, although we reckon descent and pass on property bilineally (through both sons and daughters), many societies practice unilineal inheritance and descent: either matrilineal (through females) or patrilineal (through males). It has been argued (van den Berghe, 1979) that unilineal descent - particularly common in horticultural and pastoralist societies - facilitates the formation of discrete kin groups (e.g. discrete rather than overlapping sets of first cousins) who can co-operate in common enterprises such as cultivating and herding. Bilineal descent is more common in hunter-gatherer societies, where social groups are smaller and the need for co-operative action is much more limited.

Amongst unilineal societies, only about one-quarter are matrilineal. This could seem surprising, since whereas a mother can be certain who her children are, a father cannot be so certain about his paternity of a particular child, especially if extra-marital intercourse is tolerated, or occurs with reasonable frequency, as happens in some societies. Matrilineal descent is thus a more certain guide to genetic relatedness. In, fact Gaulin and Schlegel (1980; but see Wolfe and Gray, 1981) have confirmed that low paternity certainty (as inferred from sexual customs and mores) is associated with matrilineal descent, and even more strongly with direct behavioural ways in which males might invest elsewhere than with their wive's children, for example in the inheritance of fixed or movable property.

Hartung (1976, 1982) and van den Berghe (1979) argue that the predominance of patriliny is because it is generally better for parents to invest in sons than in daughters. This is because of the greater potential reproductive success of males, discussed earlier, notably in polygynous societies with accumulation of wealth. Direct inheritance of wealth from father to son is an efficient way of aiding the son's reproductive success, with the groom's kin paying bridewealth or bride-price as part of a marriage transaction. High paternity certainty is ensured by patrilocal residence, with wives under the constant surveillance of mothers-in-law.

EXOGAMY AND INCEST AVOIDANCE

In birds and mammals there is now good evidence that an individual will tend to select as a mating partner another individual who is fairly similar to those with which it was reared, but not a sibling, parent or offspring. Incestuous matings are avoided, probably because of the likelihood of decreased fertility of the offspring of such unions; but less close relatives are preferred over complete strangers (e.g. Bateson, 1982).

Human societies typically show evidence of a similar balance between inbreeding and outbreeding in choice of marriage partners, and avoidance of incest. Close inbreeding is almost universally prohibited by incest taboos, but in addition there appears to be an unconscious mechanism by which persons with whom one is co-reared in early childhood are unattractive as adult sexual partners. Usually, one is co-reared with close genetic relatives, but two exceptions to this have been widely quoted. In the Israeli Kibbutzim, children reared together in the same children's house, usually unrelated, almost never become marriage partners although there is no adult norm against this. They just do not seem to be sexually attracted to each other. The other example is the Chinese form of sim-pua marriage, in which a girl was adopted, often in infancy, by a family whose son she was later expected to marry. The failure rate of these marriages was quite high, and in general sim pua wives bore significantly fewer children than other wives did (Bixler, 1981; van den Berghe, in press).

Many societies have rules of lineage exogamy which dictate marriage to partners who may be classified as non-kin. In practice, however, in societies with unilineal descent, the preferred, or even prescribed, marriage partners are often first cousins: cross-cousins who are in different lineages or class. Van den Berghe (1980) argues that such a system recoups some of the kin selection loss of unilineal descent systems; certain kin groups who are defined out of kinship by terminology are reconnected by marriage and reciprocity. There may be additional genetic advantages to first-cousin marriage (Hughes, 1980).

ALTRUISM, RECIPROCITY AND EXCHANGE

Kin selection theory predicts that altruistic behaviour will be directed to relatives (for conspecifics who could normally be expected to be relatives) provided that the benefit to the recipient, even when devalued by the degree of genetic relatedness, exceeds the cost to the donor. Reciprocal altruism theory (Trivers, 1974) predicts that altruistic behaviour will be directed even to unrelated individuals, provided that the benefit given can be expected to be returned on a future occasion. Kin altruism has been well substantiated in many animal species, but reciprocal altruism, which probably requires memory for the actions of conspecifics and sanctions against cheats, has only reliably been established in the primates (Packer, 1977).

The conditions for reciprocal altruism as well as kin altruism should be well fulfilled in human societies. Essock-Vitale and McGuire (1980) derived five predictions for human altruism, including that most help should be given to close kin, that friendships with non-kin will be reciprocal, and that in general the amount of reciprocity expected and received will vary inversely with genetic relatedness. That such a pattern of altruism is true generally for tribal societies was already known (see Sahlins, 1972). Essock-Vitale and McGuire examined their predictions in more detail for 13 societies for which there was excellent anthropological documentation; of the 30 predictions which could be clearly tested, 27 were confirmed, two were doubtful, and only one was disconfirmed. Feinman (1979) has carried out an analysis of the ethnographic literature on food-sharing in a similar fashion.

An example of behaviour concordant with expectations from kinship altruism comes from Morgan (1979), who studied the composition of Eskimo whaling boat crews. The only social prescription was that crew members should be from the same patriclan. However, in practice, the genetic relatedness of crew members was very high, averaging about 0.35. Morgan argues that this facilitated kin altruism in the often dangerous situations which the whaling crews encountered. As an older ethnographic study reported

> in days past the old people strongly urged that a man hunt only with his relatives, because if the boat got into trouble out on the ice a nonclansman would be less prone to help a man out of difficulty (Morgan, 1979).

Thompson (1980) has examined the implications of reciprocal altruism theory for human behaviour, taking account of research by social psychologists on the conditions under which altruistic behaviour most readily occurs. For example, the likelihood of altruism is predicted to be greater if a certain situation is likely to recur, with the roles of donor and recipient reversed: hence, greater helpfulness in smaller than larger communities. Similarly, altruistic behaviour is facilitated if the cost to the donor is small, as experimental studies have confirmed.

TERRITORIALITY AND AGGRESSION

Among mammalian species, the occurrence of territorial and aggressive behaviours has been analysed primarily in terms of resource defence, with the primary sources being food, and potential mating partners. Thus, territoriality may or may not be an optimal strategy, depending on the distribution and concentration of resources, and whether the time and energy which would be needed to defend a territory are worth it for the exclusive use of the resources therein.

Dyson-Hudson and Smith (1978) have applied a similar analysis to human societies. They developed a model taking account of resource density and resource predictability, predicting a stable territorial system when both density and predictability were high. The model was applied successfully to three locally adapted human tribal populations.

Durham (1976a) has developed an approach to tribal warfare in terms of resource competition, and the cost or benefit to an individual of taking part in an attack on a neighbouring group. He considers aspects such as the nature of resources, the size of groups and possibility of recruitment from other groups, the degree of relatedness between groups, and their relative strength and warfare technology. Animals often assess relative strength through ritualized aggression, and a functionally similar phenomenon of assessment rituals is found in tribal groups such as the Yanomamo (Chagnon, 1968) or the Maring (Peoples, 1982).

PARENTAL INVESTMENT, CARE AND ABUSE

From a sociobiological viewpoint, the successful raising of offspring is the most crucial criterion of genetic success. Predictions can be made concerning such aspects as family size, sex ratio, the specificity of parental investment, and the type and amount of investment including the possibility of parent-offspring conflict (Smith, 1983).

For hunter-gatherer peoples, with the mother carrying a young baby with her whilst out gathering, some spacing of births is essential. Blurton Jones and Sibly (1978) have argued that the actual mean spacing of births - about four years - is optimum from the mother's point of view. Closer spacing would mean more children conceived, but set against this, less likelihood of the child surviving to maturity. The energetic costs of carrying and feeding the closely spaced babies could be very considerable.

Infanticide might seem another behaviour difficult to explain in terms of reproductive success. Yet it is found widely in mammals; see Hrdy (1979b) for a review. One class of infanticide is probably due to parental manipulation, where the neglect or death of one offspring sufficiently improves the chances of survival of the mother and/or other offspring. Infanticide has in fact been a prevalent method of birth control in human societies, except for the modern industrial states (Langer, 1972). Main causes seem to have been spacing births relative to resource conditions (e.g. preferential twin infanticide, Granzberg, 1973), and the killing of deformed babies who could in fact have little reproductive potential.

Dickemann (1979) has taken the analysis of infanticide a step further in the case of highly stratified human societies, such as Northern India, Imperial China, and medieval and early modern Western Europe. Following the argument of Trivers and Willard (1973), she argues that parents high on the social scale should favour sons, who, via inherited wealth and status, can have much better than average reproductive success. Such societies were, in fact, characterized by polygyny, hypergyny (upward marriage of females), and dowry systems and, in addition, preferential female infanticide among the middle and upper classes. Preferential male infanticide might be expected in the lower classes, but is not, Dickemann argues, because of the direct contribution such males can make to subsistence. Chagnon, Flinn and Melancon (1979) found no connection with sex ratio of offspring and parental rank in Yanamamo villages, but the Yanamamo are a relatively non-stratified society. Hughes (1981) has presented a case for preferential female infanticide in non-stratified societies, based on the relative importance of co-operation and competition among sibs of the same sex.

It is possible that the increased sanctions against infanticide in modern societies have led in part to the incidence of child abuse and neglect. Sociobiologists have suggested that child abuse might be explained by lack of parental resources, or low reproductive value of offspring (as with infanticide), and/or lack of confidence in paternity (Daly and

Wilson, 1981; Lenington, 1981). Such predictions are often borne out, as abuse is more frequent from males, from step-parents, and to handicapped children (Lightcap, Kurland and Burgess, 1982).

Step-parents might be expected to be less prepared to invest in anothers' offspring, from a sociobiological viewpoint. Thus, adoption might seem difficult to explain. In fact, adoption of unrelated children was very rare in historical or in present-day non-urban communities (Goody, 1969); it was usually done by close relatives. Silk (1980) has examined in detail adoption in the Polynesian islands, where some 25 per cent of children may be raised away from their parents. She found that 80 per cent of adoptive parents were relatives; nevertheless, biological children still tended to be favoured in inheritance rights over adopted children.

FURTHER EXAMPLES

The above do not, of course, exhaust the topics treated by human sociobiologists. Among some others are infant stereotypies (Thelen, 1981), homicide (Daly and Wilson, 1982), suicide (DeCatanzaro, 1981), concealment of ovulation in the human female (Burley, 1979; Alexander and Noonan, 1979; Spuhler, 1979; Strassman, 1981), and the timing of the female menopause (Gaulin, 1980).

THE SCIENTIFIC STATUS OF HUMAN SOCIOBIOLOGY

Human sociobiology has been, and continues to be, a controversial discipline. It has been accused of having reactionary political, racist or sexist connotations; and of being unscientific, false or unfalsifiable (e.g. Sahlins, 1976; Lewontin, 1979; Gould, 1980). These accusations are well discussed by Ruse (1979). In this section, I shall discuss the purely scientific status of human sociobiology in terms of whether it can provide a unified explanation of many diverse phenomena; whether it can explain previously unexplained phenomena; whether it can make successful but falsifiable predictions; and whether it can successfully compete with other theories.

A UNIFIED EXPLANATION OF DIVERSE PHENOMENA

Potentially, human sociobiology can provide an explanatory framework for a great variety of behavioural phenomena. As the previous sections have outlined, it claims to do so for large areas of anthropology, and social and developmental psychology, in particular. It does so on the basis of a cost/benefit analysis of behaviour in terms of inclusive fitness and thus ultimately, in terms of the relative success of genes which specify or predispose to certain behavioural pathways in development.

Although the range of phenomena is impressive, it will have struck the reader that some of the phenomena explained are unsurprising, to say the least. For example, the fact that people are less willing to be altruistic to others if there is a psychological cost to themselves, such as time available (Thompson, 1980); that concentrated and predictable resources are more likely to be defended (Dyson-Hudson and Smith, 1978); or that mothers space their births if they have to carry and feed young infants (Blurton Jones and Sibly, 1978). The point here is that human sociobiologists have not directly related psychological costs and benefits to genetic inclusive fitness, and that potentially any alternative theory which postulated costs and benefits to behavioural choices could similarly explain many human behavioural phenomena, without reference to genes. This argument will be considered further when we compare human sociobiology with alternative theories.

EXPLANATIONS OF PREVIOUSLY UNEXPLAINED PHENOMENA

There are certain behavioural phenomena which human sociobiologists can in principle explain, and which point strongly to genetic advantage as being implicated in the costs and benefits of behavioural choices. Two examples are the mother's brothers phenomenon and parent-offspring conflict. Convincing alternative explanations for these have been lacking (though an attempt to provide a cultural explanation for the former has recently been made by Werren and Pulliam, 1981).

In many non-technological societies, the mother's brother has a special relationship with her children, often closer than that of the father. Apart from invoking a general matrilineal structure to the society (which itself needs to be explained), it is not clear what explanation there is for this asymmetry in kin relationships (Radcliffe-Brown, 1924). Indeed, Sahlins (1976) used this kin asymmetry as an argument against the kin selection approach of sociobiologists. However, as we saw earlier, low paternity certainty can be an explanation both for matriliny generally and for the mother's brother phenomenon in particular. As Greene (1978) and Kurland

234

(1979) have calculated, if paternity certainty is low enough then mother's brother is likely to be more closely genetically related than 'father'. Gaulin and Schlegel's (1980) analyses suggest only limited support for the specific prediction that societies with high mother's brother involvement should have low paternity certainty, but make further predictions concerning alternative investment routes, or the likelihood of rapid cultural change in societies which deviate from this prediction.

Another sociobiological prediction is of parent-offspring conflict over the amount and timing of parental investment in the offspring; this is due to the non-identical genetic interests of an individual offspring and either its parent, or its existing or potential future sibs. Parent-offspring conflict theory (Trivers, 1974) makes more specific predictions, such as higher degree of conflict in younger mothers (with more future potential offspring at stake).

Blurton Jones (1978) has provided one example of possible parent-offspring conflict in humans. Babies have an optimum birthweight at which perinatal mortality is lowest. However, if a mother's conserving resources from the present offspring increased the chances of successfully raising subsequent offspring, then it would be optimal for the mother to produce a baby of birthweight lower than that optimal for the baby. In fact, the mean human birthweight is slightly below the babies' optimum. This was known in 1952, so Blurton Jones is making a post hoc prediction; but the finding is not explained by any other theories.

MAKING SUCCESSFUL BUT FALSIFIABLE PREDICTIONS

Following the line of thought of philosophers of science such as Popper and Lakatos, human sociobiology should make predictions which are, in principle, falsifiable. In addition, most of the predictions should be successful. Considering human sociobiology as a research programme (Lakatos, 1978), incorrect predictions could lead to a modified theory with more heuristic power, or, if sustained and serious enough, the success of a rival research programme.

Many successful predictions of human sociobiology are, in principle, falsifiable. For example, altruism might not be directed preferentially to kin. If this were so, it would lead to a very different sort of human behaviour from what is known, at least in tribal societies; but since human sociobiology is attempting to describe human nature, such obvious, but in principle falsifiable, predictions are to be expected.

Other predictions are partly successful, or as yet rather untested. For example, the correlation between mother's brother involvement and paternity certainty; or between parent-offspring conflict and age of mother.

Further predictions appear to be incorrect; I will give some examples of these.

Durham (1976a), in his review of primitive warfare, proposes an analysis in terms of individual reproductive success rather than group advantage. A successful warrior, for example, might have enhanced status and greater resources to attract extra wives in a polygamous society. Yet, in his detailed analysis of Mundurucu warfare, Durham notes that a successful headhunter must abstain from sexual intercourse for three rainy seasons! This certainly tends to suggest group rather than individual advantage, and is only accommodated to Durham's argument by rather ad hoc assumptions which partially concede this.

Beall and Goldstein (1981) have analysed Tibetan fraternal polyandry to see if it is a fitness-enhancing strategy. In the area of Tibet they examined there was no female infanticide, and there were many unmarried females. As an alternative to fraternal polyandry, they found that males in monogamous unions were more reproductively successful. They conclude that sociocultural, economic and political factors can perpetuate mating systems that decrease the individual and inclusive fitness of the individuals who practice them (though see Hughes, 1982).

Other predictions which appear largely true for tribal societies seem strongly disconfirmed for modern urban societies. For example, in modern Western societies the majority of adoptions of children are by non-relatives; this is quite a widespread phenomenon, and the outcome for the children is generally good. Yet it is difficult to see how this enhances the adoptive parents' genetic fitness (Smith, 1983). Similarly, the demographic transition has led to relatively small family sizes, despite relatively plentiful resources, which any straightforward sociobiological model can do little to explain (Barkow and Burley, 1980).

HUMAN SOCIOBIOLOGY COMPETES WITH OTHER THEORIES

As mentioned earlier, many of the 'successes' of human sociobiology (though arguably not all) can be explained by other theories. For example, many reinforcement or reward theories, or simple economic models of human behaviour, can postulate certain heuristics underlying costs and benefits or choices in human behaviour, which will explain the 'obvious' predictions of human sociobiology made earlier. The distinctive feature of human sociobiology here must be the linking of such cost/benefit heuristics to ultimate genetic advantage.

I will give two examples of competition between human sociobiology and alternative theories. One concerns child abuse; the other tribal warfare and preferential female infanticide.

Lenington (1981) proposed a sociobiological model of child abuse (see earlier); she also argues that it is difficult to separate its predictions from those of 'economic' models which overlap in considering parental investment in regard to resources. She nevertheless does derive seven predictions which she argues can differentiate the two theories. One of these is that children living with grandparents should have a very low risk of abuse, since grandparents will normally be past childbearing age and will not have heavy investment in future offspring to consider. Another prediction is that a greater proportion of abuse in upper and middle class families will be by step-parents, because lack of parental resources will be a relatively less important consideration. These predictions have yet to be tested.

I have already mentioned Durham's (1976a) model of tribal warfare, and Dickemann's (1979) model of preferential female infanticide. Harris (1979) has postulated an alternative set of explanations; these are based on a minimum of 'biopsychological costs and benefits', in particular a choice of high quality diet, a desire for sex, a need for love and affection, and a principle of least effort. Cultural practices are presumed to optimize these; in addition, between-society competition is presumed to select cultural practices which will increase power and efficiency but not allow population to increase beyond available resources. Tribal warfare is seen as a population regulation device; triggered often by protein shortages, warfare involves an increased valuation of males and a corresponding devaluation of raising females, leading to female infanticide and modulation of population size. This theory makes predictions that female infanticide should be greater in more warlike societies (supported by Divale and Harris, 1976), and that tribal warfare should not occur in the absence of resource shortages. For criticisms, see Hawkes (1981) and Dickemann (1981).

Harris's (1979) cultural materialist approach provides one of the most comprehensive and well-argued alternatives to the human sociobiology research programme. Furthermore, it does admit a basic 'human nature' (cf. the naive view of Berger and

Luckmann, 1967, page 67, and many other sociologists). Nevertheless, it has severe difficulties (see Richerson and Boyd, 1980). The four biopsychological principles are so pared down that they barely describe even a mammalian 'nature', and other principles are not considered. The origins of the principles lack a more encompassing theoretical base, and there is no predictive heuristic as to how to resolve choices involving tradeoffs among the different principles.

THE THEORETICAL BASIS OF HUMAN SOCIOBIOLOGY

Aside from certain empirical successes and failures of the human sociobiology research programme, can we really expect such an approach to have any solid theoretical base? Arguments of evolutionary continuity suggest that if it applies to animals, it would not suddenly cease to apply to hominid evolution. However, the human niche is that of culture: the cumulative passing on of learnt skills and traditions from one generation to the next. As many theorists have noted, cultural transmission can be considered as an evolutionary process in its own right, with the features of variation, selection and retention (e.g. Campbell, 1975). This calls into question the theoretical basis of human sociobiology. Is there a conflict between biological and cultural evolution? Does the growth of knowledge and consciousness truly free us from the control of our genes?

This problem has been tackled independently by a number of theorists (e.g. Campbell, 1975; Durham, 1976b; Richerson and Boyd, 1978; Boehm, 1978, Lumsden and Wilson, 1981; Cavalli-Sforza and Feldman, 1981). It is generally agreed that initially - in early stages of hominid evolution - cultural behaviour must have had net biological adaptive value, else the capacity for acquiring culture would not have evolved. It is also generally agreed that as cultural evolution proceeded, the possibility for cultural behaviour to deviate from biological adaptiveness and thus not maximize inclusive fitness, is present. The question is: to what extent?

The sociobiological argument is strengthened if gene-culture links are strong. Thus, there may be 'epigenetic rules' (Lumsden and Wilson, 1981) or 'biasses' (Durham, 1976b), stemming from our genetic makeup, which predispose to certain sorts of cultural behaviour rather than others. Examples might be the physiology of the eye constraining our perception and coding of colour and hence the range of terms for colours in different cultures; and the effects of rearing co-socialization on sexual desire, and the maladaptive biological effects of inbreeding, being reinforced by cultural incest taboos (Lumsden and Wilson, 1981). The stronger such 'biasses' are, the more plausible it is that cultural behaviour will maximize inclusive fitness. Nevertheless, this is not a determinist view; changes in the human environment could produce biologically 'maladaptive' or 'nonfunctional' behaviour: an example noted being the avoidance of marriage amongst unrelated persons co-socialized in the Kibbutzim.

Another way in which cultural behaviour is more likely to be biologically adaptive, is if the lines of cultural transmission parallel the lines of genetic transmission. Durham (1976b) calls this 'symmetry'. If cultural ideas, like genes, are passed on mainly from parents to offspring or other close relatives, then behaviour which favours genetic inclusive fitness will also favour the spread of the corresponding cultural ideas. Deviations from this, even a limited sex bias in parental transmission, can produce different predictions from those of sociobiology (Werren and Pulliam, 1981).

Finally, it is possible that genes could 'track' cultural changes. Lumsden and Wilson (1981) argue that those persons most genetically suited to a particular culture (in terms of their epigenetic rules or biasses) would be more reproductively successful. This 'cultural assimilation' of the genotype, they estimate, could have significant effects over a period of some 50 generations of 1,000 years. However, this is a controversial conclusion based on mathematical models whose premises and simplifications not all critics consider acceptable.

CONCLUSIONS

Human sociobiology is almost certainly here to stay. It is a highly vigorous research programme, impacting widely in the social sciences. It can be seen as an attempt to look more deeply and precisely into 'human nature'. Accusations of ideological bias, racism and sexism miss the mark, but only provided the hypotheses of sociobiology are not taken as prescriptive or normative. There is no valid scientific reason to do so, but such dangers would be less if it is accepted that a 'naive' human sociobiology, arguing simply that human behaviour maximizes inclusive fitness, should be replaced by a wider research programme incorporating models of gene-culture co-evolution and the conditions under which cultural beliefs and sanctions may either support, or conflict with, the biological predispositions of 'human nature'.

Major conclusions in this area are premature, but it seems likely that 'naive' human sociobiology has most relevance to earlier phases of human evolution, and to less complex societies, and has a much more limited application in its unmodified form to modern industrial societies. The examples of successes and failures of human sociobiology considered earlier tend to support this supposition. As societies get more complex, 'symmetry' in transmission breaks down; wider peer groups, collective training or education and the mass media all spread cultural ideas through non-kin networks. As the cultural environment changes, the epigenetic rules are less applicable and/or less straightforwardly adaptive. It is unlikely that cultural assimilation can cause rapid enough tracking of these changes by the human genotype. Campbell (1975) argues that in complex societies, moral codes and religious beliefs act to produce behaviour more closely geared to societal than individual benefit: while Boehm (1978) points to the possibility of conscious choice, or 'rational preselection' of behaviour not dictated by inclusive fitness considerations, as our knowledge increases. One example might be moral codes or personal choices to have very small families (cf. Barkow and Burley, 1980; Smith, 1983). Another example might be personal or societal decision to try and reverse or negate certain prevalent sex differences, probably biassed by epigenetic rules; such as interest of adult males or females in child care, or in political activity (Wilson, 1978).

Naive human sociobiology will be superseded as a research programme, probably by a broader theory of gene-culture co-evolution which embraces naive human sociobiology as a limiting case. In the meantime, it deserves to be taken seriously by psychologists, not ignored; understood, not misinterpreted; and criticized, but not vilified.

REFERENCES

Alexander, R. D. (1980). Darwinism and Human Affairs. London: Pitman.

Alexander, R. D., Hoogland, J. L., Howard, R. D., Noonan, K. M. and Sherman, P. W. (1979). Sexual dimorphisms and breeding systems in pinnipeds, ungulates, primates and humans. In N. A. Chagnon and W. Irons (eds), Evolutionary Biology and Human Social Behavior. Massachusetts: Duxbury Press.

Alexander, R. D. and Noonan, K. M. (1979). Concealment of ovulation, parental care, and human social evolution. In

N. A. Chagnon and W. Irons (eds), Evolutionary Biology and Human Social Behavior. Massachusetts: Duxbury Press.

Barash, D. (1981). The Whisperings Within. Harmondsworth: Penguin.

Barkow, J. H. (1975). Prestige and culture: a biosocial interpretation. Current Anthropology, 16, 553-572.

Barkow, J. H. and Burley, N. (1980). Human fertility, evolutionary biology, and the demographic transition. Ethology and Sociobiology, 1, 163-180.

Barlow, G. W. and Silverberg, J. (eds) (1980). Sociobiology: Beyond Nature/Nurture? Boulder, Colorado: Westview Press.

Bateson, P. P. G. (1982). Preference for cousins in Japanese quail. Nature, 295, 236-237.

Beall, C. M. and Goldstein, M. C. (1981). Tibetan fraternal polyandry: a test of sociobiological theory. American Anthropologist, 83, 5-12.

Berger, P. L. and Luckmann, T. (1967). The Social Construction of Reality: A treatise in the sociology of knowledge. London: Allen Lane.

Bixler, R. H. (1981). Incest avoidance as a function of environment and heredity. Current Anthropology, 22, 639-654.

Blurton Jones, N. (1978). Natural selection and birthweight. Annals of Human Biology, 5, 487-489.

Blurton Jones, N. and Sibly, R. M. (1978). Testing adaptiveness of culturally determined behaviour: do Bushman women maximize their reproductive success by spacing births widely and foraging seldom? In N. Blurton Jones and V. Reynolds (eds), Human Behaviour and Adaptation. London: Taylor & Francis.

Boehm, C. (1978). Rational preselection from hamadryas to homo sapiens: the place of decisions in adaptive process. American Anthropologist, 80, 265-296.

Burley, N. (1979). The evolution of concealed ovulation. American Naturalist, 114, 835-858.

Campbell, D. T. (1975). On the conflicts between biological and social evolution and between psychology and moral tradition. American Psychologist, 30, 1103-1126.

Cavalli-Sforza, L. L. and Feldman, M. W. (1981). Cultural Transmission and Evolution: A quantitative approach. Princeton: Princeton University Press.

Chagnon, N. A. (1968). Yanomamo: The fierce people. New York: Holt, Rinehart & Winston.

Chagnon, N. A. (1979). Is reproductive success equal in egalitarian societies? In N. A. Chagnon and W. Irons (eds),

Evolutionary Biology and Human Social Behavior. Massachusetts: Duxbury Press.

Chagnon, N. A., Flinn, M. V. and Melancon, T. F. (1979). Sex-ratio variation among the Yanomamo Indians. In N. A. Chagnon and W. Irons (eds), Evolutionary Biology and Human Social Behavior. Massachusetts: Duxbury Press.

Chagnon, N. A. and Irons, W. (1979). Evolutionary Biology and Human Social Behavior: An anthropological perspective. Massachusetts: Duxbury Press.

Daly, M. and Wilson, M. I. (1981). Abuse and neglect of children in evolutionary perspective. In R. D. Alexander and D. W. Tinkle (eds), Natural Selection and Social Behavior. New York: Chinon Press.

Daly, M. and Wilson, M. (1982). Homicide and kinship. American Anthropologist, 84, 372-378.

Daly, M., Wilson, M. and Weghorst, S. J. (1982). Male sexual jealousy. Ethology and Sociobiology, 3, 11-27.

DeCatanzaro, D. (1981). Suicide and Self-Damaging Behaviors: A sociobiological perspective. New York and London: Academic Press.

Dickemann, M. (1979). The ecology of mating systems in hypergynous dowry societies. Social Science Information, 18, 163-195.

Dickemann, M. (1981). Comment on K. Hawkes' 'A third explanation for female infanticide'. Human Ecology, 9, 97-104.

Divale, W. T. and Harris, M. (1976). Population, warfare, and the male supremacist complex. American Anthropologist, 78, 521-538.

Durham, W.H. (1976a). Resource competition and human aggression, Part I: A review of primitive war. Quarterly Review of Biology, 51, 385-415.

Durham, W. H. (1976b). The adaptive significance of cultural behavior. Human Ecology, 4, 89-121.

Dyson-Hudson, R. and Smith, E. A. (1978). Human territoriality: an ecological reassessment. American Anthropologist, 80, 21-42.

Essock-Vitale, S. M. and McGuire, M. T. (1980). Predictions derived from the theories of kin selection and reciprocation assessed by anthropological data. Ethology and Sociobiology, 1, 233-243.

Feinman, S. (1979). An evolutionary theory of food-sharing. Social Science Information, 18, 695-726.

Fox, R. (1979). Kinship categories as natural categories. In N. A. Chagnon and W. Irons (eds), Evolutionary Biology and Human Social Behavior. Massachusetts: Duxbury Press.

Freedman, D. (1979). Human Sociobiology: A holistic approach. New York: Free Press.

Gaulin, S. J. C. (1980). Sexual dimorphism in the human post-reproductive life-span: possible causes. Journal of Human Evolution, 9, 227-232.

Gaulin, S. J. C. and Schlegel, A. (1980). Paternal confidence and paternal investment: a cross-cultural test of a socio-biological hypothesis. Ethology and Sociobiology, 1, 301-309.

Goody, J. (1969). Adoption in cross-cultural perspective. Comparative Studies in Society and History, 11, 55-78.

Gould, S. J. (1980). Sociobiology and the theory of natural selection. In G. W. Barlow and J. Silverberg (eds), Socio-biology: Beyond nature/nurture? Boulder, Colorado: West-view Press.

Granzberg, G. (1973). Twin infanticide - a cross-cultural test of a materialistic explanation. Ethos, 1, 405-412.

Greene, P. J. (1978). Promiscuity, paternity, and culture. American Ethnologist, 5, 151-159.

Gregory, M. S., Silvers, A. and Sutch, D. (eds) (1978). Socio-biology and Human Nature: An interdisciplinary critique and defense. San Francisco and London: Jossey-Bass.

Harris, M. (1979). Cultural Materialism: The struggle for a science of culture. New York: Random House.

Hartung, J. (1976). On natural selection and the inheritance of wealth. Current Anthropology, 17, 607-613.

Hartung, J. (1982). Polygyny and the inheritance of wealth. Current Anthropology, 23, 1-12.

Hawkes, K. (1981). A third explanation of female infanticide. Human Ecology, 9, 79-96.

Hrdy, S. B. (1979a). The evolution of human sexuality: the latest word and the last. Quarterly Review of Biology, 54, 309-314.

Hrdy, S. B. (1979b). Infanticide among animals: a review, classification, and examination of the implications for the reproductive strategies of females. Ethology and Sociobiology, 1, 13-40.

Hughes, A. L. (1980). Preferential first-cousin marriage and inclusive fitness. Ethology and Sociobiology, 1, 311-317.

Hughes, A. L. (1981). Female infanticide: sex ratio manipu-lation in humans. Ethology and Sociobiology, 2, 109-111.

Hughes, A. L. (1982). Confidence of paternity and wife-sharing in polygynous and polyandrous systems. Ethology and Socio-biology, 3, 125-129.

Irons, W. (1979). Cultural and biological success. In N. A. Chagnon and W. Irons (eds), Evolutionary Biology and Human Social Behavior. Massachusetts: Duxbury Press.

King's College Sociobiology Group (eds) (1982). Current Problems in Sociobiology. Cambridge and New York: Cambridge University Press.

Krebs, J. R. and Davies, N. B. (1981). An Introduction to Behavioral Ecology. Oxford and Boston: Blackwell Scientific Publications.

Kurland, J. A. (1979). Paternity, mother's brother, and human sociality. In N. A. Chagnon and W. Irons (eds), Evolutionary Biology and Human Social Behavior. Massachusetts: Duxbury Press.

Lakatos, I. (1978). The Methodology of Scientific Research Programmes: Philosophical papers, Vol.I. Cambridge: Cambridge University Press.

Langer, W. L. (1972). Checks on population growth; 1750-1850. Scientific American, 226, 92-99.

Lenington, S. (1981). Child abuse: the limits of sociobiology. Ethology and Sociobiology, 2, 17-29.

Lewontin, R. (1979). Sociobiology as an adaptationist program. Behavioral Science, 24, 5-14.

Lightcap, J. L., Kurland, J. A. and Burgess, R. L. (1982). Child abuse: a test of some predictions from evolutionary theory. Ethology and Sociobiology, 3, 61-67.

Lumsden, C. J. and Wilson, E. O. (1981). Genes, Minds and Culture. Cambridge, Mass.: Harvard University Press.

Markl, H. (ed.) (1980). Evolution of Social Behavior: Hypotheses and empirical tests. Verlag Chemie: Weinheim, Basel.

Maynard Smith, J. (1982). Evolution and the Theory of Games. Cambridge: Cambridge University Press.

Midgley, M. (1979). Beast and Man: The roots of human nature. Hassocks, Sussex: The Harvester Press.

Montagu, A. (ed.) (1980). Sociobiology Examined. New York and Oxford: Oxford University Press.

Morgan, C. J. (1979). Eskimo hunting groups, social kinship, and the possibility of kin selection in humans. Ethology and Sociobiology, 1, 83-86.

Murdock, G. P. and White, D. R. (1969). Standard cross-cultural sample. Ethology, 8, 329-369.

Packer, C. (1977). Reciprocal altruism in olive baboons. Nature (London), 265, 441-443.

Peoples, J. G. (1982). Individual or group advantage? A reinterpretation of the Maring ritual cycle. Current Anthropology, 23, 291-316.

Radcliffe-Brown, A. R. (1924). The mother's brother in South Africa. South African Journal of Science, 21, 542-555.

Richerson, P. J. and Boyd, R. (1978). A dual inheritance model of the human evolutionary process I: basic postulates and a simple model. Journal of Social and Biological Structures, 1, 127-154.

Richerson, P. J. and Boyd, R. (1980). Review of 'Cultural materialism'. Human Ecology, 8, 171-174.

Ruse, M. (1979). Sociobiology: Sense or nonsense? Dordrecht, Holland: Reidel.

Sahlins, M (1972). Stone Age Economics. London: Tavistock.

Sahlins, M. (1976). The Use and Abuse of Biology: An anthropological critique of sociobiology. Michigan: University of Michigan Press.

Silk, J. B. (1980). Adoption and kinship in Oceania. American Anthropologist, 82, 799-820.

Smith, P. K. (1983). Biological, psychological and historical aspects of reproduction and child-care. In G. Davey (ed.), Animal Models of Human Behaviour. Chichester and New York: Wiley.

Spuhler, J. N. (1979). Continuities and discontinuities in anthropoid-hominid behavioral evolution: bipedal locomotion and sexual receptivity. In N.A. Chagnon and W. Irons (eds), Evolutionary Biology and Human Social Behavior. Massachusetts: Duxury Press.

Strassman, B. I. (1981). Sexual selection, paternal care, and concealed ovulation in humans. Ethology and Sociobiology, 2, 31-40.

Symons, D. (1979). The Evolution of Human Sexuality. New York and Oxford: Oxford University Press.

Symons, D. (1980). Precis of The evolution of human sexuality. Behavioral and Brain Sciences, 3, 171-214.

Thelen, E. (1981). Rhythmical behavior in infancy: an ethological perspective. Developmental Psychology, 17, 237-257.

Thompson, P. R. (1980). 'And who is my neighbour?' An answer from evolutionary genetics. Social Science Information, 19, 341-384.

Trivers, R. L. (1974). Parent-offspring conflict. American Zoologist, 14, 249-264.

Trivers, R. L. and Willard, D. E. (1973). Natural selection of parental ability to vary the sex ratio of offspring. Science, 179, 90-92.

Van den Berghe, P. L. (1979). Human Family Systems: An evolutionary view. New York: Elsevier North Holland.

Van den Berghe, P. L. (1980). Incest and exogamy: a sociobiological reconsideration. Ethology and Sociobiology, 1, 151-162.

Van den Berghe, P. L. Human inbreeding avoidance: culture in nature. Behavioral and Brain Sciences. In press.

Werren, J. H. and Pulliam, H. R. (1981). An intergenerational transmission model for the cultural evolution of helping behavior. Human Ecology, 9, 465-483.

Wilson, E. O. (1975). Sociobiology: The new synthesis. Cambridge, Mass.: Belkmap Press.

Wilson, E. O. (1978). On Human Nature. Cambridge, Mass.: Harvard University Press.

Wind, J. (1981). Review of some books on human sociobiology. Journal of Human Evolution, 10, 443-447.

Wolfe, L. D. and Gray, J. P. (1981). Comment on Gaulin and Schlegel (1980). Ethology and Sociobiology, 2, 95-98.

Chapter 10

PHEROMONES

E. B. Keverne

Pheromones are chemical substances secreted by an animal externally with specific effects on the behaviour or physiology of another individual of the same species (Karlson and Butenandt, 1959). The term pheromone was originally defined in the context of insect communication and exemplified by such early discoveries as bombykol, an unsaturated alcohol produced by the female gypsy moth and capable of attracting males from miles around. Today, a wide variety of insect pheromones have been identified, synthesized and are not only available commercially, but are put to practical use in pest control. Because such pheromones can attract virtually the entire male population of a given species over several hectares, the farmers or the cotton growers have a powerful tool to eradicate insect pests selectively. In insects, the chemical messages conveyed by pheromones may act on the olfactory or gustatory sense, whilst in mammals pheromones appear to be exclusively olfactory.

Although the term pheromone is often used in the context of mammalian behaviour, no compounds exist that produce as powerful an attraction as can be demonstrated in insects. This is not because such compounds have yet to be discovered, but because mammalian behaviour is less capable of being stereotypically released. Most mammals use all their senses to assess their natural social environment, and while some species clearly rely on olfactory information more than others, most mammalian species do not show a fixed action pattern of behaviour in response to specific sensory cues. Even their response to nociceptive social stimuli can be modified by past experiences and the environmental context. This is exemplified by a consideration of our own species in which all the senses are well developed, and with the evolutionary enlargement of the neocortex we have the capacity to assimilate rapidly and integrate information from a number of sensory channels simultaneously. More pertinently, we have the ability to attend to whichever sensory channel is most relevant at the time, and our behaviour does not come under the obligatory domination of any one particular sense. This does not, of course, mean that olfactory cues are without behavioural significance, even to man. Most of us find certain smells attractive (the perfume industry thrives on this) and other smells aversive (deodorants are testimony to this). However, no evidence has yet been produced which clearly demonstrates a reliable behavioural effect of odours on human sexual or aggressive behaviour. Nevertheless, numerous anecdotal reports have appeared in lay scientific journals and the more popular press which might lead us to believe otherwise. Much of this reporting has stemmed from extrapolations from the findings on non-human primates.

THE IMPORTANCE OF PHEROMONES OR ODOUR CUES ON THE BEHAVIOUR OF NON-HUMAN PRIMATES

There is a wealth of behavioural data indicating that olfactory cues do play a significant part in the reproductive life of numerous primate species, particularly in prosimians and New World monkeys. The Lemuridae and Indridae are diurnal prosimians that have developed the most elaborate range of scent markings, that involve both visual and olfactory displays. Exactly what information these scent marks convey is as yet little understood, although it has been suggested they may help in sexual identification (Harrington, 1977). The scent marking of the nocturnal loris is most frequently found on the boundaries of their territory and probably serves both to deter other males and to attract females (Schilling, 1980). Among the New World primates it has been reported that female squirrel monkeys wash with their own urine during the breeding season, a factor which seems to increase the males' attention and olfactory inspections (Latta, Hopf and Ploog, 1967). Scent marking as well as intensive sniffing and licking of the partner's marks and genitals is a regular component of courtship behaviour in both males and females.

It is in this context of sexual behaviour that olfactory cues have been shown to have important communicative significance in the Old World primates. In addition to the observations reported by field workers of olfactory investigations of the females' anogenital area by males in feral monkeys and apes, laboratory studies have carefully investigated the communicatory significance of such behaviours (Keverne, 1976). Hence, when heterosexual pairs of rhesus monkeys are allowed to interact in a laboratory situation, a striking feature of their sexual interaction is the cyclicity in male sexual behaviour with respect to the females' menstrual cycles (Ball and Hartman, 1935; Michael, Herbert and Welegella, 1967), an observation also reported for free-living monkeys (Southwick, Beg and Siddiqi, 1965; Loy, 1970). This being the case, then endocrine changes which are occurring in the female at this time are being communicated to the male partner and are in turn influencing his sexual behaviour. Of course there are a number of communicatory channels other than olfaction available, not least of which is the effects that changes in endocrine state might have on a female's motivation to interact sexually with male partners. By and large though, female monkeys are prepared to receive the male at any time during their menstrual cycle and rarely refuse his sexual advances (Keverne, 1976; Baum, Everitt, Herbert and Keverne, 1976). Not only can females negate the male's initiative, but they may enhance sexual interactions by showing changes in soliciting behaviours and these also come under the influence of endocrine changes. However, many females do not show obvious increases in invitational postures around their ovulatory period when male sexual behaviour is highest (Czaja and Bielert, 1975). In fact, paradoxically they may show decreases (Michael and Welegella, 1968). Such is the interest of the male at this time that females have little opportunity to make sexual invitations, and the initiative is firmly in the hands of their partner. Moreover, in similar testing situations the sexual invitations of females can be markedly increased by giving them testosterone (Trimble and Herbert, 1968), but in the absence of female oestrogens such invitations go unheeded by the male (Michael and Keverne, 1972). Observations such as these lead to the inevitable conclusion that it is non-behavioural cues that are of some importance in communicating female attractiveness to the male, at least within the confines of a laboratory cage.

Of the non-behavioural cues available to the male, vocalizations are rare and inconsistent in promoting sexual behaviour and are certainly not governed by endocrine state. While tactile cues may be important for the mounting and thrusting performance, clearly they are not what initiates male interest, since tactile feedback occurs only after the mounting sequence has started. Of the visual cues available, rhesus monkeys do not have a sexual skin swelling but they do have a red skin coloration, the intensity of which changes with the menstrual cycle and is oestrogen-dependent (Hisaw and Hisaw, 1966). However, topical application of oestrogen cream to the sex skin area promotes an intense red coloration with little or no effect on male sexual interest and behaviour (Herbert, 1966; Michael and Keverne, 1970). Of course, this does not mean that such colour changes have no communicatory significance: they may well act as signals over a distance, but within the laboratory context these colour changes are not in themselves sufficient to stimulate male mounting behaviour.

Thus, by a process of elimination, one is drawn to the conclusion that, of the non-behaviour cues available to the male from the female, olfaction must be of some importance. With this kind of information in mind, it seemed appropriate to set up experiments which examined the role of olfactory cues in the initiation of male sexual interest and behaviour with female partners. The question asked was: could female monkeys be made attractive to males by hormone treatments which did not influence either their sex-skin colour or proceptive behaviour (sexual solicitations), and was this attractiveness communicated olfactorily? Since female attractiveness increases in the follicular phase of the cycle when oestrogens predominate, and since giving oestrogen to ovariectomized females restores male sexual interest (Herbert, 1970; Phoenix, 1973), this was the hormonal manipulation selected. However, in order to avoid any actions of the hormone on the brain, which in turn enhance soliciting behaviour, a very low dose of oestradiol was administered directly into the female's vagina. In this way, that part of the female's anatomy which most interests the male in a sexual context could be oestrogenized without any effect on either sex-skin coloration or sexual solicitations. Moreover, imposition of a mesh barrier between the male and female enabled a clearer understanding of the male's interest in the female to be achieved, since the male was obliged to work in order to gain access to the female. The work involved pressing a lever some 250 times to open a door providing access to the female (Michael and Keverne, 1968).

At the time, it seemed logical to assume that a male working with such dedication for access to a female was a male with some interest in that female. Five males were trained on this schedule and each had three ovariectomized partners, one of which received injections of oestrogen to make her attractive. Sure enough, all males pressed for access to this female partner, while four of the five showed little interest and rarely pressed for access to their ovariectomized partners receiving no hormone replacement (figure 1); nor did they show any sexual interest in these females when freely placed together in an open cage at a later time in the day. One male pressed for access to and mounted all his female partners and was therefore dropped from the study. There seemed little

Figure 1. Effects of reversible anosmia on the sexual behaviour of a male rhesus monkey and on the time taken to obtain access to three female partners in a lever-pressing situation. Lower graph (45) represents control female. When female received intravaginal oestrogen, the male only started lever pressing after olfactory activity had been restored.

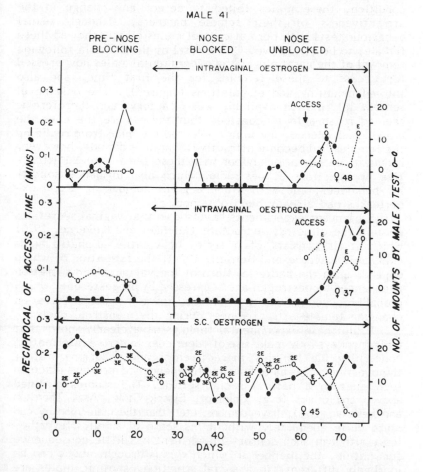

Key: o- - -o mounts by male; ●——● lever-pressing performance; E, ejaculations.

point asking this male if oestrogen made his female partners attractive when he already found them sufficiently attractive to initiate both his pressing for access and sexual behaviour.

However, of the remaining eight pairs, where males showed no sexual interest, this idea could be put to the test. These ovariectomized females were now given intravaginal oestradiol, and their male partners were made anosmic by the insertion of nasal plugs which anaesthetized the olfactory mucosa. In this condition, these males failed to detect any change in the attractiveness of their female partners, although sexual behaviour tests with normal control males clearly showed these females to be attractive. On reversal of the anosmia following removal of the nasal plugs, the experimental males now pressed for access to these females for the first time, and also showed mounting and ejaculations (figure 1). The only novel sensory information available was olfactory, and therefore it seemed reasonable to conclude that these were the cues the males used. Hence, anosmia prevented the male from realizing the females had become attractive. Anosmia did not, however, reduce male sexual behaviour with those females made attractive by injections of oestradiol which also influence soliciting behaviour, and with which a great number of sexual experiences had already been obtained.

Subsequent experiments have shown that vaginal secretions contain the olfactory attractant (Michael and Keverne, 1970) which itself consists of a series of volatile aliphatic acids (Michael, Keverne and Bonsall, 1971), the formation of which depends upon the bacterial flora of the vagina. Acid secretion is enhanced by oestrogen and suppressed by progesterone, which probably accounts for the effects these hormones have on changing female attractiveness during the menstrual cycle.

While these experimental findings have clearly shown that male monkeys may make use of odour cues to derive information concerning the females' attractiveness and endocrine status, the question arises as to how much dependence monkeys place on such cues in a natural social setting. The studies outlined above, and others (e.g. Goldfoot, Essock-Vitale, Asa, Thornton and Leshner, 1978), have demonstrated that the male monkey can mate quite adequately without his sense of smell. Nevertheless, although such sensory impairment has little consequence for mating, the manner in which this is brought about can be markedly different. In a social situation, anosmic males are responded to differently by their female partners, in that females take more initiative in promoting the behavioural interaction (Keverne, 1980). Recent studies have also shown that the volatile, fatty acid pheromones may influence the males' choice of partners in a social situation, a finding which suggests that olfactory cues are indeed important for sexual behaviour, even in their natural environment (Michael and Zumpe, 1982). Nevertheless, while we have a clear suggestion that olfactory pheromones may form one channel of female communication to the male, we are a long way from reproducing the sort of stereotyped response to pheromones seen in insects.

NEURAL BASIS OF PHEROMONE ACTION

If we consider the way olfactory information is transmitted centrally to induce a behavioural event, then at least two separate neural pathways have to be taken into account. The olfactory pathway which conveys information that results in one animal being attracted to another, for example, is clearly of a diffuse nature, since attraction in this sense can be modified by a number of variables including past experiences and partner preferences. Such olfactory information requires complex integration, and is probably represented neuroanatomically by olfactory pathways which enter the pyriform cortex, are relayed to the thalamus and on to the prefrontal area of the neocortex, before finally gaining access to the anterior hypothalamus, that area of the brain primarily concerned with sexual behaviour. In taking this indirect route, access to the neocortical neuron pool is achieved and olfactory information may be integrated and modified before being relayed to that area of the brain which is responsible for co-ordinating sexual behaviour. Hence, such olfactory cues would only lead to the onset of sexual arousal on appropriate occasions, e.g. with an attractive, receptive female and in the absence of boss males or predators. Not only does this allow for a degree of plasticity in the behavioural response to odour cues, but it also accounts for the kind of variability observed in response to sex-attractants among many mammals. If odour cues were to release a fixed-action pattern of behaviour, as seen amongst insects, this could well constitute a threat to the species (although certain mammals may behave irrationally in the presence of attractive females, none find themselves transfixed in a sexual limbo and unable to escape approaching predators).

Most mammals, the exceptions being higher primates and man, possess a dual olfactory system. The neural pathway described above is the main olfactory pathway and has its receptors located in the nasal cavity. These give rise to axons, the fila olfactoria, which ascend into the cranium through the cribriform plate to synapse on mitral cells in the olfactory bulbs. A second set of olfactory receptors, located in the epithelial lining of the vomeronasal organ also send axons, the vomeronasal nerve, through the cribriform plate. Vomeronasal nerves run medially between the main olfactory bulbs and synapse in the accessory olfactory bulbs (Barber and Raisman, 1974). The accessory olfactory bulb itself is spatially and histologically distinct from the main olfactory bulb and usually lies on the dorsal surface of the main bulbs. Attention is drawn to the vomeronasal pathway because this has given rise to the idea that two separate olfactory systems exist which may subserve distinct behavioural functions (Keverne, 1978; Scalia and Winans, 1976).

In contrast to those of the main bulb, the projections of the accessory bulb are directly into the limbic brain and terminate in the ipsilateral cortico-medial nuclei of the amygdala (Scalia and Winans, 1975). From the amygdaloid complex, fibres run in the stria terminalis to the anterior hypothalamus, preoptic area, and septal nuclei. De Olmos and Ingram (1972) divided the stria terminalis into three components and mapped the projections of specific lesions after degeneration had occurred. Their results indicated that projections from the cortico-medial nuclei of the amygdala travel in the stria to the medial hypothalamus (VMH) and the medial preoptic area. Thus the accessory olfactory pathway has a fairly direct projection to those limbic structures involved in sexual and neuroendocrine regulation, but unlike the main bulb, appears not to have access to the thalamus and in turn to neocortical regions.

OLFACTION AND ENDOCRINE REGULATION

When it comes to a consideration of olfactory effects on reproductive physiology these are best known in rodents, and in order to distinguish this type of pheromone from those which serve as attractants, the term 'primer pheromone' has been introduced (Bronson, 1968). Over the past 20 years, several different effects from primer pheromones have been demonstrated in female mice on exposure to male urine. These include the acceleration of puberty (Vandenbergh, 1969), induction of oestrus in grouped females (Whitten, 1956) and the blocking of pregnancy in newly mated females (Bruce, 1963). Exposure of female mice to female urine has the converse effect of delaying puberty (Cowley and Wise, 1973), inducing anoestrus (Whitten, 1959) and protecting against the pregnancy block (Bruce, 1963). It was commonly believed that several different primer pheromones existed which account for these different actions, but although no pheromones have actually been chemically identified in mice, recent findings have eliminated the need to postulate several different primer pheromones.

It has been demonstrated that each of these primer effects is transmitted by a specialist part of the olfactory system, namely the vomeronasal accessory olfactory system with its projection directly to that part of the brain regulating neuroendocrine activity, and that their action can be universally accounted for in terms of changes in the pituitary hormones prolactin and possibly LH (Keverne, 1982). Thus the presence of male pheromones activates the hypothalamic dopamine system, prolactin falls and LH may rise, whereas in the presence of the female pheromone the converse is true: the tubero-infundibular dopamine neurones are inhibited, prolactin rises and hence cycles are suppressed. This common neuroendocrine mechanism can account for all the reproductive effects described, the difference being the time of life and reproductive status when exposure to pheromones occurs. On the basis of these findings the need to hypothesize several types of pheromone is redundant; all that is required is a pheromone signal for 'maleness' and a pheromone signalling 'femaleness'. The olfactory block to pregnancy appears to be an exception to this simple formulation. Here 'maleness' requires the further qualification of 'strangeness', in that only males of a strain different to that of the stud will block pregnancy (Bruce, 1968). If the pheromone signal was indeed simply 'maleness', then the block to pregnancy would be induced by all males, including the stud male. Clearly, an element of strangeness is an integral part of the olfactory block to pregnancy.

THE OLFACTORY BLOCK TO PREGNANCY: IS STRANGENESS RECOGNIZED?

Although odours from a male of a strain different to that of the stud are necessary to block pregnancy, it has not been found possible to train female mice to discriminate these two strains of male bedding for food reward. However, female mice are able to discriminate, and indeed show a preference for bedding from intact males compared with that from castrated males. It is the bedding from intact males and not castrates that contain the pheromones which produce a block to pregnancy

(Bruce, 1965). If the ability of females to distinguish this bedding is prevented by selective lesions to the main olfactory system, the olfactory block to pregnancy remains unimpaired (Lloyd-Thomas and Keverne, 1982). Conversely, selective lesioning of the accessory olfactory system prevents an olfactory block to pregnancy without impairing either female discrimination or preference for the intact male bedding. These findings would imply that conscious olfactory recognition is not a prerequisite for the olfactory block to pregnancy by strange male urine odours. Hence, the recognition that occurs does so by the accessory olfactory system and its projection to the amygdala.

The block to pregnancy by strange male odours has received considerable attention from those who adopt a sociobiological approach to reproduction. It has been suggested that the mechanism has evolved to promote heterogeneity in the population, and that strange males, by possessing the capacity to block pregnancy, thereby increase their reproductive potential. However, such knowledge as we have of the territorial behaviour and social organization of mice makes this explanation less appealing, since resident males have such an advantage over intruders that access by strange males is likely to be an infrequent event. Another explanation relates pregnancy block to the effect that the pheromones have on the female's reproductive hormones in other contexts. Male pheromones can stimulate both early puberty and induction of oestrus in grouped females by suppressing prolactin secretion. Such a response, although highly appropriate to these contexts, would be extremely disadvantageous following fertilization, since lowering prolactin is known to prevent implantation. Thus, some mechanism must exist to offset the general effect of the male's own pheromone on the endocrine function of his female at such times, and this has recently been shown to be achieved by a noradrenergic mechanism.

A NORADRENERGIC 'PRINT-NOW' FOR OLFACTORY PHEROMONES

The brain's noradrenergic projections have been described as a sub-system which identifies situations of great survival value, and hence instructs the storage of relevant incoming sensory information; a kind of 'print-now' decision for important sensory events. A functional role for such a sub-system is now recognized with respect to the visual and motor systems. In the olfactory systems there are clearly occasions for 'imprinting' olfactory information that is of survival value. For example, a mother's recognition of her own offspring as opposed to that of strangers, and (of particular relevance to primer pheromones) the recognition of the stud male's odour to prevent this from blocking pregnancy. In the mouse, the noradrenergic projection to the olfactory systems is via the medial olfactory stria. Removal of this projection to the accessory olfactory bulbs by discrete neurotoxic lesions fails to impair the olfactory block to pregnancy, but does permit the stud male to block his own pregnancy (Keverne and de la Riva, 1982). Coitus thus activates the brain's noradrenergic neurones, and those centrifugal projections which terminate in the female's accessory olfactory bulb are essential to the recognition of the firing patterns of that population of receptors which code for male pheromones. The evolutionary advantage to be gained from such a group of receptors and the neuroendocrine consequences of their activation presumably apply to the acceleration of early puberty and induction of oestrus in the presence of males. This selective advantage becomes a handicap if males or their pheromones are intermittently present after mating and prior to implantation, since the consequences of activating this population of receptors at this stage induces the same chain of neuro-endocrine events which now prevent implantation. This selective disadvantage is prevented by noradrenaline release in the accessory olfactory system which enables a recognition of the pheromones of the male that mated. Males of a strain that are different to that of the stud are still able to block pregnancy only if they activate a different population of the maleness receptors, and only certain strains of mice have this capability with reference to other strains. So remote are the chances of these differing strains meeting anywhere other than by intervention in the laboratory, that natural selection has not been called upon to operate against the consequences of recently mated females meeting an alien male.

Since the olfactory block to pregnancy may be a laboratory artefact, its importance for elucidating noradrenergic mechanisms is of more significance if the principles derived from such findings can be applied to other contexts. One such context is the maternal recognition of lambs which is crucial to mother-infant bonding in the first few hours after birth. Following the birth of her lamb, the ewe characteristically licks the lamb with the emission of low-pitch bleats and suckles the young within one to two hours. After parturition, maternal responsiveness towards the lamb fades rapidly if it is removed at birth and has disappeared in 50 per cent of ewes after four hours of separation (Poindron, Le Neindre, Rak-sanyi, Trillat and Orgeur, 1980). These early hours of life are crucial for ewes to establish a selective bond with their infant and subsequently reject all lambs except their own. It is now well established that such discriminating behaviour shown by recently parturient ewes is strongly dependent on olfaction, since suppressing the sense of smell during pregnancy results in the absence of selective maternal behaviour after parturition (Baldwin and Shillito, 1974; Poindron, 1976), whilst only ewes kept sufficiently close to their lamb to be able to smell them establish this selective maternal behaviour (Poindron and Le Neindre, 1980). The neural mechanism for such olfactory recognition has much in common with the olfactory recognition which prevents the stud male mouse from blocking his own pregnancy. The neural mechanism is set in motion for a critical period by cervical stimulation (parturition in the case of sheep), and in both cases requires the presence of an intact noradrenergic nerve supply to the olfactory bulbs. Hence, vagino-cervical stimulation of non-parturient ewes rapidly enhances maternal adoption, while parturient ewes that have become selective are induced into a period of behavioural plasticity by such stimulation (Keverne, Levi, Poindron and Lindsay, 1982). Ewes that have received neurotoxic lesions to their ascending noradrenergic projection fail to recognize alien lambs and accept them at suckling as if they were their own. Findings such as these implicate an important role for the centrifugal noradrenergic projection in olfactory recognition at times critical to the survival of a species.

HUMAN PHEROMONES

Psychiatrists, particularly the analytical kind, would certainly have us believe that human pheromones exist (Clark, 1978). Long before biologists coined the term pheromone, psychoanalysts drew attention to areas of the body of classical Freudian interest that were important for odour production (breast, axilla, anal and genital regions). The proposal was advanced that the sense of smell is the primary sensory modality involved in the initial development of heterosexual responsiveness (Bieber, 1959). During the Oedipal period, the child is attracted to the odour of the heterosexual parent and repulsed by the odour of the ipsisexual parent (Kalogerakis, 1963). It has even been suggested that the conscious awareness of sexually attractive odours has been suppressed in man because of the incest taboo (Daly and White, 1930), and it has been noted that olfaction in dreams frequently refers to incestuous objects (Bieber, 1959).

Subliminal human pheromones, producing attraction or hostility below the threshold of human conscious awareness have also formed a significant line of psychiatric interest. Weiner suggested that schizophrenics are able to 'smell' moods such as hostility and fear (Weiner, 1967). Although such speculation has found favour in women's magazines and the like, it will take a good deal of careful experiment, admittedly complicated in humans by 'suggestibility', to take human pheromones out of the world of science fiction. Nevertheless, there are experimental investigations which have shown that certain body odours may influence behaviour, and that the endocrine state of the body may itself influence the perception of certain odours. Thus, a recent study provided some evidence that students, when making judgements on the basis of brief interview reports, could be influenced by the exposure to the vapour of male urinary (androstenol) or female vaginal odours (aliphatic acids). The subjects exposed to these odours modified their judgement of candidates. In particular, the women's favourable assessment of men was enhanced during their exposure to androstenol (Cowley, Johnson and Brooksbank, 1977).

Certain steroid hormones are themselves odorous, resembling musk. Perception of such steroid odours is very irregular in man with some 15-20 per cent of the population having a selective anosmia to the androstenols. Women, on the other hand, are particularly sensitive to these steroid odours, a factor of commercial concern in the marketing of pigs, the bacon from boars being unpalatable due to the musk-like odour (Patterson, 1968). Exaltolide, a lactone fixative used in perfume and also having a heavy musk-like odour is not perceived by most males or immature females, while sexually mature women perceive the odour as intense or violent (Le Magnen, 1952). Moreover, the olfactory acuity of women to this and other odours varies according to the stage of their menstrual cycle, being minimal at menstruation and maximal around the time of ovulation (Vierling and Rock, 1967; Doty, Snyder, Huggins and Lowry, 1981).

Recently, three laboratories working independently have shown that some rudimentary form of olfactory communication occurs in humans. These studies demonstrated that odours can be used by breast-feeding infants in identifying their mothers (Macfarlane, 1975), by adults in recognizing specific individuals (Hold and Schleidt, 1977), and by adults and children in determining the sex of strangers (Russell, 1976). This does not necessarily imply that such identification depends on, or is even usually acquired by olfaction, but the fact that the human nose has this capacity if called upon to make these discriminations is an interesting finding for a microsmatic mammal.

Evidence for the existence of human primer pheromones is even more rudimentary, although it is a common piece of folk-lore that women living together in colleges and hostels tend to synchronize menstruation. This anecdotal story has been given some credence by the investigations of the psychologist Martha McClintock, who found that room mates and closest friends do show a significant tendency to synchronize menstruation compared with random pairs (McClintock, 1971). This appeared to be related to the amount of time women spend together, since common environmental factors such as eating at set hours, and a common life pattern, should have produced synchrony throughout the institutionalized population. Proximity during working hours seemed to be the most important correlate of menstrual synchrony. More recent studies have suggested that underarm perspiration odours taken from women may influence the menstrual cycles of other women. Women receiving these sweaty odours applied to their upper lip showed a significant shift in the timing of their menstrual cycles which conformed closely with the donor's cycle (Russell, Genevieve and Thompson, 1980). Although oestrus synchrony has been induced in grouped female mice, this occurs on exposure to male mouse urine and not female pheromones and has receptors in the vomeronasal organ, a structure which is vestigial in the human. Hence, any parallels between the findings for man and mice are purely coincidental.

The association of eunuchoidism and anosmia (Kallman's syndrome) also led to speculation concerning human primer pheromones. Although relatively rare, patients are male, characterized by a hypogonadotrophic hypogonadism (Kallman, Schonfeld and Barrera, 1943). The syndrome is usually familial and since the gonads respond to exogenous LH, it is thought the derangement occurs at the hypothalamo-pituitary axis (Mrueh and Kase, 1968; Sparkes, Simpson and Paulsen, 1968). The fact that patients are anosmic has led to speculation that this factor is causally related to the hypogonadism. This has not been verified in either humans or experimental animals. Moreover, recent studies have shown an input of LHRH neurones to the olfactory system itself, hence a congenital absence of such a class of neurones may be responsible for both aspects of the syndrome.

REFERENCES

Baldwin, R. and Shillito, E. (1974). The effects of ablation of the olfactory bulbs on parturition and maternal behaviour in Soay Sheep. Animal Behaviour, 22, 220-223.

Ball, J. and Hartman, C. G. (1935). Sexual excitability as related to the menstrual cycle in the monkey. American Journal of Obstetrics and Gynecology, 29, 117-119.

Barber, P. C. and Raisman, G. (1974). An autoradiographic investigation of the projection of the vomeronasal organ to the accessory olfactory bulb in the mouse. Brain Research, 81, 21-30.

Baum, M. J., Everitt, B. J., Herbert, J. and Keverne, E. B. (1976). Hormonal basis of proceptivity and receptivity in female primates. Archives of Sexual Behavior, 6, 173-191.

Bieber, I. (1959). Olfaction in sexual development and adult sexual organisation. American Journal of Psychotherapy, 13, 851-859.

Bronson, F. H. (1968). Pheromonal influences on mammalian reproduction. In M. Diamond (ed.), Reproduction and Social Behaviour. Bloomington: Indiana University Press.

Bruce, H. M. (1959). An exteroceptive block to pregnancy in the mouse. Nature, 184, 105.

Bruce, H. M. (1963). Olfactory block to pregnancy among grouped mice. Journal of Reproduction and Fertility, 6, 451-460.

Bruce, H. M. (1965). Effects of castration on the reproductive pheromones of male mice. Journal of Reproduction and Fertility, 10, 141-143.

Bruce, H. M. (1968). Absence of pregnancy block in mice when the stud and test males belong to an inbred strain. Journal of Reproduction and Fertility, 17, 407-408.

Clark, T. (1978). Whose pheromone are you? World Medicine, 13, 21-26.

Cowley, J. J. and Wise, D. R. (1972). Some effects of mouse urine on neonatal growth and reproduction. Animal Behaviour, 20, 499-506.

Cowley, J. J., Johnson, A. L. and Brooksbank, B. W. L. (1977). The effect of two odorous compounds on performance in an assessment of people test. Psychoneuroendocrinology, 2, 159-172.

Czaja, J. A. and Bielert, C. (1975). Female rhesus sexual behaviour and distance to a male partner: relation to stage of the menstrual cycle. Archives of Sexual Behavior, 4, 583-598.

Daly, C. D. and White, R. S. (1930). Psychic reactions to olfactory stimuli. British Journal of Medical Psychology, 10, 70-87.

De Olmos, J. S. and Ingram, W. R. (1972). The projection field of the stria terminalis in the rat brain. Journal of Comparative Neurology, 146, 303-334.

Doty, R. L., Snyder, P., Huggins, G. and Lowry, L. D. (1981). Endocrine cardiovascular and psychological correlates of olfactory sensitivity changes during the human menstrual cycle. Journal of Comparative Physiology and Psychology, 95, 45-60.

Goldfoot, D. A., Essock-Vitale, S. M., Asa, C. S., Thornton, J. E. and Leshner, A. I. (1978). Anosmia in male rhesus monkeys does not alter copulatory activity with cycling females. Science, 19, 1095-1096.

Harrington, J. E. (1977). Discrimination between males and females by scent in lemur fulvus. Animal Behaviour, 25, 147-151.

Herbert, J. (1966). The effects of oestrogen applied directly to the genitalia upon sexual attractiveness of the female rhesus monkey. Excerpta Medica International Congress Series. Amsterdam: Excerpta Medica Foundation.

Herbert, J. (1970). Hormones and reproductive behaviour in rhesus and talapoin monkeys. Journal of Reproduction and Fertility (Suppl.), 11, 119-140.

Hisaw, F. L. and Hisaw, F. L. (1966). Edema of the sex skin and menstruation in monkeys on repeated oestrogen treatments. Proceedings of the Society of Experimental Biology, 122, 66-70.

Hold, R. and Schleidt, M. (1977). The importance of human odour in non-verbal communication. Zeitschrift fuer Tierpsychologie, 43, 225-238.

Kallman, F. J., Schonfeld, W. A. and Barrera, S. E. (1943). The genetic aspects of primary eunuchoidism. American Journal of Mental Deficiency, 48, 203-236.

Kalogerakis, M. G. (1963). The role of olfaction in sexual development. Psychosomatic Medicine, 25, 420-432.

Karlson, P. and Butenandt, A. (1959). Pheromones (ectohormones) in insects. Annual Review of Entomology, 4, 39-58.

Keverne, E. B. (1976). Sexual receptivity and attractiveness in the female rhesus monkey. In J. S. Rosenblatt, R. A. Hinde, E. Shaw and C. Beer (eds), Advances in the Study of Behaviour, 7, 155-200. New York: Academic Press.

Keverne, E. B. (1978). The dual olfactory projections and their significance for behaviour. In F. J. Ritter (ed.), Chemical Ecology: Odour communication in animals. N. Holland: Elsevier.

Keverne, E. B. (1980). Olfaction in the behaviour of non-human primates. Symposium of the Zoological Society of London, 45, 313-327.

Keverne, E. B. (1982). The accessory olfactory system and its role in pheromonally mediated changes in prolactin. In W. Breipohl (ed.), Olfaction and Endocrine Regulation. London: IRL Press.

Keverne, E. B. and de la Riva, C. (1982). Pheromones in mice: reciprocal interaction between the nose and brain. Nature, 269, 148-149.

Keverne, E. B., Levi, F., Poindron, P. and Lindsay, D. (1982). Vaginal stimulation: an important determinant of maternal bonding in sheep. Science, 219, 81-83.

Latta, J., Hopf, S. and Ploog, D. (1967). Observations on mating behaviour and sexual play in the squirrel monkey. Primates, 8, 229-246.

Le Magnen, J. (1952). Les phénomènes olfacto-sexuels chez l'homme. Archives des Sciences Physiologiques, 6, 125-160.

Lloyd Thomas, A. and Keverne, E. B. (1982). Role of the brain and accessory olfactory system in the block to pregnancy in mice. Neuroscience, 7, 907-913.

Loy, J. (1970). Perimenstrual sexual behaviour among rhesus monkeys. Folia Primatologica, 13, 286-296.

Macfarlane, A. (1975). Olfaction in the development of social preferences in the human neonate. Ciba Symposium, Parent-Infant Interaction, 33, 103-113.

McClintock, M. (1971). Menstrual synchrony and suppression. Nature, 229, 244-245.

Michael, R. P. and Keverne, E. B. (1970). Primate sex-pheromones of vaginal origin. Nature, 225, 84-85.

Michael, R. P. and Keverne, E. B. (1972). Differences in the effects of oestrogen and androgen on the sexual motivation of female rhesus monkeys. Journal of Endocrinology, 55, xl-xli.

Michael, R. P. and Keverne, E. B. (1968). Pheromones: their role in the communication of sexual status in primates. Nature, 218, 746-749.

Michael, R. P. and Welegalla, J. (1968). Ovarian hormones and the sexual behaviour of the female rhesus monkey (Macaca mulatta) under laboratory conditions. Journal of Endocrinology, 41, 4007-4020.

Michael, R. P. and Zumpe, D. (1982). Influence of olfactory signals on the reproductive behaviour of social groups of rhesus monkeys (Macaca mulatta). Journal of Endocrinology, 95, 189-205.

Michael, R. P., Herbert, J. and Welegalla, J. (1967). Ovarian hormones and the sexual behaviour of the male rhesus monkey Macaca mulatta, under laboratory conditions. Journal of Endocrinology, 39, 81-98.

Michael, R. P., Keverne, E. B. and Bonsall, R. W. (1971). Pheromones: isolation of male sex attractants from a female primate. Science, 172, 964-966.

Mrueh, A. and Kase, N. (1968). Olfactory-genital dysplasia. American Journal of Obstetrics and Gynecology, 100, 525-527.

Patterson, R. L. S. (1968). 5-androst-16-one-3-one: compound responsible for taint in boar fat. Journal of the Science of Food and Agriculture, 19, 31-38.

Phoenix, C. H. (1973). Ejaculation by male rhesus monkeys as a function of the female partner. Hormones and Behavior, 4, 365-370.

Poindron, P. (1976). Mother-young relationships in intact or anosmic ewes at the time of mating. Biology of Behaviour, 2, 161-177.

Poindron, P. and Le Neindre, P. (1970). Endocrine and sensory regulation of maternal behaviour in ewes. Advances in the Study of Behaviour, 11, 75-119.

Poindron, P., Le Neindre, P., Raksanyi, I., Trillat, G. and Orgeur, P. (1980). Importance of the characteristics of the young in the manifestation and establishment of maternal behaviour in sheep. Reproduction, Nutrition, Development, 20, 817-826.

Russell, M. J. (1976). Human olfactory communication. Nature, 260, 244-245.

Russell, M. J., Genevieve, M. S. and Thompson, K. (1980). Olfactory influences on the menstrual cycle. Pharmacology, Biochemistry and Behavior, 13, 737-739.

Scalia, F. and Winans, S. S. (1975). The differential projection of the olfactory bulb and accessory olfactory bulb in mammals. Journal of Comparative Neurology, 161, 31-56.

Scalia, F. and Winans, S. S. (1976). Olfactory and vomeronasal pathways in mammals. In R. L. Doty (ed.), Mammalian Olfaction, Reproductive Processes and Behaviour. New York: Academic Press.

Schilling, A. (1980). The possible role of urine in territoriality of some nocturnal prosimians. Symposium of the London Zoological Society, 45, 165-193.

Southwick, C. H., Beg, M. A. and Siddiqui, M. R. (1965). Rhesus monkeys in North India. In J. de Vore (ed.), Primate Behaviour. New York: Holt, Rinehart & Winston.

Sparkes, R. S., Simpson, R. W. and Paulsen, C. A. (1968). Familial hypogonadotrophic hypogonadism with anosmia. Archives of Internal Medicine, 121, 534-538.

Trimble, M. R. and Herbert, J. (1968). The effect of testosterone or oestradiol upon the sexual and associated behaviour of the adult female rhesus monkey. Journal of Endocrinology, 42, 171-185.

Vandenbergh, J. G. (1969). Male odour accelerates female sexual maturation in mice. Endocrinology, 84, 658.

Vierling, J. S. and Rock, J. (1967). Variations in olfactory sensitivity to exaltolide during the menstrual cycle. Journal of Applied Physiology, 22, 311-315.

Weiner, H. (1967). External chemical messengers. II. Natural history of schizophrenia. New York State Journal of Medicine, 67, 1144-1165.

Whitten, W. K. (1956). Modification of the oestrous cycle of the mouse by external stimuli associated with the male. Journal of Endocrinology, 13, 399-404.

Whitten, W. K. (1959). Occurrence of anoestrous in mice caged in groups. Journal of Endocrinology, 18, 102-107.

265

Chapter 11

THE COGNITIVE PSYCHOLOGY OF MUSIC

N. Spender

As many psychologists are beginning to contemplate experiments on music, it is useful to draw together some of the existing empirical work in a framework of music theory. This chapter considers approaches to how the listener makes sense of music which are based on music as language, and music as formal pattern.

INTRODUCTION

Music is communicative: its occurrence and its enjoyment is a transaction between performer and listener. As such, it persuades psychologists of the parallel to be drawn between music and natural language. In listening, we form internal representations of discrete notes or chords from the continuous soundwave, just as in continuous speech the listener extracts discrete phonemes. We respond with understanding, we can anticipate rhythmic, harmonic and melodic outcomes, and even on a first hearing we detect 'wrong notes' as making no sense. In short, we have internalized rules of musical grammar, even if, like the child in his first use of language, we may not be equipped to state the rules. A problem in regarding music as akin to natural language is that it makes sense to people who are 'native hearers' without being 'native speakers'. This obliges the psychologist to rely more heavily on the recognition paradigm in designing experiments, a difference in kind from psycholinguistics, where Chomsky's 'speaker-hearer' can be taken for granted. For the same reason, an internal generation model of music perception such as Liberman's (Liberman, Cooper, Harris, MacNeilage and Studdert-Kennedy, 1967) for the speech code might seem only appropriate to the earliest childhood development of musicality, and the most singable of melodies, whereas even the untutored listener makes some sense also of harmony, counterpoint and orchestration. Moreover, music is hardly a 'natural language' (aside from the obvious

266

objection that it lacks the semantic anchor), since the historical evolution of tonal music, through composers' innovations of the last few centuries, has been rapid to the point of extensive transmutation, even before the Schoenbergian systematic departure from the tonal system in this century. Nevertheless, many experimental paradigms from verbal learning research have proved appropriate to music, and demonstrate similar modes of perceptual organization; for instance the influence upon recognition of coding by rhythmic groups (Bower and Winzenz, 1969; Dowling, 1973). However, the absence of the semantic dimension sets important limits to the analogy.

Although music resembles language in being syntactic, communicative and a serial process extended in time, some psychologists (e.g. Jones, 1978, 1981; Handel, 1974) prefer a parallel between musical cognition and the recognition of formal pattern, whether in mathematics, plane geometry or the decorative arts. A problem with this approach is that in music the comparable features, symmetry, repetition, inversion and the like, are devices which the composer employs upon a language whose alphabet is fundamentally more complex than the series of whole numbers, or of equal lengths in plane geometry. The diatonic scale, major or minor, is no simple interval scale like centimetres on a ruler, since certain degrees of the scale, for instance the tonic and dominant, are more powerful in establishing stability of key than are others, for instance the super-tonic. Moreover, the scale is composed of a series of whole tones and semitones, but to use in experiments an equal interval scale (e.g. the whole tones C, D, E, F sharp, G sharp, A sharp and C) is to deny, in the subject's perceptual processes, the influence of practically all his or her previous musical experience. It is also noteworthy with this parallel, that spatial and temporal patterns differ in immediacy because of the crucial role of short-term memory in serial perception; for instance spatial bilateral symmetry is immediately apparent, but temporal symmetry, the palindrome, very rarely so. Eye movements in scanning are subjectively organized, whereas listening must follow the sequence of presentation. Although hearing is the more accurate temporal sense and vision the more accurate spatial one, the span of immediate memory for music varies significantly with the musical education of the individual; hence the need for careful criteria in selecting experimental groups.

Thus, musical cognition is of two closely integrated types, that which is unique to the tonal system, and that which is also operative in many other skills, ultimately in mathematics, the language of logical relations. In constructing stimulus examples, the psychologist must distinguish and control for these characteristics, for the constraints of the Western tonal system, and for the formal devices of composition which have counterparts in many other varieties of design. A prior constraint upon musical cognition is, of course, the power of resolution of the auditory system. Psychoacoustic factors in perceiving music were either intuitively or theoretically recognized by composers through the ages (e.g. Rameau, 1722; Tartini, 1754). Present-day psychoacoustic research suggests reasons for certain rules of composition of earlier centuries, and the expansion of sounds available to contemporary composers of electronic music makes a more than intuitive understanding of sensory limits to audition even more desirable. Hitherto in psychology a frontier between psychoacoustics and music psychology has sometimes been artificially maintained, or psychoacoustic experiments have failed to take systematic account of the subject's musicality.

Dimensions such as loudness, timbre and vibrato largely determine perception of orchestration and tone-quality, and although they interact with pitch and time, essentially they can be regarded as 'secondary categories' (Boulez, 1971). Making sense of music is an abstractive process using the dimensions of pitch and time to perceive musical structure. Tonal and rhythmic organization are so closely integrated, that their separate experimental study hitherto has failed to take account of the simplest, ubiquitous features which will influence perceptual grouping. For instance, ambiguous harmony on a weak beat may engender a different grouping from the same harmony falling on a strong beat. Moreover, unlike language, there can be alternative, but equally correct, parsings of a particular musical phrase, and the rules by which a certain principle of organization takes precedence in that case are difficult to define (Lerdahl and Jackendoff, 1982).

This chapter outlines the cognitive psychology of music from the point of view of tonal grammar, formal pattern, and the psychoacoustics relevant to the abstraction of tonality and rhythm. For areas relevant to the cognitive psychology of music, as well as meriting attention in their own right, the following sources are recommended. For physics and musical perception, Helmholtz, 1877/1954; Taylor, 1965; Backus, 1970; Erickson, 1975; for audition, Gerber, 1974; Tobias, 1970, 1972; Cartarette and Friedman, 1978; for neural substrates and amusia, Gates and Bradshaw, 1977; Borchgrevinck, 1982; for developmental psychology and musical aptitude, Teplov, 1966; Shuter Dyson and Gabriel, 1982; Dowling, 1982; for emotional and aesthetic responses to music, Cooke, 1959; for music theory, Piston and deVoto, 1978; Schoenberg, 1969; Schenker,

1906/1973; Yeston, 1976, and articles in The New Groves Dictionary (1981) on analysis, consonance, harmony, melody, absolute pitch and mode.

THE TONAL ALPHABET

The Western tonal system originated in the Pythagorean study of musical acoustics, as part of a general mathematical theory of the harmony of the universe. The division of their monochord string lengths according to the ratios of small whole numbers gave the Pythagoreans the basic 'consonant' intervals of our system, octave (2:1), perfect fifth (3:2), perfect fourth (4:3) and the major third, historically deemed imperfect (5:4). Throughout history, these simple ratio intervals were given cosmological (Ptolemy, Kepler, Dryden) and theological significance as the divine 'chord in nature' to which man is perceptually attuned; they occur in the first four overtones of the natural harmonic series of soundwaves which are at multiples of the fundamental frequency, and which enrich the timbre of a complex tone. When these intervals are sounded as simultaneous complex tones, the two tones of the octave share the greatest number of overtones, the perfect fifth, the next greatest and so on, a physical measure of 'consonance'. Where overtones do not coincide, but are in close proximity of frequency, as in the minor second or major seventh, the sound waxes and wanes at the rate of their frequency difference, and these beats were held to determine our experience of 'dissonance'. In the harmonic series, the fundamental and the octaves give the tonic, or keynote of a key, the next most powerful harmonic, the third one, gives the dominant, and the fifth harmonic gives the mediant (figure 1).

The tonic, dominant and mediant constitute the major triad which establishes the stability of a key, and the major scale may be regarded not so much as a linear series, but more importantly as a structure of three such triads, the tonic triad (e.g. in C major, C, E and G), the dominant triad (G, B and D), which is the tonic triad of G major, and the subdominant triad (F, A and C), which is the tonic triad of F major. Clearly, the stability of key is most powerfully maintained by the constituents of the tonic triad, and less so by notes belonging more centrally to neighbouring keys (F, A, D and B), the subdominant, submediant, supertonic, and leading note, though this latter is at least a strong indicator of progression, by a semitone step, to the stable tonic chord, as in the Ah, of the Amen cadence (see figure 2).

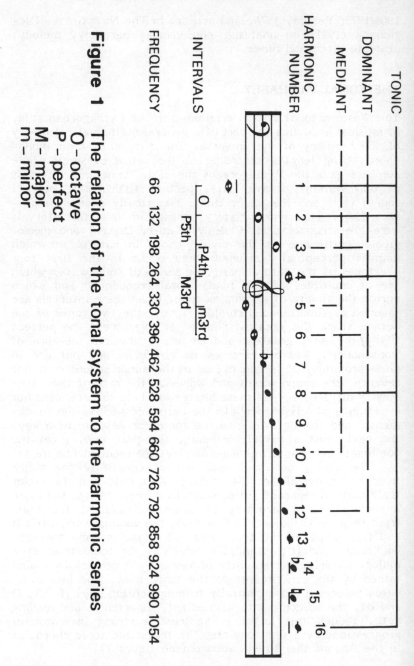

Figure 1 The relation of the tonal system to the harmonic series

O - octave
P - perfect
M - major
m - minor

270

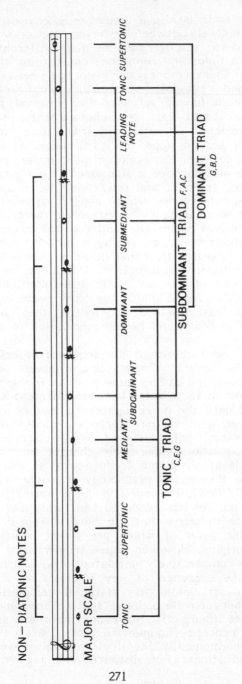

Figure 2 Major scale, showing intervening non—diatonic notes

The major scale is also a linear series composed of tone and semitone intervals between the seven notes drawn from the 12 of the chromatic scale. From the many different arrangements of seven tones and semitones constituting the ancient Greek and later Church modes, our major scale derives from the Ionian mode, and is composed of two four-note sequences called tetrachords, each having an ascending interval pattern of tone, tone, semitone. Each tetrachord also forms half of a neighbouring scale; in C major, the lower tetrachord belongs also to F major and the upper one to G major. As each tetrachord is added to form the scale on the dominant of the previous key, the leading note is sharpened (see figure 3).

This sharing of triads and tetrachords forms a continuous system of key-relatedness which appears symmetrical (see figure 4), but the dominant, or sharpening direction is based on successive moves of the key centre to the dominant. As it derives from the first non-octave harmonic, the dominant is a more powerful direction than that based on moves to the subdominant, the flattening direction. Of course, non-diatonic notes (i.e. those of the chromatic scale not included in a given major scale, for C major the black notes on the keyboard) are the least stable of all; indeed, they can serve to destroy a key stability and herald modulation to a different key.

Figures 3 and 4 represent the sequence of key relationships using the natural simple ratio intervals where, for instance, D flat is not at the same pitch as C sharp. For this reason, freedom of modulation between different key centres was hampered until the early eighteenth century introduction of 'equal temperament' tuning. Here the octave is divided into 12 equal intervals, only some of which coincide with the natural ones, but where 'enharmonic' changes are now possible, since D flat is at the same frequency as C sharp. For an account of the theory and psychology of tuning systems, see Helmholtz (1877/1954), Barbour (1951) and Ward (1970). Thus, the 'chord in nature' was rendered unnatural, and it may be argued by some theorists that the tonal system is a cultural convention, the rules of which are learnt uninfluenced by their natural origins. However, equal temperament facilitated modulation to comparatively unrelated keys, and led to conceptualizing the sequence of key relations as a circle, a rationalization not unlike the artificial completion of the colour circle between the opposite spectral frequencies of red and indigo (see figure 5). However, there are grounds for resisting this concept (Longuet-Higgins, 1962a, 1962b), not least that enharmonically identical intervals have different harmonic implications. For instance, the augmented fourth

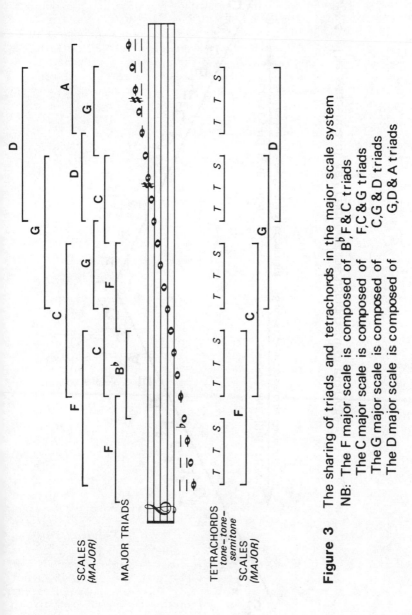

Figure 3 The sharing of triads and tetrachords in the major scale system

NB: The F major scale is composed of B♭,F & C triads
    The C major scale is composed of F,C & G triads
    The G major scale is composed of C,G & D triads
    The D major scale is composed of G,D & A triads

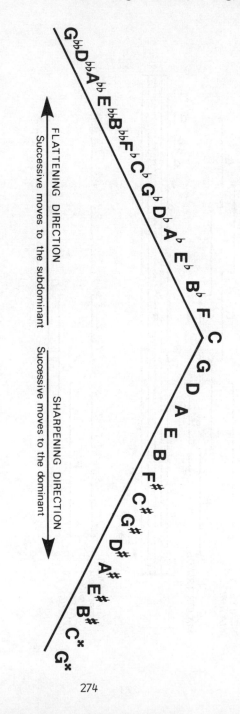

Figure 4 The sequence of key relationships using natural intervals

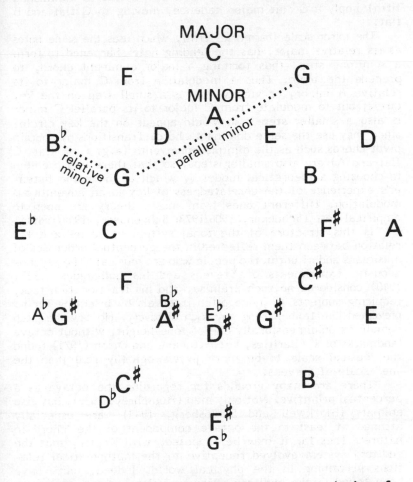

Figure 5 The equal temperament circle of key relationships

chord, F and B implies a C major cadence, moving to E and C, whereas the same keyboard notes F and C flat (a diminished fifth) imply a G flat major cadence, moving to G flat and B flat.

The minor scale (harmonic form), which uses the same notes as its relative major, has the leading note sharpened to form a semitone step, thus forming a major dominant chord, to precede the tonic. Thus a modulation from C major to its relative A minor, or vice versa, is a small step on the key circle; but to modulate from C major to its parallel C minor is also a smaller step than would appear on the key circle, since they use the same dominant chord. Transitions by certain pivot chords such as the diminished seventh (e.g. C, E flat, G flat and A) are also smaller steps, so that there is a problem in choosing a theoretical model by which to judge the listener's experience of the unrelatedness of key in an adventurous modulation. Different ones from music theory are open to empirical test (Schenker, 1906/1973; Schoenberg, 1954/1969).

Is this structure of the tonal system of scales and the relation between them reflected in the perceptual processes of musicians and of untutored people who are musical? The psychoacoustic experiments of Stevens and his colleagues (1937, 1940) considered no such premise, and his fractionation task, requiring subjects to judge pitch intervals by bisecting them, prevented him from making any such discovery. He saw the pitch domain as unidimensionally one of tone-height, without octave landmarks or similarities, but Attneave and Olson (1971) found the musical scale to be more psychologically real than the 'mel' scale of Stevens.

There are many grounds for regarding the octave as a perceptual primitive. Not only man (Humphrey, 1939), but also animals (Blackwell and Schlosberg, 1943), are especially attuned at least to the octave component of the 'chord in nature'. Thus far it may be supposed, with Kepler, that the auditory system evolved receptive to the mathematical relations pertaining in the physical world. Indeed, units have been found in the auditory pathway which respond to two or three 'best' frequencies in octave relation to each other (Evans, 1974). People often sing an octave higher or lower than required without realizing that they are doing so, and octave confusions are prevalent in experiments and aural training of musicians. Nevertheless, people's preference for tuning the octave very slightly sharp, the 'stretched octave', has been known since the ancient Greeks, and more recently attested (Stumpf and Meyer, 1898; Ward, 1954): it varies with fatigue (Elfner, 1964), and it seems to be independent of culture, since it is found in Indian musicians (Burns, 1974).

Terhardt (1974) attributes octave stretch to very early learning due to the mutual masking of overtones causing them to be slightly displaced in pitch, and later learning may also be a factor, since pianos are typically tuned sharp. It is likely that octave perception is primitive, but that certain margins of tolerance are learnt. This view would extend to other intervals where, in spite of the belief of musicians that string players' intonation gravitates towards the pure ratios of Pythagorean tuning, experiments show that broadly it conforms to equal temperament with a slight tendency to play sharp. The subject is well reviewed by Ward (1970).

Apart from this anomaly, the compelling similarity of tones in corresponding position in different octaves, called chroma, or octave equivalence, has elicited many models representing experienced pitch as the tone height continuum spiralling round a cylinder or barber's pole with all notes of the same name falling on the same vertical, and the orthogonal plane to the vertical showing the chromatic scale as the chroma circle (Drobisch, 1846; Bachem, 1950; Revesz, 1954; Shepard, 1964). Octave equivalence should also account in some measure for the perceptual similarity of triads to their inversions; but the single note in music is above all defined by its context; it not only has tone-height and chroma, but also functions at a particular moment as a particular degree of the scale, say tonic, supertonic or leading note. In the course of modulation to a new key its function will change, so that a G previously acting as the dominant of C major may become the leading note of A flat major, for instance. The previous models could not accommodate this characteristic.

Several multidimensional scaling studies have shown that the listener uses a kind of matrix of tonality when hearing a sequence of tones. Krumhansl and Shepard (1979) found a hierarchy of preferences for the most suitable note to follow a major scale sequence, the most preferred being the tonic, followed by dominant, mediant, other notes of the diatonic scale, and non-diatonic notes being the least preferred. However, quartertones, midway in frequency between each of the 12 semitones, do not evoke different preferences from their semitone neighbours. This suggests a highly overlearnt category system for semitones, hierarchically structured as to tonal function, and an inability to perceive quartertones as other than inflection or faulty intonation, if indeed the fault is perceived at all. Ethnomusicologists sometimes have the greatest difficulty in perceiving the smaller intervals of other systems as independent from the Western tonal system. Krumhansl (1979) represents her experiments on the psychological relatedness of tones by modifying the cylinder to a cone, and the fact that the triad takes its place at the vertex argues for the salience of tonal structure as against tone-height proximity. Later work (Krumhansl and Kessler, 1982) describes experiments on the perceived relation to the key centre of the single note, the chord, and finally the progression of chords in a musical phrase. They show that the implicit tonal structure used in listening is orientated to the key centre, and accommodates the experience of various changes of key which can be represented as spatial distances, and there is a trend of correspondence between degree of musical training and the salience of perfect fifths and major thirds, only the unmusical group responding simply to tone height and chroma. The experienced distances of various changes of key conform to those in music theory, particularly to the model of Schoenberg (1969), i.e. not only measured by steps around the circle of fifths, but also modified by the comparatively swift change across the circle to a parallel rather than related minor, and the swift reorientation of key effected by certain pivot chords. It would be interesting to test experimentally the model of Longuet-Higgins (1962a, 1962b; Longuet-Higgins and Steedman, 1971); and Balzano (1977) has done so with a model essentially similar to it which he has developed in terms of group theory.

Shepard's (1982) classic account of successive geometric models of perceived tonal structure puts very cogently the case for having altered the orthogonal plane, originally of the chroma circle, to the circle of fifths with two vertical interleaved whole tone scales describing a double helix. He draws a parallel between perceiving changes of key, and mentally rotating spatial figures, suggesting perhaps that there are universals in structure perception despite the unique nature of the tonal system. Comparisons with the musical systems of other cultures would have to consider not only number and size of intervals in the scale, but also the extent of their harmonic structure. It is not enough to regard the listener as operating a scalar category system. That the sequence of childhood acquisition of tonality seems to follow that of the importance of tonic, dominant and mediant to key stability is significant (Krumhansl and Keil, in press). For an account of the development of a tonal sense in childhood, see Imberty (1969). Thus, a musical person who is untutored but can 'carry a tune' is abstracting features of the melody which include local ones such as contour (the pattern of ups and downs without regard to interval size), or exact intervals. It is, however, tonal relations, which include key centre, triadic steps and their inversions, which must have a particular salience.

TONAL CODING PROCESSES

The importance of clear criteria for the choice of experimental groups must be strongly emphasized, since coding processes differ in kind between individuals according to their musical training. Musical yet untrained people can code by pitch intervals, although they lack the verbal labels for them. Those with musical training recognize pitch intervals as for instance, major third, octave or augmented fourth, but need to be given the name of either starting note or keynote, before they can translate, readily, these intervals into a name of note code, for instance E, C or F sharp. Those trained in solfege also have a code for the function of a note within the key (Doh, Re, Mi, etc.), and can use it for the change of that function when the music modulates to a new key. The possessor of absolute pitch can code instantly into notenames, as you would instantly recognize a colour, though his or her training gives the other codes as well. In addition, instrumentalists have kinaesthetic codes for their fingerings, and visual ones for the score and for their fingerings, all of which are integrated with the auditory imagery for the sound; so much so that it may to some extent operate unconsciously when they are only listening to music, or silently reading a score. Any of these codes can co-exist and assume different salience at different moments. Added to this is the fact that conventional patterns in music, such as arpeggios or Alberti basses are so ubiquitous that they are immediately 'chunkable' like familiar words or simple repetitive wallpaper designs. Musical experience makes a great difference to coding processes directed to these highly redundant configurations, which may be perceived as continuous harmonic texture. The relation of vertical (harmonic) to horizontal (melodic) perception has as yet received very little experimental attention.

PRINCIPLES OF PERCEPTUAL ORGANIZATION

Musical perception is largely concerned with which sounds belong together. The ear combines the harmonics of complex tones so that continuity of timbre perceptually assigns a melody to a single source, yet it can separately discern the components of a chord. Modern electronic control of sound production enables us to explore the effects of selectively altering the strength of components of a complex tone, so that it is no longer easy to maintain the clear distinction between harmony and timbre, between a chord and the single complex

279

tone (Risset, 1970; Erickson, 1975; Kubovy, 1981; McAdams, 1982). Just as the Gestalt psychologists explored a fluctuating frontier between innate and cognitive processes in visual perceptual organization, so constraint upon the formation of tonal Gestalten (for instance, of grouping into melodic configurations) may be seen as psychoacoustic or musically conventional in nature. Often the evolution of a musical convention will have been due to composer's awareness of the psychoacoustic factors; for instance, rules of part-writing from Palestrina's time prescribed the scale step approach to, or departure from, any large melodic interval leap in any voice in polyphony. Clearly, the difficulty of monitoring melodic leaps was well known to composers and theorists. Two psychoacoustic explanations may be invoked. First, there is the 'critical band', a theory that the ear functions neurally as a series of overlapping band-pass filters. Since critical bands are found in many mammalian species (Watson, 1963; Miller, 1964; Gourevitch, 1965), and exhibit an orderly correlation for each species between bandwidth and equal numbers of cochlear nerve cells, 1,300 in man (Zwislocki, 1965), it suggests the limitation of a neural tracking mechanism as basis for a rule of musical composition.

Alternatively, the 'existence region' may contribute to the effect. A complex tone can be quite clearly heard when, in the physical stimulus, the fundamental is missing and only an adjacent few of its harmonics are present. The most effective harmonics to evoke this perception of the missing fundamental lie in a limited frequency region below 2,000 Hz, called the 'existence region' (Ritsma, 1962, 1967; Bilsen, 1973; de Boer, 1976). It is likely that those complex tones, most of whose harmonics fall outside the existence region, will be differently processed by the nervous system, so as to influence the perception of large melodic leaps.

However strong the psychoacoustic influences upon melodic tracking may be, they can at times be overcome by musical grammar; the harmonic transitional probabilities in the tonal system are strong organizing factors which are compounded with those of rhythmic organization. The relative influences upon attention, of continuity of timbre versus tonal grammar, invite experimental test.

The Principle of Tonal Proximity

In spite of the compelling similarity of octaves, a well-known tune which preserves chroma but in which each note is distributed randomly in different octaves, is very difficult to recognize (Deutsch, 1972a); but if the identity of the tune is already known, it is more easily perceived, for in matching each note as it arrives to a prepared template, the higher cognitive process helps to overcome the psychoacoustically taxing nature of wide interval tracking. However, a tune with wide octave spacing which preserves the original contour is more easily recognized (Dowling and Hollombe, 1977). Indeed, where intervals are reduced instead of augmented, contour alone can be a sufficient cue for recognition, either where all intervals are reduced to one semitone (White, 1960), or where absolute interval size is reduced, but relative interval size is proportionate to the original (Dowling and Fujitani, 1971; Kallman and Massaro, 1979). Contour appears to be a cue used in recognition which is marginally effective where intervals are augmented, but more powerful where they are diminished.

Deutsch (1975) describes an auditory illusion which exemplifies the principle of tonal proximity overcoming that of good continuation, at least to the extent that a complete major scale 'continues' better than a scalar sequence with one change of contour. She simultaneously presented an ascending and a descending scale dichotically, but alternating each successive note between ears, so that each ear received a wide interval zigzag tune. It was perceived, not as a succession of wide interval contour changes to each ear, but as an upper U-shaped scale step sequence, and a lower inverted U-shaped sequence; thus two different frequency bands were distinguished, and this overcame both a possible zigzag percept, ear by ear, and a possible percept of two scales in contrary motion crossing in the middle. Butler (1979) extended these findings by using sequences in which the alternate notes from each ear yielded tunes with small intervals and many more changes of contour; again frequency proximity was the dominant organizing factor. This research has implications for how people perceive two or more tunes at once in contrapuntal music. As Sloboda and Edworthy (1981) indicate, degree of key-relatedness is influential in perceiving interval jumps in two-part music.

The importance of frequency proximity to coherent perception is also shown in the research on auditory stream segregation, the perceptual splitting into two concurrent streams of a rapidly alternating two-tone sequence like a trill. This phenomenon has long been exploited by composers intending to give a polyphonic percept from a single voice instrumentation (e.g. in Bach's solo violin partitas). There is a reciprocal relation between frequency separation and tempo; the faster the tempo the smaller the interval at which two separate streams are perceived. Miller and Heise's (1950) trill threshold occurred as two streams when at a rate of 10 alternations per second, the frequency separation was augmented to 15 per cent. A further study (Heise and Miller, 1951), using 11-tone sequences of scalar or V-shaped contour, yielded streaming between one and the several other component tones, if it was at a sufficient frequency separation from them. Van Noorden (1975) maps the frequency-tempo relationship indicating the important effect of prior focussing of attention. Listening for streaming ('fission') gives a very different curve from listening for an integrated perception ('coherence'), and his 'ambiguous region' between the two curves shows the degree to which cognitive processes may overcome the limits associated with the fine grain of the nervous system (see figure 6). The power of coherence is also evident in Dowling's (1973) experiment, where two well-known tunes interleaving alternate notes are unrecognizable when in an overlapping pitch range, and are only identifiable when the frequency separation between them is increased and the overlap diminished.

An interesting issue, as yet not comprehensively explored, is how far a musical factor, harmonic relation, could overcome proximity in perceptual organization. Streaming has been studied using eight note sequences which, as tempo is increased, perceptually split first into an upper and lower stream, then four and finally, at a very fast tempo, only a continuous inharmonic chord is heard. Rhythmic factors in the composition of the sequence have an influence on its streaming. Bregman (1978b) reported a middle note in a repeating sequence as 'captured' either by the upper or the lower stream; the impossibility of its belonging to both resembles figure-ground segregation in vision. One can construct an eight-tone sequence so that a middle tone may be captured either by three widely spaced but harmonically related tones on one frequency side of the capturable tone, or by inharmonic tones in close proximity on the other. Harmonicity appears to be a strong influence in the capture. For good reviews of this work, see McAdams and Bregman, 1979; Bregman, 1978a and 1978c.

There are temporal effects which interact with the proximity factor; they are interpreted as indicating the extra processing time taken to shift between frequency bands. Fitzgibbon, Pollatsek and Thomas (1974) presented a six-tone sequence of three high and three low tones, and found that a 20 msec gap was undetected when it occurred between the tones which made a large frequency leap, but between tones in the same frequency range it was reliably perceived. Perrott and

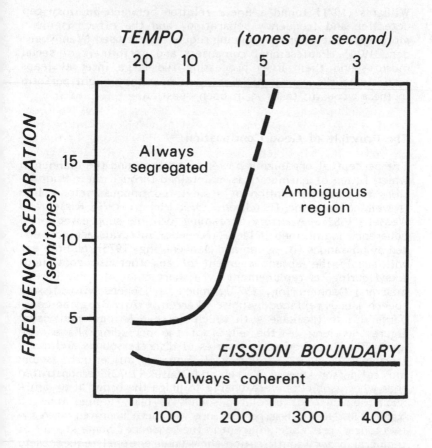

Figure 6 Three perceptual regions in the relationship between two alternate tones (duration 40msecs). The *ambiguous* region represents attentional factors
(After McAdams & Bregman 1979 using Van Noorden's 1975 data)

Williams (1971) found a linear relation between auditory gap detection and frequency separation, and the effect is much more apparent where continuing sequences are used (Van Noorden, 1975). Professional composers and performers of serial music spend their lives processing the large interval leaps intrinsic to their musical idiom, and how they might perform in these acoustic tasks is in open question.

The Principle of Good Continuation

The perceptual organizing power of timbre, and the manner in which fusion of harmonics is maintained through their fluctuations to yield perception of a single continuous melodic line is well documented (Erickson, 1975; Plomp, 1976; Risset and Wessel, 1982). Auditory streaming can be suppressed, and coherence maintained if large frequency intervals are connected by glissandos (Bregman and Dannenbring, 1973); and the ear will supply the absent segment of an otherwise continuous sound during its replacement by a short burst of noise (Bregman and Dannenbring, 1977), much as happens with missing speech sounds replaced by noise (Warren, 1970). Bregman compares this to the ease with which we read an occluded visual figure, as long as the edges of the occluding shapes are apparent. Yet even with a series of discrete sounds and many frequency changes, similarity of timbre is influential, as any musical person knows. Warren and Obusek (1972) demonstrated that where subjects were unable to judge the order of a continuous sequence of unrelated sounds (a hiss, a high tone, a buzz, a low tone) their performance was much improved when the two tones were made adjacent in the sequence. Some studies of temporal order identification show unidirectional sequences to be easier to perceive than those with more changes of contour (Divenyi and Hirsch, 1974; Nickerson and Freeman, 1974; McNally and Handel, 1977). However, good continuation is demonstrably less effective than proximity in other, more musical tasks, as is apparent in the Deutsch and the Butler experiments mentioned above. One is led to speculate how far tonal relatedness is playing a part in this effect.

RHYTHMIC ORGANIZATION

Rhythm is essentially temporal pattern. Lashley (1951) emphasized the rhythmically ordered central control of all motor organization, and claimed that this connects the performance and the perception of speech or music. Objective rhythmic pattern in music makes the timing of non-adjacent sounds in a sequence predictable; attention can therefore be preorganized by higher levels in the syntactic structure, and the continuous monitoring required for arhythmic sequences is not essential. The more regular the objective grouping, the higher the structural level of monitoring; for instance, repetitive sequences of eights can be more easily grouped by fours, hence twos, than by alternate fives and threes, whether in perception or performance; but subjective rhythm contributes greatly to order in perception. When a continuous sequence of identical sounds is without accent, subjective grouping is imposed by listeners (usually more by fours than threes), as evidenced by the periodic irregularity of their tapping with the stimulus, which lengthens the first of each group (Bolton, 1894; McDougall, 1903; Woodrow, 1951; Temperley, 1963).

Music has two coexistent rhythmic organizations, that of the time signature or beat, originally related to pace or step, and that of the phrase, originally related to the singer's span of breath; their structural boundaries often do not coincide. Although the phrasal surface structure can be analysed in terms of small groupings derived from the metric feet of Greek poetry (Cooper and Meyer, 1960; Anderson, 1973), these are not necessarily contained by bar-line structure, and this overlap of phrase and measure will pertain consistently through higher levels of analysis. Thus, objective rhythm uses within-bar meter (as in 4/4 time, the first beat is strongest, the third next, and the second and fourth relatively weak), but imposed accents on weak beats, rests or tied notes on strong beats, phrasing (e.g. legato or staccato), and the significance of tonal progression may severally contradict this scheme. Sometimes the listener misconstrues the position of the main beat because of these phrasal features of the performance, and having thus got off on the wrong foot, it may take some bars before he mentally adjusts to the correct first beat of the bar (see the 'stretch' routine, Longuet-Higgins and Lee, 1982). What is it that determines the listener's perceptual imposition of rhythmic order?

Spontaneous Grouping

Any change of an objective characteristic of tones from total uniformity, even that of pitch alone, evokes subjective experience of rhythm, which organizes expectancy. Garner and his colleagues (Garner and Gottwald, 1968; Preusser, Garner and Gottwald, 1970; Garner, 1974) describe a series of experiments where continuous sequences of recurring pattern, like auditory wallpaper are presented, eight or 10 events per pattern, varying only between two pitch levels. The subjects must tap the pattern as soon as they have perceived it, the response measure being the latency, and which of the eight (or 10) equally correct starting tones is chosen to indicate the pattern boundary. He cites holistic organizing principles, since subjects choose as pattern boundaries either the first of many repetitions of the same pitch (the 'run' principle), or the last of a run (the 'gap' principle). This is interpreted as analogous to figure ground segregation, though it is questionable how much, in real music, even in an alternating passage of Bach, the stationary pitch achieves the total neutrality of ground. In some Garner patterns, figure and ground are made reversible as in an Escher design, and they can also be made incompatible when more variability of the chosen pattern response occurs (Preusser, 1972). However, subjects also perceive some patterns as starting with a series of regular alternations; this more clearly resembles musical structure, particularly where the experimenter varies durations rather than pitch, like the longs and shorts of traditional prosody (Handel, 1974). Moreover, the figure-ground effect disappears where punctuation by pauses is introduced. Handel (1973) segmented repeating eight or nine element patterns into groups of two, three, seven, eight or nine by pauses occurring compatibly or incompatibly with pattern length. Identification of the pattern was (predictably) much better with compatible segmentation, but in the other stimuli the pattern was perceived by its temporal grouping rather than by its previously preferred structure. Whichever pattern is initially perceived exerts a strong influence on subsequent processing. This is similar to Dowling's (1973) finding, that where tunes of 20 notes were presented in groups of five, a recognition probe of five notes was better recognized if it fell within one group than across the gap between two groups. This paradigm merits further test with systematic variation of predictable tone patterns (for instance, small repetitive tonal patterns) cutting across rhythmic ones. Which boundaries would be more salient? This possibility of rhythmic grouping overcoming tonal sense would resemble Bower and Springston's (1970) verbal experiment where grouping by pauses overcame meaning.

Hierarchic Rhythmic Structure

Hierarchic organization of perception and performance is discussed by Martin (1972), who points out that if too many speech syllables, or musical notes occur between accents, a subsidiary accent is often subjectively introduced, and that emphasizing a certain syllable will subtly reorganize the structure of the whole phrase. Hierarchic perception is also shown where subjects estimate the number of taps occurring in sequences accented mainly in 16s with subsidiary accents in fours, since errors predominate in multiples of four and 16 (Perkins, 1974). Sturges and Martin (1974) found recognition memory less good for 14-element sequences, than for the longer 16-element ones, which can be organized at higher levels.

However, in performing the polyrhythms of classical music it is often necessary to suspend consciousness of the lower level of organization; in an outstanding example, the double concerto (1961) of Elliot Carter, 3 against 5 is sustained in ensemble with 4 against 7 (see Carter, 1977). Three groups of three in the 9 against 5 of Scriabine, op. 42, no. 1 are easily realized, yet even simpler polyrhythms, for instance 3 against 4 (as in Beethoven, op. 79) can be difficult to teach. Handel and Oshinsky (1978) found threes to dominate fours with this rhythm, surprisingly. Unfortunately, there is little indication of their subjects' degree of training, and in any case, in music such dominance depends upon context. In general, many of the rhythm experiments might be replicated with subject groups graded for musicianship.

At the level of surface structure, Fraisse (1956) found that, with equal durations, alternating intensities are more often perceived as trochees (strong-weak) than as iambs (weak-strong), as in the musical up-beat. Vos (1977) varied durations of two or three element sequences, which subjects classified as iambs trochees, dactyls (- v v), anapests (v v -) or amphibrachs (v - v). He extracted three grouping principles: tones separated by a short gap are grouped together, a tone after a long gap starts a new group (both simple proximity principles), and long tones seem accented, short ones not. However, in music the structure of the whole phrase will govern these alternatives, and tonal shape will be a factor. 'Any abstract grouping pattern could stand equally for local and global events in musical structure' (Lerdahl and Jackendoff, 1982).

Rhythm and Tempo

Since rhythm would not be perceived at all were it not for immediate memory which retains very recent events in the 'psychological present', tempo is a crucial variable. Garner and Gottwald (1968) make a distinction between the active memory coding elicited by a slow tempo, and the more passive, Gestalt-like experience evoked by a rapid tempo. At which tempo there is a change from one to another of these perceptual processes will, of course, depend on interactions with other features. According to Fraisse (1963) and Woodrow (1934), the 'indifference' interval of time, the length at which it is neither over nor under-estimated, is 600 msecs, midway in the range between the shortest interval when the order of two separate events can be discerned (20 msecs; Hirsch, 1966) to the largest at which they can belong to the same present (1.5 to 2 seconds). This is the tempo of musical march-time, and the relation of rhythm perception to natural pace is apparent in a great deal of research reviewed by Fraisse (1974). In studies of timing by musical performers there are systematic variations from strict metronomic time, particularly in the overestimation, or time value given to smaller note values (Gabrielsson, 1974; Sternberg, Knoll and Zukofsky, 1982). In general, a performance response measure is more often used for rhythm than for tonal research, but it is difficult to draw any conclusions, as yet, which would have generality for the subjective organization of rhythm by skilled and unskilled musical people. The question pursued in a large and confusing literature on rhythm remains unanswered. It is whether musicians' systematic distortions from exact timing, which certainly seem more lively and natural, are a set of interpretive conventions introduced simply to make the whole musical structure more apparent, or whether they succeed in so doing, because they entrain that substratum of neural systems in the listener which Lashley describes as the rhythmic basis of all serial behaviour.

MUSIC AS FORMAL PATTERN

Hierarchical organization in music is also evident in the use of those transformational rules by which phrases are perceived as the 'equivalent' one either repeated, elaborated, doubled or halved in time value, transposed in pitch, inverted, turned backwards (retrograde), or both retrograde and inverted. These compositional devices account for a large share of our enjoyment in its design. Elaboration preserves the harmonic and rhythmic structure, usually ornamenting it by faster moving note values, and is exemplified in variation form. Augmentation or diminution of time values equally does not modify harmonic structure. The remaining devices are more problematical.

The banal example presented in figure 7 shows the repetition of a simple pattern which is also repeated in augmentation at the higher level. It is represented by a simple tree diagram, and could be translated into digits, letters of the alphabet, or spatially arranged lights, as used in experiments by Restle and Brown (1970), Kotovsky and Simon (1973) and Jones (1974). Or could it? To preserve the exact interval size it would have to be translated into the whole tone scale (see figure 7). Although the tonal system is not a mathematical interval scale, the very numbering of the interval names would suggest that an enduring number system to the base eight is built into the child's learning, so that the highly overlearnt major scale must to some extent be perceived as such, and used as basic in perceiving transformations. In listening to fugues we accept with ease the alterations to interval size, where perfect fourths and perfect fifths are interchangeable to accommodate the tonal answer. Any transposition within the same key will involve changes of exact interval size, so that only contour is preserved. It follows that there are two types of 'equivalence' judgements used in perceiving transformations; tonal transformations preserve key-centredness, altering tones to semitones and vice versa in the process; but transformations which preserve exact interval size demand the cognitive leap of a change of key centre. Moreover, the smallest transposition in pitch level, say C major to C sharp major, requires almost the largest possible move around the circle of key relation. When a tune is presented, its tonality will have acquired some perceptual priority, and it is likely that even for untutored people a trip around the circle is unsettling. Dowling's (1978) experiment distinguishing 'scale and contour' illustrates this.

On the other hand, atonal sequences do not evoke the tonal matrix of expectancies within which musical transformations have hitherto been heard by the subject. Dowling (1972) presented five-note atonal tunes to non-musician subjects for recognition of their transforms. As any musician would expect, identity was the easiest, followed by inversion retrograde, with retrograde inversion the most difficult. With the last two, the well-known strong salience of forward temporal order is violated; to compare the first interval to the last in reverse, the second to the penultimate and so on, makes great demands on short-term memory for a once-heard tune. Since in real live music, both tonal and rhythmic configuration aid the initial encoding, and any small easily recognized pattern within a longer tonal sequence (scale or triadic steps, for instance) would considerably aid a four-alternative forced choice task, this line of enquiry needs further attention.

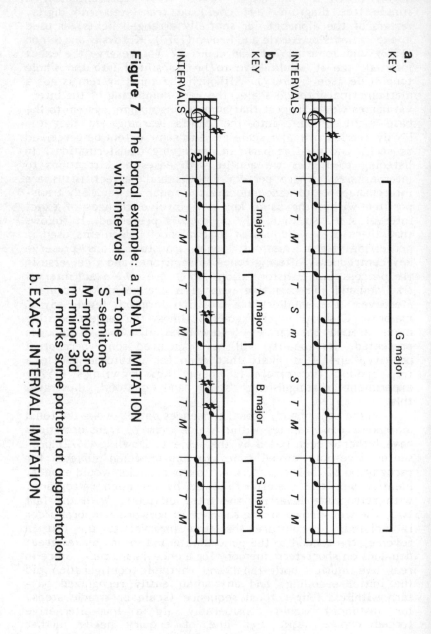

Figure 7 The banal example: a.TONAL IMITATION with intervals

b.EXACT INTERVAL IMITATION

T — tone
S — semitone
M — major 3rd
m — minor 3rd
⌢ marks same pattern at augmentation

Deutsch (1981) presented simple tonal 12-note sequences composed of four 3-note imitative patterns, and also 'unstructured' 12-note control sequences randomizing the same notes. Tonal structure was also grouped compatibly or incompatibly with rhythmic structure. Although the musician subjects taking the tunes down from dictation retained the imitative, rhythmically compatible sequences with predictable ease, it is difficult to assess the rest of the experiment, since any musician would scarcely fail to find structure in the so-called 'random' control sequences (p. 382, figure 1B). This illustrates the difficulty of achieving randomness in generating musical control sequences which are constrained by the pitch classes used, and should also be controlled for number of contour changes. Very few possibilities are left to the random generator.

With formal patterns imposed upon the tonal system, two cognitive processes are simultaneously operative in listening to tonal music, each with its own transitional probabilities and redundancies, each its own tree diagram. One can anticipate, for instance, that this phrase will end in two bars from now on the tonic cadence, and also that its repetitive pattern of imitation is going to complete its cycle satisfactorily. The ultimate question is how the tree diagrams proper to the analysis of formal pattern, can be combined with those of tonal and rhythmic structure, and how the listener acquires this integrated predictive faculty.

MUSIC THEORY, ARTIFICIAL INTELLIGENCE AND PSYCHOLOGY

Whether or not it is presented as an algorithm, a musical theory of grammar describes the intuitions of listeners familiar with music; thus it is a psychological theory. Since the 1960s there have been models of musical grammar using principles analogous to Chomsky's generative grammar or those of Schenker's prior theory of musical structure (see Yeston, 1977). Schenker's theory resembles that of Chomsky in that he relates 'foreground' to 'background' by rules used recursively, much as surface and deep structure are related. Narmour's (1977) theory questions whether Schenker's thoroughgoing top-down approach can describe the listener's intuitions, rather as the altogether holistic stance of Gestalt psychology was criticized. In linguistics, the instances of a sentence having more than one meaning, and hence more than one structural description, are few indeed compared to music, where legitimately different parsing schemes of a phrase are more commonplace. This difference in the role of ambiguity between linguistics and music theory is accommodated in Lerdahl and Jackendoff's (1982) theory by their distinguishing between 'well-formedness' rules and 'preference' rules which deal with these legitimately competing principles of organization. Having analysed both phrasal and metric structure, their 'tone-span reduction' assigns structural importance to events by their positions in the first two analyses, and they also have a system for expressing the 'tensions and resolutions' of a musical passage. This has been well discussed descriptively some years ago by Cooke (1959), but formal theories provide the psychologist with testable models.

Hitherto, psychologists have often used experimental techniques which do not sufficiently recognize that music is nodal. It does not proceed from note to note with uniform structural importance, yet this is often how experimental stimuli are generated. Unaccented passing notes for instance may, as it were, stand in for a glissando from one node to the next, as in a fast chromatic scale from strong beat to strong beat. Thus non-diatonic notes will differentially disturb key-centredness according to their structural importance. The expectations of the listener as to these nodes are multiply determined by melodic motion, harmony, phrasal and metrical rhythm, and formal pattern. Tolerance of tension between the nodes will vary with the listener's experience; to the sophisticated listener, a phrase may reach great harmonic and rhythmic predicaments of atonality and metrical irregularity, and yet be perceived as retrievable.

However, how the listener makes sense of the simplest music is problem enough. Winograd's (1968) programme analysing tonal harmony, based on Halliday's systemic grammar, produced satisfactory parsings of Schubert dances and Bach Chorales which could account for modulations. Simon and Sumner (1968) were concerned with pattern repetitions which the programme finds by starting at very small units. Longuet-Higgins and Steedman's (1971) programme assigned the correct key and time signatures to the 48 fugue subjects of Bach. Their rhythmic algorithm used the dactyl as a powerful small unit detector of correct bar-lines. The tonal algorithm uses a matrix of perfect fifths major thirds (and octaves), a theoretical choice subsequently supported by the empirical work of Shepard and Krumhansl. The problem of key-centre arose in the B minor fugue subject (Book 1), where chromatic intervals function both as passing notes and as modulation to the dominant (see figure 8). Exactly where, in this progression, the listener's expectations become committed to F sharp minor, is the interesting question. Musicians show intuitive certainty as to

Figure 8 Bach: B minor Fugue Book 1, *48 Preludes and Fugues*

whether a passage has arrived at a changed key-centre, or is only 'flirting', or passing through it to another destination, yet it is extremely difficult to model this perceptual process. The question for AI models, which hitherto have dealt separately with tonal and rhythmic parsing schemes, is to envisage how they might be integrated. Indeed, this integration, which the listener seems to accomplish with such ease, is the problem, and an exciting one, for experimental psychology.

REFERENCES

Anderson, W. (1973). Word accent and melody in ancient Greek musical texts. Journal of Music Theory, 17, 186.

Attneave, F. and Olson, R. K. (1971). Pitch as a medium: a new approach to psychophysical scaling. American Journal of Psychology, 84, 147-165.

Bachem, A. (1950). Tone height and tone chroma as two different pitch qualities. Acta Psychologica, 7, 80-88.

Backus, J. (1970). The Acoustical Foundations of Music. London: John Murray.

Balzano, G. J. (1977). Chronometric studies of the musical interval sense. Doctoral dissertation, Stanford University. Dissertation Abstracts International, 38, 2898B (University Microfilms No. 77-25, 643).

Barbour, J. M. (1951). Tuning and Temperament. East Lansing, Michigan: Michigan State College Press.

Bilsen, F. A. (1973). On the influence of the number and phase of harmonics on the perceptibility of the pitch of complex signals. Acustica, 28, 60-65.

Blackwell, H. R. and Schlosberg, H. (1943). Octave generalisation, pitch discrimination, and loudness thresholds in the white rat. Journal of Experimental Psychology, 33, 407-419.

Bolton, T. L. (1899). Rhythm. American Journal of Psychology, 6, 145-238.

Borchgrevinck, H. M. (1982). Prosody and musical rhythms are controlled by the speech hemisphere. In M. Clynes (ed.), Music, Mind and Brain. New York: Plenum Press.

Boulez, P. (1971). Boulez on Music Today. London: Faber & Faber.

Bower, G. and Springston, F. (1970). Pauses as recoding points in letter series. Journal of Experimental Psychology, 83, 421-430.

Bower, G. and Winzenz, D. (1969). Group structure, coding and memory for digit series. Journal of Experimental Psychology Monographs, 80, No. 2, Part 2, 1-17.

Bregman, A. S. (1978a). Asking the 'what for' question in auditory perception. In M. Kubovy and J. R. Pomerantz (eds), Perceptual Organisation. Hillsdale, NJ: Erlbaum Associates.

Bregman, A. S. (1978b). Auditory streaming: competition among alternative organisations. Perception and Psychophysics, 23, 391-398.

Bregman, A. S. (1978c). The formation of auditory streams. In J. Requin (ed.), Attention and Performance, VII. Hillsdale, NJ: Erlbaum Associates.

Bregman, A. S. and Dannenbring, G. L. (1973). The effect of continuity on auditory stream segregation. Perception and Psychophysics, 13, 308-312.

Bregman, A. S. and Dannenbring, G. L. (1977). Auditory continuity and amplitude edges. Canadian Journal of Psychology, 31, 151-159.

Burns, E. M. (1974). Octave adjustment by non-western musicians. Journal of the Acoustical Society of America, 56, S25-S26.

Butler, D. (1979). A further study of melodic channelling. Perception and Psychophysics, 25, 264-268.

Carter, E. (1977). The orchestral composer's point of view. In E. Stone and K. Stone (eds), The Writings of Elliott Carter. Bloomington, Ind.: Indiana University Press.

Carterette, E. C. and Friedman, P. (1978). Handbook of Perception, Volume IV: Hearing. New York: Academic Press.

Cooke, D. (1959). The Language of Music. Oxford: Oxford University Press.

Cooper, G. and Meyer, L. B. (1960). The Rhythmic Structure of Music. Chicago: University of Chicago Press.

De Boer, E. (1976). On the 'residue' and auditory pitch perception. In W. D. Keidel and W. D. Neff (eds), Handbook of Sensory Physiology, Volume V/3. New York: Springer Verlag.

Deutsch, D. (1972a). Octave generalisation and tune recognition. Perception and Psychophysics, 11, 411-412.

Deutsch, D. (1975). Musical illusions. Scientific American, 233, 92-104.

Deutsch, D. (1981). The processing of structured and unstructured tonal sequences. Perception and Psychophysics, 28, 381-389.

Divenyi, P. L. and Hirsch, I. J. (1974). Identification of temporal order in three-tone sequences. Journal of the Acoustical Society of America, 56, 144-151.

Dowling, W. J. (1972). Recognition of melodic transformations: inversion, retrograde, and retrograde inversion. Perception and Psychophysics, 12, 417-421.

Dowling, W. J. (1973). Rhythmic groups and subjective chunks in memory for melodies. Perception and Psychophysics, 4, 37-40.

Dowling, W. J. (1978). Scale and contour: two components of a theory of memory for melodies. Psychological Review, 85, 342-354.

Dowling, W. J. (1982). Melodic information processing and its development. In D. Deutsch (ed.), The Psychology of Music. New York: Academic Press.

Dowling, W. J. and Fujitani, D. S. (1971). Contour, interval and pitch recognition in memory for melodies. Journal of the Acoustical Society of America, 49, 524-531.

Dowling, W. J. and Hollombe, A. W. (1977). The perception of melodies distorted by splitting into several octaves: effects of increasing proximity and melodic contour. Perception and Psychophysics, 21, 60-64.

Elfner, L. (1964). Systematic shifts in the judgments of octaves of high frequencies. Journal of the Acoustical Society of America, 36, 270-276.

Erickson, R. (1975). Sound Structure in Music. Berkeley, Ca.: University of California Press.

Evans, E. F. (1974). Neural processes for the detection of acoustic patterns and for sound localization. In F. T. Schmitt Worden (ed.), The Neurosciences, a Third Study Program. Cambridge, Mass.: Massachusetts Institute of Technology Press.

Fitzgibbon, P. J., Pollatsek, A. and Thomas, I. B. (1974). Detection of temporal gaps within and between perceptual tonal groups. Perception and Psychophysics, 16, 522-528.

Fraisse, P. (1956). Les structures rythmiques. Louvain: Editions Universitaires.

Fraisse, P. (1963). Psychology of Time. New York: Harper.

Fraisse, P. (1974). Psychologie du Rythme. Paris: Presses Universitaires de France.

Gabrielsson, A. (1974). Performance of rhythm patterns. Scandinavian Journal of Psychology, 15, 63-72.

Gates, A. and Bradshaw, J. C. (1977). The role of the cerebral hemispheres in music. Brain and Language, 4, 403-431.

Garner, W. R. (1974). The Processing of Information and Structure. Hillsdale, NJ: Erlbaum Associates.

Garner, W. R. and Gottwald, R. L. (1968). The perception and learning of temporal patterns. Quarterly Journal of Experimental Psychology, 20, 97-109.

Gerber, S. E. (1974). Introductory Hearing Science. Philadelphia, Pa: Saunders.

Gourevitch, G. (1965). Auditory masking in the white rat. Journal of the Acoustical Society of America, 37, 439.

Groves Dictionary of Music and Musicians (1980). In S. Sadie (ed.), Absolute pitch, Volume 1, Natasha Spender. Analysis, Ian Bent. Consonance, Volume 4, 668-671, Mark Lindley and Natasha Spender. Harmony, Volume 8, 175-188, Carl Dahlhaus. Melody, Volume 12, 112, Alexander Ringer. Mode, Volume 12, 376-450, Harold S. Powers. London: Macmillan.

Handel, S. (1973). Temporal segmentation of repeating auditory patterns. Journal of Experimental Psychology, 101, 46-54.

Handel, S. (1974). Perceiving melodic and rhythmic auditory patterns. Journal of Experimental Psychology, 103, 922-933.

Handel, S. and Oshinsky, J. (1981). The meter of syncopated auditory polyrhythms. Perception and Psychophysics, 30, 1-9.

Heise, G. A. and Miller, G. A. (1951). An experimental study of auditory patterns. American Journal of Psychology, 64, 68-77.

Helmholtz, H. (1877/1954). On the Sensations of Tone (4th edn). New York: Dover.

Hirsch, I. (1966). Auditory perception of speech. In E. Cartarette (ed.), Brain Function, Volume 3: Speech, Language and Communication. Berkeley, Ca.: University of California Press.

Humphrey, L. F. (1939). Generalisation as a function of method of reinforcement. Journal of Experimental Psychology, 25, 361-372.

Imberty, M. (1969). L'acquisition des structures tonales chez l'enfant. Paris: Klinksieck.

Jones, M. R. (1974). Cognitive representations of serial patterns. In B. M. Kantowitz (ed.), Human Information Processing: Tutorials in Performance and Cognition. Hillsdale, NJ: Erlbaum Associates.

Jones, M. R. (1978). Auditory patterns: studies in the perception of structure. In E. C. Cartarette and M. P. Friedman (eds), Handbook of Perception, Volume VIII. New York: Academic Press.

Jones, M. R. (1981). A tutorial on some issues and methods in serial pattern research. Perception and Psychophysics, 30, 492-504.

Kallman, H. J. and Massaro, D. W. (1979). Tone chroma is functional in melody recognition. Perception and Psychophysics, 26, 32-36.

Kotovsky, K. and Simon, H. A. (1973). Empirical tests of a theory of human acquisition of concepts for sequential patterns. Cognitive Psychology, 4, 399-424.

Krumhansl, C. L. (1979). The psychological representation of musical pitch in a tonal context. Cognitive Psychology, 11, 346-374.

Krumhansl, C. L. and Kessler, E. J. (1982). Tracing the dynamic changes in perceived tonal organization in a spatial representation of musical keys. Psychological Review, 89, 334-368.

Krumhansl, C. L. and Keil, F. C. Acquisition of the hierarchy of tonal functions in music. Memory and Cognition. In press.

Krumhansl, C. L. and Shepard, R. N. (1979). Quantification of the hierarchy of tonal function within a diatonic context. Journal of Experimental Psychology: Human Perception and Performance, 5, 579-594.

Kubovy, M. (1981). Concurrent pitch-segregation and the theory of indispensable attributes. In M. Kubovy and J. Pomerantz (eds), Perceptual Organization. Hillsdale, NJ: Erlbaum Associates.

Lashley, K. (1951). The problem of serial order in behaviour. In L. A. Jeffries (ed.), Cerebral Mechanisms in Behaviour: The Hixon Symposium. New York: Wiley.

Lerdahl, F. and Jackendoff, R. (1982). A Generative Theory of Tonal Music. Cambridge, Mass.: Massachusetts Institute of Technology Press.

Liberman, A. M., Cooper, F. S., Harris, K. S., MacNeilage, P. F. and Studdert-Kennedy, M. (1967). Some observations on a model for speech perception. In W. Wathen-Dunn (ed.), Models for the Perception of Speech and Visual Form. Cambridge, Mass.: Massachusetts Institute of Technology Press.

Longuet-Higgins, H. C. (1962a). Letter to a musical friend. Music Review, 23, 244-248.

Longuet-Higgins, H. C. (1962b). Second letter to a musical friend. Music Review, 23, 271-280.

Longuet-Higgins, H. C. and Lee, C. S. (1982). The perception of musical rhythms. Perception, 11, 115-128.

Longuet-Higgins, H. C. and Steedman, M. J. (1971). On interpreting Bach. In B. Meltzer and D. Michie (eds), Machine Intelligence, 6. Edinburgh: Edinburgh University Press.

Martin, J. G. (1972). Rhythmic (hierarchical) versus serial structure in speech and other behaviour. Psychological Review, 79, 487-509.

McAdams, S. (1982). Spectral fusion and the creation of auditory images. In M. Clynes (ed.), Music, Mind and Brain. New York: Plenum Press.

McAdams, S. and Bregman, A. (1979). Hearing musical streams. Computer Music Journal, 3, 26-43.

McDougall, R. (1903). The structure of simple rhythm forms. Psychological Review Monograph Supplements, 4, 309-416.

McNally, K. A. and Handel, S. (1977). Effect of element composition on streaming and the ordering of repeating sequences. Journal of Experimental Psychology: Human perception and performance, 3, 451-460.

Miller, G. A. and Heise, G. A. (1950). The trill threshold. Journal of the Acoustical Society of America, 22, 637-638.

Miller, J. (1964). Auditory sensitivity of the chinchilla in quiet and in noise. Journal of the Acoustical Society of America, 36, 2010.

Narmour, E. (1977). Beyond Schenkerism. Chicago: University of Chicago Press.

Nickerson, R. S. and Freeman, B. (1974). Discrimination of the order of the components of repeating tone sequences: effects of frequency separation and extensive practice. Perception and Psychophysics, 16, 471-477.

Perkins, D. N. (1974). Coding position in a sequence by rhythmic grouping. Memory and Cognition, 2, 219-223.

Perrott, D. R. and Williams, K. N. (1971). Auditory temporal resolution: gap detection as a function of interpulse frequency disparity. Psychonomic Science, 25, 73-74.

Piston, W. and DeVoto, M. (1973). Harmony. London: Gollancz.

Plomp, R. (1976). Aspects of Tone Sensation: A psychophysical study. New York: Academic Press.

Preusser, D. (1972). The effect of structure and rate on the recognition and description of auditory temporal patterns. Perception and Psychophysics, 11, 233-240.

Preusser, D., Garner, W. and Gottwald, R. L. (1970). Perceptual organisation of two-element temporal patterns as a function of their component one-element patterns. American Journal of Psychology, 83, 151-170.

Rameau, J. P. (1722/1971). Treatise on Harmony. New York: Dover Publications.

Restle, F. and Brown, E. R. (1970). Serial pattern learning. Journal of Experimental Psychology, 83, 120-125.

Revesz, G. (1954). Introduction to the Psychology of Music. Norman, Oklahoma: University of Oklahoma Press.

Risset, J. C. (1970). An Introductory Catalog of Computer Synthesized Sounds. Mimeo with recorded examples no. 550. Murray Hill, NJ: Bell Telephone Laboratories.

Risset, J. C. and Wessel, D. L. (1982). Exploration of sound by analysis and synthesis. In D. Deutsch (ed.), The Psychology of Music. New York: Academic Press.

Ritsma, R. J. (1962). Existence region of the tonal residue. Journal of the Acoustical Society of America, 34, 1224-1229.

Ritsma, R. J. (1967). Frequencies dominant in the perception of the pitch of complex sounds. Journal of the Acoustical Society of America, 42, 191-198.

Schenker, H. (1906/1973). Translated and edited by O. Jonas. Harmony. Cambridge, Mass.: Massachusetts Institute of Technology Press.

Schoenberg, A. (1954/1969). Structural Functions of Harmony. New York: Norton.

Simon, H. A. and Sumner, R. K. (1968). Pattern in music. In B. Kleinmutz (ed.), Formal Representation of Human Judgment. New York: Wiley.

Shepard, R. N. (1964). Circularity in judgments of relative pitch. Journal of the Acoustical Society of America, 36, 2346-2353.

Shepard, R. N. (1982). Geometric approximations to the structure of musical pitch. Psychological Review, 89, 305-333.

Shuter Dyson R. and Gabriel, C. (1982). The Psychology of Musical Ability (2nd edn). London: Methuen.

Sloboda, J. and Edworthy, J. (1981). Attending to two melodies at once: the effect of key relatedness. Psychology of Music, 9, 39-43.

Sternberg, S., Knoll, R. and Zukofsky, P. (1982). Timing by skilled musicians. In D. Deutsch (ed.), Psychology of Music. New York: Academic Press.

Stevens, S. S. and Volkman, J. (1940). The relation of pitch to frequency: a revised scale. American Journal of Psychology, 53, 329-353.

Stevens, S. S., Volkman, J. and Newman, E. B. (1937). A scale for the measurement of the psychological magnitude of pitch. Journal of the Acoustical Society of America, 8, 185-190.

Stumpf, C. and Meyer, M. (1898). Maasbestimmungen uber die Reinheit consonanter intervallen. Beitrage zür Akustik und Musikwissenschaft, 2, 84-167.

Sturges, P. T. and Martin, J. G. (1974). Rhythmic structure in auditory temporal pattern perception and immediate memory. Journal of Experimental Psychology, 102, 377-383.

Tartini, G. (1754/1966/1973) Trattato di musica secondo la vera scienza dell'armonica. Padua.

Taylor, C. A. (1965). The Physics of Musical Sounds. London: The English Universities Press.

Temperley, N. M. (1963). Persona: tempo and subjective accentuation. Journal of General Psychology, 68, 267-287.

Teplov, B. M. (1966). Psychologie des Aptitudes Musicales. Paris: Presses Universitaires de France.

Terhardt, E. (1974). Pitch, consonance and harmony. Journal of the Acoustical Society of America, 55, 1061-1069.

Tobias, J. (1970, 1972). Foundations of Modern Auditory Theory, Volumes I and II. New York: Academic Press.

Van Noorden, L. (1975). Temporal Coherence in the Perception of Tone Sequences. Eindhoven, Holland: Instituut voor Perceptie Onderzoek.

Vos, P. J. (1977). Temporal duration factors in the perception of auditory rhythmic patters. Scientific Aesthetics, 1, 183-189.

Ward, W. D. (1954). Subjective musical pitch. Journal of the Acoustical Society of America, 26, 369-380.

Ward, W. D. (1970). Musical perception. In J. Tobias (ed.), Foundations of Modern Auditory Theory. New York: Academic Press.

Warren, R. M. (1970). Perceptual restoration of missing speech sounds. Science, 167, 392-297.

Warren, R. M. and Obusek, C. J. (1972). Identification of temporal order within auditory sequences. Perception and Psychophysics, 12, 86-90.

Watson, C. (1962). Masking of tones by noise for the cat. Journal of the Acoustical Society of America, 35, 167-172.

White, B. (1960). Recognition of distorted melodies. American Journal of Psychology, 73, 100-107.

Winograd, T. (1968). Linguistics and the computer analysis of tonal harmony. Journal of Music Theory, 12, 2-50.

Woodrow, H. (1934). The temporal indifference interval determined by the method of mean error. Journal of Experimental Psychology, 17, 167-188.

Woodrow, H. (1951). Time perception. In S. S. Stevens (ed.), Handbook of Experimental Psychology. New York: Wiley.

Yeston, M. (1976). The Stratification of Musical Rhythm. New Haven, Conn.: Yale University Press.

Yeston, M. (ed.) (1977). Readings in Schenker Analysis. New Haven, Conn.: Yale University Press.

Zwislocki, J. (1965). Analysis of some auditory characteristics. In R. D. Luce, R. R. Bush and E. Galanter (eds), Handbook of Mathematical Psychology, Volume 3. New York: Wiley.

Chapter 12

PSYCHOLOGY AND MATHEMATICS

Arthur Still

INTRODUCTION

Not many psychologists have the mathematical training necessary to evaluate a text in mathematical psychology, and it is
easy to see this as an esoteric branch of the subject, its
devotees pottering away harmlessly above the heads of the
workers producing real data, the experimental psychologists. A
glance through recent numbers of the Journal of Mathematical
Psychology may confirm this impression, but it is misleading.
Learned developments in measurement theory having no foresee-
able relevance to empirical concerns are certainly occurring
in the name of mathematical psychology, but they are at one
extreme of a dimension which has a steady empiricism at the
other end, and lots of useful mathematics sharing the centre
with theoretically guided experimentation. This chapter will
look at the role played by this mathematics in the centre, and
it is written with non-mathematicians in mind. The author of
the first chapter of Psychology Survey I found that 'The
context of some twenty years work is necessary in order to
understand why some questions have arisen, others have
changed, and some have been entirely neglected' (Rabbitt,
1978). That was on visual selective attention, a relatively
recent invention. Mathematics is much older than psychology,
and to understand its role we need to go back (briefly) much
further.

Nowadays, mathematics seems so much a part of physics and
other sciences that it is a surprise to read (Bochner, 1966)
that they were once thought opposed in their interests. Thus
the Greeks were ambivalent about mathematics. It was a pure
and lofty pursuit remote from the disorder of daily life, or,
depending upon your point of view, an idle pastime having
little usefulness. Francis Bacon was inclined to the latter
view, but Galileo and Descartes were among the first to become
fully aware that the apparent haphazardness of sub-lunar
physical events did not make them permanently at odds with

mathematics in its perfect orderliness. For Descartes mathematics was the very science needed to bring order out of disorder. 'What,' he asked, in an early work which he held back from publication when he heard of Galileo's persecution and which was published posthumously,

> characterizes the mathematical? As I considered this more attentively, it finally became clear that only those subjects in which order or measure are considered are regarded as mathematical, and it makes no difference whether such measure is to be sought in number, or figures, or stars, or sounds, or any other object whatever. It then follows that there must be a certain general science which explains everything which can be asked about order and measure, and which is concerned with no particular subject matter, and that this very thing is called 'pure (literally 'universal') mathematics', not by an arbitrary appellation, but by a usage which is already accepted and of long standing, because in it is contained everything on account of which other sentences are called parts of mathematics (Descartes, 1961; first published in 1628).

Thus, Descartes dispels the old ambivalence. The mathematical statements of the laws of nature may be idealizations, never to be observed in their pure form, but ordinary physical events are not, in principle, beyond their reach. They are merely the outcome of complex conditions and the combination of different laws, and it is our inadequate descriptive powers which make them seem distant approximations to the ideal mathematical order. Although ordinary physical events are presumably enclosed in the mathematical net which physics throws over the world, experimental physicists are not concerned with them directly, but with their own contrived physical idealizations in the laboratory, which are much better approximations to the mathematical ideal. Thus, abstract laws are discovered from concrete experiments designed to approximate the conditions of the laws; and it has proved possible, to an astonishing extent, to make use of these laws in the everyday world. This is partly because the machines we find so useful, such as motor cars, computers, televisions, refrigerators and bombs, are insulated from the world like laboratories, and hence can embody the mathematically idealized laws of nature to a good enough approximation to be predictable and useful to us.

PSYCHOLOGY AS PHYSICS

The goals of experimental psychology are similar to those of physics. Mathematical laws have been proposed to govern the transformation of a physical energy into sensory experience (Fechner, 1964; first published in Elemente der Psychophysik, 1860), judgements of all kinds (Thurstone, 1927), learning (Hull, 1943), choice (Luce, 1959), detection (Swets, Tanner and Birdsall, 1961), problem solving (Newell and Simon, 1972), etc., and laboratory idealizations have been created in order to test the validity of these laws. These are the topics of mathematical psychology, and they blend imperceptibly into the rest of core experimental psychology, which is also concerned to reveal formal laws, though not necessarily stated in the language of mathematics. However, the spirit is similar, and is part of the 'general science which explains everything which can be asked about order and measure'.

Thus, in both physics and psychology there are mathematical laws regarded as idealizations which can never be exactly fulfilled in practice. They are, however, thought useful because there are laboratory experiments which approximate the conditions required of the laws, and which prove, to this degree of approximation, the truth of the laws. Some good examples from psychology are given in the book on signal detection theory by Green and Swets (1966). In the experimental realization of this theory an observer is required to detect a signal in noise. He bases his decision (according to the theory) upon a number which is treated as a sample from a distribution of likelihood ratios formed from two distributions, one of noise alone, and one of signal plus noise. The ideal observer also takes account of the payoff matrix, which lists the costs and benefits of correct detections, false alarms, and the other possible categories of response.

Under very carefully controlled conditions, a well-trained observer will approximate to the ideal, and produce results which accord almost exactly (with a margin of statistical error) with the theory. As in the theories of physics, the theory or theories of signal detection can be stated qualitatively, and this has been found useful in laboratory experiments where ideal, exact control is not possible, but where fruitful results can nevertheless be obtained. The interpretations of such experiments usually imply that the principles that govern the behaviour of the ideal observer also govern the behaviour of the non-ideal observer, although they are overlaid with many other factors, so that predictions must be approximate or merely qualitative, rather than precise and quantitative. In much the same way, full descriptions of experiments and observations in the physical sciences may be removed from the ideal laws which are the source of the explanatory power. Think, for instance, of the relationship between the laws of motion and the study of avalanches. No one doubts that, amongst other laws, avalanches follow the classical laws of motion, and that their initiation and progress could, in principle, be understood in terms of those laws. Yet it is unlikely that the laws could be applied with exactitude to any instance of an avalanche. Thus, in both physics and psychology the conceptual appeal of mathematical idealizations extends their power into regions where precision is neither possible nor necessary.

Here, then, is a pleasant picture of a satisfactory relationship between mathematics and science, whether the science in question is physics or psychology. In both cases, a lawful orderliness is described and the rules of this orderliness are used, by appropriate measurement, to impose order upon the apparent disorder of the everyday world of the behaviour of physical objects or human beings. Even so, the ancient ambivalence about mathematics, long dead in physics, remains to plague scientific psychology; for it is a much repeated commonplace that the social sciences, including psychology, have wrongly aped the methods of physics. Is there any justice in this claim? Is mathematical psychology to be held partly responsible?

EXPERIMENTAL PSYCHOLOGY AND MEASUREMENT

Experimental psychology came into being, not as a science which happens to use measurement, but as the science of measurement. The science, that is, which investigates the way in which observations are translated into numbers.

In the early seventeenth century, Descartes had firmly demarcated mind and matter, thus setting aside the material world as the legitimate field for mathematical physics, devoid of mind. This had a liberating effect upon physics, but raised difficult problems about the possibility of knowledge. How could knowledge of the world of matter be acquired by another world, that of mind or thinking substance? Obviously it was being acquired, but on the Cartesian view of a mind shut up inside its body, in only indirect contact with the world outside, the world of physics, it should not have been possible. Measure and order were the key, but measurement has a subjective aspect, so how can scientists be sure that it is the objective way to orderliness in the world?

Scientists themselves did not wait for the philosophers to solve this problem and continued to muddle along with increasing success. They were not indifferent to it. By the eighteenth century, mathematicians were studying the theory of error, thus laying the foundations of modern probability theory (Hacking, 1975), and attempts began to be made to study empirically the ways in which errors of observation occur, in order to be able to predict them and to control or allow for them. It was out of this study of measurement that psychology emerged.

A well known event which captures these preoccupations occurred in 1796, when Maskelyne, the Astronomer-Royal, dismissed his assistant, Kinnebrook, for a consistent 'error' in determining the moment in time at which a star viewed through a telescope crossed a wire. A few years later, a report of this reached Bessel, the astronomer at Konigsberg, who, according to Boring (1950), was 'an investigator with a special interest in instrumental errors of measurement', and had already carried out an experiment to compare his judgements with that of a colleague. More experiments followed, but the problem was eventually solved for astronomers by taking readings automatically, relying upon a satisfactory theory of how the reading device worked. This is always the potential solution of particular problems of this kind, and is reminiscent of Winston Churchill's epistemological theory, as described by Popper (1979). For Churchill, the problem of knowledge is solved if scientific predictions are fulfilled, especially when the observations are, or can be, made by 'automatic calculating machines'. More generally, the problem should be solvable by showing that the human observer is an automatic calculating machine, which is equivalent to discovering the laws, and hence discovering the algorithms, which underlie human observation. In Cartesian terms, we require the laws which will enable us to describe the mapping between numbers corresponding to the energies in the world of matter, and numbers corresponding to experiences in the world of thought, not forgetting eventually to take account of the further transformation into the observer's report, since error may occur through a shaky hand or a faulty memory, not only through failure of perceptual judgement.

THE DEVELOPMENT OF MATHEMATICAL PSYCHOLOGY

Fechner (1964; first published in 1860) proposed a subjective scale based on just noticeable differences (jnd) between neighbouring stimuli varying along a physical dimension such as intensity of light or sound. Fechner assumed that jnds at different points along the physical scale form identical subjective units, and drawing on the experimental work of Weber and himself, which showed that the physical change necessary to give rise to a jnd is proportional to the physical intensity, he deduced the first law mapping physical onto mental quantities.

$$S = k. \log R \qquad (1)$$

where S is sensation, R the stimulus magnitude, and k a constant.

If the subjective intensity can be represented by a number which is constructed by a concatenation of units (jnds) then the numbers should form a subjective scale. This is a testable hypothesis which has given rise to much experimentation and is the foundation of psychophysics, or at least of the psychophysics of scaling. The Weber-Fechner law was eventually replaced for prothetic continua (concerned with how much, as in intensity, rather than where as in pitch or colour) by the more precise power law:

$$S = k.R^n \qquad (2)$$

where the exponent n depends on the continua being tested (Stevens, 1957; see also Poulton, 1968, for a critical evaluation of the power law).

However, the mathematical ideal underlying psychophysics, the mapping of physical onto subjective quantities, was an influence of far greater scope than this refinement by Stevens of the original law.

THURSTONE'S LAW OF COMPARATIVE JUDGEMENT

Thurstone (1927) proposed a law of comparative judgement, which he saw as a generalization of the Weber and Fechner laws, being 'applicable not only to the comparison of physical stimulus intensities but also to qualitative comparative judgements such as those of excellence of specimens in an educational scale'. Thurstone argued that when we are comparing stimuli 'there must be some kind of process in us by which we react differently', and he called this, in a 'non-committal way', the 'discriminal process'. This discriminal process fluctuates, so that judgements are not always consistent. One stimulus or specimen may be preferred to another not always but on, say, 75 per cent of occasions, and on the basis of such proportions, 'the psychological continuum or scale is so constructed or defined that the frequencies of the respective discriminal processes for any given stimulus form a normal distribution of the psychological scale' (Miller, 1964). This scale is an artificial construct, the numbers given to the 'modal discriminal process' for a given stimulus being chosen to form a normal distribution around the mode. Thus, if A and B are two stimuli close together on the physical dimension, sometimes A will be preferred, sometimes B, giving rise to an observed frequency, or a proportion, which is a measure of the 'dominance' of A over B. Given a number of points on the stimulus dimension, the observed proportional preferences from, for instance, pairwise comparisons, are used to construct a set of normal distributions that would generate such proportions through a process of random sampling. The method for constructing the scale in this way is given in Torgerson (1958). Thurstone's formal statement of the law of comparative judgement is as follows:

$$ S_1 - S_2 = X_{12.} \sqrt{\sigma_1^2 + \sigma_2^2 - 2r\sigma_1\sigma_2} \tag{3} $$

where S_1 and S_2 are the psychological scale values of the two compared stimuli; x_{12} is the number of standard deviation units separating S_1 and S_2, 1 and 2 are the standard deviations of the distributions of the discriminal processes, and r is the correlation between them. Thurstone considered five cases, which differ in simplifying assumptions. The best known is case V, which involves the assumptions that all the discriminal processes have equal variance and are uncorrelated, so that (3) becomes:

$$ S_1 - S_2 = \sigma X_{12.} \sqrt{2} \tag{4} $$

The process of deriving a scale is very simple in this case, though obviously such sweeping assumptions are not always justified. When they are not justified, the best fitting scale will, in fact, fit the data rather poorly, and tests of

308

significance are available to evaluate the fit (Torgerson, 1958). Thus, the scale values that give the best fit to the data are obtained using a simple algorithm; and the null hypothesis that the observed variation in the data is due to chance acting upon the scale values is then tested. This process was called functional scaling by Anderson (1970), since the process of testing a theory and developing a scale go hand in hand. The success of a scale, tested empirically by seeing whether it stands up under the permissible operations, such as concatenation and bisection if it is what Stevens (1946) calls a ratio scale, is also the success of a theory about the mapping of physical onto sensory space. As Luce (1972) has written 'man ... is, among other things, a measuring device, in function not unlike a spring balance or a voltmeter, which is capable of transforming many kinds of physical attributes into a common measure in the central nervous system'.

THE INFLUENCE OF THURSTONE

The extent of Thurstone's influence has not, I think, been recognized. It is greater in some ways than that of behaviourism. Hull's habit strength which was at the centre of the learning theory which dominated American psychology until the 1950s, is formally identical to Thurstone's discriminal process. The stochastic consequences of Hull's theory were spelled out in Bush and Mosteller's (1955) linear model, one of the twin pillars of mathematical learning theory, the other being Estes' (1950) stimulus sampling theory. Mathematically, these two theories amount to much the same thing, and the relationship between them is shown in elementary form in the textbook by Coombs, Dawes and Tversky (1970); see also Atkinson, Bower and Crothers (1964). Both predicted the matching law, which states that an organism will distribute its choices according to reinforcement probability, so that if it receives reinforcement with a probability of 0.6 in one arm of a T-maze, 0.3 in the other, it will distribute its choices 2:1 in favour of the 60 per cent arm, even though the optimal strategy, if optimal means maximum reinforcement with given effort, would be always to choose the 60 per cent arm. For then it would receive 60 per cent reinforcement, instead of 50 per cent if it distributes its choices in this ratio.

The matching 'law' has now entered learning theory as a possible solution to the question of optimization, within a context provided by the ethological notion of optimal foraging

(Rachlin, Battalio, Kagel and Green, 1981). Thus, what was part of mathematical psychology has become absorbed into general experimental psychology, and in a similar way, the idea of an underlying process which can be given a varying numerical value (and called modal discriminal process or habit strength) continues in modern learning theory as associative strength (Dickinson, 1980). Mathematical learning theory has, as it were, completed its work, and its useful results have entered mainstream psychology. Excellent accounts of these results and methods have appeared (e.g. Wickens, 1982), but the word 'learning' now scarcely ever appears in the titles of articles in the Journal of Mathematical Psychology (it appears in just over 2 per cent of paper titles in volumes 17-22 compared with 29 per cent in the first six volumes of the journal).

Other developments of Thurstone's ideas include signal detection theory (Tanner and Swets, 1966), in which statistical decision theory is brought to bear on an updated version of discriminal processes, and theories of choice and scaling. The mathematical consequences of assuming an underlying process or strength underlying choice were worked out by Luce (1959) in a book which may prove to be as much a landmark for mathematical psychology and for psychology as a whole, as the work of Fechner and Thurstone. Luce started with the assumption that given a number of choices, including x and y, the ratio of the probability of choosing x to the probability of choosing y is independent of the other choices available. This is a version of what he called the choice axiom. From this assumption he showed how it is possible to construct an interval scale, known as the v-scale, such that if v_x is the value for x and v_y for y, then the probability of choosing x from y is given by

$$P(x,y) = \frac{v_x}{v_x + v_y} \qquad (5)$$

while the ratio of the probabilities, whatever the available alternatives, is v_x/v_y. He deduced various theorems which are easily tested.

Although the title of Luce's book is 'Individual Choice Behaviour', and although he gave examples where predictions from theorems derived from the choice axiom were confirmed, he was under no illusion that its truth is universal. His suggested counter example was the choice of roast beef, and its dependence upon the alternatives on the menu. Suppose the customer chooses meat rather than fish nine times out of 10, whatever the meat or fish available, but chooses veal rather than beef four times out of five, when both are available. Then when beef, veal and cod are the only options, the ratio of the probabilities of choosing beef and cod will be .9 x .2/.1=1.8, while when only beef and cod are available the ratio is .9/.1=9. So the ratio of probabilities is not independent of the available alternatives.

Since Luce's book there has been much empirical and theoretical work on the choice axiom (Morgan, 1974; Yellott, 1977; Luce, 1977; Strauss, 1981). It is not easy to know what to make of the empirical work. As we have seen, a thought experiment is quite sufficient to demonstrate that it will not always hold, and to suggest conditions under which it will break down. Luce is the first to admit that 'the conditions under which the choice axiom holds are surely delicate' (Luce, 1977), and he concludes that it is not so much a potential law as a normative rule. 'Perhaps the greatest strength of the choice axiom, and one reason it continued to be used, is as a canon of probabilistic rationality' (Luce, 1977). He continues: 'It is a natural probabilistic formulation of K. J. Arrow's famed principle of the independence of irrelevant alternatives, and as such it is a possible underpinning for rational, probabilistic theories of social behaviour'. This sounds an attractive idea which would make the relationship between the choice axiom and studies designed to test it similar to that between logic and studies of reasoning (Wason and Johnson-Laird, 1972), arithmetic and studies of arithmetic reasoning (Young and O'Shea, 1981), or between linguistic competence and linguistic performance (Chomsky, 1965). In all these cases, behaviour can be described in relation to an ideal which it fails to meet, and the burden of explanation is to account for the apparent failures. Logic and arithmetic might seem fairly unchangeable as normative ideals, but in the case of probabilistic choice, the study of behaviour in different situations will lead to the development of a more elaborate model of rationality. Thus, as we have seen, the main failure of the axiom as a model of choice is where some of the alternatives are similar, so that there are subsets of choice items between the members of which the chooser is relatively indifferent. One example was that given above concerning choice of foods, and another offers the choice between a trip to Paris, a trip to Paris plus £1, and a trip to New York. Given these alternatives, the trip to Paris on its own should never be chosen, and yet if Paris plus £1 is not on offer, Paris alone may well be chosen over New York. Luce was able to deal with this case by means of an exclusion clause which leaves out of the choice set any members which are never chosen when paired with another member. Thus, a mere trip to Paris, which is presumably never preferred over the same trip plus £1, is left out of the calculations, and the choice axiom will hold for the remaining alternatives. One way of describing this example is that the utilities of a trip to Paris, and a trip to Paris plus £1 are perfectly correlated (Restle, 1961). Strauss (1981) has extended this idea in a model which allows for intermediate correlations between utilities, which would include the choice of foods for example, since to say that a chooser has a superordinate preference which guides his choice between meat and fish and which precedes the choice of a particular meat (if meat is chosen) is one way in which the utilities for the different meats can be correlated.

The other interesting theoretical development is the clarification of the relationship between Thurstone's law of comparative judgement and the choice axiom. An exceptionally shaky prediction from Thurstone's model with normal distributions processes is that if a subject has to choose one of n different books, and there are k copies of each book, choice probability will depend upon the value of k. Yellott (1977) showed that this is not predicted if the discriminal processes are distributed according to a double exponential, and that when they are distributed in this way it is equivalent to Luce's choice model. This may be small comfort for Thurstone's theory, since it still has all the difficulties that it shares with Luce's theory, but at least Yellott brings out the similarity in the theorizing of these two psychologists committed to understanding the human being as a measuring device.

PSYCHOLOGY AND ENGINEERING

Much of the mathematics in psychophysical scaling and thematical learning theory has come directly from probability theory and has been developed by psychologists or by mathematicians working within psychology. Since 1945 there has been a steady influx of ideas from electrical engineering, culminating in computer systems and artificial intelligence. This seems so far from the mainstream of mathematical ideas in psychology that Estes, reviewing the state of the art and future prospects, declared an identity crisis. 'Suddenly, the all but omnipresent computers are taking over one after another of the functions formerly served only by mathematics' (Estes, 1975); but he concludes, reassuringly, that

Psychology and Mathematics

mathematical and computer simulation models may prove more complementary than competitive. The computer programme offers means of working with ideas that are insufficiently explicit for mathematical expression and techniques for simulating behavioural protocols that are too complex to be fitted by tractable mathematical models. But mathematics remains our principle vehicle for the flights of imagination that smooth our experiences and extract from varying contexts the relationships that would hold among events under idealized noise free conditions (Estes, 1975).

I believe that Estes is mistaken in maintaining such a sharp separation between mathematics and computer programming, but one sees what he had in mind. Reports (protocols) on their strategies by subjects solving problems have shown an impressive match with the corresponding reports by programs written to solve similar problems (Newell and Simon, 1963). There is no mathematics in this, and little new has been discovered about the psychology of thinking by such methods, since ideas about human thinking were already well advanced (Wertheimer, 1961). However, there was progress of a kind, since talk about strategies and hypotheses became acceptable to members of an empiricist tradition which had never assimilated the concepts of psychologists such as Wertheimer whose roots lay elsewhere. Reduction to a computer program provides the same kind of seal of respectability as reduction to mathematics.

The study of computer problem solving eventually brought its own kind of mathematics, and it is instructive to compare Wertheimer's approach with more recent work on production systems (Newell and Simon, 1972). A production system consists of a set of rules connecting conditions with actions. On the one hand, production systems are implemented as programs, on the other, they provide a formal language for describing the processes involved in problem solving. Wertheimer himself sometimes used a formal language. He used diagrams and symbols in order to get across his discoveries about how children or adults go about solving certain kinds of problems, usually involving an initial false attempt or attempts, leading eventually to insight and solution. In a geometrical problem, for instance, sometimes a child would blindly apply B-responses, learnt responses which continue to be used inappropriately when the figure is changed; but sometimes A-responses would appear, which are sensible adaptations of the old responses, and which are accompanied by insight into the principles underlying the solution. In a recent study of errors in children's subtraction, Young and O'Shea (1981) set up a production

313

system which will correctly carry out subtraction. It is, thus, an algorithm which consists of a set of rules, which forms an ideal to which children learning subtraction will eventually attain. By deleting or adding rules, other production systems can be created by a programmer which will make errors, and in this way it is possible to use productive systems to model the pattern of errors shown by individual children.

Superficially, Wertheimer and Young and O'Shea may seem to be writing about the same kind of thing, and in languages that are at least commensurable or translatable from one to another. The child with A-responses is using a production system which ranges over a wider range of conditions than a child with a B-response. The difference, as in Young and O'Shea, is revealed by the types of error made. When Wertheimer asks about the cause of this difference between A- and B-responses, it is apparent that he and the others are miles apart. For Young and O'Shea it can only be a difference in production systems, whereas for Wertheimer the B-responders are able to view the operations 'from the vantage point of the inner structure of the whole procedure, as they function within the context and fit its requirements' (Wertheimer, 1961). The well trained empiricist will bridle at such talk, but its purpose is clear: it is to make us understand learning and thinking by an appeal to mental processes that are <u>ostensively defined.</u> 'Inner structure' cannot be reduced to a production system or to any mathematical description, but by reading Wertheimer we may come to recognize what he means, and thereby to understand the difference between A- and B-responders. It is true that a wider ranging production system could view the operations from a 'vantage point', but this would destroy the open-endedness of Wertheimer's psychology, which enables him to analyse the thinking of Galileo, Gauss, and Einstein within the same framework as that of children solving geometrical problems. He may have been wrong, but he knew what he was trying to do, and one task for the future must be to investigate the limits of mathematical models and production systems in this area. Such mapping of limits has been carried out rigorously for the simple classificatory devices known as Perceptrons (Minsky and Papert, 1969), which are discussed below.

COMPUTATIONAL PERCEPTION

Another important influence from engineering over the last few years is the computational approach to perception, which can be seen as a technological updating of the traditional measurement basis for mathematical psychology. The traditional law of scaling is a function, mapping a physical dimension into a psychical. Multidimensional scaling is also possible, where a point in psychical space is picked out by a multidimensional point in physical space (Beals, Krantz and Tversky, 1968).

The points in psychical space could be identified with a state of an information processing system, which in turn might one day be identified with a state of a physiological system. The terminology is of less importance than the common idea of a state, like Thurstone's discriminal process, to which a number can be attached. A Perceptron is a special instance of this mapping process. It is a device which combines several quantitative inputs by computing their weighted sum, and giving an output of 1 or 0, depending upon whether or not this sum exceeds a given threshold value (Minsky and Papert, 1969). It is thus a classification device which combines linearly several sources of evidence, and it has been a popular model of pattern recognition with some plausibility in the very restricted environment of the visual laboratory. It is also a powerful model of learning (Nilsson, 1965), since the weights of the input may be modified by correlating them with reinforcement. Inputs that predict the correct output well will have the value of their weights increased, while those uncorrelated with the correct output will be reduced. These principles formed the basis of one of the great early successes of computer intelligence, Samuel's checkers (or draughts) player (Samuel, 1959), while correlation, prediction and linear combination play an important part in modern theories of associative learning (Dickinson, 1980).

In perception, however, functions have been replaced by functionals. A function transforms a number into another number, whilst a functional transforms a function into another function. Both are transforms. In his very lucid book on the Fast Fourier Transform, Brigham (1974) begins by introducing the concept of a transform, and takes the logarithmic transform as an example with which all his readers will be familiar. Arithmetic operations such as multiplication are simplified by transforming the numbers in logarithms, carrying out the appropriate operations in the logarithmic domain, and then transforming back again into ordinary numbers to get the answer. Brigham points out that the same logic applies to Fourier transforms. The Fourier transform of a waveform separates it into the sinusoids of different frequencies that make it up. The value of the transform at any point is given by a complex number which corresponds to amplitude and phase of the frequency in the original waveform. By applying the inverse transform, the original waveform may be reconstructed. Just as with logarithms, the Fourier transform and its inverse may be used to simplify calculations. Thus the transfer function of a linear system indicates how much energy passes through the system at different frequencies. To calculate the output waveform from the input, take the product of the transfer function and the Fourier transform of the input. The inverse transform of this product is the output.

In general, the integral transform involves the operation of one function on another to produce a third function. Thus the basilar membrane of the ear, which approximately carries out a Fourier Transform, may be said to operate upon the input waveform to produce a function of frequency. Since Campbell and Robson (1968) there has been much empirical and theoretical research in vision starting from the idea that the visual system carries out a Fourier analysis of the input. The input is described as a function of light intensity at different points on the retina. This is transformed by the operation of a function (presumably embodied in the retinal mechanisms) into a third function. The integral need not be a Fourier transform however. More general transforms, closely related to the Fourier, are convolution and correlation, and these, too, have appeared in research on perception and the central nervous system (Caelli, 1981; Murdock, 1979).

Marr and his colleagues (Marr and Hildreth, 1980; Marr and Poggio, 1979) have described a device that will take a grey level 'retinal' input and transform it into a 'raw primal sketch' which picks out contours significant for vision. Thus one function is transformed into another and it is by means of the so-called (because of its shape) Mexican hat operator. The raw primal sketch is, in turn, transformed by another operator, and the sketches from the two eyes are combined to form the '$2\frac{1}{2}$-D sketch'; the implicit theory is that there is a series of such transformations, from function to function, ending with the 3-D representation of the human visual world.

This is perhaps the most elaborate and complete application of integral transform analysis in psychology. Several examples involving the application of similar principles will be found in a recent book edited by Grossberg (1981), to which Grossberg contributes a chapter with the title 'Adaptive resonance in development, perception and cognition'. Suppose a system has to discriminate between two patterns, A and B, represented as functions which assign a number to every retinal point. These functions are operated upon by another function, g, and the output, the transformed function, should make it possible to distinguish between the two inputs, possibly after further transformations. If the use of g leads to the two inputs being mistakenly treated as the same (or different), this information is fed back to modify g, until it is successful in setting up the discrimination. Such a model manages to incorporate most of the practical developments in mathematical psychology over the past 30 years. It brings together in a well digested form the insights of information theory (Attneave, 1959), a signal detection theory, mathematical learning theory, control theory (Toates, 1975), perceptrons, integral transforms, and the considerable mathematical skills of Grossberg himself. Perhaps the theory is too powerful, and there seems a slight incongruity when it is applied to some earthbound data from a Skinner box. It is worth heeding Estes' warning that if 'the technology had been available, computer simulation models for the motions of the planets based on the conception of epicycles, or for the process of combustion in terms of phlogiston could never have been rejected' (Estes, 1975).

As Brigham (1974) explains, the logic of a logarithmic transform, which as a function converts one number into another, is similar to that of an integral transform, which as a functional converts one function into another. Does this not mean that the logic underlying Fechner's law, which used a logarithmic transform to convert a number representing physical energy into another number representing perceived intensity, is similar to the logic of Grossberg's adaptive resonance theory, or Marr's model, which converts a grey level function into a raw primal sketch? They all provide models for highly controlled idealized environments in which the subject's (or the eye's or the brain's) activities can be reasonably compared to measuring, classifying and machine-minding activities of human beings and other organisms (like many modern machines, a Skinner box has levers and flashing lights). These activities are extremely important, but are they all there is?

CONCLUSION

In recent years, mathematical ideas have had their source from outside experimental psychology. They have their day and eventually get assimilated and are carried along the mainstream, where they help to keep theory abreast with the latest developments in devices for measuring and ordering the world. Theories are like specifications of such devices. They may be normative, specifying what is required, as Luce suggested for his choice axiom, as is obvious in the ideal observer of signal detection theory, and as is implicit in the cognitive scientist's investigations into the abstract structures of (machine) intelligence (Simon, 1981). Alternatively, they may be blueprints for a device like Churchill's calculating machine which solves the problem of knowledge, and like Marr's successive transformations from whose final output it should be possible to draw conclusions about the world outside. Thus scientific psychology, guided to some extent by mathematics, has its place in the Cartesian world of physics. It investigates the fallible human link in the chain transforming the physical world into a system of knowledge. If this is so, the ambivalence noted earlier about the benefits of mathematics and the desirability of taking physics as a model are understandable. For superficially at least, people and animals do more than merely measure and order and classify the world, and the philosophy that makes these their main activities fits uneasily within a Darwinian framework. The deeper workings of the world regarded as a Cartesian machine give rise to natural selection and evolution, but the products of evolution, like ourselves, are first of all at home in the macroscopic world of earth, air, fire and water, rather than the microscopic abstractions of modern physics; but it is the latter rather than the former which provide the inspiration for the modern psychological laboratory.

Such considerations lie behind Gibson's (1979) proposal for an ecological physics, in which the scale of description, while still austerely physical, is appropriate to the evolutionary adaptation that has actually taken place. Instead of the light energy falling upon the retina and providing evidence of objects in the 'external' world, as in the Cartesian model, the information available in the light reflected from surfaces specifies the layout of the environment. The metaphor of external knowledge by inference based upon evidence required devices for measuring, ordering and inference, and mathematics took the lead in providing models of such devices. The mathematics required was that of formal measurement theory, probability, decision processes and computation. If the light specifies the layout, the emphasis will not be on inferential processes, but on a description of the layout and how it is specified by reflected light in relation to a moving organism, and on an account of the means for picking up the available information. Mathematics (using differential geometry) has played some part in describing the environment (Gibson, Olum and Rosenblatt, 1955; Lee, 1974; Longuet-Higgins and Prazdny, 1980), and the mathematics of control systems may eventually be expected to play some part in this approach, as well as the mathematics used by biologists studying the ecology of behaviour (Smith, 1982).

REFERENCES

Anderson, N. H. (1970). Functional measurement and psychological judgement. Psychological Review, 77, 153-170.
Atkinson, R. C., Bower, G. H. and Crothers, E. J. (1965). An Introduction to Mathematical Learning Theory. New York: Wiley.
Attneave, F. (1959). Applications of Information Theory to Psychology. New York: Holt, Rinehart & Winston.
Beals, R., Krantz, D. H. and Tversky, A. (1968). Foundations of multidimensional scaling. Psychological Review, 75, 127-142.
Boring, E. G. (1950). A History of Experimental Psychology. New York: Appleton-Century-Crofts.
Bochner, S. (1966). The Role of Mathematics in the Rise of Science. Princeton: Princeton University Press.
Brigham, E. O. (1974). The Fast Fourier Transform. Englewood Cliffs, NJ: Prentice-Hall.
Bush, R. R. and Mosteller, F. (1955). Stochastic Models for Learning. New York: Wiley.
Caelli, T. (1981). Visual Perception: Theory and practice. Oxford: Pergamon.
Campbell, F. W. and Robson, J. G. (1968). Application of Fourier analysis to the visibility of gratings. Journal of Physiology (London), 197, 531-566.
Chomsky, N. (1965). Aspects of the Theory of Syntax. Cambridge, Mass.: MIT Press.
Coombs, C. H., Dawes, R. M. and Tversky, A. (1970). Mathematical Psychology, an Elementary Introduction. Englewood Cliffs, NJ: Prentice-Hall.
Descartes, R. (1961). Rules for the Direction of the Mind. New York: Bobbs-Merrill.
Dickinson, A. (1980). Contemporary Animal Learning Theory. Cambridge: Cambridge University Press.
Estes, W. K. (1950). Toward a statistical theory of learning Psychological Review, 57, 94-107.
Fechner, G. T. (1964). The fundamental formula and the measurement formula. In G. A. Miller (ed.), Mathematics and Psychology. New York: Wiley.
Gibson, J. J. (1979). The Ecological Approach to Visual Perception. Boston: Houghton Mifflin.

Gibson, J. J., Olum, P. and Rosenblatt, F. (1955). Parallax and perspective during aircraft landings. American Journal of Psychology, 68, 372-385.

Green, D. M. and Swets, J. A. Signal Detection Theory and Psychophysics. New York: Wiley.

Grossberg, S. (ed.) (1981). Mathematical Psychology and Psychophysiology. Providence, RI: American Mathematical Society.

Hacking, I. (1975). The Emergence of Probability. London: Cambridge University Press.

Hull, C. L. (1943). Principles of Behaviour. New York: Appleton-Century-Crofts.

Lee,D. N. (1974). Visual information during locomotion. In R. B. MacLeod and H. L. Pick (eds), Studies in Perceptual Theory. Ithaca, NY: Cornell University Press.

Longuet-Higgins, H. C. and Prazdny, K. (1980). The interpretation of a moving retinal image. Proceedings of the Royal Society (London). B. 208, 385-397.

Luce, R. D. (1959). Individual Choice Behaviour. New York: Wiley.

Luce, R. D. (1972). What sort of measurement is psychophysical measurement? American Psychologist, 27, 96-106.

Luce, R. D. (1977). The choice axiom after twenty years. American Psychologist, 15, 215-233.

Marr, D. and Hildreth, E. (1980). Theory of edge detection. Proceedings of the Royal Society (London).B. 207, 187-217.

Marr, D. and Poggio, T. (1979). A computational theory of human stereo vision. Proceedings of the Royal Society (London) B, 204, 301-328.

Miller, G. A. (1964). Mathematics and Psychology. New York: Wiley.

Minsky, M. and Papert, S. (1969). Perceptrons: an introduction to computational geometry. Cambridge, Mass.: MIT Press.

Morgan, B. J. T. (1974). On Luce's choice axiom. Journal of Mathematical Psychology, 11, 107-123.

Murdock, R. B. (1979). Convolution and correlation in perception and memory. In L. G. Nilsson (ed.), Perspectives on Memory Research. Hillsdale, NJ: Lawrence Erlbaum Associates.

Newell, A. and Simon, H. A. (1963). GPS - a program that stimulates human thought. In E. A. Feigenbaum and J. Feldman (eds), Computers and Thought. New York: Wiley.

Newell, A. and Simon, H. A. (1972). Human Problem Solving. Englewood Cliffs, NJ: Prentice-Hall.

Nilsson, N. (1965). Learning Machines. New York: McGraw-Hill.

Popper, K. R. (1979). Objective Knowledge: An evolutionary approach. Oxford: Oxford University Press.

Poulton, E. C. (1968). The new psychophysics: six models for magnitude estimation. Psychological Bulletin, 69, 1-19.

Rabbitt, P. M. A. (1978). Visual selective attention. In B. M. Foss (ed.), Psychology Survey no. 1. London: Allen & Unwin.

Rachlin, H., Battalio, R., Kagel, J. and Green, L. (1981). Maximization theory in behavioural psychology. Behavioural Brain Sciences, 4, 371-417.

Restle, F. (1961). Psychology of Judgement and Choice. New York: Wiley.

Samuel, A. L. (1959). Some studies in machine learning using the game of checkers. IBM Journal of Research and Development, 3, 210-223.

Simon, H. A. (1981). Cognitive science: the newest science of the artifical. In D.A. Norman (ed.), Perspectives on Cognitive Science. Hillsdale, NJ: Lawrence Erlbaum Associates.

Smith, J. M. (1982). Evolution and the Theory of Games. Cambridge: Cambridge University Press.

Stevens, S. S. (1946). On the theory of scales of measurement. Science, 103, 679-680.

Stevens, S. S. (1957). On the psychophysical law. Psychological Review, 64, 153-181.

Strauss, D. (1981). Choice by features: an extension of Luce's choice model to account for similarities. British Journal of Mathematical and Statistical Psychology, 34, 50-61.

Swets, J. A., Tanner, W. P. and Birdsall, T. G. (1961). Decision processes in perception. Psychological Review, 68, 301-340.

Thurstone, L. L. (1927). A law of comparative judgement. Psychological Review, 34, 273-286.

Toates, F. M. (1975). Control Theory in Biology and Experimental Psychology. London: Hutchinson Educational.

Torgerson, W. S. (1958). Theory and Methods of Scaling. New York: Wiley.

Wason, P. C. and Johnson-Laird, P. N. (1972). Psychology of Reasoning: Structure and content. London: Batsford.

Wertheimer, M. (1961). Productive Thinking. London: Tavistock.

Wickens, T. D. (1982). Models of Behavior: Stochastic processes in psychology. San Francisco: Freeman.
Yellott, J.I. (1977). The relationship between Luce's choice axiom, Thurstone's theory of comparative judgement, and the double exponential distribution. Journal of Mathematical Psychology, 15, 109-144.
Young, R. M. and O'Shea, T. (1981). Errors in children's subtraction. Cognitive Science, 5, 153-177.

Acknowledgement

I thank Dr John Findlay for reading through the manuscript and making some helpful comments.

Chapter 13

WRITING AND READING TECHNICAL INFORMATION

Patricia Wright

1. WHY AN INTEREST IN TECHNICAL INFORMATION?

Anyone who has been puzzled by a timetable, or who has had difficulties following the instructions for putting together some home-assembly furniture, or who has only tenuously grasped the concepts an author was developing in a journal article, knows that technical communication can make heavy demands on the problem-solving skills of both readers and writers. Nickerson (1981) has discussed the difficulties of interpretation facing road users confronted by cryptic messages such as SLOW ANIMAL CROSSING or END ROAD WORKS. Nickerson points out that although 'the grammar of signs, if there is one, is not consistent', nevertheless, when read in context usually such messages are readily understood. Of course, there are exceptions. Chapanis (1965) drew attention to the problems of comprehending messages such as 'please walk up one floor walk down two floors for improved elevator service'. Similarly, Clark and Clark (1977) have discussed how people construe the tacit implications of notices such as 'Dogs must be carried' (but if you have left yours at home there is no need to go back for it) in contrast to admonitions such as 'Passes must be carried' (in which case you had better go back for it).

When reading technical material people will draw upon a wide range of psychological processes, including those associated with the comprehension of oral language. It is, however, important to note at the outset that the phrase 'technical information' is being used here to mark a contrast with fiction materials (stories, poems, novels). It covers materials as diverse as educational textbooks, government forms, explanatory leaflets, notices for operating machines and, of course, technical manuals. Often the successful communication of technical information relies much more on spatial format and typographic cueing than does narrative fiction. Consider the non-linear structure of application forms such as those included in a travel agent's brochure, where information from row and column headings must be combined to generate the question. Many of these formatting conventions have no counterpart in oral language. We seldom articulate lists of items, and more complex visual structures such as a matrix are nearly impossible to communicate by speech alone. Inevitably, the communication of technical material poses novel psycholinguistic problems both with respect to its production and its comprehension. As yet there are no theories of the broad-based literacy skills that enable people to understand and use a great diversity of visible language systems, including non-sentence-based information such as maps and diagrams, directories and indexes: whether the Yellow Pages or Psychological Abstracts.

The relation between spoken and written language is far from simple (Olson, 1977). It may, therefore, not be necessary to accept the argument of Stubbs (1980) that 'A systematic theory of literacy must be based, first of all, on an account of the relationship between spoken and written language'. For the many people who do not read for pleasure, the written language of most relevance to their literacy skills is technical information (Williams, 1976). Here many of the problem-solving skills and strategies for decoding visual signals will have no counterpart in oral language, so a theory of literacy may need to turn to other cognitive theories for conceptual support.

Urgent Practical Problems

The adequate design of technical information has considerable practical relevance. There can be no doubt that technological advances make increasing demands upon literacy skills. Much more information is being made directly available to the public, for example through computer-based systems such as Prestel. Moreover, the rising cost of wages means that it is cheaper for many organizations to provide information in leaflets and posters rather than through their trained personnel. Information about welfare benefits, the operation of domestic appliances and the training course for learning how to talk to personal computers all rely heavily on the reader's successful interaction with printed material. Campaigns for Plain English, both in Britain and the United States, have highlighted numerous instances where written information has been designed in a way that presents the reader with a formidable task (e.g. Cutts and Maher, 1980; Rose, 1981). Some psychologists have been concerned about the causes of poor written commmunication (e.g. Flower and Hayes, 1980), others have sought to develop procedures or guidelines for improving technical writing (e.g. Hartley, 1981a). If psychologists are willing to respond to the demands of society (e.g. Fishman and Neigher, 1982) then the domain of technical information is undoubtedly an area where help is being urgently requested.

Value to Cognitive Psychology

The variety of problems to be found in the domain of technical information raises two quite different issues for cognitive psychology. One issue concerns the relevance of contemporary cognitive theory. Can psychologists familiar with the research literature on how people communicate and process information make a useful contribution to the solution of design problems? A second issue concerns the theoretical relevance of pragmatically successful communication techniques. Do the problems of information design, and the research findings which have come from exploring design issues, have any contribution to make to the development of psychological theory? The remainder of this chapter will seek to show that the answers to both questions are varying shades of YES.

The reason why neither question can be answered with an unequivocal YES is that there exist numerous difficulties in applying psychological theory to a practical problem. For example, although we know a great deal about memory processes, there is nothing inherent in any theory of memory which would speak to the question of how to design a rows by columns matrix. Yet it would appear that consulting such matrices involves memory processes, because reducing these memory requirements makes the table easier to use (Wright, 1977). One contribution that cognitive psychology can offer may be a way of analysing the cognitive processes required by alternative information displays.

Simplistic mapping from psychological theory to practical application is seldom possible because even when the theory appears adequate and relevant, its predictions may be completely overshadowed by other factors. For example, when constructing a question and answer matrix, the designer must decide whether the main content of the question goes in the row heading or the column heading. Since most people work along the rows of such a matrix, it might seem highly compatible with memory strategies to have the item about which the questions were asked as the row heading. Having located this item in memory, people could now answer several questions about it as they worked across the page. However, an experimental comparison found this display to be almost twice as error prone as having the questions in the row headings and the items in the column headings (Wright and Barnard, 1978). The most likely explanation seemed to be in terms of the kinds of questions being used. These questions were very detailed, but when they were in column headings people gave up rereading them thoroughly as they worked down the page; as a consequence, mistakes were made. In row headings, these questions only needed to be read carefully once and so mistakes were fewer. Successful application of cognitive psychology to information design depends upon an ability to analyse in detail how readers will interact with the written material.

The advantages of moving back and forth between theory and application have been cogently argued elsewhere (e.g. Broadbent, 1971; Baddeley, 1981). The need for a practical solution can force recognition of theoretical inadequacy that may otherwise be undetected. One example of this is the growing recognition of the need for theories of writing (e.g. Gregg and Steinberg, 1980). Certainly, theoretical developments are able to provide insights which can guide information design: see for example the work of Burton and Brown (1982) on the design of materials for computer-assisted instruction. However, few psychological studies of reading have been concerned with non-prose information; nor has there been much interest in the display characteristics of technical material. Therefore, for many kinds of technical information relevant psychological theories are in short supply.

Although there is an absence of theory, there is no shortage of data. For over 50 years, behavioural studies have explored the effects of numerous typographic variables such as the size and style of the typeface, the uses of white space, etc. The findings from some of these studies are briefly summarized in the next section.

2. MAKING TECHNICAL INFORMATION USABLE

Terms such as legible, comprehensible, readable and usable have not always been clearly distinguished in the literature. Legible refers to the quality of the physical signal; comprehensible refers to the attainment by the reader of the writer's intended meaning; readable refers to the relative ease of achieving the intended understanding: thus it can be a composite of both legibility and comprehensibility factors. Usable refers to the ease with which the reader can apply that understanding (e.g. to answering a question on a form or to carrying out some procedural sequence).

Legibility Factors

There is a large literature on legibility, both for print on paper and for electronic displays (see the reviews by Tinker, 1965; Spencer, 1969; Watts and Nisbet, 1974; Hartley, 1978; Grandjean and Vigliani, 1982). The most serious attempt to create a theoretical framework for this domain can be seen in the work of Twyman (1982). He has suggested sub-dividing the features of verbal graphic language into those which are intrinsic to the characters themselves (e.g. the range of the character set, the style of the letter forms, including bold and italic variations, the size of the letter forms) and the numerous extrinsic features relating to the way the character sets are configured on the page (e.g. the use of space between characters, between words and between lines). It is primarily the extrinsic factors which can be related to psychological processes. For example, recent developments concerning the spacing of letters in text suggest that letters may have a 'perceptual centre', and that in well-designed material the letters are spaced to be equidistant from these centres (Kindersley, 1976). This aspect of the visual spacing between letters may be analogous to the finding in the auditory modality that when words are adjusted to appear equally spaced in time, people are responding to the perceptual centre of the word (Morton, Marcus and Frankish, 1976). As yet, no detailed theoretical explanation of the visual effect has been proposed.

Because the constraints on legibility are in part physically determined, there is some consistency in the literature as to what size of type, or colour contrast between print and background (i.e. Twyman's intrinsic factors) will cause difficulties for readers. For example, Tinker and Paterson (1931) reported that people took 40 per cent longer to read a dark brown text on a dark green background than to read the same text printed in black on a white page; but it should be noted that brightness contrast is much more critical than the colour difference itself (Poulton, 1968; 1969a and b).

Although there may be some consistency at the extremes of the legibility domain, for the most part typographic factors have been found to interact with each other (illustrations of many of these interactions will be found in Watts and Nisbet, 1974). Perhaps the most obvious example is the interaction between length of line and size of type. The width of newspaper columns is only feasible with a print size smaller than that used for newspaper headlines. Less obvious is the research finding that the white space between lines needs to be greater for longer lines (Tinker, 1965). Indeed, the potency of white space as a determinant of legibility raises several issues. Reynolds (1979a) reported that when text was printed on both sides of very thin paper, readers found it easier if the text was aligned so that the print on both sides coincided, thereby preserving the white space, rather than having the text on one side coincide with the white space on the other. The psychological explanation of this finding is not obvious. One possibility is that conceptually-driven (top-down) processes in reading are able to filter out the signal from the noise on the line being read, but when the noise shows through more prominently in the white space between the lines perhaps data-driven (bottom-up) processes are captured, with the result that the reader is distracted by the noise. This explanation is testable, since it predicts that visual noise on the line will interact with the cohesiveness of the text being read (i.e. the less cohesive the text, the more disruptive the noise), whereas noise between the lines will result in a constant decrement, no matter what the text characteristics. However, few researchers concerned with legibility effects have gone beyond the phenomenology of their data to explore the cognitive processes responsible for such effects. Perhaps there has been a tacit assumption that such effects are caused by physiological rather than psychological mechanisms; but only in special circumstances does this seem likely to be the case, given the considerable evidence from cognitive psychology for the role of conceptually-driven processes in adult reading.

One physiological mechanism that may be highly relevant to reading is the tendency of the spatial frequency analysers in the visual system to respond to the pattern of dark stripes formed by the lines of text on a page (Wilkins, personal communication). There could be a relation between the eye strain some people experience when reading and cortical patterns of epileptogenic activity elicited by striped patterns (Wilkins, Binnie and Darby, 1981). If such a relation is found, this would have direct implications for the presentation of written materials, both technical and fictional.

Our theoretical understanding of the processes involved in word recognition (e.g. see the review by Allport, 1979) provides an underpinning for the research finding that words written in lower case are easier to read than words written entirely in capital letters (e.g. Starch, 1914; Poulton, 1967). Tinker (1955) suggests that for a 20-minute reading period the slowing down is in the order of 14 per cent when the text is entirely in capital letters. The explanation would seem to be that the outline of many word shapes is much more distinctive in lower case than in capitals, and so provides additional information for the reader.

It seemed only a short extension of this reasoning about how words were recognized to argue that introducing visual noise into the contours of the word (e.g. by having each letter written in a separate box, a requirement of many forms) would make the information harder to read. Although there are data confirming this prediction (e.g. Barnard and Wright, 1976; Barnard, Wright and Wilcox, 1978), it is difficult to explain why partial boxes (just small marks segmenting the line on which the answer was written) were more disruptive than full boxes for each character. Wing (1979) showed that the small segmentation lines were less disruptive if placed at the top of the answer box rather than at the bottom. The explanation appeared to be that when the marks were at the top, people reduced the size of their manuscript and so wrote entirely under the segmentation marks.

Comprehension Factors

For the most part, when readers have problems understanding a Government leaflet or a computer manual, these problems are not related to legibility but to comprehensibility and to usability. This does not mean that the problems are entirely verbal or linguistic. Presentation factors can often contribute to readers' confusion: see the analysis of a college prospectus by Burnhill, Hartley, Young and Fraser (1975). Guidelines exist which stress the need for function to be the over-riding consideration when designing information (e.g. Hartley, 1981a), and illustrate the relevance of gestalt principles to computer-generated displays (e.g. Stewart, 1976). Nevertheless, there is no theoretical approach to information presentation that corresponds to the models of text processing that are being developed for narrative materials (e.g. Kintsch and van Dijk, 1978).

There are many reasons for doubting that any exclusively text-based approach to the meaning that readers derive from written information will ever be fully adequate (Nystrand, 1981a and b). Psychologists have emphasized the contribution of readers' prior knowledge (e.g. Bransford, 1979). It is also the case that the graphic presentation of the information on the page (the use of headings, variation in type style, indentation, column width, etc.) can all influence the reader's

329

interaction with the text. Hartley (1982) reported that students who were asked to study and recall a recipe tended to reproduce it in a graphic format (list or paragraph) that was similar to the format they had been studying. This correspondence can depend, however, on there being an obvious rationale underlying the visual organization (Broadbent, Cooper and Broadbent, 1978).

Waller (1980) has coined the phrase 'macro-punctuation' to refer to the presentation options available for displaying text. There are many different ways of instantiating such punctuation. For technical material such as scientific papers, some of the presentation options are illustrated in the papers by Jewett (1981), Shebilske and Rotondo (1981) and Jonassen (1981), which are helpfully published as successive articles in the same journal issue. An even more radical re-structuring of the visual impact of a page, together with evidence of its effectiveness and acceptability to the intended readership, has been provided by Wendt (1979). As yet there are few studies of the use which readers make of running headings, section headings and marginalia. Twyman (1981) has developed a notation for discussing the presentation of headings and sub-headings. As to their verbal content, there are reports that headings can be unintentionally misleading (Swarts, Flower and Hayes, 1980) as well as facilitative (Schwarz and Flammer, 1981).

Studies of how information display affects comprehension can have implications not only for information design, but also for understanding the reading strategies adopted for technical materials. For example, Whalley and Flemming (1975) showed that a circuit diagram was ignored by many readers when it occurred at the top of the second column on a page where it was referred to about half way down the first column. Moving the illustration to be in the first column, immediately after it was referred in the text, greatly increased the number of people who studied it. This suggests that readers may perceive place-keeping as a hazardous component of following the writer's request to look at an illustration. Editorial decisions that locate graphic material appropriately can reduce the hazards of readers getting lost.

3. RESEARCH APPROACHES TO TECHNICAL COMMUNICATION

The reference to editors serves as a reminder that there are often multiple 'authors' of technical information. This is another characteristic which distinguishes technical

information from the class of written materials which are read
for pleasure. The creation of usable technical material
requires people who are skilful at capturing the essential
content (e.g. from the product developer, the administrative
or legal departments), people who are skilful at translating
this into a verbal and visual display, and people who are
skilful at seeing these design decisions implemented through
the appropriate production processes. Inevitably the constraints of the real world require that all this be done with
minimal cost and by tea-time tomorrow. Given such constraints,
the need to integrate many diverse skills, and to resolve
conflicting demands - e.g. to format the bibliographic references to comply with the recommendations of research (Hartley, Trueman and Burnhill, 1979; Hartley, 1981b), or to
continue with a well-established convention such as the BPS or
APA standards -the contribution of researchers is sometimes
seen by technical writers as rather peripheral to their needs
as information designers. It is appropriate for psychologists
to consider to what extent this is true, and where true,
whether it is inevitable. Clearly, psychologists cannot make
an equal contribution to all components of the design process.
Given the present stage of cognitive theory, psychology may be
able to help designers understand the way readers interact
with technical materials. In the long term, other kinds of
help may also be possible.

Modelling the User

Apart from ad hoc research, there are three main approaches
that can be adopted when trying to design or to improve some
specific piece of written information. All three draw upon
cognitive psychology. One approach is to work from a model of
the reader or user of the information. The design objective is
then to present the information in a way that is cognitively
compatible with the user's needs and processing resources. One
example of this approach would be Sticht's development of the
concept of 'reading to do' (as distinct from 'reading to
learn'). Sticht has explored the relationship between the
reading skills of US military personnel and their more general
skills of language comprehension (Sticht, 1972; 1977). The
value of such an understanding of the reader's knowledge and
skills is that these set boundary conditions for information
design.

   In a different domain, namely the design of user-friendly
computer interfaces, a similar approach has been advocated
(e.g. by Morton, Barnard, Hammond and Long, 1979). Here too,

the concern is with cognitive limitations which set boundary conditions for design. As a basic design principle, Morton and his colleagues have argued that the information displayed needs to be compatible with the user's cognitive structures. This has led them to consider how such structures might be characterized. This, in turn, has resulted in their advocating the need for a variety of psychological models, each capturing different facets of the user's interaction with the system. Much of their analysis seems highly relevant to the reader/ user of technical information, as the following summary shows.

Barnard, Hammond, Morton and Long (1981) have outlined five theoretical perspectives. One focusses on the user's prior knowledge. For written materials it has been shown that the reader's prior knowledge of the content area (Rothkopf, 1978a) and assumptions about the text characteristics (Rothkopf and Coatney, 1974) will change reading performance. Compatibility of the written information with that prior knowledge is perhaps at its most essential when new technical terms and concepts are being introduced. A second, and closely related analysis, seeks to characterize the way readers draw upon their knowledge whilst interacting with the display. Riesbeck (1980) has argued that, at least during the first casual reading of a text outlining a route to be driven, no internal map is generated. Instead, the reader's concern is with whether the directions seem clear and sensible. Prior knowledge undoubtedly plays a vital role in such evaluation. A third analytic perspective seeks to model the user's goal structures. There is evidence that reading purpose will change details of the micro-structure of reading performance, such as the allocation of pauses (Aaronsen and Scarborough, 1976) and control of eye movements (Rothkopf, 1978b; Rothkopf and Billington, 1979). In principle, the information about readers' goals and the strategies selected for attaining these goals could be used to determine the sequence in which information is presented in a text and the access structures which need to be provided for readers. A fourth kind of analysis seeks to capture the way in which users will modify their knowledge and beliefs as they interact with information displays. The use of concrete examples and analogies can be particularly critical in this respect (e.g. Hayes and Tierney, 1982). The issues relating to when readers will change their conceptualization as they read have been discussed by Bransford and Nitsch (1978), who have emphasized that readers often need to acquire information which they can use rather than information they simply 'know about'. The fifth proposed perspective relates to human information processing as developed by contemporary cognitive psychology. Just and Carpenter (1980) illustrate such an approach to reading comprehension, but the implications of this class of models for information design are not obvious.

Although Barnard, Hammond, Morton and Long explicitly designed their five-pronged approach for application to people's interaction with computer systems, it would seem to have wider relevance to people's interaction with technical material in general. It is too soon to say whether the separation of these five facets of a reader's interaction with written communications is in practice necessary or valuable. Much may depend on the way different facets can be combined to address specific design problems. In contrast, an artificial intelligence approach might integrate several of these facets into a single, albeit more complex, model. For example, the second, third and fourth perspectives might be merged in a way that enabled reading purposes to be related to the selection of reading strategies and the consequent change in the reader's knowledge.

Undoubtedly, understanding the constituents of the reader's interaction with the text, constituents such as knowledge and goals, can be a very valuable aid to information design. Sleeman and Brown (1982) have shown how AI models of the user/reader's knowledge can have a salutary impact on the design of course-ware for computer-assisted instruction systems. There is, however, no reason for thinking that an understanding of the reader will itself be sufficient to ensure that technical communication succeeds: even when fully informed, writers can still have communication problems.

Modelling the Writer

A quite different approach, and one taken much less often, focusses not on the reader, but on the writer. There have been descriptions of how students write essays (Branthwaite, Trueman and Hartley, 1980) and how scientists write journal articles (Wason, 1970). As with the study of reading, the contrast between skilled and unskilled writers can yield insights into the underlying cognitive processes. For example, Atlas (1979) found differences both in the way ideas were generated and the way they were incorporated into the subsequent text. Novice writers simply listed the ideas they wanted to mention in the text, whereas experts generated plans. These plans in turn prompted new ideas as the plan was translated into text. Another way to explore some of the cognitive processes is to examine the contribution of the writer's knowledge of the subject matter (e.g. Voss, Vesonder and Spilich, 1980). These writers suggest that domain-related knowledge has similar effects on text generation and text comprehension, but there are undoubtedly some aspects of writing (e.g. 'writer's block') that seem to have no counterpart in comprehension processes (Flower and Hayes, 1977).

One of the few detailed accounts of the writing processes available at present has drawn heavily on the techniques of AI. This approach has had considerable success in analysing highly skilled human problem-solving (e.g. Hayes, 1981). Indeed, it is very appropriate to think of technical communication as a problem solving task, both for the writer and the reader. Hayes and Flower (1980) have outlined some of the constituents of writing, constituents such as generating the text, monitoring and editing it. As Kolers (1981) points out, the model is undoubtedly at a preliminary stage of development. Nevertheless, it provides an orientating and co-ordinating framework within which further research can be conducted on specific sub-processes such as revision (e.g. Flower, Hayes and Swarts, 1980).

Most studies of writers have focussed on the generation of verbal materials, particularly prose. Creating technical information, however, often involves not only control of the language, but also the control of the visual presentation. People who are good with words are not necessarily sensitive to the visual characteristics of a display. Perhaps there is a link between people's use of imagery as a preferred encoding representation and their ability to visually edit a display. Such questions have not yet been asked by cognitive psychologists. When we know more about how writers write, we may be in a better position to decide how to train writers to create texts that meet the reader's requirements.

Exploring the Effects of Design Variables

A third approach to information design has sought to create a mapping between presentation variables on the one hand and performance effects on the other. Such an approach is not focussing on the question of how readers read or writers write. Instead, it attempts to answer questions about when certain effects will obtain (e.g. for what kinds of texts or reading purposes will headings or summaries be helpful?). 'When' questions are relevant because there appear to be very few universal truths relating to information design. This has been illustrated in a number of studies. For example, when people consult an information display in order to answer a question, the details of that question can significantly affect which display is found easier to use (e.g. Wright and Reid, 1973). Similar interactions have been reported for the design of command structures in computer languages (e.g. Barnard and Hammond, 1982). The command string which worked well in one task environment was not the one used most easily in another task.

Among the advantages of exploring these interactions is that they potentially have direct relevance to decisions about information presentation. Unfortunately, a functionalist approach which involves simply mapping between design factors and performance is liable to deteriorate into numerous piece meal findings which yield no co-ordinated picture that designers could use. Such deterioration has often occurred and numerous 'failures to replicate' are reported. For evidence, see the reviews of variables such as underlining in prose (Foster, 1979), the use of questions in educational materials (Rickards and Denner, 1978), and the use of section summaries in textbooks (Hartley and Davies, 1976; Hartley and Trueman, 1982). In all these areas conflicting research findings abound and reviewers seek some touchstone by counting heads. Meanwhile the design problems continue to be tackled in an ad hoc fashion. As Fishman and Neigher (1982) point out, there seems to be a need for psychology to develop a 'technological' paradigm of applied research if it is to have any useful impact on practical problems.

A modification of this functionalist approach comes from the suggestion that a detailed analysis of the cognitive processes being drawn upon by the reader could provide a bridge between design factors and psychological knowledge about human information processing (Wright, 1978; 1980a). This is similar in spirit to the recent developments in relating performance on psychometric tests to cognitive components (Sternberg, 1981). The essence of the suggestion is that the interactions among presentation variables arise because of changes in the detailed processing that the reader carries out with the information. Universality of general principles is assumed to obtain at the micro-level of cognition (e.g using fewer cognitive resources will always be easier than using more). Nevertheless, adequate design decisions may require that writers know how to trade off the support needed for the various sub-processes when creating a total design package (e.g. more space and a smaller type size versus larger type and less white space).

Whilst it appears plausible to analyse design options in terms of their cognitive requirements, and to map these on to theories of cognition, in practice there appear to be several drawbacks to using the familiar labels of cognitive psychology. Often these labels are themselves not very precise and may be too global. Variations in the reader's 'decision-making process' when looking up information in a table may subsume presuppositions about the structure of the table (Wright and Threlfall, 1980), linguistic factors such as the asymmetric difficulty of 'more' and 'less' (Wright and Barnard, 1975), memory factors when more than one location must be searched (Wright, 1977) and response integration if information must be combined from several sources (Wright and Fox, 1972). While these terms may be convenient post hoc labels, purporting to account for the performance effects observed, there remains the difficulty of structuring them as conceptual heuristics which designers themselves can use.

An alternative approach, which may turn out to be more appropriate as a design tool, is to follow the lead given by those studying human problem-solving. Within this framework, the objective is to analyse readers' interaction with technical information in terms of the goals that they set up and the paths they select for achieving these goals (Wright, 1983). In effect, this is a move away from cognitive psychology in the direction of cognitive science. Whether there is any residual benefit from using the familiar psychological labels in order to relate design choice points to the psychological literature remains to be seen; so does the effectiveness of this approach as a tool for designers.

Comparison of the Three Approaches

The three approaches to technical communication which have just been outlined (studying the reader, the writer, and the effects of design variables) have a complementary relationship to each other. The first two fall easily within the traditional scope of psychology. Research focussing on readers and writers is going to enhance our understanding of human cognitive processes; if, however, one pauses to ask the question, 'How easily can this understanding be applied to the solution of practical communication problems?', it becomes clear that some bridging techniques are required. In particular, techniques are needed to indicate which sub-set of cognitive processes will be relevant to a particular communication. For example, it has already been suggested that memory processes may be an important factor even though the information remains continually visible; but how is the designer to know when this is the case and when not? Heuristics for answering this question by performing a cognitive 'task analysis' have been proposed (e.g. Wright, 1980a), but these heuristics may only be usable by people with a background in cognitive psychology. Moreover, such techniques are usually better for detecting trouble spots than for suggesting remedies. This is where the third approach, that of exploring the effects of design variables, is potentially helpful. It not only indicates preferred solutions, but provides some basis for the designer evaluating the overall cost-benefit of alternative proposals. Nevertheless, the major weakness of this third approach concerns the safety with which generalized conclusions can be drawn from any given study. Thus it becomes vital to be able to link the observed performance effects to underlying cognitive processes. In this sense, the third approach is heavily dependent upon the other two; but the other two have less direct relevance to the problems facing those who design technical information.

4. GROWTH POINTS FOR RESEARCH

In at least four domains the need for research is being increasingly recognized: sometimes by psychologists, sometimes by those trying to solve practical problems of communication. One domain concerns procedural instructions, whether verbal or pictorial; a second concerns the display aspects of printed materials as diverse as educational textbooks and application forms; a third arises from the technological advances encouraging the dissemination of computer-based information systems; the fourth relates to the creative processes of writing and design. Some of the background for each of these growth points is sketched briefly below.

Procedural Instructions

Although most insructions are couched in words, this is not always the case. Non-verbal instructions range from single pictographs (e.g. the numerous warning signals provided in modern cars) through to pictorial sequences describing procedures (e.g. how to put on a life jacket if your plane should come down over the sea). Cross-cultural comparisons often become part of the necessary ground-work when designing such displays (e.g. Zimmer and Zimmer, 1978). Research on single pictographs becomes of interest to cognitive psychologists when message complexity increases, for example by the need to convey prohibitions (Jones, 1978) or when the illustrations serve as aids to problem-solving (Szlichcinski, 1979).

Work on pictorial sequences, although less common, has raised some interesting parallels with readers' interpretation of verbal sequences. Barnard and Marcel (1982) note that people apply systematic parsing rules to divide a pictorial sequence into successive actions, each action being linked with its consequent state. This seems analogous to the finding of Dixon (1982) that when interpreting verbal imperatives people create action plans in which the action is the dominant component, and any conditional information appears to be secondary. The generality of this finding may be challenged, but there remain many interesting psychological questions concerning how people create and implement action plans. As yet unexplored are the role of the reader's prior knowledge and assumptions, the operational task constraints, and the critical display variables, all of which may determine the characteristics of such action plans.

One important observation arising from Marcel and Barnard (1979) was the discrepancy between people's interpretation of pictorial instructions when they were asked to 'read them aloud' and their interaction with the same instructions when asked to carry them out and operate the machine. The reading data showed that the instructions were comprehensible; but the operating data showed that certain misunderstandings were common and that some of the displayed information was ignored. This is one of the respects in which the reader's interaction with technical information is very different from the reading of narrative prose. A preliminary exploration of people's tendency to ignore instructions yielded data consistent with the hypothesis that people formulate questions before turning to the technical information to find the answer (Wright, 1981a). Consequently, if there is no question being asked by the reader, then the technical information is not read. The question asked by Marcel and Barnard's subjects appeared to be 'What do I do next?' Information that was not part of the answer, such as details concerning changes in the internal state of the machine, were overlooked.

Text Design

For any printed information, the design issues can be thought of as falling roughly into three classes: content, presentation and evaluation. These classes are by no means totally independent (Nystrand, 1981a). For example, a decision to ask form-fillers about date of birth rather than age illustrates the interplay between content and presentation factors. Nevertheless, these three classes can serve as a convenient framework for relating the design of written information to cognitive psychology. Where content is concerned, decisions must be made about what should be presented to the reader, what can be assumed, what must be explained. Here a detailed knowledge of the semantic structures of the readership would be very useful. In particular, a number of government agencies would find it helpful if more were known about fuzzy concepts such as 'income' and 'family'.

Among the decisions about presentation, answers must be found to questions as diverse as how should the information be sequenced? Should it be pictorial, verbal or both? How important is the arrangement of elements on the page? The problems of sequencing technical information have received scant attention from psychologists. Among the exceptions are Meyer (1977) and Kieras (1980), who have shown that thematic variables in narrative factual information (Scientific American articles) have similar effects to those found with fiction materials. The vital link would seem to be the writer's use of a 'narrative' prose style, but quite different expository styles may be used in explanatory leaflets and maintenance handbooks.

One way of circumventing the sequencing issue is to rely on the interaction being driven by readers' questions. The writer's task then becomes one of providing adequate means for readers to find whatever information is required. Many other presentation issues currently have the status of ill-formed questions, in the sense that although an answer could be found for a specific communication, it would be extremely difficult to know how to characterize either the text or the readers so that generalizable conclusions could be drawn (e.g. concerning the sequencing of questions on a form, or the relation between questions and notes).

The problem of achieving generalizable statements about information display seems a particularly thorny one for technical communications. For example, Ehrenberg (1977) has illustrated the value of rounding numerical values to two significant figures if readers are seeking to detect trends or discrepancies in multi-column tables such as financial statements. Similar rounding might be helpful in a table showing average hours worked in different occupations or in different countries, but it would clearly not be appropriate to apply such rounding to a train time-table. This example illustrates the need for precision in our analysis of how people interact with written information, that analysis cannot be exclusively text-based since it appears helpful to round some time values but not others. The critical determinant here seems to be the use to which the information will be put by the reader. Broadly characterizing the interaction as 'decision-search-read-decide' carries few design implications, but each of those terms can be further elaborated. A more detailed analysis of the final 'decide' would be likely to show whether rounding was feasible or foolish.

In any text, ambiguities and miscommunication can arise from many sources. This is why empirical evaluation plays a vital part in determining the adequacy of technical material for its intended purpose. There are numerous procedures available for such evaluation, but all of them have shortcomings. Selecting appropriate techniques, and interpreting the data obtained, calls for special skills. It may be relatively easy to discover that readers have problems on page two. Understanding the nature of these difficulties and knowing how to reduce them lies outside the scope of most undergraduate training, both in design departments and in psychology departments.

Computer-based Information

A wide variety of technical information is being transferred to computer-based displays: library catalogues (Seal, Bryant and Hall, 1982), welfare rights information (Ottley and Kempson, 1982), and management support systems (Spence and Apperley, 1982), including medical diagnosis (Fitter and Cruikshank, 1982). Developments such as cable television and inexpensive personal computers will accelerate the use of television screens for information displays in the homes of the general public. Such information systems differ from print in many ways, but particularly in making explicit some facets of the reader's interaction with the material, and indeed often imposing constraints on the nature of this interaction. The reader scanning a newspaper's entertainment section may have made no conscious choice between the theatre or cinema. An interactive display may demand such a choice. Indeed, the access structures provided for electronic displays can be critical determinants of whether the information is used successfully. This is evident from the comments on Prestel by Sutherland (1980) and Young and Hull (1982). The use of access structures relates to the cognitive psychology of problem-solving and decision-making rather than to the issues normally addressed by those studying reading. A similar need to broaden the notion of 'reading' was noted earlier when discussing tables. Using technical information often involves much more than just reading. In time, one might hope that theories from cognitive psychology will have implications both for the teaching of these broader-based information skills (Brake, 1980; Wray, 1982) and also for the design of displays which will assist readers during the problem-solving process.

A rather different area of computer-based information is that known as intelligent tutoring systems. This is a development of computer-assisted instruction which started in the mid-1960s. Recent research has focussed on creating supportive learning environments in which the reader learns by doing, so transforming factual knowledge into experiential knowledge. Those generating such tutorial environments have found it helpful to work with an explicit model of the reader's changing knowledge and belief systems. The models thus generated may well facilitate a cogent theory of learning and mislearning. Moreover, an increased understanding of such models may have implications for information display in other fields. A useful review of contemporary research on intelligent tutoring systems is given in Sleeman and Brown (1982).

Creative Processes of Writing and Design

Only a few psychologists have given serious attention to the psychological processes underlying the production of written information (e.g. Wason, 1970; Hayes and Flower, 1980). More generally, there seems to have been a tacit assumption that if one understood speech production and understood how people could translate between graphemes and speech, then no interesting questions would remain. This simplistic view has been contested for reading (Kolers, 1970; Rubin 1980), but one can still note the absence of any discussion of written communication in books on the psychology of language; see, for example, the excellent text by Clark and Clark (1977).

For technical information the disparity between oral and written language is considerable. The communicative potential of the spatial and typographic resources available on the printed page have no counterpart in speech. Some things have to be written down to be easily understood (Simon and Hayes, 1976; Olson, 1977). Once written, the format of visible language may impose further constraints that have no counterpart in oral language. For example, Galbraith (1980) has illustrated how an author's ability to revise a text can be hampered by the conflicting goals of reading and understanding what there is on the page while simultaneously striving to express particular ideas in effective ways. Helping readers to separate these goals, perhaps dealing with them sequentially rather than simultaneously, and giving the expressive goal priority, may be one way of developing a writer's editing skills.

Belatedly, and in part as a result of technical advances, researchers are starting to explore the issues arising from communicating in different media, such as print on paper, microfiche, or visual display units (Lefrere, 1982). Some studies using relatively simple production tasks, such as letter writing, have found little effect of medium (e.g. Gould, 1981; 1982) on anything other than time. Yet for more complex information, such as computer-assisted instruction, there have been reports of the inappropriate transfer of design skills from the static medium of print on paper to a dynamic electronic display (Jenkin, 1981). Teachers tend to design the screen from the top, just as they would a typewritten page, whereas focussing on the interactive elements on the screen may be a more appropriate strategy.

Advances in technology have one other impact on the writing process. When an author's material is being handled by a word-processing system, a number of supports for the writer become available. Appropriate software can let writers know when sentences become too long or technical terms too frequent (Frase, Keenan and Dever, 1980). In the long term, it is conceivable that intelligent software may be able to monitor the thematic structure of the material and let authors know when problems arise at this level. Some writing aids will inevitably be more successful than others (Woodruff, Bereiter and Scardamalia, 1981). Knowing what advice to give authors, as well as how and when to give it, are among the issues remaining to be explored.

Word-processing facilities make it much easier for authors to check back to see whether they have already covered a particular item, and for designers to explore alternative page displays. Sophisticated editing facilities also make it possible for psychologists to explore fundamental aspects of human symbolic communication. For example, Card, Moran and Newell (1980) have suggested that some aspects of a manuscript-editing task can be treated as a 'routine cognitive skill'. They were concerned to model the implementation of changes which had already been decided. Little is known about how people make these editorial decisions to change the text. In order to exploit the potential of the various writing support systems that are becoming available, we need to know much more about the generative aspects of writing and design. As yet we have only a preliminary outline of the cognitive process underlying the production of written materials (Flower and Hayes, 1980), and only a few detailed accounts of the creation of specific communications (e.g. Levelt, 1981). Nevertheless, the generative processes underlying written communication will undoubtedly be an area that sees considerable development in the next few years.

5. FUTURE PROSPECTS

Following the Government White Paper on administrative forms (Anon., 1982), many departments are reconsidering their procedures for communicating with the public. Departments are often willing to enlist whatever expertise is available. In principle, psychologists could make a variety of contributions to this effort. They could act as translators between non-psychologists and the research literature; they could make behavioural skills available at the analysis, planning and the evaluation stages of document creation (Duffy, 1981); they could help departments formulate the general issues which recur for specific classes of communication, and through basic research provide the psychological underpinnings for the development of appropriate design solutions.

The potential for contributions of this kind is by no means confined to government departments. Computer companies have started to be concerned about their manuals. Other manufacturers are discovering that the product gets blamed for what is essentially a documentation problem. Information providers on Prestel and teletext systems have found out the hard way that not all displays communicate effectively (Reynolds, 1979b). Socially concerned organizations have specified the information needs of particular target groups such as the elderly (e.g. Epstein, 1981). As awareness increases concerning the problems of technical communication, so does the willingness of the information providers to consult or recruit professional expertise.

However, at present there is a sizeable gap between psychologists' potential contribution and what happens in practice. Few psychologists in the UK have shown either interest or expertise in this area. The picture is only marginally better in the USA, where the military and the National Institute of Education have supported major research programmes on technical information. This reluctance of psychologists to explore the cognitive problem of technical information is understandable. Real communications are so complex that the prospects for progress in understanding human behaviour must seem much more assured in virtually all other directions.

Nevertheless, as has already been pointed out, applied psychology is by no means one-way traffic from theory to application. Technical information provides the opportunity to explore some aspects of cognition that are otherwise difficult to bring into the laboratory. For example, Baddeley (1981) has emphasized the need for links to be forged between cognition and motivational factors. It is sometimes the motivational or emotional aspects of technical information, especially bureaucratic information, that cause problems for readers. Thus technical information may provide a useful domain for exploring the interactions between thinking and affect, at least for negative affects such as annoyance and frustration. Perhaps if the information were well enough designed then positive affect might also be found. Over a decade ago, Popper pointed out that 'instead of growing better memories and brains, we grow paper, pens, pencils, typewriters, dictaphones, the printing press and libraries' (Popper, 1972). Understanding how people use these cortical adjuncts would seem to be a legitimate concern for cognitive psychology.

Readers' interaction with technical information requires skills that go beyond those normally taught in reading classes. This fact was recognized in the government report of the Bullock committee on A Language for Life (Bullock, 1975). There will undoubtedly be psychologists interested in the processes of comprehension who feel uneasy about the present proposals to broaden the notion of reading to include processes before and after the encounter with the text (e.g. formulating a question, implementing an action plan). Nevertheless, one of the advantages of such broadening is that is necessitates detailed examination of people's interaction with text. This in turn has enabled similarities in reading activities to be seen across materials as diverse as numerical tables and prose paragraphs (Wright, 1980b; 1981b). In an area overcrowded with variety (of content, of presentation medium, of reader characteristics, etc.), there may be some advantage to any framework that can bring a semblance of unity to the field.

Undoubtedly, a number of research investigations of people's interaction with technical information have asked questions which, in research terms, are ill-formed: for example, how many colours should you have on a page? Such a question has no answer because so much depends upon the functions for which colour is being used. One reason for the lack of a clear conceptual focus for investigations is that in related design areas no theoretical framework has been developed, or appears to be missed, by those working in the discipline. Ergonomics might be taken as an illustrative example. Traditionally, ergonomists have been concerned with tailoring machine design to human physical limitations. These limitations were immutable in that machine operators were not going to grow a third hand or an extra long leg. So firm facts and figures that had clear design consequences could be obtained. When people are interacting with information rather than machines, then the limitations become less physically determined and more strategy-bound. These strategies can and do vary: with experience, with training, with subject matter and with fatigue. There may plausibly be occasions when it is more appropriate to change readers' information-handling strategies (e.g. teaching students study skills: Augstein and Thomas, 1978) than to design written information to fit the user's present strategies (Wright and Bason, in press). There are, however, also occasions when readers' presuppositions about the structure of an information display may be so strong that although incorrect, these resist being changed either by instruction or experience (Wright and Threlfall, 1980). Perhaps the most common example occurs with multiple columns of information, when each column includes pairs of elements (e.g. a page index or a conversion chart). If the gap within the related pair is larger than the gap between columns, the resulting perceptual effect prompts readers to associate the wrong elements together. For psychologists familiar with gestalt principles such an outcome seems highly predictable. Yet most cases are not so simple. Take a particular example of technical communication, such as the instruction manual for your new word processor or an application form available from you local post office, and ask of contemporary psychology whether there would be advantage in changing readers' strategies or modifying the written information or both. The question may serve to highlight how much remains to be discovered about the production and comprehension of technical information.

REFERENCES

Aaronsen, D. and Scarborough, H. S. (1976). Performance theories for sentence coding: some quantitative evidence. Journal of Experimental Psychology, 2, 56-70.

Allport, A. (1979). Word recognition in reading. In P. A. Kolers, M. E. Wrolstad and H. Bouma (eds), Processing of Visible Language, 1. New York: Plenum Press.

Anon. (1982). Administrative Forms in Government. Cmnd 8504. London: HMSO.

Atlas, M. A. (1979). Addressing an Audience: A study of expert-novice differences in writing. Washington DC: American Institute for Research, Document Design Project, Technical Report No. 3.

Augstein, S. Harri and Thomas, L. F. (1978). Is comprehension the purpose of reading? In E. Hunter-Grundin and H. U. Grundin (eds), Reading: Implementing the Bullock Report. London: Ward Lock Educational (for the United Kingdom Reading Association).

Baddeley, A. D. (1981). The cognitive psychology of everyday life. British Journal of Psychology, 72, 257-269.

Barnard, P. J. and Hammond, N. V. (1982). Usability and its multiple determination for the occasional user of interactive systems. Proceedings of the 6th International Conference on Computer Communication, London, September 1982.

Barnard, P. J., Hammond, N. V., Morton, J. and Long, J. B. (1981). Consistency and compatibility in human-computer dialogue. International Journal of Man-Machine Studies, 15, 87-134.

Barnard, P. J. and Marcel, A. J. (1982). Representation and understanding in the use of symbols and pictograms. In R. Easterby and H. Zwaga (eds), NATO conference on Visual Presentation of Information. Het Vennenbos, The Netherlands, 1978. Chichester: Wiley.

Barnard, P. J. and Wright, P. (1976). The effects of spaced character formats on the production and legibility of handwritten names. Ergonomics, 19, 81-92.

Barnard, P. J., Wright, P. and Wilcox, P. (1978). The effects of spatial constraints on the legibility of handwritten alphanumeric codes. Ergonomics, 21, 73-78.

Brake, T. (1980). The Need to Know: Teaching the importance of information. London: British Library Research and Development Report No. 5511.

Bransford, J. D. (1979). Human Cognition: Learning, understanding and remembering. Belmont, Ca: Wadworth Publishing Company.

Bransford, J. D. and Nitsch, K. E. (1978). Coming to understand things we could not previously understand. In J. F. Kavanagh and W. Strange (eds), Speech and Language in the Laboratory, School and Clinic. London: MIT Press.

Branthwaite, A., Trueman, M. and Hartley, J. (1980). Writing essays: the actions and strategies of students. In J. Hartley (ed.), The Psychology of Written Communication. London: Kogan Page.

Broadbent, D. E. (1971). Relation between theory and application in psychology. In P. B. Warr (ed.), Psychology at Work. London, Harmondsworth: Penguin books

Broadbent, D. E., Cooper, P. J. and Broadbent, M. H. P. (1978). A comparison of hierarchical and matrix retrieval schemes in recall. Journal of Experimental Psychology: Human Learning and Memory, 4, 486-497.

Bullock, A. (1975). A Language for Life. London: HMSO

Burnhill, P., Hartley, J., Young, M. and Fraser, S. (1975). The typography of college prospectuses. In L. Evans and J. Leedham (eds), Aspects of Educational Technology IX. London: Kogan Page.

Burton, R. R. and Brown, J. S. (1982). An investigation of computer coaching for informal learning activities. In D. Sleeman and J. S. Brown (eds), Intelligent Tutoring Systems. London: Academic Press.

Card, S. K., Moran, T. P. and Newell, A. (1980). Computer text-editing: an information analysis of a routine cognitive skill. Cognitive Psychology, 12, 32-74.

Chapanis, A. (1965). Words, words, words. Human Factors, 7, 1-17.

Clark, H. H. and Clark, E. V. (1977). Psychology and Language. New York: Harcourt, Brace Jovanovich, Inc.

Cutts, M. and Maher, C. (1980). Writing Plain English. Salford, UK: Plain English Campaign.

Dixon, P. (1982). Plans and written directions for complex tasks. Journal of Verbal Learning and Verbal Behavior, 21, 70-84.

Duffy, T. M. (1981). Organizing and utilizing document design options. Information Design Journal, 2, 255-266.

Ehrenberg, A. S. C. (1977). Rudiments of numeracy. Journal of the Royal Statistical Society A, 140, 277-297.

Epstein, J. (1981). Informing the elderly. Information Design Journal, 2, 215-235.

Fishman, D. B. and Neigher, W. D. (1982). American psychology in the eighties: who will buy? American Psychologist, 37, 533-546.

Fitter, M. J. and Cruikshank, P. J. (1982). The computer in the consulting room: a psychological framework. Behaviour and Information Technology, 1, 81-92.

Flower, L. S. and Hayes, J. R. (1977). Problem solving strategies and the writing process. College English, 39, 449-461.

Flower, L. S. and Hayes, J. R. (1980). The dynamics of composing: making plans and juggling constraints. In L. W. Gregg and E. R. Steinberg (eds), Cognitive Processes in Writing. Hillsdale, NJ: Lawrence Erlbaum Associates.

Flower L. S., Hayes, J. R. and Swarts, H. (1980). Revising Functional Documents: The scenario principle. Technical Report No. 10, Document Design Project. Washington DC: Document Design Center.

Foster, J. (1979). The use of visual cues in text. In P. A. Kolers, M. E. Wrolstad and H. Bouma (eds), Processing of Visible Language, 1. New York: Plenum Press.

Frase, L. T., Keenan, S. A. and Dever, J. J. (1980). Human performance in computer aided writing and documentation. In P. A Kolers, M. E. Wrolstad and H. Bouma (eds), Processing of Visible Language, 2. New York: Plenum Press.

Galbraith, D. (1980). The effect of conflicting goals on writing: a case study. Visible Language, 14, 364-375.

Gould, J. D. (1981). Composing letters with computer-based text editors. Human Factors, 23, 593-606.

Gould, J. D. (1982). Writing and speaking letters and messages. International Journal of Man-Machine Studies, 16, 147-171.

Grandjean, E. and Vigliani, E. (eds) (1982). Ergonomic Aspects of Visual Display Terminals. London: Taylor & Francis Ltd.

Gregg, L. W. and Steinberg, E. R. (eds) (1980). Cognitive Processes in Writing. Hillsdale, NJ: Lawrence Erlbaum Associates.

Hartley, J. (1978). Designing Instructional Text. London: Kogan Page.

Hartley, J. (1981a). Eighty ways of improving instructions text. IEEE Transactions on Professional Communication, 24, 17-27.

Hartley, J. (1981b). Sequencing the elements in references. Applied Ergonomics, 12, 7-12.

Hartley, J. (1982). Information mapping: a critique. Information Design Journal, 3, 51-58.

Hartley, J. and Davies, I. K. (1976). Pre-instructional strategies: the role of pretests, behavioural objectives, overviews and advance organisers. Review of Educational Research, 46, 239-265.

Hartley, J. and Trueman, M. (1982). The effects of summaries on the recall of information from prose: five experimental studies. Human Learning, 1, 63-82.

Hartley, J., Trueman, M. and Burnhill, P. (1979). The role of spatial and typographic cues in the layout of journal references. Applied Ergonomics, 10, 165-169.

Writing and Reading Technical Information

Hayes, D. A. and Tierney, R. J. (1982). Developing readers' knowledge through analogy. Reading Research Quarterly, 17, 256-280.

Hayes, J. R. (1981). The Complete Problem Solver. Philadelphia, Pa: The Franklin Institute.

Hayes, J. R. and Flower, L. S. (1980). Identifying the organization of writing processes. In L. W. Gregg and E. R. Steinberg (eds), Cognitive Processes in Writing. Hillsdale, NJ: Lawrence Erlbaum Associates.

Jenkin, J. M. (1981). Some principles of screen design and software for their support. In P. R. Smith (ed.), Computer Assisted Learning. Oxford: Pergamon Press.

Jewett, D. L. (1981). Multi-level writing in theory and practice. Visible Language, 15, 32-40.

Jonassen, D. H. (1981). Information mapping: a description, rationale and comparison with programmed instruction. Visible Language, 15, 55-66.

Jones, S. (1978). Symbolic representation of abstract concepts. Ergonomics, 21, 573-577.

Just, M. A. and Carpenter, P. A. (1980). A theory of reading: from eye fixation to comprehension. Psychological Review, 87, 329-354.

Kieras, D. E. (1980). Initial mention as a signal to thematic content in technical passages. Memory and Cognition, 8, 345-353.

Kindersley, D. (1976). Optical Letter Spacing for New Printing Systems. The Wynkyn de Worde Society, London: Lund Humphries.

Kintsch, W. and van Dijk, T. A. (1978). Toward a model of text comprehension and production. Psychological Review, 85, 363-394.

Kolers, P. A. (1970). Three stages of reading. In H. Levin and J. P. Williams (eds), Basic Studies on Reading. New York: Basic Books.

Kolers, P. A. (1981). Righting Writing. Contemporary Psychology, 26, 700-701.

Lefrere, P. (1982). Beyond word-processing: human and artificial intelligence in document preparation and use. In P. J. Hills (ed.), Trends in Information Transfer. London: Frances Pinter.

Levelt, W. J. M. (1981). The speaker's linearization problem. In H. C. Longuet-Higgins, J. Lyons and D. Broadbent (eds), Psychological Mechanisms of Language. London: The Royal Society and British Academy. Also published in Philosophical Transactions of the Royal Society of London, series B, 1981, 295, 213-423.

349

Marcel, A. J. and Barnard, P. J. (1979). Paragraphs of pictographs: the use of non-verbal instructions for equipment. In P. A. Kolers, M. E Wrolstad and H. Bouma (eds), Processing of Visible Language, 1. New York: Plenum Press.

Meyer, B. J. F. (1977). The structure of prose: effects on learning and memory and implications for educational practice. In R. C. Anderson, R. J. Spiro and W. E. Montague (eds), Schooling and the Acquisition of Knowledge. Hillsdale, NJ: Lawrence Erlbaum Associates.

Morton, J., Barnard, P., Hammond, N. and Long, J. B. (1979). Interacting with the computer: a framework. In E. J. Boutmy and A. Danthine (eds), Teleinformatics, 79. Amsterdam: North-Holland Publishing Company.

Morton, J., Marcus, S. and Frankish, C. (1976). Perceptual Centers (P-Centers). Psychological Review, 83, 405-408.

Nickerson, R. S. (1981). Understanding signs: some examples of knowledge-dependent language processing. Information Design Journal, 2, 2-16.

Nystrand, M. (1981a). Elaborating and buttressing: the writer-reader interaction model of readability. Paper presented at the convention of the College Conference on composition and communication. Dallas.

Nystrand, M. (1981b). The structure of textual space. In M. Nystrand (ed.), What Writers Know: The language, process and structure of written discourse. New York: Academic Press.

Olson, D. R. (1977). The bias of language in speech and writing. Harvard Educational Review, 47, 257-281.

Ottley, P. and Kempson, E. (1982). Computer Benefits? Guidelines for Local Information and Advice Centres. London: National Consumer Council.

Popper, K. R. (1972). Objective Knowledge. Oxford: Clarendon Press.

Poulton, E. C. (1967). Searching for newspaper headlines printed in capitals or lower case letters. Journal of Applied Psychology, 51, 417-425.

Poulton, E. C. (1968). The measurement of legibility. Printing Technology, 12, 1-6.

Poulton, E. C. (1969a). Skimming lists of food ingredients printed in different sizes. Journal of Applied Psychology, 53, 55-58.

Poulton, E. C. (1969b). Skimming lists of food ingredients printed in different brightness contrasts. Journal of Applied Psychology, 53, 498-500.

Reynolds, L. (1979a). Progress in documentation-legibility studies: their relevance to present-day documentation methods. Journal of Documentation, 35, 307-340.

Reynolds, L. (1979b). Teletext and viewdata - a new challenge for the designer. Information Design Journal, 1, 2-14.

Rickards, J. P. and Denner, P. R. (1978). Inserted questions as aids to reading text. Instructional Science, 7, 313-346.

Riesbeck, C. K. (1980). 'You can't miss it': judging the clarity of directions. Cognitive Science, 4, 285-303.

Rose, A. M. (1981). Problems in public documents. Information Design Journal, 2, 179-196.

Rothkopf, E. Z. (1978a). On the reciprocal relationship between previous experience and processing in determining learning outcomes. In A. M. Lesgold, J. W. Pellegrino, S. D. Fokkema and R. Glaser (eds), Cognitive Psychology and Instruction. New York: Plenum Publishing Co.

Rothkopf, E. Z. (1978b). Analysing eye movements to infer processing styles during learning from text. In J. W. Senders, D. F. Fisher and R. A. Marty (eds), Eye Movements and the Higher Psychological Functions. Hillsdale, NJ: Lawrence Erlbaum Associates.

Rothkopf, E. Z. and Billington, M. J. (1979). Effects of task demand on eye movements during goal guided reading. Journal of Educational Psychology, 71, 310-327.

Rothkopf, E. Z. and Coatney, R. P. (1974). Effects of readability of context passages on subsequent inspection rates. Journal of Applied Psychology, 59, 679-682.

Rubin, A. (1980). A theoretical taxonomy of the differences between oral and written language. In R. J. Spiro, B. C. Bruce and W. F. Brewer (eds), Theoretical Issues in Reading Comprehension: Perspectives from cognitive psychology, linguistics, artificial intelligence and education. Hillsdale, NJ: Lawrence Erlbaum Associates.

Schwarz, M. N. K. and Flammer, A. (1981). Text structure and title - effects on comprehension and recall. Journal of Verbal Learning and Verbal Behavior, 20, 61-66.

Seal, A., Bryant, P. and Hall, C. (1982). Full and Short Entry Catalogues: Library needs and uses. Bath: University Library Centre for Catalogue Research.

Shebilske, W. and Rotondo, J. A. (1981). Typographical and spatial cues that facilitate learning from textbooks. Visible Language, 15, 41-54.

Simon, H. A. and Hayes, J. R. (1976). Understanding complex task instructions. In D. Klahr (ed.), Cognition and Instruction. Hillsdale, NJ: Lawrence Erlbaum Associates.

Sleeman, D. and Brown, J. S. (1982). Intelligent Tutoring Systems. London: Academic Press.

Spence, R. and Apperley, M. (1982). Data base navigation: an office environment for the professional. Behaviour and Information Technology, 1, 43-54.

Spencer, H. (1969). The Visible Word. London: Lund Humphries.

Starch, D (1914). Advertising. Chicago: Scott, Foresman.

Sternberg, R. J. (1981). Testing and cognitive psychology. American Psychologist, 35, 1181-1189.

Stewart, T. F. M. (1976). Displays and the software interface. Applied Ergonomics, 7, 137-146.

Sticht, T. G. (1972). Learning by listening. In J. B. Carroll and R. O. Freedle (eds), Language and Comprehension and the Acquisition of Knowledge. Washington DC: V. H. Winston & Sons.

Sticht, T. G. (1977). Comprehending reading at work. In M. A. Just and P. A. Carpenter (eds), Cognitive Processes in Comprehension. Hillsdale, NJ: Lawrence Erlbaum Associates.

Stubbs, M. (1980). Language and Literacy: The sociolinguistics of reading and writing. London: Routledge & Kegan Paul.

Sutherland, S. (1980). Prestel and the User: A survey of psychological and ergonomic research. London: Central Office of Information.

Swarts, H., Flower, L. S. and Hayes, J. R. (1980). How headings in documents can mislead readers. Technical Report No. 9, Document Design Project. Washington DC: Document Design Center.

Szlichcinski, K. P. (1979). Diagrams and illustrations as aids to problem solving. Instructional Science, 8, 253-274.

Tinker, M. A. (1955). Prolonged reading tasks in visual research. Journal of Applied Psychology, 39, 444-446.

Tinker, M. A. (1965). Bases for Effective Reading. Minneapolis: University of Minnesota Press.

Tinker, M. A. and Paterson, D. G. (1931). Studies of typographical factors influencing speed of reading: VII. Variation in colour of print and background. Journal of Applied Psychology, 15, 471-479.

Twyman, M. (1981). Typography without words. Visible Language, 15, 5-12.

Twyman, M. (1982). The graphic presentation of language. Information Design Journal, 3, 2-22.

Voss, J. F., Vesonder, G. T. and Spilich, G. J. (1980). Text generation and recall by high-knowledge and low-knowledge individuals. Journal of Verbal Learning and Verbal Behavior, 19, 651-667.

Waller, R. H. (1980). Graphic aspects of complex texts: typography as macropunctuation. In P. A. Kolers, M. E.

Wrolstad and H. Bouma (eds), Processing of Visible Language, 2. New York: Plenum Press.

Wason, P. C. (1970). On writing scientific papers. Physics Bulletin, 21, 407-408. Reprinted in (1980) J. Hartley (ed.), The Psychology of Written Communication, London: Kogan Page.

Watts, L. and Nisbet, J. (1974). Legibility in Children's Books: A review of research. Windsor, Berkshire: National Foundation for Educational Research.

Wendt, D. (1979). An experimental approach to the improvement of the typographic design of textbooks. Visible Language, 13, 108-133.

Whalley, P. C. and Flemming, R. W. (1975). An experiment with a simple recorder of reading behaviour. Programmed Learning and Educational Technology, 12, 120-123.

Wilkins, A. (1982). Personal communication.

Wilkins, A. J., Binnie, C. D. and Darby, C. E. (1981). Inter-hemispheric differences in photosensitive epilepsy. I. Pattern sensitivity thresholds. Electroencephalography and Clinical Neurophysiology, 52, 461-468.

Williams, A. (1976). Reading and the Consumer. London: Hodder & Stoughton Educational.

Wing, A. (1979). The slowing of handwritten responses made in spaced character formats. Ergonomics, 22, 465-468.

Woodruff, E., Bereiter, C. and Scardamalia, M. (1981). On the road to computer assisted compositions. Journal of Educational Technology Systems, 10, 133-148.

Wray, D. (1982). Research insights into extending reading. Reading, 16, 31-42.

Wright, P. (1977). Decision making as a factor in the ease of using numerical tables. Ergonomics, 20, 91-96.

Wright, P. (1978). Feeding the information eaters: suggestions for integrating pure and applied research on language comprehension. Instructional Science, 7, 249-312.

Wright, P. (1980a). Usability: the criterion for designing written information. In P. A. Kolers, M. E. Wrolstad and H. Bouma (eds), Processing of Visible Language, 2. New York: Plenum Press.

Wright, P. (1980b). The comprehension of tabulated information: some similarities between reading prose and reading tables. National Society for Performance and Instruction Journal, 19, 25-29.

Wright, P. (1981a). The instructions clearly state ... Can't people read? Applied Ergonomics, 12, 131-141.

Wright, P. (1981b). Tables in text: the subskills needed for reading formatted information. In L. J. Chapman (ed.), The

Reader and the Text. London: Heinemann Educational Books Ltd.

Wright, P. (1983). Document Design: Psychological research and theory. Cambridge: Cambridge University Press.

Wright, P. and Barnard, P. (1975). Effects of 'more than' and 'less than' decisions on the use of numerical tables. Journal of Applied Psychology, 60, 606-611.

Wright, P. and Barnard, P. (1978). Asking multiple questions about several items: the design of matrix structures on application forms. Applied Ergonomics, 9, 7-14.

Wright, P. and Bason, G. Detour routes to usability. International Journal of Man-Machine Studies. In press.

Wright, P. and Fox, K. (1972). Explicit and implicit tabulation formats. Ergonomics, 15, 175-187.

Wright, P. and Reid, F. (1973). Written information: some alternatives to prose for expressing the outcomes of complex contingencies. Journal of Applied Psychology, 57, 160-166.

Wright, P. and Threlfall, S. (1980). Readers' expectations about format influence of the usability of an index. Journal of Research Communication Studies, 2, 99-106.

Young, R. M. and Hull, A. (1982). Cognitive aspects of the selection of viewdata options by casual users. In Pathways to the Information Society. Proceedings of the 6th International Conference on Computer Communication. London.

Zimmer, A. and Zimmer, F. (1978). Visual Literacy in Communication: Designing for development. Bucks, UK: Halton Publications Ltd.

TABLE OF CONTENTS OF PSYCHOLOGY SURVEY, No. 1

355

TABLE OF CONTENTS OF PSYCHOLOGY SURVEY, No. 2

TABLE OF CONTENTS OF PSYCHOLOGY SURVEY, No. 3

AUTHOR INDEX

(Underlined numbers indicate that name appears in references)

SUBJECT INDEX

Accommodation, visual 7-10
Acoustics, Pythagorean 269
Acuity, visual 5-7, 10, 14, 18
Adoption 233, 236
  studies and crime 110
Aging, information processing 65-67
  intelligence 67-70
  life satisfaction 77-79
  memory 63-65
  personality 71-73
  stages and events 74-76
Aggression 110, 112, 115, 231
  see anger
Alcohol and crime 123
Alexithymia 137
Altruism 224-225, 230-231, 234, 235
Amblyopia 17
Analgesics 177
Anger 155-157
Anosmia 260
Anthropology and sociobiology 226
Anxiety, effect on pain 186-187
Apes, see primates
Arousal 118
Artificial intelligence 291-294, 333
Assertion training 120
Asthma 137
Astigmatism 10
Attention 45
  development 14-15
Auditory system 268
Autokinetic effect 92
Awareness 45
Behaviour, experimental analysis of 38-45, 53
  predictability of 43
  see operant
Behaviourism 45
Benton Visual Retention Test 66
Binocular vision 15-17, 19
Biofeedback 189-190
Biology of criminals 109-111
Birth-spacing 232
Birthweight 235
Bombykol 247
Borstal 111
Bradburn Affect Balance Scale 78
Brain function in mystical experience 217-218
  see epilepsy
Brightness discrimination 12
Broken homes 113-114
Cardiovascular disorder 155-156, 160
Cat vision 17
Child abuse 232, 237
Child rearing 229
Choice behaviour 45, 51, 310, 311
Chromosome abnormalities 110
Clinical psychologists 144
Clock, internal 53
Cognitive control of pain 190-191
Cognitive learning theory 50-54
  and crime 117-118
Cognitive psychology and communication 325-326
Colour vision 11-13
  judgements 95
Communication, technical 323-345
Computers, in communication 340-341
  programs 322
Conditioning see operant
  classical 46, 47, 51, 114-115
  instrumental 46
Conflict 138
  parent-offspring 231
Conformity 92-96, 101
Consciousness, altered states 203-220
Constancies, perceptual 25-27
Contagion of criminal acts 122
Contingencies of reinforcement 41, 47

Contour orientation 22
Contrast sensitivity 5-7, 11, 22
Conversion 95
Crime, psychology of 109-127
  situational approach 124
  theories of 109-117
Criminal justice 116
Criminology 116
Criminals and body-build 110-111
  female 116-117
Critical periods, visual 17-18, 20
Cross-cultural studies 226
Cues 41
Cultural evolution, see evolution
Cumulative record 40
Dark adapted sensitivity 13
Decision making 89-91
  see choice behaviour
Deja vu 218
Delinquency, 111-114
  female 117
Depression 75-77
Depth perception 18-22
Dermatitis 138
Desensitization 172
Design of buildings etc. and crime 124-126
Design in communication 333-336, 338-343
Dichromacy 12
Diet 156
Discrimination, colour 11-13
  visual 2-5
Discriminative control 41, 44, 45
Displacement activities 47
Drinking, see alcohol
  see polydipsia
Drugs, in operant 42
  and mystical experience 204-205
  psychotrophic 159-160
ECG 145
EDA 145
EEG 145, 189
Effect, correlated law of 50, 53
Electrodermal activity 137, 145
EMG 176, 189
Emotion 156-158
Endorphins 171-172
Engineering and psychology 312-314
Environment and psychosomatic disorders 158-160
Environmental influences on behaviour, see operant
Epilepsy 205, 207-213
Episiotomy 183
ERG 11
Ergonomics 345
ESP 219-220
Ethology 46
Events, life 74-76
Evoked potentials (VEP) 3, 11
Evolution, see sociobiology
  biological v. cultural 226, 238, 239
Exogamy 229
Extraversion 111, 112, 180
Eye contact 121, 123
Eye movements 2, 13-14, 24, 27
Face perception 23-24
Factor analysis 112
Fading 41
Families, criminal 113-114, 119, 120, 189-190
Female criminals 116-117
Fitness (evolutionary), see inclusive fitness
Fixed action pattern 247
Flicker, perception of 11
Focussing eyes 7
Fourier transform 315-317
Fovea centralis 10
Functional scaling 309